PRAYER

PRAYER

A STUDY IN THE HISTORY AND PSYCHOLOGY OF RELIGION

by Friedrich Heiler

translated and edited by
SAMUEL McCOMB

with the assistance of
J. EDGAR PARK

A Galaxy Book

New York · Oxford University Press
1958

264.1
H466p

91379

AUTHOR'S PREFACE TO THE
ENGLISH EDITION

THE present work appeared during the World War. Some
parts of it were written in a hospital, where the author served
as attendant on the patients. It was published a few months
before the end of the war.

For the inspiration of the work and its psychological method
I have to thank my teacher, Dr. Aloys Fischer, who now occupies the Chair of Pedagogy and Philosophy in the University
of Munich.

The religio-historical method and religious view-point I had
learnt through the writings of the Lutheran Archbishop Söderblom of Upsala, who died last year. For the friendly reception
which the work has met with in Protestant Christendom I have
in no small measure to thank his favorable judgment. Besides
the above-named, I have been under special obligations (in the
course of my religious and theological development) to two
Roman Catholic scholars, Dr. Karl Adam, Professor of Catholic Dogmatics in Tübingen University, and to the great Roman
Catholic lay-theologian, Friedrich von Hügel. It was the
latter, moreover, who first urged the publication of an English
translation; however, this appeared impossible, until the present translator with great energy, undertook the difficult task.
And here I would express to him my most cordial thanks for
the time and for the painstaking care he has unselfishly devoted to this work.

The book was written before the great oecumenical movement for unity arose after the war. It could not — certainly
in this form — have been written unless the author, born a
Roman Catholic, had fought his way up to an oecumenical position through his studies and experience of life.

The path which the author has trod after completing this
book — from Roman Catholicism to Evangelical Catholicism,
from the Roman community to the Lutheran, and to kindly
relations with the Anglican and the Eastern Orthodox Churches

— was but the sequel to that oecumenical attitude to which the book owes its origin.

Prayer is the great bond of union of Christendom; and not only of Christendom, but of all mankind. Prayer is the most tangible proof of the fact that the whole of mankind is seeking after God; or — to put it more correctly — that it is sought by God. Mankind at prayer is a proof of the universal *revelation* of God. For it is precisely in prayer that we have revealed to us the *essential* element of all religion, which Friedrich von Hügel, as well as Nathan Söderblom, were never tired of pointing out, viz.: the " prevenience and givenness " of the grace of God. Prayer is not man's work, or discovery or achievement; but *God's* work in man — " for we know not what we should pray for as we ought: but the Spirit Himself maketh intercession for us with groanings which cannot be uttered." (Rom. 8. 26).

FRIEDRICH HEILER

TRANSLATOR'S NOTE

FROM the time when this work fell into my hands till now, my enthusiastic admiration of it has remained unabated. And I was delighted to find that my judgment was confirmed by two such men as Dean Inge and the late Baron von Hügel. The more I studied the book the more I felt that English and American readers interested in the living religious issues of our time should not be prevented from appropriating its riches by the barrier of a foreign tongue. There were difficulties in the way. The work, in its fifth edition, contains about a quarter of a million words and more than two thousand quotations. The printing of all this material would mean that the price of the book would be prohibitive and its perusal a sore trial to the patience of the English reader. The author, with much self-abnegation, consented to the excision of those portions of the work which did not touch vitally his main argument. I have, therefore, omitted certain sections which are of only secondary importance, and other sections which are of less interest to an English than to a German reader. Much, too, of the illustrative material had to be left untranslated. On the other hand it is hoped that the essentials of the book, more particularly the chapters dealing with prophetic and mystical prayer, are adequately represented in the present translation. And perhaps the reader will agree that a sufficient quantity of illustrative citations has been included.

My thanks are due to the author for his cordial co-operation and valuable suggestions, to Mrs. Elwood Worcester for her beautiful verse-rendering of Tersteegen's lines on p. 178, and to Baron von Nettelbladt who has added to his many kindnesses that of putting into English verse Lermontow's poem on p. 292 and Jalâl-ed-dîn-Rûmî's lines on pp. 294 seq. I owe a special debt of gratitude to my friend and fellow-countryman, Dr. J. Edgar Park, whom I have persuaded to permit his name to appear upon the title-page, inasmuch as he has devoted time and thought as well as his mastery of the German idiom to the revision of the manuscript. If the book is in any degree readable it is to him that in no small measure the credit is due. A few footnotes in square brackets are mine, all others are Dr. Heiler's.

THE TRANSLATOR

CONTENTS

INTRODUCTION

CHAPTER I

PRIMITIVE PRAYER

Occasions and motives of prayer, 2. Form of prayer, 8. The praying person. The individual and society in primitive prayer, 12. The content of, 15. Attitude and gesture in, 40. The higher beings invoked in, 42. The conception of God underlying primitive prayer, 53. The relation of man to God expressed in, 58.

CHAPTER II

RITUAL PRAYER

Transformation of free prayer into ritual prayer, 65. The obligatoriness of the wording of the prayer, 66. The fixedness of prayer formulas, 68. The content of ritual prayer, 69. The mechanization of prayer, 70.

CHAPTER III

PRAYER IN THE RELIGION OF GREEK CIVILIZATION

Characteristics of Homeric religion, 74. Sense of dependence in Greek religion, 75. As expressed in prayer, 76. Freedom of Greek prayer, 77. Its content, 78. Its social character, 80. Eudaemonistic prayer, 80. Prayers of cursing and vengeance, 81. General prayers, 82. Sense of proportion, 83. Character of the gods addressed in prayer, 84. Friendly relation to the gods, 85. Appraisal of Greek prayer, 86.

CHAPTER IV

CRITIQUE AND IDEAL OF PRAYER IN PHILOSOPHICAL THOUGHT

CHAPTER V

PRAYER IN THE EXPERIENCE OF GREAT RELIGIOUS PERSONALITIES

CHAPTER VI

GENERAL CHARACTERISTICS OF MYSTICISM AND PROPHETIC RELIGION

CHAPTER VII

PRAYER IN MYSTICISM

CHAPTER VIII

THE VARIANTS OF MYSTICAL PRAYER

CHAPTER IX

PRAYER IN PROPHETIC RELIGION

CHAPTER X

THE PERSONAL PRAYER OF GREAT MEN.
POETS AND ARTISTS

CHAPTER XI

PRAYER IN PUBLIC WORSHIP

INTRODUCTION

1. *Prayer as the Central Phenomenon of Religion*

RELIGIOUS people, students of religion, theologians of all creeds and tendencies, agree in thinking that prayer is the central phenomenon of religion, the very hearthstone of all piety. Faith is, in Luther's judgment, " prayer and nothing but prayer." " He who does not pray or call upon God in his hour of need, assuredly does not think of Him as God, nor does he give Him the honor that is His due." The great evangelical mystic, Johann Arndt, constantly emphasizes the truth that: " without prayer we cannot find God; prayer is the means by which we seek and find Him." Schleiermacher, the restorer of evangelical theology in the nineteenth century, observes in one of his sermons: " To be religious and to pray — that is really one and the same thing." Novalis, the poet of romanticism, remarks: " Praying is to religion what thinking is to philosophy. Praying is religion in the making. The religious sense prays, just as the thinking mechanism thinks." The same thought is expressed by the gifted evangelical divine, Richard Rothe, when he says, " . . . the religious impulse is essentially the impulse to pray. It is by prayer, in fact, that the process of the individual religious life is governed, the process of the gradual fulfilment of God's indwelling in the individual and his religious life. Therefore, the non-praying man is rightly considered to be religiously dead."

One of the most eminent evangelical theologians of our time, Adolf Deissmann, holds that " religion, wherever it is alive in man, is prayer." The profoundly religious philosopher, Gustav Theodor Fechner, says in his impressive way: " Take prayer out of the world and it is as if you had torn asunder the bond that binds humanity to God, and had struck dumb the tongue of the child in the presence of his Father." C. P. Tiele, one of the founders of the science of comparative religion, expressed himself similarly, " Where prayer has wholly ceased, it is all over with religion itself." And this agrees with the judgment of the distinguished philosophical student of religion, Auguste Sabatier, " Where the prayer of the heart is wanting, there is no religion." William James, the pioneer in the psychology of religion, subscribes to this opinion of Sabatier. A celebrated Catholic apologist (Hettinger) describes prayer as " the first, highest, and most solemn phenomenon and manifestation of religion "; a popular writer of Catholic books of devotion (Alban Stolz) calls it " the blood and the circulation of the blood in the religious life "; a Jesuit divine (M. Meschler) calls it " the soul of the public worship of God and the chief means of grace for the inner life." The acute Biblical critic, J. Wellhausen, sees in prayer " the only adequate form for a confession of faith "; another Old Testament investigator (E. Kautzsch) believes it to be " the absolutely necessary activity of the religious life, the unconscious, indispensable breathing of the religious spirit "; a third (R. Kittel) calls it " the natural and necessary expression of every religion." A New Testament theologian, P. Christ, describes it as " the culmination of the religious process in man." E. von der Goltz, a church historian who has devoted careful study to prayer in early Christianity, speaks of prayer as " the breath of all piety "; another, Paul Althaus, who has investigated the literature of prayer in the sixteenth century, calls it " the soul and very heart-beat of piety." For Rothe " prayer is the potent agency for obtaining power to live a religious life, the specific remedy for religious weakness "; for R. Kähler it is " a fundamental element in all genuine piety, the central point of all personal Christianity "; for a modern theologian, Samuel Eck, it is " the essential and characteristic expression of the religious consciousness "; and for the French divine, F. Ménégoz, it is " the primary phenomenon of religion," " the primary fact of the religious life." A classical philologist, K. F. Hermann, describes prayer as " the simplest and most direct way by which man puts himself into relation with the Deity." In Sabatier's view the peculiarly religious phenomenon is distinguished by prayer from similar allied phenomena, such as, for example, the aesthetic sense or the moral feelings. And even the most radical of the critics of religion, Feuerbach, who set down all religion as an illusion, declares that " the innermost essence of religion is revealed by the simplest act of religion — prayer."

Accordingly, there can be no doubt at all that prayer is the heart and centre of all religion. Not in dogmas and institutions, not in rites and ethical ideals, but in prayer do we grasp the peculiar quality of the religious life. In the words of a prayer we can penetrate into the deepest and the most intimate movements of the religious soul. " Examine the prayers of the saints of all ages, and you have their faith, their life, their ruling motive, their work," says Adolphe Monod, the famous Calvinistic preacher. The varied world of religious conceptions and actions is always nothing less than the reflection of the personal religious life. All the various thoughts of God, creation, revelation, redemption, grace, the life beyond, are the crystallized products in which the rich stream of religious experience, faith, hope, and love, gains a firm outline. All the manifold rites and sacraments, consecrations and purifications, offerings and sacred feasts, sacred dances and processions, all the working of asceticism and morality, are only the indirect expression of the inner experience of religion, the experience of awe, trust, surrender, yearning, and enthusiasm. In prayer, on the other hand, this experience is directly unveiled; prayer, as Thomas Aquinas said, " is the peculiar practical proof of religion "; or, as Sabatier excellently puts it, " Prayer is religion in action, that is, real religion."

Just because prayer is the elementary and necessary expression of the religious life, it is also, as the evangelical theologian, Palmer, has it, " the perfectly accurate test by which the existence or the non-existence of religion in persons and systems must always be tried: it is the standard by which the degree of religion alive in men or possible to them, must be measured." K. Girgensohn stresses the same idea in his thoughtful *Addresses on the Christian Religion*. " Prayer," he says, " is a perfectly accurate instrument for grading the religious life of the soul. Did one only know how a man prays, and what he prays about, one would be able to see how much religion that man has. When a man, without any witnesses, speaks with his God, the soul stands unveiled before its Creator. What it has then to say shows quite distinctly how rich or how poor it is."

But not only are the religious differences of individuals revealed in prayer, but the same thing is true of entire peoples, ages, types of culture, churches, religions. Auguste Sabatier remarks: " Nothing reveals to us better the moral worth and the spiritual dignity of a form of worship than the kind of prayer it puts on the lips of its adherents." Althaus writes in the introduction to his study of prayer in the literature of the Reformation: " Prayer is, as hardly anything else can be, the most reliable indication of this or that type of piety. Next to hymns, prayers reflect in the clearest manner the outstanding quality of the religious life in any given stage of its development." Dr. L. R. Farnell, perhaps the most eminent contemporary English historian of religion, observes by way of introduction to his sketch of the development of prayer: " There is no part of the religious service of mankind that so clearly reveals the various views of the divine nature held by the different races at the different stages of their development, or reflects so vividly the material and psychologic history of man, as the formulas of prayer." Hence, as Deissmann says, " one might, without more ado, write a history of religion by writing a history of prayer."

2. Sources for the Study of Prayer

PRAYER is that expression of religious experience in which, as Deissmann says, " the life and movement of real piety is revealed most clearly and where at the same time it is most shyly veiled." Genuine, personal prayer conceals itself in delicate modesty from the eyes and ears of the profane. Even primitive peoples are extremely reserved in imparting information about their religious life. Many an explorer and missionary has sojourned for years among primitive peoples before he succeeded in learning anything about their religious thought and action or even in overhearing their prayers. What is true of primitive man is still more true of devout individuals. The personal devotional life of men of religious genius is lived in secret. The worshipper stands before his God " alone with the Alone." The great men of religion fly for prayer to solitude, to the quiet chamber or the open spaces of Nature. Seldom has the ear of man heard or his pen recorded that which they have poured out in prayer to God in such hours of solitude. They have indeed spoken of their devotional life to their disciples and have taught them how and for what one ought to pray, but hardly ever have they opened their mouths in the presence of others to hold intimate converse with their God. Paul often exhorts to prayer in his letters, and at times he discloses something of his way of praying and of his mysterious and wonderful experiences in the prayer-state, but in " his religious chastity he shrinks from praying a written prayer even in confidential letters to his churches." To be sure, we know thousands and thousands of prayers which have come down to us chiselled on stone or printed in letters, prayers from ancient temple libraries, and prayers in modern books of devotion; from altars and pulpits we also hear solemn words of prayers, the liturgical inheritance of the Christian Church. But all these are not the genuine, spontaneous prayers that break forth from the deepest need and innermost yearning of the human heart. Such prayers speak a different language; nay, sometimes do not speak at all, but are only a silent adoration and contemplation or a mute sighing and yearning. Formal, literary prayers are merely the weak reflection of the original, simple prayer of the heart. Most sources of prayer are, therefore, only indirect evidences; on the one hand, intimations about the experiences of prayer and instructions in prayer, and on the other, formulas of prayer and devotional compositions. Consequently it is no easy task to get an exact picture of real prayer. And yet we shall succeed in doing this if we carefully collect the various specimens of prayer and grade them according to their psychological value and if, in addition, we supplement them by the individual and general utterances on prayer which we have from the lips of the great men of prayer.

(a) Prayers

Prayers born of powerful psychic convulsions are apt to be loud cries to God. This is always true among primitive people and very frequently among great men of religion. Sometimes it happens, accidentally or intentionally, that other persons succeed in overhearing one who thinks himself to be alone with God in prayer, and afterwards in writing down the very words. Sometimes the distress and joy of the heart are so great that the individual breaks out into involuntary prayer in the presence of others or even in some public place. The impression of such passionate and fervent prayers on the hearers is so deep and lasting, the language itself is so concisely and pregnantly formulated, that it indelibly impresses itself on the memory and so makes possible an exact, unaltered reproduction. Missionaries and ethnographers either openly or secretly have frequently observed savages at their spontaneous prayers and have subsequently noted down the words. Such loud cries have been transmitted from even the greatest men of prayer. We have from Jesus four prayers which spring directly from the heights of His experience. They were heard by His disciples and were transmitted from mouth to mouth until finally they were written down in the Gospels. In spite of the fact that they were committed to writing only after the lapse of years their genuineness is, nevertheless, fully guaranteed. (His invocation in Gethsemane, " Abba," and His cry of anguish on the Cross, " Eloi," were handed down by the primitive community with such literal fidelity that even the Greek translator of the Gospels reproduces them in the Semitic wording.) A rich man of Assisi invited Francis to spend the night at his house with the intention of overhearing him at his prayers and he heard him repeat through the livelong night the fervent words: " My God and my All." He was so deeply moved by the ardour of the prayer that he forthwith became a disciple of the saint's. Veit Dietrich writes about Luther to Melanchthon: " I once had the good fortune to hear him pray from his heart in a clear voice." Then he describes Luther's way of praying and the powerful impression he received from it. Oliver Cromwell, two days before his death, uttered a heartfelt prayer in loud tones which was heard by those about him and was preserved by his valet Harvey in almost its exact wording.[1] These testimonies of others, for which accident is to be thanked, are the most valuable first-hand pieces of evidence because they preserve for us the " actual fact in its momentary present "; they are, of course, the most difficult to find.

Side by side with these are such spontaneous prayers as were written down by those who actually prayed them. But the words fixed in writing do not perfectly correspond to those uttered in the prayer. The very act of writing brings with it the transformation of the authentic words of the prayer into literary form. Experiences intelligible only in a certain mood are translated into the language of common experiences. That which was confused and disarranged is harmonized. Fragments of thought disconnectedly following each other are somehow linked together. There is an element of truth in Bunyan's exaggeration: " A man that truly prays one prayer shall after that never be able to express with his mouth or pen the unutterable desires, sense, affections and longing that went to God in that prayer." Whenever a suppliant writes down in words his most fervent prayer, he feels only too deeply that the written words are but a faint reflection of the burning prayer of the heart.

---

[1] This prayer will be found on p. 291 seq.

Some prayers have been directly written down immediately while the devotional mood in which they were uttered has not yet altogether passed away. Thus the prayer of praise which Francis of Assisi uttered after he had received the *Stigmata* was put into writing immediately after by himself on a card intended for Brother Leo. More frequent by far is the writing out from memory of genuine prayers in autobiographies and confessions. It is evident that the wording of such prayers could only be preserved accurately when they were very brief cries. Prayers of this kind are to be found in the confessions and writings of Old Testament prophets such as Amos and Jeremiah, and in the letters and autobiographies of religious persons of modern times, such as Ignatius Loyola, George Fox, John Bunyan and J. H. Wichern.

In religious literature there is another kind of prayer written down by its author, which is also of great value as a source, that is to say, those prayers which flowed freely to the pen of the devout author as he was writing in a state of inspiration, when, at the remembrance of God's mercy or of his own sinfulness and weakness, he fell into a devotional mood. Such prayers are literary prayers yet none the less genuine. They are not deliberately composed formularies, even though they have been prayed not with the speaking lips but with the writing pen. In the case of Jeremiah the account of the stirring destinies of his prophetic vocation often passes directly into a spontaneous address to Jahve. The anxious doubts and questionings of the author of the book of Job frequently find relief in passionate cries to God. Augustine prefaces the profound philosophical discussions of his *Soliloquies* with a fervent prayer to God, the Source of all goodness, beauty and truth. Symeon, the " new theologian," opens his remarkable *Divine Hymns* with a powerful prayer to the Holy Spirit. Luther's preface to his *Commentary on Genesis* concludes with a prayer for the coming of the Kingdom of God.

Religious confessions especially contain prayers written by the authors themselves, such as the *Confessions* of Augustine, and the autobiographies of Gertrude of Helfta, St. Teresa, and Madame Guyon. They are really only extended prayers, for they are addressed not to man but to God. Augustine's expression *confessio* means not so much a self-unveiling before man as rather a prayer of praise, penitence, and thanksgiving addressed to God. " And now, Lord, I confess to Thee in writing." The motive which urged Augustine and Teresa to the composition of their confessions was doubtless a genuine impulse to pray; an attempt at expression and self-revelation in the presence of the Most High. They are real prayers, though interspersed with passages of narration and self-analysis composed in the style of prayer, and they give us a graphic representation of the real life of devotion experienced alone with God. Literary and poetic qualities appear in those prayers which are contained in mystical dialogues, especially in the revelations of Mechthild of Magdeburg and in the *Imitation of Christ* of Thomas à Kempis. The mystical communion in prayer with God is here set forth as a conversation of the soul with Christ. Typical examples of literary prayers which yet faithfully reflect the personal prayer of the heart are the *Pater noster* of Margaret Ebner, and the *Exercitia Spiritualia* of Gertrude of Helfta. Here also belongs the prayer of Pascal *For the Right Use of Suffering* which no doubt is a literary creation, but yet must be reckoned among genuine prayers and not among mere literary compositions, for the motive is truly devotional. By the writing of this prayer Pascal seeks inwardly to come to terms with his own severe physical suffering.

It has sometimes been possible to note down prayers after they have been offered, in accordance with information given spontaneously by the maker of the prayer or in answer to express questioning. The majority of prayers which we have from primitive tribes have been preserved in this way. Sometimes also explorers who had listened to the prayer of a savage had it afterwards repeated and dictated by the individual who had prayed it. In this way, also, have prayers been handed down from great religious leaders, as in the case of Suso who personally communicated his prayers to his spiritual daughter Elsbeth Stagel. Finally, even those examples are of value in which the content of the prayer is only referred to or suggested; for instance, the prayer of Jesus for Peter, Paul's prayer for deliverance from " the thorn in the flesh," his intercession for his young churches, as well as the lists of subjects of liturgical prayers such as are found in early Christian writers.

In addition to " prayed " prayers, there is a second, larger group of sources: prayers which have been definitely thought out, composed or put into rhythmical form; these are nearly always of a literary kind. First of all there are prayers which are *pattern prayers*, which are in part personal but more frequently general, and are intended to give pastoral guidance in prayer to others. Of such instructions in prayer the most important is that which Jesus, after the manner of Jewish Rabbis, gave to His disciples: the Lord's Prayer. It is by no means intended as the " foundation of a non-personal liturgy for a new type of worship; but Jesus, the man of prayer, by means of this pattern prayer, teaches his disciples how to pray." In the petitions of the Lord's Prayer we do not hear Him conversing with His Father; and yet they bear inestimable testimony to His praying. " They are the ripe fruits of His own prayer-experience."

The results of deliberate composition are much more evident in formularies composed for the purposes of ritual and liturgy or of private edification. To this class belong sacrificial and ritual prayers composed by the priests of ancient religions, the vast majority of the liturgical prayers used in the Jewish Synagogue and in Christian Churches and the numberless prayers which may be found in the prayer-books and books of devotion of the Christian communions. The value of these formularies as a source for the knowledge of the individual devotional life is very unequal. Among them are to be found those in which the free, creative and profound prayer of distinct personalities is unmistakably revealed. This is true of not a few early Christian prayers, of some of the prayers of Anselm of Canterbury, of the liturgical prayers which were composed by Calvin, and of the prayer-books of the first half of the century of the Reformation. But there are many prayers whose character makes it evident at the first glance that they are conscious, deliberate, artificial products. They had never been prayed in the form in which they were written down, but excogitated and composed for the use of the multitude, "manufactured," as the compiler of a book of prayers in the sixteenth century says in his preface, or as Luther pungently put it, "composed by the fireside." Whilst genuine prayers are distinguished by a forceful brevity, composed prayers exhibit a verbosity and prolixity of expression often wearisome. Spontaneous prayer is shown in a simple and free naturalness of expression; the literary elaborations are recognizable by the artistic structure of the sentence, the fulness of imagery, the rhetorical splendour. Naïve prayer is untroubled by any logical consideration, it is a real asking and thanking; thought-out prayers are deliberative, didactic, hortatory. Genuine prayer is the spontaneous expression of one's own experience or at least the fruit of what one has experienced and gained in struggle; artificially composed prayers are meant for other people, and are to edify, instruct, and influence them in religious and moral ways; they are rather dogmatic catechisms, moral homilies, sermons. Indeed, most of these artificially constructed prayers are not even the independent work of the authors of books of prayers. The research of Althaus has thrown an astonishing light on the way in which these books were composed by compilation, even by plagiarism. The formularies are taken from older collections, copied, combined, or hastily revised.

In addition to model prayers and liturgical prayers there is a third class of composed prayers — poetic prayers in which the liturgical or edifying is clothed in an artistic garb. The ancient cultual hymns are a form of prayer produced in accordance with fixed models and they occupy a place similar to the prose formulas of prayer. Much of this artistic devotional poetry issues from personal experiences in prayer and is a source of our knowledge of genuine, personal prayer, as for instance, the hymns of the ancient religions in their highly individualized final phase, the Latin hymns of ancient and mediaeval Christianity, and the hymns of the various national Churches. But it is only a part of these hymns which is the independent expression of a personally experienced devotional mood. Many are only prose prayers re-cast in form.

Literary prayers of a fourth variety are found in the secondary prayer of epics and dramas of great poets. The poet is a discriminating psychologist like the creative sculptor or painter who knows and interprets the most delicate and secret movements of the heart. The prayers which he puts in the mouths of his heroes have never indeed come in this form from human lips and yet they are learnt from living reality; they are " prayed " not " invented " prayers. The formularies of priests, theologians and edifying writers may be said to be the reflected image of the spirit of prayer in a given stratum of culture, era of piety, or religious communion, but the prayers of poetic genius are rather first-hand records of the simple piety of naïve people. If we think of the natural prayer in Homer and the Greek tragic poets, or of Gretchen's " Ah, incline thou, Mother of Sorrows " in Goethe's *Faust,* or of the hymn " O Virgin Mother " in Dante's *Paradiso,* we must place among the most significant testimonies to prayer these creations of the great poets.

(b) Personal Testimonies About Prayer

The words of the prayers themselves are always the most important sources for the study of prayer, but if they are to be correctly interpreted the utterances of great men of prayer about prayer must also be considered. These reveal still more clearly to the psychologist the psychic events which take place in the process of prayer; motives, feelings and results. It is true that great men of genius do not speak frequently of their devotional experiences in the first person. Humility and fine religious feeling generally restrain them from giving direct and detailed descriptions of their most intimate emotions. Nay, they seldom venture to illumine with the harsh light of scrutinizing analysis the mysterious twilight in which are veiled the most sacred things of their intercourse with God. They frequently hide their most secret devotional experience from their own reflective thought as well as from the questions of others. Their precious personal witness is hidden behind their general and standard statements about true prayer. Yet it is true that in the ideal of prayer which great men of prayer have proclaimed, they have drawn a picture of their own praying. When we strip off the husk of what is merely standard or polemical material, we have in our hands genuine, first-hand evidence. Personal testimony should not, as with so many psychologists of religion to-day, be limited to mean only direct, psychologically coloured descriptions and analysis of religious states and experiences. For in the study of the psychology of art, the instructions of the great artists to their pupils are looked upon as much important sources.

First let us consider how some of the *great men of prayer* have given directions which are quite untheological, unsystematic, and without any psychological intention. In His brief and scattered remarks about true and false prayer, Jesus has described His very self. His sharp criticism of the prayer-methods of the hypocrite and the heathen gives us an outlook on the fashion of *His own* praying. The hypocrites pray at the corners of the streets, He prays in His inner chamber. The heathen and the Pharisees babble wordy liturgies, His prayers are short and concise. Through His words, " But thou, when thou prayest," we see Himself in those lonely desert places on His knees throughout the livelong night. His injunction to pray for our enemies springs out of His own prayer-life; even on the Cross He intercedes for His murderers. It is His own childlike confidence and unshakable assurance of being heard which speaks in His vigorous exhortation to vehement prayer, and in the words of the promise which he gives to believers who pray. When Augustine in his letter to the widow Proba sketches a spiritual ideal of prayer, he discloses his own purely spiritual way of praying. When Nilus of Sinai in his *Sentences* gives lessons in praying to the monks of the desert he permits us a glance into his own devotional life. When Luther outlines " the way in which one ought to pray," or enumerates " the things which are necessary to right prayer," we are getting to know, in the main, how he himself prayed and believed. In the *Discourse Touching Prayer* of John Bunyan, there is revealed in a systematic form not to be found in Luther the remarkable emotional power and spontaneity which marked the spiritual life of the Bedford tinker.

More reflective and deliberate than these perfectly ingenuous self-revelations are the *general and standard utterances of*

great modern theologians and preachers which are to be found
in their sermons and religious writings. Among these may be
named Schleiermacher, Tholuck, Monod and Robertson.[2] The
individualistic spirit of our own age gives rise to a deeper
and more delicate psychological observation and description
of religious experiences. The little book *From the World of
Prayer* by Monrad, the Danish Bishop, is a pearl in modern
religious literature. It is a proof as much of a simple piety of
the heart as of a trustworthy religious psychology.

The self-revelations of the *mystics* about prayer, whether
personal statements or general introductions to prayer, occupy a place by themselves. Mysticism leads the individual
back to his inner life. The continual concentration and self-
absorption, the preoccupation with himself leads to genuine,
psychological self-scrutiny. Thus it happens that the utterances of great mystical leaders — so far as they do not permanently cling to the naïve and fanciful notions of nuptial
symbolism — have in many ways a psychological character.
Buddhist monks and Christian quietist mystics have developed
to perfection this self-scrutiny. St. Teresa, with her masterly
analysis from which every modern psychologist may learn,
stands unsurpassed among all the mystics and one might call
her the woman psychologist among the saints. Yet in her the
simplicity and intensity of her experience are not injured by
the psychological self-analysis. Her achievement has been to
experience and at the same time to observe the experience.
She describes her mystical prayer-states while she experiences
them and it is with her " as if she had a model before her and
copied from it." Psychologists of religion are apt to fall into
the mistake of using these mystical self-revelations as if they
were the chief source of their inquiry into the nature of religion.
In doing so they forget that they have before them in these
psychologizing examples only one great type of personal religion. Self-revelations coming from prophetic personalities
are just as valuable for their purpose. Even in them psychological reference seems to be wholly wanting, nevertheless they
very often express (one thinks of Luther and Bunyan) inner
experiences with astonishing verbal felicity.

[2] [To these may be added Martineau and Jowett.]

Theologies of prayer as they lie before us in the numerous systematic discussions " on prayer " by Origen, Tertullian, Cyprian, Alexander of Hales, Thomas Aquinas, Suarez, Melanchthon, Calvin, and many other theologians, are of secondary value. Their contents are determined for the most part by related problems of philosophy; ethical and religious points of view modify the simple, religious experience. But even when the theological presuppositions are not determined by extra-religious philosophical motives, but are taken from religious experience itself, still faithfulness to the actual facts of the life of prayer may be sacrificed to these determining ideas. This is never so in the case of the great non-theological men of prayer. And yet such theologies of prayer help us in many ways to gain some knowledge of the religious experience of the author, sometimes even valuable psychological hints, as in the section dedicated to prayer in Calvin's *Institutes of the Christian Religion.*

(c) Purely External Testimonies

Prayers heard and preserved by others must be held to be really personal testimonies, but observations of the bodily expression, ritual gesture and deportment of the worshipper are purely external testimonies, and are found partly in literary accounts and partly in artificial representations. The reports of ethnologists and of ancient authors contain notes on the conventional bodily attitudes in prayer. We possess but scanty information about any personal bodily expression during definite devotional experiences in the case of great men of prayer such as Jesus and Francis. Artistic representation of praying persons in ancient, mediaeval, and modern painting and sculpture are more important and fruitful for knowledge of bodily expression.[3] To be sure, works of religious art portray the traditional and conventional gestures of prayer, but they also reveal just those individual characteristics of religious experience, especially in the play of facial expression, which can be only imperfectly described by reports in writing. The value of artistic representation for the study of the mode

[3] [Reference may be made to the Praying Hands of Dürer.]

of expression accompanying spiritual experiences is particularly great since the two main types of personal prayer, the mystical and contemplative, and the prophetic and emotional are to be found in the representations of praying persons in painting and sculpture.

CHAPTER I

PRIMITIVE PRAYER

THE free spontaneous petitionary prayer of the natural man exhibits the prototype of all prayer. It is an echo of that primitive prayer which once — when and how we know not — broke from the lips of prehistoric man and opened devotional communion between him and the divinity. But it is at the same time an anticipation of those noble creations of prayer which are achieved in the highest experience of religious genius. We grasp it in its purest form in the prayer of primitive man. In the popular religions of highly developed civilized peoples it lives with native energy and simplicity, but it is strongly repressed by ritual prayer and the fixed forms of exorcism and the magic spell. Moreover, not a few hymns, as for example, of the Rig-Veda, and poetic prayers as in Homer and the Greek tragedians, in their charming simplicity and in the vigour of their language are seen to be an echo of genuine prayer.

The stocks which we classify together by the now generally adopted but not very exact terms " primitives," " nature-peoples," " savages," " non-civilized peoples," are in their cultural life as little as possible really primitives and nature-peoples. Rather do they reveal an entire gradation of stages, strata, and spheres of civilization. There is a great difference between the civilization of a Wedda pygmy, a Central Australian, a West African Negro, and a North American Indian, as even a superficial comparison can recognize. Moreover, the religious notions and forms of worship reveal quite important differences and distinctions of spiritual level.

There is, however, a real justification for speaking comprehensively of a primitive culture and for contrasting with it the advanced culture of the ancient world, although primitive culture comprises a series of stages and ancient culture conceals within itself numerous primitive survivals. The funda-

mental distinction lies in the absence of literature among the
lower races and its possession by ancient peoples. This distinction is, for religion and especially for prayer, the immense
significance. The literary fixation of ritual prayers and hymns
brings about a restriction of free prayer which is not possible
to the same extent among non-literary peoples. This one
factor, indeed, quite apart from the uniformity of all primitive
prayers, justifies the classification as a unit of all nature-
peoples in the following exposition of the spontaneous prayer
of primitive man.

I. Occasions and Motives of Prayer

A momentary, concrete, immediate need in which the primary interests of life, either of the individual or the group, are
threatened — this forms the original incitement to prayer.
Famine and drought, danger to life in storm and lightning,
attacks by enemies and wild beasts, disease and pestilence,
but also accusations and complaints, such as those caused by
the shame of childlessness, urge primitive man with fervid force
to pray to the higher beings. Momentary, or habitual and
permanent, emotional states of high intensity, such as fear,
anxiety, vexation, wrath, hate, sorrow, worry, are the psychic
experiences produced by such situations as act as motives of
prayer. The emotional life of primitive man is far more sensitive, more intense, and less restrained, than that of civilized
man, who lives under a great number of restrictions. The
smallest stimulation suffices to bring about a quite dispropor-
tionate discharge, as H. Schurtz remarks. Excited by the
emotion, the will to live expresses itself in a passionate struggle
and urgent longing for self-preservation, deliverance from the
present situation, the turning aside of the threatened danger.
The consciousness of absolute weakness, of complete dependence on higher, mightier beings whose strong hands mould the
destinies of humanity, pervades the entire life of primitive
man. In the moment of danger and need it awakens a vitality
hitherto non-existent. The connection between the feeling of
dependence and self-asserting effort gives birth to hope; the
Being who is lord of my fate can also help and save me.

Spontaneously and unconsciously this leads to an invocation of the divinity and a prayer for help. When such trust no longer exists and yet the feeling of dependence possesses the man, despairing complaint takes the place of confident petition; he does not beg or demand, he only pours out his need and misery before the divinity. Of course, all these events do not happen in the soul of primitive man in succession; they rather penetrate each other mutually in a unitary collective experience. Yet it is also possible that fear and hope alternate for a long time until at length trust becomes so strong that words of petition are wrung from the lips of the distressed individual. Fear, therefore, may be described as the impelling, and hope as the releasing motive of prayer.

Faith in the existence of supernatural, anthropomorphic beings must be already provided, before man, not without profound emotional disturbance, enters into relation with those beings by invoking them in prayer. Or to use religious language, God must have revealed himself to man before man, on his side, comes to Him; God Himself must open up intercourse with humanity. It is not possible that, as Schopenhauer and Feuerbach thought, faith in God arose merely as the projection of a wish, or that, as the ancient poet believed, fear alone created the gods. Von Hartmann had already correctly recognized that the psychic events in which fear, hope, and the longing for blessedness are bound up, " may be described as a theogonic process only in the sense that he makes already existing objects of consciousness into objects of religious relation, that is, into gods. . . . The recognition of objects must precede the entering into a religious relation with them if the religious relation is to attain absolute assurance, and to stand on the ground of real truth." Man must therefore already possess an idea of God. The feeling of weakness and dependence awakened in distress can only raise this idea to a firm conviction, it cannot evoke it out of nothing. Men take over faith in God from the community in which they were born; but how it first arose cannot here be discussed; doubtless it flowed from a whole series of psychological sources.

" Necessity teaches man to pray." But if once through necessity the intercourse with higher beings is opened up and help and deliverance follow on the prayer, man is thereafter led to pray, not only by the menace to his bare existence, but by the desire for an intensification, enhancement, and enrichment of life. The primitive hunter desires success in hunting, the fisherman a plentiful catch, the merchant abundant profit, the farmer a rich harvest, and so on. Thus the *wish* appears as the second motive of prayer. The original meaning of one of the Greek words for " to pray "[1] is " to wish." Since the fulfilment of the effort and the desire is not in the hands of man, the feeling of dependence is awakened; but the consciousness that all happiness rests on the will of higher beings, who have already given their aid in times of stress, kindles a trust which then releases the naïve expression of the wish in prayer to God. Even here the inducement to pray is concrete and momentary. When primitive man goes hunting he prays for game, when he sows he prays for a good harvest; the uprising wish spontaneously changes itself into a prayer.

The definite occasions of prayer repeat themselves again and again, the needs impelling to prayer remain constantly the same. Thus it happens that primitive man does not wait until he falls into distress or cherishes a wish, but he regularly brings to the higher beings in a general comprehensive form his permanent needs and wishes. And so, besides the extraordinary occasions of prayer there are the regular, customary ones suggested by seasonal changes, sunrise and sunset, the changes of the moon, seedtime and harvest. Morning and evening prayer is not customary merely in Christendom or among such ancient peoples as the Egyptians, Greeks, and Romans; it is practised by numberless primitive tribes. Every Ovambo in South Africa appears in the morning before his tent door, spits towards the sun, throws out a handful of grass or leaves and at the same time expresses his wishes. Among the Bantu tribes the appearance of the new moon is a constant occasion of prayer.

The members of primitive society are bound together primarily by a strong tribal instinct and by a self-sacrificing altruism. Social sympathy is expressed not only in prayer when there is a common need, but also in the mutual inter-

[1] εὔχεσθαι.

cessory prayers of the members of a social circle, especially the family, as also of the clan and the tribe. The individual suffers in the distress and need of the man socially bound to him as if it were his own, and out of this altruistic feeling he prays to the powers above for the other's happiness and welfare. Nay, even beyond the limits of the tribe does this social feeling extend. We read occasionally of heartfelt prayers which members of primitive peoples offer to their gods for Europeans, alien in race and blood, who have won their confidence and goodwill. The intercessory prayer of an African chief runs thus: " I and the white man are as near each other as if we were of the same mother." Primitive man is indeed a naïve eudaemonist, but so far as he has not under various influences lost his primitive quality, he is no rude antisocial egoist, as so many anthropologists describe him. We must therefore include *altruistic sympathy* among the motives of primitive prayer.

It is often asserted that less civilized tribes know neither gratitude nor giving of thanks, and that consequently a prayer of thanksgiving is not possible in their religious life. We are referred to primitive languages which have no word meaning " to thank," and it is recalled that in the rich verbal treasury of the Rig-Veda the same defect is found. It cannot, indeed, be denied that, as Schurtz observes, " the giving of thanks as an express form of intercourse is not a universal trait of humanity," although among many primitive peoples it is one of their social customs. Wherever a primitive communism rules there exists but little occasion for testifying gratitude. Yet it is indisputable that the feeling of gratitude belongs to the primary social impulses which are peculiar to man as a social being, and that this feeling is expressed in gesture, countenance, and speech. Many tribes, like the Dajak, are credited by investigators with a great feeling of gratitude; others, as for example, the West African tribes, practise the giving of thanks even to excess. It is clear from many records that the emotion of joyful gratitude is among the motives of prayer. It is true that the joy seldom passes over directly into a prayer of thanksgiving. As a rule petition precedes thanksgiving; the thankful mood follows upon the desired deliverance from some need, or the prayed-for fulfilment of a positive wish. The feeling of joy is bound up with the consciousness of dependence. It is not to himself or to other men, but to the supernatural being to whom he had first offered sacrifices and prayers, that man gives thanks for the preservation of his life, the blessings of food and property. An African pygmy who was successful in his search for food, prayed: " O Waka, thou hast given me this buffalo, this honey, this wine." Here also, as in petitionary prayer, the occasion is momentary and concrete. But as with petitionary prayers so it is the regular occasions that have called forth thanksgiving. Primitive man was originally a hunter and gatherer of plants. In his search for food he had to trust to fortunate finds; the consciousness of being wholly dependent on higher powers with regard to the satisfaction of the need for food, is expressed most deeply by giving thanks for food and drink. The regular recurrence of the occasion gave rise to the custom of grace before meat, which became habitual among various primitive tribes. Batchelor says that he was greatly surprised when he saw many Ainu (the original inhabitants of Japan) give thanks before eating. Moreover, he never met an Ainu who did not salute his god before drinking wine and who did not thank him for his kindness. This pious custom of a blessing at table is therefore a primitive usage which persisted in Greece and Rome, in Israel and Mazdaism, and as time went on was deepened and intensified by religion. An especial occasion for the prayer of thanksgiving was harvest time. In China, where the forms of primitive religion have been preserved with great fidelity down to historical times, thanksgivings were always offered after the harvest. The harvest thanksgiving to-day still has a place in Christian churches.

Certainly in many cases the pure feeling of gratitude in returning thanks is mingled with a simple-minded eudaemonistic desire to insure the future favour of the god by expression of thanks. Yet it would be unjustifiable on that account to consider the prayer of thanks as nothing more than an expedient born of a calculating egoism and recital with a view to new proofs of divine favour. Only when sacrifice rules the religious life and becomes a formal commerce with supernatural powers, does thanksgiving fall into the background; man believes that on the ground of his sacrificial offerings he has obliged the god to fulfil his wishes, so that he does not need to be further grateful to him. This might explain why in the great ancient religions — which were certainly sacrificial religions — we meet with the prayer of thanksgiving much less frequently than among primitive tribes.

In petition and thanksgiving man's most personal interests drive him to God, but already in the prayer of primitive man there is a hint at that form of prayer which reaches its highest perfection in mysticism, the self-forgetting adoration which has lost itself in God. Awe in the presence of the Holy stands beside need and gratitude as another motive of prayer. The Holy is at once awesome and fascinating, and it is from that specifically religious feeling or primeval emotion of anxious dread and enraptured fascination that the mysterious, wonderful " power," the magic " force," *mana* and *tabu*, is born, which is one of the most important roots of belief in God. It is an undifferentiated emotion which includes fear and hope, anxiety and trust, dread and bliss, trembling and surprise. The English language has for this experience a fairly appropriate term in the word *awe*. Among many peoples this emotion expresses itself in an involuntary cry. The names of the " power," *mana, tabu, wakanda, manitu,* and so forth, originally go back to the spontaneous cry which bursts forth from the religious emotion. They do not however indicate any address in prayer, because the object presupposed in the emotion, " the Holy," does not possess the features of a human personality. But wherever the notion of the " power " is bound up with a personifying animistic set of ideas, when belief in *mana* goes hand in hand with belief in spirits, the direct address in prayer may issue out of reverential dread. Whenever primitive man passes by an object in which dwells a mighty spiritual being, a divinity, he manifests his reverence by a few words of greeting and veneration and lays down an offering, even though only a symbol. No Herero passes by the sacred tree without at least laying a stone at its foot, with the words: " Hail! Father! "

The mystic is absorbed in a non-sensuous, spiritual world;

the contemplation of primitive man is fastened on a sensuous object. But if we could hear the secret utterances of these naïve worshippers we should discover the same blissful yet dread experience of the " Holy," the " Highest Good " in which the mystic's soul is entranced.

Moreover, that other form of mystical prayer, ecstatic praise, seems to be already existent in primitive religion at least in germ. Ecstasy as an experience of physiologically abnormal individuals as well as a mass-epidemic, is not a rarity in the primitive or ancient world. Mysticism has elevated it from being a mere physical intoxication, induced by a variety of narcotics, to become the sublimest spiritual experience, that of the identity of the pure, world-renouncing ego with the Infinite and the Eternal. But the religious interpretation is the same in the one as in the other. Ecstasy means a passing out from the ordinary physical life, a being obsessed and engulfed by the superhuman and the divine. Therefore the loud cries by which the ecstatic state is revealed may be cries and prayers of praise to the divinity. It appears that the brief, concluding cries of ancient hymns were originally ecstatic shouts of joy, the *triumpe* of Roman prayers, the *hailly* of old Mexican hymns, the refrain of the ancient Greek songs of Dionysos.[2] Thus we may also count amongst the motives of prayer ecstatic enthusiasm, although naturally rapturous inspiration and reverential awe are less frequently motives of prayer than need and gratitude.

II. Form of Prayer

The rudiments of a pre-historic form of invocation which seem to go back to a time in which the human language was as yet undeveloped, are the purely natural sounds of clicking the tongue, whistling and roaring which have been preserved in many ancient cults and primitive customs of prayer. Among the African Duala people he who prays begins with a long, drawn-out whistle that the god may pay attention, and after each sentence the whistle is repeated in order that he may not fall asleep again! Even the wordless and formless cry to the

---

[2] ἄξιε ταῦρε.

divinity, which doubtless exhibits a primitive kind of prayer, is still to-day found among primitive peoples. The Ewe of West Africa, when an epidemic breaks out, utter no prayer, but raise a loud lament, beseeching the spirits to save them.

The prayer welling up from deep emotions and desires is a free outpouring of the heart, a direct expression of psychic stimulation. The language of prayer is therefore wholly free, informal, unpremeditated, impromptu. He who prays does not borrow his words from others, they come naturally to him, he speaks from his heart, in his own impulsive words, corresponding entirely to the momentary situation and the particular circumstances. Marcus Aurelius, referring to the prayer of the ancient Athenians, strikingly describes it as " a simple and free prayer." [8]

Thus prayer is a free creation of the moment, an independent, creative act on the part of the worshipper. Probably no tribe on earth is without this free, direct prayer. Among peoples in the lowest grade of culture, the Pygmies and allied tribes, it still appears to be the sole type of prayer. Skeat asserts of the semi-Pygmy natives of the Malayan peninsula that they, with very few exceptions, have not reached the stage of fixed forms of prayer. " The petitioner is usually satisfied with expressing his wish to the great divinities of his tribe in quasi-conversational phrase." P. W. Schmidt is therefore correct when he writes of the Pygmy peoples: " Fixed external forms and formulas in religion are still but little developed. The religious life seems rather to express itself to a certain extent without any rule or form, or rather the form of its expression changed with person, time, place, and occasion, almost to the same extent as the spontaneous manifestations of the rest of the mental and spiritual life from which it has not yet been differentiated. A valuable parallel to the free prayer of primitive man is to be found in the songs which they sing at work, which are in no way bound to traditionally fixed forms. Among many tribes, as for instance, the Indians of South America, even the lament for the dead is improvised."

The perfectly free prayer has never completely died out in the history of religion; it could not be suppressed even through the formation of fixed forms in public worship. It is true that in many primitive tribes, free individual appeals to higher beings are not regarded as part of the religion of the tribe, that is, of their sacred social rites, their regular religious customs; but this fact proves that the conventional, regular forms of cultual worship do not satisfy the religious instincts. Individual needs and stresses were so varied that even in the great sacerdotal religions of antiquity ritual forms and cultual hymns could not wholly put an end to free prayer. Just because here prayer had become the official business of the priest, the individual's deep personal need, again and again, moved him of his own accord and quite independently to turn to the divinity. Especially in the vow, corresponding to the ever-changing object of sacrifice, voluntary prayer has preserved its original informal character. Even to-day the ordinary man, in his own personal concerns and needs, in sickness, in anxiety about wife and child, danger to life by storm, flood, or fire, is accustomed not to say the Lord's Prayer or any other prayer learned by heart, but in free, passionate words to beseech God and the beloved saints.

By the regular recurrence of the occasions of prayer there was gradually formed a scheme of prayer. The formal outlines, the succession of thoughts, and particular turns of expression became fixed, though, of course, the wording varied in accordance with the special circumstances of the moment. Prayer, " from being at first utterances, free and flexible as requests to a living patriarch or chief," as E. B. Tylor says, begins to harden and enters on a process that ends in ritual and liturgy. We may speak here of a half-free or a half-rigid, variable prayer. A formal scheme of vowing among present-day Syrians runs thus: " I need this and this and if thou wilt do this for me I will bring thee an offering." The majority of prayers of primitive peoples which are spoken in matters common to all belong to this intermediate form. The progressive hardening of the entire worship leads gradually to the complete fixation of originally free prayer into stereotyped formulas, the wording of which is sacrosanct.

The element of spontaneity does not wholly exclude fixity of expression. A man in need frequently catches hold of a prayer-formula quite unconsciously and unintentionally, or, to put it better, the formula suggests itself to him, and in it he pours forth his emotion. Here the hard, impersonal formula is filled with personal life. Even the short, ejaculatory prayers: " Help me! " " Hear me! " " Have mercy upon me! " are fixed and formal modes of speech, and yet they well up from the depths of the soul. The terms of reproach, the imprecations with which a man in anger overwhelms his neighbour are indeed mostly worn-out expressions, although their emotional quality is unmistakable. The emotion or desire joins together certain phrases out of the words and formulas stored up in memory, and discharges itself in them. Man's entire life of expression, gesture, mimicry shows the same union of emotional spontaneity and conventional fixity. Nay, even regular prayers which have a traditional inviolable form need not therefore be wanting in the quality of feeling. The ancient prayers which the Kekchi Indians say on definite occasions were uttered with a devotion, reality, and sincerity, that astonished the European spectator.

Originally prayer consisted only in the invocation of the god and a cry for help, or a petition which was repeated in the same form. In the moment of supreme need the original impulse to prayer comes about in this way again and again. In most cases, however, the petition is varied in many ways and includes all sorts of expression which are intended to win an answer from the divinity. Thus by repetition there grows out of a short appeal in prayer an extensive talk in prayer, which sometimes means a wearisome verbosity. The few thoughts which could be expressed in two or three sentences are again and again repeated with small formal variations. The prayer which an Indian chief offered as he was about to begin a journey by sea lasted, as the observer calculated, from five to ten minutes. The Baronga have even a word (*bukutjela*) for a long, drawn-out prayer in which the speaker repeats the same thing over and over again. As primitive prayer is the genuine reflection of social fellowship, frequent repetition in prayer exactly corresponds to its customs in daily life. " In the villages of South American Indians or Negroes," writes Schurtz, " delightful chatter is accustomed to last far on into the night, but its intellectual substance could be expressed in a few short sentences." Even the pictorial richness and charming poetry of many primitive prayers are no symptoms of a lack of simplicity and in no way prove that these prayers are the product of consciously creative art. These qualities emanate rather from a liveliness of fancy, which is characteristic of the more highly developed primitive peoples. " The mind of the Bantu peoples," writes the missionary Junod, " is distinguished by imaginative liveliness and quickness which enables them to grasp the similarities between things. The Negro likes to speak in pictures. There is nothing more singular than to listen to the addresses of native Christian preachers who faithfully preserve the picturesqueness of their conversational style." There are, however, lower tribes who in their intercourse with those socially superior consciously cultivate the art of phrase-making. " No Batak," writes the missionary Warneck, " speaks out clearly what he would have, but heaps up circumlocutions. The gods claim the same kind of address, rich in expression and in idiom to be learned off by heart, as is addressed to any man of repute. The longer the formula of prayer, the greater is the honor to him to whom it is addressed." Here prayer is about to become from a simple expression a premeditated piece of work. Rhetoric, parade, and expansion of style found their perfection in the ancient prayers and hymns of cultual worship, which are the conscious literary elaborations of the priests.

III. The Praying Person — The Individual and Society in Primitive Prayer

The need which impels to prayer within the primitive world is for the most part not the need of the individual but of an entire group; therefore, in the main, it is not the individual that prays but a group of individuals socially bound together, the family, the village community, the tribe, the clan, the league. The oldest form of collective prayer is doubtless to be sought in the confused cries which arise from a group of people in a supreme moment of common need. This form of common prayer, *the chaotic prayer of the multitude,* is found extremely seldom in the primitive peoples of to-day. As in ordinary intercourse with strange tribes and authorities, so also in their religious intercourse with the higher Powers a group expresses their common wishes and cares by the mouth of the person who is their central figure. The other members of the group express their wishes silently, as by gesture and bodily posture. *The father of the family* prays when it is a question of family concern. The *chief* of the village or of the tribe prays in the name of the village or of the tribe. This sociological form of prayer is the most frequent among the less civilized peoples. In tribes which are not monarchically but oligarchically organized, one of the *elders* prays. Where the religious functions are in the hands of special priests, the *priest* prays in the name and by the authority of the community. The representative prayer, however, of the official priest for a social group is much later than that of the head of the family, village, or tribe. The performance of cultual acts by professional priests already presupposes a certain separation of religion from ordinary life. As the magician took over the magical functions of the father of the family and the chief, so the priest took over the religious functions, that is to say, sacrifice and prayer.

While the chief or priest puts the request of the people before the god, those present listen to the words of his prayer in reverent silence. In many tribes the speaker prefaces his prayer with an express request for silence. But not only in devout silence and with reverent gestures does the assembly share in the prayer of the chief or the priest; it actually joins in the prayer by taking up the closing words of the leader in a common choral response or answers the words of the prayer with a formal phrase of acquiescence. The exchange of prayer of the officiant and the response of the congregation as seen in the Jewish and Christian liturgies is already a characteristic of primitive prayer. At the sacrifices of the Amazulu people the chief opens his prayer with these words: " All hail! Spirit of our tribe! " and all present respond: " All hail! "

Though the short choral responses are nearly always formally fixed, the words which the paterfamilias or the chief speaks are often free and improvised. Relatively seldom do we find among primitive tribes a prayer spoken in common by a choir which presupposes a fixed form. Such collective prayers are generally sung in rhythm. It is possible that the song to which primitive man ascribed weird and secret powers was from magical motives made use of in prayer.

Individual prayer which a single person utters in his need, though subordinate in primitive tribes to collective prayer, is almost nowhere wanting. He who is overtaken by a thunderstorm, or is in danger of his life, or is charged with a crime, or is stricken with disease, sends up passionate cries to a divinity. As the individual in need and anxiety prays in his own interest, so also he gives thanks for the happiness vouchsafed him, for deliverance from danger, for the acquisition of food and success in business. Individualism in prayer among the North American Indian tribes even goes so far that the worshipper withdraws into solitude in order to pray. Thus the Osage Indian goes away from his camp or his companions when he offers his morning prayer. In ancient religions in which the priest or state official prays about matters of common concern, the prayer of the individual about personal affairs is more prominent than among primitive peoples. The typical form of collective primitive prayer, that is, the prayer-meeting in which the chief leads and the congregation responds, almost completely disappears among ancient civilized people.

The authorized individuals appear not only as representative offerers of prayer by the authority of the group, but also by the special direction of an individual in his personal concerns. Thus among African tribes, the chief prays in the name of a sick person for his recovery. But it is especially the sacrificing priest who is commissioned to pray in personal matters. He is in constant communion with the divinity whose loyal servant he is, and because he is closer to him than the layman he can much better than the latter influence him and gain the accomplishment of the prayer. As in common prayer, so here the petitioner and offerer of sacrifice is accustomed to be present at the ceremonial act of the priest, which consists of prayer and sacrifice. Among the primitive peoples of to-day, who for the most part have only magicians and fortune-tellers, but no professional sacrificing priests, this form of individual prayer is unusual. It is found chiefly among the Ewe tribes of West

Africa. In the ancient as in the modern Brahmanic religion, individual prayers are addressed to God through the mediation of the Brahmans. In the popular religion of all centuries, the priest is regarded as the one qualified to pray; he is in continuous, immediate contact with the god, therefore his prayer possesses an incomparably greater power than that of other men; the sacrificial act performed by him is much more efficacious than the offering which the individual presents.

An intermediate form between the prayer of the individual and that of an assembly consists in this, that on a common occasion of worship the individuals utter a prayer one after the other. Thus in a ceremonial beer-drinking of the Kikuyu, one rises up after the other to pray, whilst the rest make responses.

The problem now arises; which form of prayer, the individual or the social, came first? The nature-peoples of to-day mostly exhibit both forms beside each other. Common prayer always shows a tendency to take on a fixed and formal outline, but individual prayer, on the contrary, retains in the main its original freedom and elasticity. The question of priority, like that of origin, cannot be answered with certainty. Still, it is probable that the prayer of individuals in personal need is older than the perfectly formless and unregulated prayer of a group. Moreover, the formless prayer of a group goes back in the long run to a praying individual, for indeed it has always been an individual who first uttered a cry which the entire group then quite spontaneously took up, and which it repeated or even varied in chaotic confusion. These prayers and responses spoken in common, once the free cries of the multitude, survive in standardized and fixed forms.

IV. The Content of Prayer

The most prominent characteristic of primitive prayer is its ingenuousness. Everything that stirs in the soul of him who prays, anxiety, urgency, desire, trust, vexation, depression, is expressed freely. L'Houet in his *Psychology of the Peasant* says: " Artlessness is the unembarrassed revelation of the soul's psychic content, whether it be good or bad. It is

well expressed in the Biblical saying — ' Out of the abundance
of the heart the mouth speaketh.' Artlessness is the agreement of a man's speech and actions with his thought. It is
simplicity in the original meaning of the word, concord between
a man's inner and outer life." The praying of primitive man
is a real " pouring out of the heart before God " as the Old Testament metaphor, with fine psychological insight, phrases it.

Invocation

Every prayer opens with an invocation to the divine being.
The personal name of the god is used, or the descriptive title
of that group of gods whose attributes he possesses. The attention of the god is thus called to the presence of the worshipper, or the god is summoned from a distance to hear him.
Sometimes a loud cry precedes the god's name, or to it is added
some such word as " Hear! " This word is the standing introduction of the prayers in Homer. " Hear me," " hear us,"
" hear our voice," " hear my supplication ": all these primitive
prayer-formulas are familiar to us in the language of the
psalmists. Sometimes the worshipper is so ceremonious that
he formally apologizes, and begs only for a moment's attention. " Let one word only be heard, only one word, if thou
wilt really give heed," is a formula among the Cora Indians.
A word is frequently added to the god's name claiming a social relation to the supernatural beings, such as father, mother,
lord, chief, and this word sometimes actually takes the place
of the divinity's name; or several such modes of address are
strung together. The Kekchi Indian prays: " O God, thou
my Lord, thou my father, thou my mother, thou lord of the
mountains and the valleys." The address frequently contains
a reference to the dwelling-place of the god. Forms like these
are found among the most primitive peoples: " O thou great
Spirit up yonder! " " O God who art above! " " O Lord on
high! " " O God who dwellest in the highest heaven! " Thus
even from the lips of primitive worshippers there sounds the
Christian " Who art in Heaven."

Sometimes we find the feeling expressed that the tribe and
its gods belong to one another. The Ovambo in prayer call the
divinity " Our Kalunga," that is, " Our Creator." The West

Africans apostrophize God thus: " God of our country," " God
of our fathers," reminding us of Israel's invocation, " Jahve,
thou God of Israel, thou God of our fathers."

Complaint and Question

Some primitive prayers contain no petition in the strict sense,
but consist of a passionate complaint addressed to the divinity,
of a solemn protest, of an indignant, reproachful question;
" O Karai Kasang! Do behold! O Karai Kasang! I lie not,
O Karai Kasang, I steal not, O Karai Kasang, I am innocent "
— so cry the Katchins when anyone brings a charge against
them. " O Karai Kasang," they complain, " see how I am
mocked," when anyone ridicules them. " Tsui-Goatse, thou
alone knowest that I am free from guilt " — so runs the Khoi-
Khoi's formula protesting innocence. If they are in anxiety
they ask with a sigh, " Tsui-Goatse, what have I done that
I am so severely punished? " If it thunders, the Amazulu call
anxiously, " O Lord, what have we destroyed? What sin have
we committed? We have committed no sin." If a Baronga
has learned by divination that the spirits of his private shrine
have caused him to fall sick, he approaches the altar and asks
with a sigh: " Ba Ngoni, why are ye angry with me? " The
mysteries of a theodicy such as baffled Theognis, the Oedipus
of Sophocles, and Job, the terrible problems of suffering and
of unanswered prayer and the enigma of death tortured the
hearts of men even in primitive times.

Petition

The heart of all prayer is petition, from which indeed it
takes its name.[4] The aim of all petition is the asserting,
strengthening or enhancement of one's own desire for a natural
and healthy life and the satisfaction of one's deepest needs.
It is partly negative when it aims at deliverance from an evil
or at protection against danger; it is partly positive when
it has in view the granting of possessions and advantages.
Primitive man prays almost exclusively for things which are
useful or contribute to personal happiness. Even when he
prays for things of aesthetical or social value, as he some-

---

[4] Cf. the German *beten* to pray, and *bitten* to ask.

times does, there will be found in his prayer a touch of selfish hedonism. To be sure, he knows what ethical values mean and his experience of them is indeed religious, for the sovereign validity of the ethical demands is for him an expression of the will of the supreme God. According to the belief of countless primitive types the Father and Creator of all things enjoined on man a number of moral commandments. As Söderblom says: "With due precaution against a very great anachronism, one might here speak of a certain system of morals in the primitive world." But in spite of his belief in the divineness of the moral law primitive man hardly ever makes morality for its own sake the subject of a prayer. He sees morality only from the standpoint of a social or divine obligation. His personal experience of it as such is not intense enough to kindle his emotion and desire and to form a motive of prayer.

If the occasion for the prayer is specific his prayer is specific and is concerned solely with the need of the moment. If the occasion is stated and regular the petition is formulated in general terms; in that case he expresses not only one wish but in a general way all the wishes of his daily life.

First among the subjects of primitive prayer are life and health. When an Indian is in danger of his life, he supplicates his god: "Be peaceful and do not injure me!" When the Melanesians are in a storm at sea they pray to their ancestral spirits: "Save us in the deep, save us from the storm, bring us to land!" "O thou, dear divinity. I am sick and my body is weak, please help me soon!" prays the Ainu. The primitive man prays not only in such moments for life and health, but in all possible circumstances: "Give me strength and life, Waka!" (African Pygmies). "I ask thee to give me long life!" (Sioux Indians). "We ask for life" (Marshall Islanders). "May the muscles of my arms and legs be strong" (Ewe). The Ewe even express in prayer the paradoxical wish that alcohol may have no injurious effects on them: "Mawu Sogble! Grant that brandy does not make me drunk."

Savage man knows the dangers and difficulties of a journey by land or water; therefore he prays for divine protection beforehand: "O Oki who dwellest in this place, I offer to thee tobacco. Help us, save us from shipwreck, defend us against our enemies, grant us good trade and bring us back home again in happiness " — so runs the prayer of the Huron Indians for travellers.

Protection of life, acquisition of food and drink, the growth and preservation of crops, increase of flocks and herds, large families, occupy a prominent place in primitive prayer. " O Cagn! O Cagn! Are we not thy children? Seest thou not our hunger? Give us food! " — so pray the Bushmen. The Ewe who goes to hunt at the full moon prays: " O Full Moon, grant that I may find game to kill in this bush." The Hottentots cry: " Let me find honey and roots! " In tropical countries water is often more difficult to find than food. The Ewe tormented by thirst pray: " The heart of thy children has become hot. They are thirsty and must die. Therefore have we come to ask thee to grant us a little coolness, a coolness even to the throat." The Wanyika people in the tilling of the fields cry to their supreme deity and to their ancestors: " O Mulungu, I pray to thee. I cultivate this field. I do this that I may obtain food, so as to keep in good health. O ye ancestors, I till this field. May the corn spring up richly in this field! " As material civilization advances, growing needs are taken up into prayer. The Ewe pray to a river-spirit: " Give us clothes to put on and give us cowry shells! " The Duala prays: " Forget not, O God, to give me a European lamp and oil as well! " Protection of property against thieves, help against attacks of enemies, wisdom to interpret rightly oracles and dreams, success in acts of magic. The naïveté of primitive prayer is shown in the quite undisguised egoism which comes to light. One does not shrink from calling down upon other people the calamity which one seeks to escape by the help of the gods. Since praying is the spontaneous expression of a wish, therefore, such wishes as are branded as non-moral and irreligious by a purer piety are the subject of petition. An Ewe prays to a spirit: " Him who has taken from me what has been lost, I give over with all that belongs to him into thy hands. Punish him for me! "

Among the most heartfelt prayers of the primitive world is the following which the chief of the Khonds offers in a time of great drought: " Mbamba! Kiara! Thou hast refused us rain; send us rain that we die not. Save us from starvation! Thou art indeed our father, we are thy children, and thou hast created us; wherefore is it thy will that we die? Give us maize, bananas, and beans. Thou hast given us legs for running, arms for working, and children also; give us rain as well that we may reap the harvest."

It is a symptom of naïveté when the primitive suppliant in unembarrassed importunity heaps up his petition upon petition. The Kikuyu pray: " May the clouds give much rain. May our wives be fruitful. May no disease touch our children. May our herds grow fat and multiply, and may our goods be plentiful! " The same naïveté is seen in the undisguised egoism of some prayers. For example, the shipmasters on Lake Tanganyika pray to the spirit of the lake while they offer pearls: " Thou exalted spirit, thou great ruler, thou takest away all men, thou killest all men; only let us alone." While purely material things are the principal subjects of the primitive man's prayer, still there are rare examples of prayer for higher things, blessings of the intellectual, moral, and social order. For example, the Toba Bataks have such a highly developed feeling of the worth of personality that they pray that others may hold them in high esteem. " Sanctify and magnify us so that our repute may be that of those who are reputable, that our happiness may be that of the happy! " The Ewe pray for family peace and harmony: " May the calabash agree with the pot! " that is, " May husband and wife live together in peace." " Give us peace with our neighbours," pray the Ruanda people to their ancestors. After a death in the family, the oldest brother among the Barongas asks the gods " to bless the family and to remove from it evil feelings and quarrelling."

At a higher stage of primitive prayer, we find that the subject of the prayer is sometimes quite generalized. Here we have the germ of a more philosophical ideal of prayer: " Give us what is good and watch over us! " " Bless us graciously! " " Look on me and be always with me that I may live happily! " — these are specimens of the prayers of the Ainu and Amazalu people. The Khonds of Orissa pray: " We know not what is

good or for what we ought to pray. Thou knowest. Give it
to us." Even the yearning for communion with a divine being
is not wholly unknown amongst advanced nature-peoples.
Thus an Ewe priest prays: " Let me abide with thee, and do
thou abide with me." In the great religions of antiquity, the
primitive materialism of prayer continues with undiminished
force, above all in popular religion, but also in the cultus
which is in the hands of the priests or of state officials; most
of the poetry of their hymns is, however, an exception.

Chinese prayers for rain and a good harvest, for riches and
a long life, do not differ from primitive prayers. The Babylonian and Assyrian kings do, to be sure, sometimes pray for
higher things, such as the fear of God and a righteous government. But what they especially implore their gods to grant
are always earthly blessings, " long life," " numerous off-
spring," " health," " fulness of life," " subjection of enemies,"
and " conquest of an enemy's country." In the popular religion of early Israel, people prayed for the preservation of
life, children, help against oppressors, deliverance from
plagues, destruction of enemies, signs and wonders. Nor was
it otherwise in ancient India. How primitive sounds the following prayer from the Sama-Veda: " Indra, that hurlest lightning, bring to us all good things with both hands; . . . pour
upon me great riches, possession of cattle, for Thou art great."
But even in the Rig-Veda we find all the primitive materialistic
prayers for long life and well-being, strong sons, food, wealth,
plenty of cattle and horses, protection against enemies and
victory over them. Seldom is prayer offered for such things as
right thinking or that one may not do what the gods punish.
In Assyrian and Vedic hymns the petitions for cleansing from
guilt hardly ever arise out of genuine ethical self-condemnation
or a religious consciousness of sin, but generally seek only
deliverance from disease or the removal of a curse. The
Homeric heroes pray for help in time of need, but almost never
for a boon which is specifically moral or spiritual. Xenophon
prays for " health, bodily strength, honour among the citizens,
fellowship with friends, safety in battle, and riches " — all subjects which meet us in the prayers of primitive peoples. The
Athenian State prayed for the health and the welfare of the

Athenian people, for wives and children and the whole country.
The spirit of prayer in Roman religion is revealed in the prayer
of Tibullus: " Give an abundant harvest and good wine! "
The prayers of the people of antiquity — so far as they are
real praying and not merely the formal recitation of a ritual
— are primitive prayers. We see here, as is clear also in
other ways, that in the great civilizations of antiquity, religion
had not advanced inwardly, but only outwardly, not in depth,
but only in breadth. The religions of antiquity are therefore
simply primitive religions, only more complex, embellished by
external splendour, overgrown with ritualism, mythology,
astrology, and magic. It is true that the religion of ancient
Greece at the zenith of its civilization occupied, as will be
shown later, a place by itself among ancient religions. It had,
indeed, inwardly developed, deepened and purified the primitive element; but even this religion had not risen to a new level
of religious thought.

Christian ideals of prayer have only had a superficial effect
on the praying of simple people, especially of country folk.
The spontaneous prayers of the early Christians to the martyrs
move along the same lines as ancient prayer in general; feelings of veneration, of adoration, nay, even of gratitude, are but
rarely expressed; it is essentially a petitionary prayer, " prayer
for life and happiness." Prayer at the present day among
Catholic and Protestant peasants is, as in the Middle Ages, so
far as it is quite spontaneous and free, generally unadulterated
primitive prayer. The well-known themes of prayer among
primitive peoples recur — life and health, rain and sunshine,
harvest blessings, good luck in all enterprises.

Intercession

Intercessory prayer, springing from social feelings, finds a
larger place in primitive devotion than we might expect. It
is primarily concerned with the members of one's own family.

The father of the family prays for wife and child on special
occasions as well as in his regular devotions. The Ku-Bushman
calls to Hue: " Why is my son sick? Make him well again! "
Especially is parental solicitude manifested when a daughter
is affianced or married. Among the Ainu, the father of the

bride on the occasion of the engagement, offers a prayer to his fire divinity for his daughter and son-in-law: " We have, here and now, agreed to join in marriage our son and our daughter, therefore, O Goddess of Fire, hear thou and be a witness thereof. Guard this pair from disease and watch over them that they may grow to old age."

The prayer of uncivilized tribes for a European foreigner who knows how to win their confidence is not infrequent. H. M. Stanley tells how his guides, subjects of King Komat of Waganda, threw pearls into the lake and prayed: " Be gracious to the white man, O Nyansa, I beseech thee. Give him a safe and happy voyage across the wide waters! "

Intercession for persons with whom one was connected closely during life reaches beyond death. Where there exists the idea of a place of happiness in the world beyond the dead are prayed for. This is, however, true only of some primitive peoples; among others the life after death is conceived as a sojourn in the ancestral grave, or as reincarnation. Among the Euahlayi people of Australia when an initiate into the tribal mysteries dies, the Supreme Father Baiame is besought to grant the dead man an entrance into heaven since he has observed the laws of the " Boorah " (Ritual).

Sacrifice, Sacrificial Formulas, and Vows

Prayer was originally quite independent of sacrifice, and it remains so still, whenever in a moment of profound emotional disturbance a cry of distress or of gratitude rises up to God. But if the sense of need and fearfulness gives place to the glow of desire and hope, then man conceives the idea of winning by means of a gift this supernatural power which thinks and feels humanly like himself. He knows that among men gifts and presents are able to open the heart. He is not accustomed to come with a petition to the mighty ones of this earth without a gift. Even to-day it is deeply rooted in the popular consciousness that no one can hope for great tokens of favour and of generosity in return for nothing. And what is valid in intercourse with man, is still more valid in man's relations with supernatural powers. " Ye shall never appear before Jahve empty," runs a saying in Deuteronomy in

which the primitive faith in the indispensability of sacrifice
for the winning of divine favour is clearly expressed. Among
the Greeks the idea of bringing round the gods to one's desires
by means of gifts had become proverbial,[5] and even Ovid
sings: " Believe me, gods and men are won by gifts. Jupiter
himself is softened by sacrifices."

The simple man then conceives of his god as an egoist, who
is, like himself, avid of possession and enjoyment. Therefore,
he hopes to move him to a generous disposition by offering a
useful or valuable object which is designed, as an Ewe priest
expresses it in sincere simplicity, " to make warm his breast."
Thus, out of prayer sacrifice develops as a means of giving it
weight and efficacy. Jacob Grimm was not wrong when he
defined sacrifice as a " prayer offered up with gifts." " Prayer
is always an occasion for sacrifice." Köberle describes sacrifice as " embodied prayer." Auguste Sabatier says: " sacrifice was originally only a form of prayer." Prayer and sacrifice are closely connected with each other; nearly all the
prayers of primitive peoples, as of the peoples of antiquity, are
accompanied and strengthened by sacrifices. The only exceptions are brief, impulsive cries of fear or appeals for help. The
terminology itself points to a close connection between prayer
and sacrifice.[6]

Prayer is one of the roots of sacrifice; it is undoubtedly the
older of the two. Among some of the Australian aborigines
to-day there are tribes who know of prayer, but not of sacrifice. There are also divine beings to whom one prays in time
of need and danger, but who receive no sacrifices. They are
those mysterious, apparently monotheistic Supreme Fathers
and Creators, the " high gods " as Andrew Lang calls them,
who in many primitive tribes possess no cult of their own, and
therefore, for practical religious purposes, rank far behind the
spirits and ancestors greedy of sacrifice.

Originally, sacrifice was completely at the service of prayer.
" This is our greeting with which we ask " is spoken of the
sacrificial offerings in a Batak prayer. But it gradually rose

    [5] πείθειν δῶρα καὶ θεούς.
    [6] In Greek λιτή and λίσσομαι and in Latin litare can mean "prayer" or
"sacrifice." The Hebrew âtâr originally means "to sacrifice."

out of a subordinate into a commanding position. Already in many less civilized tribes, but especially in the peoples of ancient culture, it stands at the centre of religion, whilst prayer is thrown back to its circumference. Of the Batak peoples in Sumatra, Warneck writes that " the rich sacrificial system is the real essence of religion and worship." But wherever sacrifice in support of prayer predominates, the level of religion is inevitably lowered. The feeling of absolute dependence upon God which animates the worshipper is weakened by the thought of a service rendered to God, which obliges God to render a service in return; it is completely crowded out by the belief that the gods live on man's offerings and are, therefore, dependent on man. Thus in the sacrificial transaction, it frequently appears that the worshipper, instead of being in subordination to God, is on an equality with Him, or even superior to Him. The sacrifice which accompanies the prayer is, as the word implies in many languages, a present from man to God, intended to move Him to the fulfilment of the wish expressed in the prayer. Plato makes these definitions: " Sacrifice is the bringing of gifts to the gods "; " prayer is asking the gods for some thing." Similarly, Tylor says: " As prayer is a request made to a deity as if he were a man, so sacrifice is made to a deity as if he were a man."

The gifts are as various and as manifold as man's vital needs. Everything that he requires for life or whatever can enrich or beautify his life is offered to the supernatural being. Nowhere in religious worship is the material civilization of a people or a period so clearly mirrored as in the objects offered in sacrifice, such as food and drink, holy gifts in the form of objects of use and adornment. Sacrifice was originally an occasional gift; gradually it became a regular tribute and in some ancient religions a complete maintenance and support of the god which rested in the hands of the priests.

Man is not always in a position to offer sacrifices to the divinities. In many cases tribes and peoples who have attained a high stage of civilization shrink from continuing the gruesome offerings of an earlier age. Moreover, it dawns upon many races that the offerings do not at all serve the gods as food but are only a sign of reverence, dependence, and gratitude. All these motives explain that in place of the older offerings of food and drink and other valuable objects, symbolical sacrifices of less value make their appearance. Instead of a human being, animals or parts of the human body, such as the blood or the hair, are offered.

Even in the substituted offering the original meaning of sacrifice as a gift to the divinity is not wholly lost. The sacrificial idea lives on in this original meaning through the centuries in popular religion to the present time. In early Christianity the people offered to the martyrs the same gifts which ancient peoples dedicated to their gods. But gradually the offered objects changed. Indeed, the food offerings still exist to-day in European folklore in some small measure; gifts still adorn the walls of churches to which pilgrimages are made. But other pious acts have taken over the religious function of sacrifice, such as, for example, church attendance, participation in acts of public worship, pilgrimages, donations, fasting, almsgiving, in short all that is practised as a meritorious work as service rendered to God in a hope of receiving a benefit in return and an answer to prayer.

The doctrine of " the meritoriousness of good works " in the great legalistic religions, Mazdaism, Judaism, Islam, and Catholicism, is fundamentally only a moralizing and a sublimation of the primitive thought of sacrifice. The essential idea of a positive, definite service *to* God which establishes a claim to a counter-service *from* God has remained the same.

The idea of the presentation of gifts is not the only one which is influential in primitive and ancient sacrifice; rather is the idea of *communion* frequently bound up with it. Gifts are offered to the divinity not only in order to obtain its favour and to appease its resentment, but it is invited as a guest to the festive meals which the family or the tribe celebrates in its honour. By this eating and drinking with the mighty divinity the participants would absorb into themselves its mysterious power.

Because sacrifice is offered for the purpose of helping the prayer, special reference is made in the petition preceding or accompanying it to the gifts offered or to the meal prepared. There are prayers, indeed, in which the simultaneously offered sacrifice is not mentioned, nay, there are tribes who hand over their offerings dumb and speechless with a mere gesture of reverence and entreaty. But generally the sacrificial offering is specially noted. Warneck writes of the Toba Batak tribes: " Every sacrifice, small or great, must be accompanied by an utterance of prayer, however short, the object of which is to deliver the offering and to set forth the meaning of the worshipper's pleading approach. This accompanying prayer was originally the chief element in the sacrifice and occupies a large place in the greater festivals, for it makes the gift what it is meant to be, an act of respect on the part of the humble petitioner, with which he lends weight to his prayer." The sacrificial prayers are not generally offered with such a passionate excitement as the cries for help which an anxious soul utters out of its distress. The mood is comparatively calm and manifests a certain ceremonial solemnity.

The sacrificial formula exhibits, for the most part, a brief reference to the offering to which a short petition is directly joined. In detailed prayers the offering is frequently hinted at in a few words only. But not infrequently the worshipper calls the attention of the god to his offering. The content of the actual formula often amounts only to this, that attention is called to the sacrificial object and the god is told that the offering is intended for him: " Here is thy ram! (Ewe). " Here is your ox!" "Here is your meat!" (Amazulu). "I have brought you an offering!" (Navahoes). Since primitive man believes that sacrifice really serves as nourishment of supernatural beings, in presenting the sacrifice he frequently calls upon them to eat and drink what is offered. The Papuans pray to Tanna: " Merciful Father! Here is some food for thee; consume it; be gracious to us for the sake of this gift!" Divine beings who are not immediately near to man but live afar off are usually summoned expressly to come to the place of sacrifice and to take possession of the sacrificial gifts. For example, an Ainu prays: " O Creator of the world, come down and receive this wine!" Sometimes the offerer refers to his gifts with special emphasis; he informs the god that his sacrifice is something special. "We shall offer thee a sheep, a very valuable sheep," the Kikuyu chief announces to the Supreme Father

Ngai. And a Baronga village chief commends his sacrifice with these words: " Thou Mombo-wa-Ndlofu, Lord of this land . . . look on my offering! Is it not a fine offering? I am quite alone. If I had not brought it, who would have given thee anything? " Sometimes the offerer apologizes for the faultiness of his offering. The Kekchi Indian prays: " A very little of thy food and drink have I brought thee now. It is indeed neither much nor good that I give thee." The Electra of Sophocles excuses herself to Apollo that she comes before him without a gift, with mere words of petition —

> " And now Lykeia King, Apollo, hear;
> With all I have, I kneel, pray, supplicate."

Originally man, when he prays with hands uplifted to the god, brings a gift in order to gain approval of his desires. But not always is the fulfilment of the prayer granted him. He is made wiser by experience; he no longer trusts the god wholly. Therefore, he does not want to plunge into useless expense, he wants first to experience the help of the god and then afterwards bring his offering as a reward and thanksgiving in return for it. He thus lures the god in a conditional way, with an offering which he pledges to give if his prayer should be granted. Frequently he links this vow with the presentation of a gift of small value as compared with the gift which he has promised, a kind of earnest of the real sacrifice. The *vow* is doubtless to be traced to a later date than the simple prayer accompanying sacrifice. The childlike confidence in the efficacy of the gift is already somewhat shaken. As B. Stade says, " One seeks to tempt the gods by means of a promise and is clever enough to avoid a possibly useless gift." The feeling of dependence is thereby weakened, so that man bargains and haggles with the higher beings and so stands not beneath them, but on a level with them.

Frequently a humble petition and reverent offering of a gift ends in an ordinary business transaction. " Give me and I will give you," occurs in an Indian sacrificial text. " If thou hastenest with the answer, we also can hasten; but if thou haltest, we must also halt," so pray the Ewe. The secondary character of the vow appears already from this that it is found

only among the more civilized nature-peoples, such as the
North American Indians, the Bantu, and the Malays, whilst
tribes at a lower stage of culture know only a prayer which is
at the same time strengthened by a sacrifice. Vows in the
earliest epoch of the Indian religion are seldom found; only
in the post-Vedic Brahmanical period do they become more
frequent. There can, therefore, be no doubt that the vow is of
later origin.

Means of Persuasion

It is not only by means of a tangible sacrificial gift that
primitive man seeks to have his god alter his purpose and
to regard him favourably, but he uses all possible means
of persuasion to this end. In this process he frequently betrays a remarkable amount of craft. He is polite to the higher
powers, he flatters them, he shows them that the fulfilment
of his prayer is in their own interest; nay, if that does not
help, he resorts to threatening. He appeals to their power,
their former assistance, the social bond which binds gods and
men together. He sounds his own praises, but often also wails
and yells before them. He continues to storm at them until
they surrender. He accuses himself, humiliates himself, excuses himself, and implores forgiveness. He uses with the
gods every verbal artifice with which he seeks to win an
advantage in his intercourse with his fellows and especially
his rulers.

His prayer often opens or closes with a word of salutation
such as is used in the ordinary greetings of daily life — expressing friendship, reverence, devotion, or goodwill. "Wel-
come" — so begins the prayer of the Hottentots to the new
moon. A Baronga, before his offering, claps his hands and
says "Good morning, Ba-Ngoni!" Some invocations of the
Wedda in Ceylon begin with the words "Hail! Hail!" "Long
life! Long life!" are the introductory formulas of other sacrificial prayers.

The god is thought of as a human being who rejoices not
only in food and drink and beautiful gifts, but likes to have
his worth recognized in respectful words, flattering to his self-
esteem. And so man works upon his weak side. He flatters

his vanity that the god may be better disposed to give. It is true that primitive man uses also spontaneous expressions of praise which spring out of a genuine enthusiasm for the god and reverence in his presence, and not out of some selfish interest of the worshipper. But generally the words which express reverence and homage found in the petitionary prayers are meant to back up the petition and to put the supernatural beings in good humour so that they may gladly and quickly answer the prayer. As Euripides writes:

> " For even to the gods this appertains
> That in the homage of mankind they joy."

Many Bantu tribes when they pray to their ancestors enumerate the titles of honour which they won in battle with their enemies and praise the deeds which they achieved in their lifetime. The Amazulu people laud an ancestral spirit thus: " We praise thee with all titles of honour, we reckon up thy achievements. Be no longer angry with us! " Sometimes behind the short, respectful epithets, " great," " kind," " lord," there is concealed a flattering servile significance, though originally they expressed the feeling of dependence and trust.

The fact that one flatters and pays homage to supernatural beings already presupposes a development of one's own self-consciousness. Men must first themselves rejoice in praises and in fine titles before they can attribute such rejoicing to the gods. Therefore, words of praise in connection with prayer are generally found only in the case of the more advanced Bantu and Malay tribes, and among the peoples of historical antiquity, while the more primitive races do not as yet adorn their prayers with formulas of adoration.

The god of the primitive man is the same naïve egoist as the man himself; therefore, man makes use of the god's egoism as a means of satisfying his own. He *appeals to his personal interest:* he explains to him that the fulfilment of his wish is for the god's own advantage. The blessings which may be apportioned to man will return to the god for his own good in the shape of sacrificial offerings. For example, the Ewe pray: " O Kapelè, give heed! Grant that we may keep well, so that

later we may come to thee and pour out some palm-wine upon
the earth." A Xosa Kaffir supplicates his ancestral spirits:
" I pray that ye fill my kraal with cattle, my sheds with corn,
my houses with children, so that ye may be always remembered." Sometimes the god's jealousy is stimulated. Thus a
Zulu said to his ancestral spirits: " Other ancestral spirits
bless their people." One pictures to the god what one would
do, if the roles were reversed. " Were I thou, O Agni," says
the singer of the Rig-Veda, " and thou wert I, thy wishes
would be realized."

But primitive man does not confine himself to friendly
words in order to move the Higher Powers to the fulfilment
of his wishes. An appeal to the gods' own interests not seldom develops into open threats. In particular he tells them of
his withdrawal of the sacrificial meals, for thereby he thinks he
touches their most vital needs. The following prayer of a
Zulu is a precious example of naïveté: " When have we failed
to sacrifice and to repeat thy titles of honour? Why art thou
then so niggardly? If thou dost not amend, we will let all thy
titles of honour fall into forgetfulness. What then will be thy
fate? Then thou canst go and eat grasshoppers! Do better,
else we will forget thee! What is the good of our sacrificing
and praising thee with thy titles? Thou dost not render us any
thanks for all our trouble."

He does not shrink from severe reproaches and wild asper-
sions. Warneck reports of the Batak that they are a people
who, " finding themselves in misfortune, curse God and heap
reproaches on Him." Junod, writing of the Baronga, says:
" If a great mishap is the motive of the prayer, then a regular
formula of insult to the gods precedes or follows the petition.
There are two terms wherewith they describe this strange part
of the prayer: rukatela, which properly means " insult," and
holobela, " to scold the gods." " Ye are good for nothing, ye
gods! " runs one such abusive prayer. " Ye only vex us! For
although we bring you offerings, ye do not answer us! We
are robbed of everything. Ye are full of hate. Ye do not
enrich us! " The Homeric worshippers do not hesitate to
cast harsh reproaches on Zeus, the sender of misfortune. In

the *Odyssey*, Philoetius breaks out into a complaining cry to Zeus: "Father Zeus, none other god is more baneful than thou; thou hast no compassion on men that are of thine own begettin̬ but makest them to have fellowship with evil and with bitter pains."

A purer piety sees blasphemy in the threats and insults offered to the divinity, because here the religious relation to the god, which is one of dependence, is reversed. But one must not take these impulsive utterances of primitive man too seriously. His expressions of emotion are stronger and less restrained than those of civilized man, who is able to repress movements of his inner world. Moreover, man tends to treat superhuman beings in the same way as he treats other men. He uses threats and hard words in order to get other men to comply with his demands, so he tries by the use of the same means to get results from the gods when the fine arts of persuasion miscarry. But the feeling of dependence and impotence is too deeply rooted in man for him to be able to keep himself in a permanently hostile attitude toward the higher powers, or permanently to break off intercourse with them. As soon as the show of resentment has abated, the religious sense of dependence comes back. Often indeed in the same prayer, savage threatening passes over into humble entreaty. The missionary Nassau saw in West Africa a woman in the same breath alternately scold the spirits and try to persuade them to let alone the child whom they were tormenting with cramps.

An efficacious means of winning divine favour is *self-praise*. Surely the god will much more willingly listen when he knows what an admirable person the petitioner is. He is reminded how constantly the worshipper is thinking of him and making him to rejoice by offerings and praises. "We have done thee no injury; beer and milk have we not withheld from thee" — so runs a Ruanda prayer. Sophocles makes Electra pray to Apollo — "O Lord Apollo, favourably hear them and me also who with generous hand so often sacrificed to thee of all that I possessed." Moreover, the appeal to one's own moral excellence is not at all unusual in primitive prayers. Moral laws really originate from the gods; they are the guardians and avengers of the moral order. Therefore, the gods must rejoice to hear how men obey their commandments. The Duala Negro prays to his god Nyambe: " Thou knowest that I have never stolen nor committed murder or adultery. I have always told the truth, I have paid for the wife I bought and for my slaves. I owe no one anything. O righteous God, thou knowest that I have never cast an envious eye upon my neighbour's house, wife, or slaves, nor upon his ass or his goats or his grain, nor upon his new hat which he has lately bought himself."

An appeal to the sympathy of the god is frequently a part of the prayer in the hope that the higher powers, like men, may be disposed to tenderness by heart-touching lamentations. " Have pity on my child and on my wife! " " Be merciful, I am very poor! " " Pity us! " — these are specimens of primitive supplications. Ulysses beseeches the mighty river-god — " Pity me, O King! " Electra in the *Choephoroe* addresses her dead father: " Pity me, O Father! "

Among many Indian tribes crying and lamenting is a part of their prayers. According to MacCoy's testimony the praying Osage " cries with pretended or real weeping in an unusually loud voice and in a whining tone." Among the accessories of prayer in the Sioux and Dakota tribes Dorsey reckons ceremonial crying and shrieking. When among the Romans, in times of need and danger, the Senate ordered a " supplication " the matrons flung themselves on the ground weeping and screaming. In the early Christian popular religion, it was well-nigh obligatory that in every prayer addressed to the martyrs, the petitioners should pour out streams of tears and bedew with them the graves of the saints. This lamenting, groaning, and weeping must not be taken any more seriously than the praise, which the primitive worshipper lavishes upon himself. Man exaggerates and puffs himself up in order to gain his ends with gods as with men, not quite intentionally nor as the result of reflection and deliberation. He simply unconsciously grasps at all possible means of influence which may spontaneously occur to him. It is not a matter of dishonesty and hypocrisy, either here or in the excessive flattery of the god and self-praise; for the exaggeration mingled with these is involuntarily produced by the strength of the wish and the fervour of the hope. Misfortune and distress, especially sickness, is for primitive man a consequence of the wrath of a higher being who has, in some way or another, been roused to anger through a violation of a ceremonial or ethical law. According to the primitive notion of retribution, misfortune is the punishment and vengeance imposed by a supernatural being who, often quite unintentionally, has been outraged and provoked by man, or who, simply because he is a wayward and capricious being, is sometimes angry without a cause. Therefore, tortured by fear and anxiety, man tries to soften the ill-will of the mighty by fair words. He seeks to justify and excuse himself; he tells them that they had indeed no reason for being angry with him. A Batak prayer runs: "If thou art the spirit of so-and-so whom we have buried, do not come near us. We are not those who are weary of thee. We love thee. Be angry with the spirit who took thee away."

Self-accusation and self-humiliation develop in many primitive tribes into a detailed confession of sin. Confession before a friend, a sorcerer, or a priest, is not at all unusual. In most instances it precedes acts of magic ritual which serve for the removal of dangerous occasions of sin. But prayers containing confessions of sin to God are also not unknown among primitive races.

The self-accusation and self-humiliation before higher beings are not ends in themselves, but means to an end. Primitive man does not seek freedom from guilt and moral regeneration because moved by a genuine feeling of sin; but he is interested in getting the misfortune removed which has befallen him, or escaping the danger which threatens him. His penitential prayer is, therefore, only a variant of petitionary prayer, or, to speak more correctly, a method of changing the mind of a higher power, of reinforcing the plea for deliverance or protection from evil. Moreover, his acknowledgment of sin and request for forgiveness refer by no means exclusively to moral transgression but just as much to ritualistic omissions. There is nothing new in the content and purpose of the ancient Babylonian and Vedic penitential psalms when they are compared with these primitive penitential prayers. They too are designed to soften the divine anger aroused by moral or ritualistic transgressions, to deliver man from disease and evil. Nevertheless, we find here, as in primitive prayers for forgiveness, the beginning of a genuine religious feeling for sin, the depressing consciousness of weakness, of littleness, and of nothingness, the tormenting feeling of moral unworthiness.

The primitive worshipper does not grow weary of entreaty even if his wish is not immediately granted. Nay, he holds fast by his faith that his persevering, vehement, and importunate prayers will finally move the god to grant a hearing to his petition. When among the Khonds of Africa, in spite of their fervent prayers, the scorching aridity of the soil continues and the wished-for rain fails to come, again and again they repair to the same place to pray until they are heard. Among the Omaha of North America the chosen leaders in war were accustomed by night and by day to cry unceasingly: " O Wakanda! Have pity on me! Help me in this time of need! " A Tyrolese peasant woman related that she had prayed incessantly before a picture of Christ until she succeeded in bringing our Lord God into compliance with her wish, and her husband recovered his health. She was quite proud of her forceful prayer. It is true that this indefatigable importuning is intended to soften and change the god who shows himself so hard and unyielding and to harass him until, worn out by the constant begging, he grants the prayer. This shameless praying the Romans characterized as " wearing God out." [7] But it is doubtless more than a mere will to persuade and to influence; it expresses an invincible confidence in the higher powers which does not collapse even when a passionate desire is not immediately satisfied. It is significant that just this feature of naïve prayer is most conspicuous in the devotional life of prophetic personalities.

Expression of the Feelings of Dependence, Trust, and Resignation

When we study the prayers of primitive man we find that in his invocation and praise, in his self-accusation and petitions for pardon, although primarily designed as means to

---

[7] *Fatigare deos.*

persuade and win over the higher powers, another and a higher element begins to appear, transcending what is merely materialistic and egoistic, namely, reverence, admiration, humility, and confidence. But this higher element appears even more clearly in the appeal to the power of God, to His help in former times and to His Fatherhood. He makes use of this at first only for the purpose of impressing the god, and inclining him favourably to his petition. His power, his former goodness and readiness to help, and the closeness of his relationship with men are mentioned in order that he may be inclined to give to them and assist them. But apart from the intention of the worshipper, from out of these arts of persuasion, and appeals to God, and arguments in favour of the petition, is born an independent expression of the two fundamental feelings of religion: the feelings of dependence and of trust. Hence among the petitionary prayers of primitive man we catch the notes of a higher and purer piety, which at first surprise us. But they testify to the presence even in the prayers of primitive man of those deep religious feelings which, although unuttered, underlie all prayers and all religious acts: humility and trust. "We have no power," confess the Anloer when they are attacked by enemies. They beg their god to put himself at the head of their army. "But as for us we are children who can do nothing! Thou art the possessor of power. I have no spittle in my mouth. Thou hast spittle " — says an Ewe priest when he begs Mawa that his medicine may have good effect. "Ye alone are mighty," confesses the Cora Indian. The Watje Negro in the Caribbean Islands prays daily: "O God, I know thee not. Thou knowest me. I need thee!"

The hope of impressing the god is operative also in the appeal to the divine fatherhood. But in the prayers of the more advanced nature-peoples we do come upon unadulterated expressions of religious assurance and confidence from which every selfish thought of converting the god to the worshipper's desire is absent, so that the worshipper lives only in the joyful assurance of being safe under the protection of the Most High. Yet it is true that this expression of trust stands in intimate connection with the naïve request, and grows out of it with self-evident naturalness. Hope and confidence, which are already at work as a motive of prayer, banish all anxiety and fear, and rise to joyful assurance. The wish and the yearning yield to a sense of an inner appropriation and possession. In the midst of the prayer the pious man discovers that a profound psychological change has taken place within him. When he has poured out his need and uttered his desires, he finds himself filled with such confidence that he is indubitably certain that his prayer has been answered.

We know of course that the naïve self-expression of such prayer does intensify one's confidence in life, for it changes the tone of the inner life from fear and anguish to a peaceful hope. But it is a sign of a distinctive spiritual experience when man expresses in prayer not only his unhappy feelings and fervent wishes, but also finer impulses and moods, quiet confidence and courage. The evening prayer of the North African Galla tribe ends thus: " In Thy hand I pass the day, in Thy hand I pass the night. Thou art my mother! Thou art my father! "

It is true that it is very seldom we find the feeling of dependence and trust attaining such purity and strength that all selfish wishes break down, and man, full of confidence and consolation, commits himself wholly to the power of the higher being. Yet the very prayer of resignation, which is so often praised as the ideal of all prayer, is found occasionally in the primitive world. The Jesuit, de Smet, tells of an Indian who had lost three tobacco pipes — a greater loss is inconceivable to an Indian — and in his distress he turned to the Great Spirit: " O, great God, Thou who seest everything and upholdest everything, grant, I pray Thee, that I find that which I seek! " He frankly utters to his God the fervent wish that possesses him. Then his desire is quiescent, he leaves the fulfilment of his prayer to the Great Spirit, submits his will to the will of the great God: " and yet let Thy will be done." Thus does our authority render the words of his prayer. Here the petition ends in submission. The highest and finest prayer which the history of religion knows comes here from the lips of a pious child of nature. Another example is the prayer of the Ho, one of the Ewe tribes: " O Mawa

Sodza, Mother of man and beast! If thou givest to men, thou givest to men. If thou withholdest from men, thou withholdest from men. In thy greatness I am great. I am at one with that which thou dost will."

In many primitive prayers a transition is effected from speech with God to soliloquy, from praise and the expression of humility and trust to meditation and contemplation. Primitive man in his prayer pictures to himself the nearness, greatness, might, goodness, and protecting care of God. The Cora Indian has the river-god in his mind's eye as he prays: " If thou art here, though I know nothing of thee, still thou dost hear me."

We thus find in the prayer of primitive races the striking two-fold character and aim of prayer peculiar to all personal religion and more particularly to mysticism. Prayer is real speech with another who is conceived as present, a Being represented after a human fashion. It is address to a Thou, and at the same time it is a soliloquy, a speech addressed to oneself. In prayer man seeks to exercise a real influence upon the divinity, he seeks to move him to help and grant what he desires, and at the same time he seeks unconsciously to work upon himself through the realization of what God means to him, to strengthen, to renew, and to refresh his own inner life.

Thanksgiving

Whilst the expression of dependence and trust is, in reality, only a part of petitionary prayer, thanksgiving is an independent form of prayer existing alongside of petition and intercession. The prayer of gratitude consists in the humble and happy acknowledgment that God has bestowed help or a gift on man, whether unexpectedly or in answer to an expressed desire. Nor is it at all necessary that a special word for " thanks " be used. The languages of many tribes do not possess such a word, although, as a fact, they do give thanks. Whenever one acknowledges to the Giver that one has received from Him some special favour, that is thanksgiving. In the language of the African Kiziba, the words " thank you " are generally rendered only by " Thou hast done it." " O Waka, thou hast given me this buffalo, this honey, this wine " — such is the

thanksgiving of an African Pygmy. " Thou hast rescued me,
O God," says a Khond, when he has escaped a great danger.
The objects for which thanksgiving and petition are offered
are the same, the satisfying of primal needs and desires, and
like petition they are almost always accompanied by the offering of gifts. But whilst petition was originally independent,
and only later was strengthened by an offering, thanksgiving,
or at least thanksgiving for food already obtained, was from
the beginning accompanied by an offering. Primitive man
brings the first fruits of all that is designed for food to the
higher powers, especially to the Supreme Father and Creator
God: the firstlings of the fruits which he finds in the primeval
forest, of the wild animals which he kills in the chase, of the
harvests of his fields, of the yield of his herds, of the intoxicat-
ing liquors which he prepares. We find these offerings of first
fruits over the entire earth. They are said to be found among
a race of so low a stage of culture as the Pygmies as the only
form of sacrifice. Aristotle and many modern investigators
of religion, such as Brinton and P. W. Schmidt, consider them
to be the primitive form of sacrifice. Certain it is that they
spring from other motives and notions than the customary
offerings of gifts which are intended for the nourishment, or at
least the refreshment, of exalted beings. The first fruits are
offered as a simple expression of reverence, acknowledgement,
and gratitude, but the other conception of sacrifice can of
course be easily connected with this quite different one. In
the religion of the Old Testament too, both ideas run together.
The devout man testifies by the presentation of the first fruits
that he owes his food and drink to the beneficence of the divinity; he acknowledges his absolute dependence upon the
powers on high, and their sovereign claims over all allotted
to him.

Closely allied to these offerings of first fruits we find such
thank-offerings as are presented when a life is saved or on
other happy occasions, as well as stipulated gifts, offered in fulfilment of a vow. These have more of the character of a gift
or a present as in the case of the offering which goes with a
petition. Yet some of these pledged offerings are given as a
mere act of reverence. The Malinki present to their highest

god the object that is pledged, but they also give it to the poor, to friends, and to children, who eat the food uttering a blessing. Moreover, like the petitional offering the thank-offering is explained by a short sacrificial formula or by a reference to the object offered, or sometimes by an invitation to accept it.

Because the naïve offerer of prayer is always a sincere and childlike egoist, he does not allow the opportunity for thanks-giving to pass without expressing to the god a few wishes which lie close to his heart, or without putting in a plea for future favours and assistance.

V. Attitude and Gesture in Prayer

Just as speech is only one method of psychic expression and is always associated with certain bodily attitudes, facial expressions, and gestures, so prayer consists not of spoken words alone, but of the accompanying bodily posture, movements, and expression of the countenance. Nay, if it were right to say that conversation by gestures is older than conversation by sounds, we might assume that the prayer gesture is older than the word of prayer, that prayer originally consisted in definite attitudes, and that these were only later, when speech had developed, accompanied by sounds and words. Indeed, it is told of South American tribes that they pray silently, that only with reverential gestures do they implore the higher powers and offer their gifts. The Australian Yuin, in their tribal mysteries, raise their hands and weapons to their divine progenitor in Heaven and pray without words. The question whether attitude precedes sound, the prayer gesture the prayer, cannot be decided here. But it is established that wherever we find prayer we meet with a certain definite form of gesture. The deep psychic experiences which are the very basis of prayer are apt to influence not merely a part of the system of physical expression but the system as a whole. In the cleatest and most evident fashion, the manifold and ever-changing passions, moods, feelings, volitions, and wishes, stirring in the soul of the praying man, express themselves in his gestures. In this way fear and anxiety, care and trouble, reverence and admiration, astonishment and rapture, yearning and surrender, longing, confidence, and hope, betray themselves. But it is impossible for us to catch these gestures expressive of experiences in prayer. We must infer them, as we infer the experiences causing, accompanying, or rising out of the prayer, solely from the words of the prayer. Only the sculpture of the peoples of antiquity, chiefly of the Greeks, gives us a faint conception of the outer appearance of primitive man at prayer. But it can represent only one side or phase of the experience of prayer, not the change of feelings reflected in mimicry. We know infinitely more of primitive man's and especially of ancient man's bodily attitudes and gestures than of his mimicry. They are originally just as free as speech and the play of feature. But the posture and gestures of prayer became bound up in conventionally restricted forms, much more quickly than were words of prayer restricted to formulas of prayer.

To pray is to enter into fellowship with the divinity and the form of the fellowship corresponds to that of men's social relationships. Hence in praying primitive man reproduced spontaneously and unconsciously the bodily attitudes which he assumed in similar circumstances when he spoke with his parents, his master, or his chief. When he wanted something from God he raised his hands towards Him as he did when he proffered a request to his parents; to show his reverence he threw himself upon the ground as he did before his chief; he approached God with the same ceremonial which he used when he saluted his sovereign or his guest. These usages when transferred from the social to the religious sphere became obligatory and sacrosanct.

The *standing* posture is the most frequent in prayer, then comes *kneeling*, with which *squatting, cowering,* or *sitting* are allied. *Prostration* often precedes prayer, the throwing of one's self to the earth, *bending,* or the bowing of the upper part of the body, or the nodding of the head. A peculiar but certainly very ancient custom is hopping or skipping during prayer. Among the various postures of the hands in prayer the most original and the most frequent are the lifting of them up or the holding of them outspread. Prayer is very frequently begun, accompanied, and concluded by the *clapping of the hands. Striking the breast,* still practised in present-day piety, is very ancient. The folding of the hands and the interlacing of the fingers are also found in ancient times. The *crossing of the hands over the breast* is an oriental custom. A widespread usage is the *kissing of cultual objects,* the throwing of kisses by the hand, as also the uncovering of the feet, the head, the upper part of the body, etc. We find also the opposite custom of *veiling the head* in prayer, as among the Romans and the Israelites.

As a whole, gestures and usages in prayer go back to ordinary gestures and forms of intercourse, especially to modes of salutation. There was originally no specific posture in prayer which was the peculiar expression of religious feelings or of magical conceptions. Most attitudes and gestures in prayer which were formerly interpreted as gestures of *petition* are in reality gestures of greeting. Only the spreading out and the folding of the hands may have been practised in many tribes as ordinary gestures of request, and then were elevated to be gestures of prayer. Gesture in prayer arising out of a dim primeval time has come down unaltered to the present, a living witness of that dramatic realism which is peculiar to the devotional intercourse of primitive man with his god.

VI. The Higher Beings Invoked in Prayer

1. Many and various are the beings to whom primitive men turn in petition and adoration. Prayers and petitions are addressed most of all to the various *nature-spirits and nature-gods,* higher, mighty beings which are identified with a perceptible natural object in which they live and work. All natural objects and phenomena which impress primitive man as extraordinary, which move him to such strong emotions as fear, awe, wonder, and hope, which promise him happiness and advantage, or threaten to bring down upon him unhappiness and danger, may become the object of prayer and adoration. Such are, for example, an oddly shaped stone, a prominent, jagged rock, a snow-covered, gigantic mountain peak; a bubbling spring with its power to refresh human beings, a murmuring brook which makes fruitful the fields, a mighty stream

that overflows its banks, a treacherous lake that draws so many victims into its depths; a great and venerable tree, offering an abundant shade, an evergreen stem, a medicinal herb, the nutritious and germinating seed-corn; the corn field, the fruitfulness of which is believed to be centred in the divinity dwelling in this field; the lightning-flash, the thunder, the wind; the flaring fire, a source of endless blessing to man's work, and, at the same time, a protection against wild beasts and evil spirits; the maternal soil from which, according to primitive ideas, all vegetable and animal life springs, and to which all living things return again; the luminous sun which bestows warmth, light and growth, the radiant moon which lights up the nocturnal darkness, the stars which sparkle in the firmament at night. Besides the spirits at work in lifeless and vegetable Nature, there are the animal-gods, forms of life which, like the elephants, by their very size make an impression on man, or such as inspire him with fear on account of their strange aspect, especially the serpent; then the various totem-animals with which a closely organized group (or clan) feels itself intimately connected and which are sometimes regarded as the original founders and creators of the clan.

Not only does primitive man address lifeless and animate natural objects and offer them sacrifice, he even reverences *the works of his own hands* as divine beings. Even in objects fabricated by human art which have a practical bearing on human life and work, the energy and power of a supernatural being is revealed. Thus the Ewe tribesman offers sacrifices at the yearly yams harvest to the bush-cutter, the axe, the plane, the saw, the bell, in short, to all the tools at his service. But primitive man likes especially to regard manifold objects and preparations which are filled with supernatural magical power (*Mana*) as animated and indwelt by spiritual beings like to man, and he therefore invokes in petition and worship these representatives of the supernatural. The implements of sacrifice as well as those other instruments which are employed in worship, such as magic wands and especially fetishes, may be objects endowed with power. By a fetish is to be understood, according to the etymology of the word (Portuguese *feitiço* from *facticius*), a power-laden, magical object which is artificially " made," constructed, or prepared by man; in contrast to it, natural objects such as stones, trees, plants are honoured and revered in their original, native form as power-filled, spirit-animated supernatural beings. Whilst fetishes, in spite of all artificial elaboration, are yet, after all, only natural things which happen to possess supernatural *Mana*, idols and images which, at a higher stage of culture, grew out of rude fetishes, are a free, artistic, creative shaping of imaginative thoughts about strongly anthropomorphic supernatural powers. This artistic presentation always presupposes some advance in mythological thought. Yet the simple character of the mighty beings lives on even in the artistic idols. The material out of which the Greek pillars of Hermes were constructed was always stone. The animal heads of the images of the gods in Egypt prove the originally animal character of the gods.

Not only natural objects, and phenomena in which mysterious power and vital energy are manifested, become objects of worship; sacrifices and prayers also are offered to the soul-substance which gives to the human body life, strength, and health, a refined, material, energizing substance which one seeks to preserve for oneself and which one, in every way possible, would strengthen and promote — this faith and custom are particularly alive among the Malay peoples. The *genius* which every ancient Roman husband possessed, like the *juno* which every Roman matron had, is nothing else than the invisible material of the soul which confers vital energy. The worshipful reverence which was shown to it in order to assure and intensify it resulted in the development of a personal, supersensuous soul-substance into a personal, divine, guardian-spirit, as is clear from the evolution of the Roman conception of the *genius*.

Besides the nature powers there is a second great group of supernatural beings, the active gods. These are not, like the various nature divinities, inseparably bound up with definite visible objects, but are in themselves perfectly invisible, being visible and apprehensible only in the effects which issue from them. Strange and sudden ailments are traced back to the working of sinister spirits which enter the body of the sick person or in some other way are responsible for its mischief.

Primitive man very frequently conceives of these evil spirits as inhabiting the air and as brought into the human body through the air; it is as if he surmised the part played by atmospheric air in the spread of the germs of disease. In most cases acts or words of exorcism are used to deliver one from these uncanny guests; sometimes, however, humble petition and gifts of sacrifice are offered to them by men filled with a deep sense of complete dependence.

Another class of these active gods is formed by the " departmental gods," as Andrew Lang calls them, or " patron gods," which are not related to any natural phenomena but control and superintend human activities and occupations, and so make manifest that these are supernaturally contrived. The most widely spread of these patron gods are the gods of war which are to be found among the more highly developed primitive peoples such as the African Ewe and the Polynesians. The Ewe merchant honours the divinity of the market-place as Mercury was honoured by the Roman merchant. In almost every human action from the cradle to the grave, in daily work and business or in the rare emergency, the Greek invoked a special divinity which helped him there and only there. Thus sacrifice was offered at Athens at the women's festival of Thesmophoria to Kalligeneia, that is, to the giver of a happy birth. Among the Romans every single action of the peasant was believed to be under the patronage of a special god.

Particular local divinities [8] are a variant of the patron gods. They stand in close relation to specifically defined places and countries. Among the Kekchi Indians every village has its own Tzultaccá, the " lord of mountains and valleys " to which one prays and offers sacrifices. " In ancient Egypt," says G. Steindorff, " every city, village and hamlet had its own guardian divinity, its patron saint. The inhabitants turned to him in supplication for help in days of distress and danger." In Greece every city and village had its own divinity who granted protection to his worshippers and only to these. Among the Romans every town and province, every street and every property had its protecting spirit, every house had its *lar familiaris*, just as every man had his *genius*.

[8] θεοὶ πολιοῦχοι or ἐγχώριοι.

All these higher beings are not unlimited in their operations, but are restricted to their own exactly circumscribed sphere of influence, the nature spirits to their respective phenomena of nature, the patron gods to the actions and occupations under their superintendence, the local divinities to the places and countries belonging to them. Their power is, therefore, not absolute, but limited to their own particular province of action. Hence one is accustomed to turn to them not in any concern whatever but only in such matters of interest as have reference to their particular sphere of activity. For this reason they are not appealed to in any sort of matter but only with such desires and petitions the fulfilment of which is within their power.

Originally, therefore, the nature gods and patron gods were invoked only in those special affairs that concerned them, and the local gods only within their own territory; the tribal, folk, and national gods were invoked only by their tribe or stock, the gods of the family by their own families, the guardian geniuses only by those individuals under their protection. But whenever a nature spirit, a fetish, or a special god hears the prayers of his worshippers and shows himself favourable on account of their gifts, the multitude of his worshippers grows accordingly. One begins to apply to him in all possible affairs; the province of his power extends, he ceases to be a specialist and becomes a helper and hearer of prayer in general. So now prayers are offered to the god of the mountains for health, to the spirit of a pool for abundance of children, to the god of the earth for long life, and so on. The second factor which enlarges a god's sphere of activity and province of power is the process of fusion which takes place among the various individual gods and produces great divine figures. The beginnings of this simplifying process are already found in not a few of the more highly developed primitive peoples; in its completed form, however, it is found only in the religions of antiquity. This fusion of the conceptions of the divine is indeed the characteristic mark of the idea of the gods in the ancient world as contrasted with the primitive. Nearly all the great figures of the gods in the Assyrian, Egyptian, Vedic, Greek, Roman, and Mexican pantheons are the product of an immense syncretism. It is a discriminating observation of Wundt that the great anthropomorphic figures of the gods in national religions resulted from a fusion of the ideal human being with the *demon* of primitive magic; the demon raises the hero into the realm of the supernatural, the hero gives to the demon the features of an individual human personality. When once such great and mighty gods have arisen, they absorb the innumerable little local divinities and assume their functions.

In popular religion in all the centuries one turns in particular circumstances to the special gods, great and small, who can best help and work in their own province of power. And so not a few saints in the popular Roman Catholic and Mohammedan religions are seen to be the real successors of pre-Christian and pre-Mohammedan gods, especially of those particular gods who are usually invoked for help in special anxieties and distresses; as, for example, St. Wendel in cattle disease, St. Blasius in sore throat, St. Lucia in affection of the eyes, St. Appollonia in toothache. St. Anthony helps to find things that are lost, St. Katharine helps maidens to get husbands, St. Valentine is the patron saint of lovers, the Mother of God is the powerful helper of women in the pains of labor.

2. *Ancestral spirits* form a second great class of supernatural beings addressed in prayer and honoured by sacrifice. Among many peoples and groups of peoples, the spirits of their progenitors form the almost exclusive object of religious adoration. Thus among the African Bantu peoples and the Indonesian stocks their religion tends to become purely and simply ancestor worship. Among civilized peoples it is among the Chinese that reverence for the divine ancestors has the most important religious place. Among other groups of peoples, on the contrary, the development of the cult of the dead is relatively weak, as among North American Indians and the Semitic races.

In ancient Greece worship was offered the dead father with prayer and sacrifice. The vitality and fervour of children's communion in prayer with their dead father is nowhere so clearly reflected as in the *Choephoroe* of Aeschylus. Next to the father, reverence is paid to the mother, the dead grandparents, brothers and sisters and children, nay, to all the kinsfolk. In the sacrificial prayers addressed to the ancestors, the entire family tree is often enumerated. The Baronga when he sacrifices calls in the first place his father and begs him to bring his grandfather, and then asks the latter to bring his ancestors and so on until the last is named. The progenitors in the direct line are then commissioned to call all the departed on the collateral lines. Important and influential persons, especially powerful magicians who are respected and feared on account of their rich *Mana*, their mysterious magical powers, are worshipped after their death even outside their family by offerings and invocations. The spirit of a strong and skilful man remains among the Veddas in enduring remembrance and receives constant sacrifices even after the death of the nearer relatives. Here we recognize the beginnings of the hero cult which developed greatly among the Greeks and which is one of the roots of the early Christian reverence for saints. For religious veneration is given not to all the dead without distinction, but only to the progenitors and members of families on the one side, and on the other, to individuals pre-eminent by their social dignity or their magical power. As for the *profanum vulgus* of the discarnate, no worship is offered them; on the contrary they are regarded as malevolent, to be banished by incantations or placated by an offering.

The spirits of ancestors are with special frequency invoked in cases of sickness in the family, since their wrath is considered to be the cause of such misfortune. But to primitive man they are not only ordainers of every kind of evil, but also the bestowers of happiness and blessing. Ancestors are therefore specially besought for good fortune, riches, and family success, for rescue when death threatens, for health, a happy life, and so forth. The sphere of the influence and activity of the divine progenitors is, therefore, considerably wider than that of the nature spirits, active gods and patron spirits who are bound to a limited province.

3. Behind and above these beings innumerable lower tribes in all parts of the earth have in their religion conceived strange and mysterious supernatural figures, " high gods," primitive

beings who rise up quite distinctly from those lower spirits. In the ethnology and science of religion of to-day they have become the subject of an animated exchange of opinion. Max Müller, Andrew Lang, P. W. Schmidt, N. Söderblom have busied themselves in throwing light on these religious conceptions. The " high gods " occupy a special place in the world of religious ideas of nature peoples. At all events they do not stand in genetic connection either with belief in spirits or with ancestor worship. Knowledge of these divine figures is absolutely necessary in order to answer the question of the origin and primary form of prayer. The " high gods " (Lang), " supreme beings " (Marett), " highest beings," " heavenly gods " (P. Schmidt), " all-fathers," " first fathers," or " originators " (Söderblom) stand at a greater distance from man than nature spirits or ancestors, and rise above them in might, greatness, and sublimity. They are the originators and creators of all that exists. They are also founders and lawgivers. They are the cause of all civilization, culture, and moral ideals. Thus the primitive conception contains both elements of the fully formed idea of God — God as the source of all existence and of all values.

Among the prevailing majority of nature-peoples the highest being is more than originator, creator, founder, and legislator in a far-distant past; he is at the same time the maintainer of his work, the god of destiny, the guardian of his laws. Tira-wa, the highest god of the Pawnee tribe, is also called " the Power from on high; who rules the world and superintends all things." The absolute might of God is expressed in this, that He is Lord of life and death. But anthropomorphic traits are not wanting in the image of the first father. Most of the high gods have wives and children. On the other hand, we are struck by the purity, the spirituality, and the loftiness of the faith of certain tribes in these highest beings. The primal father is uncreated, eternal. The high gods are called " heavenly man," " heavenly chief," or simply " heaven." Not infrequently they are simply called " might " or " mighty." But the oldest and most widespread name is the name " father." They are called " father " and " our father " among many African and Australian tribes. If we listen more closely this " father " and

" our father " sounds to us like a prelude from a remote antiquity of the Christian belief in God. In spite of their greatness and exaltation they are not the object of a rich sacrificial cult like the numerous nature spirits and souls of the dead who stand near to man. Since no regular offerings and gifts are dedicated to them, regular prayers are seldom addressed to them, while the lower powers are besought with petitions in the most varied stresses and situations. Ethnologists and missionaries assert that among many stocks these high gods are not at all invoked in prayer. It is true, we do not hear very often of the ceremonial prayers of a tribe to its Supreme Father and Creator God, and yet the facts would contradict us if we assumed that primitive man never, or only exceptionally, turned in petition to those high beings. " One sometimes applies to them when forced by need and danger. Such prayers are the impulsive expressions of a soul which feels itself oppressed and has sought in vain the expedients of official religion. They are not a community affair and this means that they are not a part of religion in the sense of ordered rites and mysteries." These words of Söderblom go to the heart of the matter. Prayer to the Supreme Father is generally the spontaneous and informal outpouring of an individual, not the regulated expression of a social whole. What missionaries and ethnographers tell us of the religion of primitive peoples relates, for the most part, to religious rites and notions so far as these people are bound together in close social bonds and are inwardly linked to a society of individuals as their organ. But here in prayer to the Supreme Being is unveiled to us the *personal* prayer of primitive man in all its fervour and passion. The testimony of the most varied races agrees that when in need or danger, they do call upon those high Beings spontaneously and freely, without sacrifice and vow. They constitute the court of final appeal.

As primitive man, when in sore need, supplicates the Supreme Being, so he also thanks him when he is happy. He sends up to him fervent words of gratitude when he brings to him as a sign of acknowledgement the offering of first fruits. Wherever these offerings to the Supreme God become a regular custom, there also communion with him in prayer became a matter of regular occurrence; it was not limited to extraordinary occasions.

Among some races the Supreme Father in the course of development stood out in a stronger relief, and they finally served him, as they did other supernatural beings, with a rich and ordered sacrificial ritual. But also the contrary course of development may not infrequently be seen. Since these high beings had no set ritual like nature spirits and ancestors, they tended to fall behind these revered powers, and in the end disappeared wholly from the religious consciousness. Since prayers were not regularly offered to them, they finally were not offered at all. Yet we must estimate very cautiously that ethnological evidence which reports that the highest god of a tribe was never at all addressed in prayer. In many instances what is lacking is only the formal ritual prayer, not free and spontaneous prayer. But we do possess unquestionable testimonies that in many tribes, as a matter of fact, prayer is almost never addressed to the Supreme God. Moreover, interesting expressions of savages are communicated to us which disclose the reasons for the infrequency or the total lack of prayers to this Being. There are, in the main, two reasons which explain the neglect of the " high gods," belief in their sublimity and remoteness and belief in their goodness. In the thought of many primitive peoples the Supreme Father has a thoroughly *deistic* character. He created the world and humanity and when He had accomplished His creative work, He withdrew Himself from the world and now He lives in a far-distant elevation as an idle deity, careless of the course of the world and of human destiny. " He made us " — so runs the view of the West African Bantu tribe — " but after he had made us he left us to ourselves; he does not trouble himself about us — why should we trouble ourselves about him? He does not help or hurt us."

The second reason for neglect of the Supreme Being is the conviction of his goodness and clemency on the one side, and fear of numerous evil spirits on the other. All the calamities which befall primitive peoples every day, especially sickness and premature death, are a work of supernatural beings who have continually watched their opportunity to do man an injury. He defends himself against these evil demons by acts of adjuration of every kind, he scares them away by fire, noise, and threats, but he also seeks to propitiate them by humbly suppliant words and to make them favourably disposed by offerings of all sorts. Yet these malicious beings are not to be satisfied. Again and again they send disease and other evils, again and again he must appease their appetite for sacrifices. He turns to them first in unhappiness, for they are the causes of it. To them he prays in his distress, not to the exalted, kindly spirit enthroned in heaven. To the question — " Why then do you not sacrifice to Ndjambi? " the Hereros reply — " Why should we bring offerings to him? He, indeed, does us no harm like our Ovakuru (spirits)."

The recession of the Supreme Father behind the nature and ancestor spirits results in this, that his figure completely vanishes from the religious life of many tribes and only with difficulty continues in the sacred traditions and in stereotyped pious expressions of everyday life.

To sum up: we find three distinct groups of Supreme Beings among various tribes. (1) High gods who (apart from offerings of first fruits) receive no sacrifices, but to whom in time of need spontaneous and informal prayers are offered. (2) High gods to whom sacrifices and prayers are offered as to all other powers which are the objects of worship in the strict sense. (3) High gods to whom no offerings are brought and to whom prayers are never, or almost never, addressed.

4. *Intercession.* The feeling of the sublimity and majesty of the Supreme God may be so strong that man does not dare to come into direct intercourse with him. As he sometimes turns to his lord and chief not directly, but indirectly, by asking his lord's friends and servants to bring his situation before the throne, so also he addresses his prayer to the God of heaven not personally and directly, but invokes the lower divinities for their intercession. In many instances this request for intercession is only a help to the personal petition to the highest being. The suppliant lays his petition before this being, then turns to the lower gods in order that they may intercede for him. One is indeed accustomed to do the same thing on

earth: one asks the friend of the ruler to speak favourably of the request which has been addressed to him.

The invocation of lower spirits as mediators and intercessors with the higher divinities or with the Supreme God is doubtless a secondary phenomenon. When the childlike trust in God died away and men began to represent God as a sovereign Lord to be approached with difficulty, then they sought, in harmony with earthly, social analogies, to win God's favour and goodwill by the mediation of such beings as, on the one side, stood near to God, and on the other, were intimate with human beings. But it is significant that the thought of the "intercession of the saints" is found among the illiterate tribes of Australia, Africa, and among the oldest civilized peoples. It is rooted in the tendency revealed in the entire religious life to carry over the relations of social life into our relation to God. The invoking of the interceding saints and angels which plays a conspicuous rôle in the great monotheistic and prophetic religions, in post-exilic Judaism, Christianity, and Islam, proves itself accordingly to be a very ancient form of religious intercourse with God deeply founded in human needs and tendencies.

VII. The Conception of God Underlying Primitive Prayer

The higher beings in whom primitive man believes and whom he reveres are supernatural. To be sure, they are always connected with natural objects of sense which are their dwelling-places or the spheres of their activity. But they are always *supernatural* since they are never wholly identical with natural objects, and a god, in spite of his anthropomorphic character, is never perceived with a human form and human face, for then he were a god become man. This supernaturalness is, however, not the essential mark of a god. All over the world in tribes in which animism is expanded into panpsychism, every stone, plant, tree, river, lake, animal, nay, every utensil has its "spirit," its soul, its invisible, supernatural substance of a refined material nature. All Nature is governed by spirits. As primitive man personifies all these lifeless and living objects, he speaks with them as with his equals. To-day one may observe the same thing in a child. But this speech is not praying, these spiritual beings are not gods to whom man stands in a relation of worship. He brings offerings and prayers only to some of these spirits, to those upon whose power he feels himself dependent and in whose presence he feels himself impotent. God and demons are to primitive man not merely supernatural spiritual beings who exist but concern man no further; they are beings who have power and make man feel this power. But the essential characteristic of the divinity does not lie in his transcendental character but in his supernatural and superhuman might, in his great strength and "holiness." It is its mysterious, wonderful, magically powerful *Mana,* by virtue of which they direct and shape the course of Nature and of human destiny. *Mana* is a source of blessing and vital vigour, but *Mana* can also work harm and destruction, can bring a curse; thus, its negative side stands out in the Polynesian word *tabu,* "dangerous." On account of this double-sided power, the gods can bestow and deny, give and take, do good and harm, bless and curse.

Power is only one constituent in the idea of God which gives birth to prayer. Power alone does not constitute the essential nature of a god to whom prayer is offered. Primitive man knows an endless number of objects and living things which are filled with power, charged with magical virtue — sacred stones, sacred plants, sacred trees, sacred animals, sacred cultual vessels, sacred weapons, sacred places. He stands in the presence of these objects with the same feelings and ideas which animate him when in communion with the gods; if he draws near to them, trembling and astonishment, dread and wonder, anxiety and confidence take hold of him. These objects are to him something supernatural, mysterious, enigmatic, "numinous." They are to him a source of life, power, and happiness, but also something dangerous, a "*noli me tangere,*" bringing destruction upon him who without any right comes into contact with them. They are at once *Mana* and *tabu.* Sacred objects have an immeasurable importance in the religious life of primitive man. He reverences them in devout awe but he does not pray to them; he offers them neither petition nor thanks. They are *impersonal;* therefore he cannot come into personal relations with them. In order to be an object of prayer, the " power," the " numen " must be borne by a personal being; it cannot simply be there, it must be active, governed and controlled by a personal will. It is only by connecting the idea of *Mana* with personifying animism, or, as expressed in Otto's phraseology, " the rationalization of the non-rational " in the idea of the divine, that the presupposition of prayer is created. A supersensuous being equipped with supernatural, superhuman power, a being like to man, is the object of prayer and sacrifice. He is a god. The third characteristic of the god invoked in prayer is therefore *anthropomorphism.* Man can pray only to a being like to man. To the thought of him who prays, God has the same psychological and especially the same psychical structure as man; he is created " after his image and in his likeness."

The divinities of primitive man are never incorporeal or immaterial; they have a material body, whether this be conceived as an animal or a human body. Like man, they are of a definite age; awe of them leads to their being represented generally as aged; they are addressed as " father," " mother," " grandfather," or " grandmother." They are nearly always distinguished as to sex, gods or goddesses. Sometimes, of course, they are represented as hermaphrodite; in their character as double-sexed is sought the secret of their origin and procreative power. They have the same organization of the senses as man, only greater and more refined, a " perceptive faculty substantially the same as our own, only formally superior and raised to a higher power." The language of the Old Testament has preserved in a remarkable way the sensuous anthropomorphism of the primitive conception of God when it speaks of God's eyes and ears, mouth and hands. God sees, hears, and smells. He perceives, like every human being, by means of His organs of sense. Man comes before Him in prayer with reverent demeanour and gesture; God sees him and addresses him by name; God hears his voice. Together with the capacity to perceive by the senses the god also has the capacity to *enjoy* by the senses. Moreover, the god longs for food and drink, nay, even for sexual enjoyment; since he has the same sense organization as man, he has also the same animal impulses and needs.

All divine beings to whom primitive man addresses his prayers possess the capacity for sensuous perception, but not all possess the capacity for sensuous enjoyment. These ruder anthropomorphic features are nearly always absent from the lofty image of the High Gods, the Supreme Fathers, who are exalted above man's physical needs and require offerings neither of food nor of drink.

The god of the primitive worshipper has not only the same sense organization as man; he has something still more important, his mental life is exactly the same as man's. He has the same powers of perception, imagination, and thought, the same feelings, moods, emotions, the same power to desire and to will, the same consciousness of life and self. As he sees and hears men he imagines their doings, he remembers their earlier acts, he ponders and considers (" speaks in his heart "), he rejoices (" his breast grows warm ") when men keep his commands cr when they bring him gifts and presents; he feels himself honoured when men acknowledge his might and praise his deeds; he is full of affection and " love " for those who obey him, worship and honour him; he has " sympathy " and " compassion " for him who supplicates him for help in distress and misery. But even the painful emotions of man are not alien to him. Wrath, sullen rage, ill-will seize him when man despises his worship and his laws, when he neglects or insults him. Sometimes he even regrets that he has made man, and meditates vengeance against the evil doers. His wrath can be hardened into permanent hate against a man. But his anger is not always a righteous anger. The lower spiritual beings are especially incalculable in their humours; they bring evil on man without a reason. Yet the suppliant can reconcile even the angry god, can appease his resentment. God pardons and forgives the man who casts himself humbly in the dust before him, and confesses openly his guilt. He can prevail on God, change his mind, propitiate him. *The changeableness of God is an essential presupposition of primitive prayer.* Seeing that a petition is presented to him as to a man, he can let himself be determined by the petitioner and can grant his wish; but just because like man he has a free will, he can also refuse the suppliant, deny his help, and withhold his gifts.

The anthropomorphism of the idea of God embraces its social as well as its physical and psychical aspects. Wherever a primitive pantheon has been formed, the higher beings begin at once to be ranked in social categories. In the main they stand to one another in a genealogical relation. The Supreme Fathers of the most various tribes have mothers, brothers, wives, and children. This conception of a social order of divine beings is the presupposition of the invocation of mediators and intercessors. In the ancient religions a rich theological and mythological speculation surrounded and grew exuberantly around the national faith in gods, and so gave to the order of social precedence of the gods a still greater significance.

The god of primitive man is a human being, only greater and mightier and more blessed than any inhabitant of earth. To his anthropomorphic character is due his relative finiteness and narrowness. All the predicates which a philosophical theology seeks to acquire by the *via negationis* and the *via eminentiae* in order to describe the nature of God are absent in primitive man's idea of prayer or are — as in the idea of the Supreme Fathers — only hinted at. The god of the primitive worshipper is not omnipresent and spaceless but bound indissolubly to a point in space, to a material object. He is not omniscient, but must first be informed by man concerning the nature of his request. He is not almighty, but his power is limited to a special sphere of influence, to a natural object or phenomenon, a province of human activity, a limited region, a circle of human individuals. He is not perfectly good nor perfectly righteous, but is sometimes ill-tempered, jealous, revengeful, full of hate. He is not unchangeable. He alters his plans and makes new ones and is accessible to human influence and persuasion. He grants man's petition because of prayer and sacrifice, which, without these, he would not have done. Only the First Fathers stand out above the mass of strongly anthropomorphic spirits and gods. Yet nearly all these all-too-human features can be found even among them; still, their anthropomorphism is finer, milder, purer, relates itself more to the psychical than to the physical side. The highest being is more spiritual and more exalted than the motley host of nature spirits, active gods, and ancestor spirits.

VIII. The Relation of Man to God Expressed in Primitive Prayer

Primitive prayer is no soliloquy, no meditation, but a cry to God, a speech with God. Face to face with an " I " is a " thou," with man another manlike being; the " I " and the " thou " man and the other come into relation with each other. *Prayer is a social phenomenon.* In prayer there takes place a real communion, an intercourse, an interchange between men and a present God. In keeping with the anthropomorphic character of God this intercourse takes place wholly in the form of men's social relations with one another. Prayer is, as a whole, the reflex of human social relations. The forms of prayer are as manifold as are the forms of human speech; appeal and address, greeting and benediction, complaint and petition, praise and thanks, invitation, allurement, persuasion, threatening, insult, accusation, and apology — all these modes of speech reappear in prayer. As man's speech is not only utterance, communication, but also aims at a real influence, a prevailing upon, a change of another's point of view, so prayer especially is of use in moving the god to grant help or to fulfil man's desire. Plato speaks of changing the course of the gods by prayers.[9] The poet of the *Iliad* says with great distinctness: " Nay, even the very gods can turn. . . . Their hearts by incense and reverent vows and drinking and burnt-offering men turn with prayer, as often as any transgresseth and doeth sin." [10]

All the coarse and fine means of persuasion which man employs in order to exercise an influence on his fellow man and to induce him to be favourable, are also used by him who prays in order to obtain a favourable hearing from his god. As in intercourse with men, so also in devotional communion with God, gesture accompanies speech. The gesture in prayer is like the language of prayer, two things at once; it is the ex-

[9] θεοὺς εὐχαῖς παράγεσθαι.   [10] Lang's translation.

pression of the feelings which animate the soul: reverence and weakness, yearning and desire, joy and love, as a means for influencing God; moreover, by attestations of courtesy and humility it is of value in winning the favour of God.

The idea that human prayer has a real effect on the will of the divinity forms the presupposition of belief in the answer to prayer, a belief with which primitive prayer stands or falls. In the inscriptions of ancient temples and in the votive tablets of modern churches to which pilgrimages are made — everywhere there meets us the unaffected testimony of afflicted people who called to God for help and to whom the fulfilment of their prayer was vouchsafed. " I have prayed humbly and Nanar, my King, has heard me," confesses an ancient Babylonian ruler; and a countless company of suppliants give thanks in similar words. They are all convinced that they have prevailed upon or changed the will of the god, that they have obtained, by reason of the prayer, what, without the prayer, would have remained denied to them.

The social relation in which the praying man stands to God is one of subordination and dependence. God is greater and mightier than man, man's destiny is in His power. This relation of dependence is always a *faithful reflection of an earthly social relation,* mostly one of kinship or of subjection. This social relation supporting the prayer is nearly always expressed in the introductory words. " The idea of the kinship of man with God," says Dr. Farnell, " belongs to the alphabet of true prayer." " In the liturgies of primitive peoples as of advanced religion the divinity is ordinarily addressed in the relations of kinship." Aeschylus makes the chorus in the *Suppliants* cry: " O Mother Earth, O Mother Earth! Turn from us what is terrible! O Father, Son of Earth, Zeus! "

The relation of the praying man to God as a filial relation is a primitive religious phenomenon. In this address to God, Pygmies and Australians, Bantu-peoples and Indians, clasp hands with Greeks, Romans, Assyrians, and Hindus. Primitive men call the Creator and Heavenly Father, the mysterious First Cause, by the name " Father," and with this name they address him in prayer. They boast to him of their filial relation. " Art thou not our father? Are we not thy children?

Thou art our father and we are thy children." Ancestors and nature spirits, divinities of trees and water, stars, the brilliant sun, the radiant moon, the native " lord of the mountains and valleys," even cultual objects, fetishes, and magic wands are so addressed by primitive peoples. " Thou, O Agni, art our father, we are of thy kin," prays the singer of the Rig-Veda to the god of fire. A pure devotional religion and a refined idea of prayer protest against the name " father " being given to many gods and even to fetishes and idols; but these very protests at the same time testify to the tenacious continuity of primitive prayer. Jeremiah, the great man of prayer, cries out: " They, their kings, their princes, and their priests and their prophets (are ashamed) who say to a stock, Thou art my father; and to a stone, Thou hast brought me forth." The application of the name " father " to different gods is for Lactantius, the apologist, a weighty argument for the absurdity and unnaturalness of belief in a plurality of gods. Like the name " Father," the name " Mother " is also used as a title of honour and respect. Thus it happens that even feminine divinities other than the goddesses of the Earth and " Fruitfulness " are addressed as mothers, as, for example, the Moon-goddess of the Cora Indians. " Mother " as the title of a divinity like the name " Father " is a primitive religious phenomenon which meets us throughout the whole world. In the Christian cult of the Virgin Mary this primitive picture of man's relation to the divinity as a child's relation to his mother awakened to new life, religiously deepened, morally purified, and aesthetically transfigured.

Among some peoples such as the central American Indians, the Sumerians, and the Egyptians, we come across the remarkable fact that in the invocation of prayer, the terms " father " and " mother " are applied to one and the same divine being. " Thou my mother, Thou my father! " the Kekchi Indians say to Tzultaccá, the lord of mountains and valleys. The Egyptian addresses Isis: " O my father, my brother, my mother, Isis! " And in a prayer to Marduk it is said: " As a father and a mother thou dwellest with thy people." Did these worshippers intend merely to heap up titles of honour? Or did they think that the goodness of God

embraces a father's solicitude and a mother's love? Or were
they, as Radau asserts of the Sumerians, influenced by the
notion of the hermaphrodite character of the divinity? The
question is without importance for our discussion. The important point is only the fact that in all the world men believe
that they stand in a filial relation to divine beings, that they
speak with them as children with their parents.

Awe in the presence of higher beings is the reason why one
approaches them as young people approach their elders.
"Grandfather" and "grandmother" are frequent modes of
address in prayer among primitive peoples. Among the Sioux
Indians masculine divinities are invoked as "grandfather," and
feminine divinities as "grandmother." The Hottentots call
their Supreme Father, Tsui-Goab, "grandfather." "Grandfather, Venerable man!" is the prayer of the Santee Indians
to the buffalo. The address "uncle" and "elder brother"
are also found sometimes in primitive prayers. The Cora Indians address the morning star as "elder brother." "Thou art
my brother," says an Egyptian to Isis.

The relation of servant to God is expressed in prayer much
more frequently than that of friend, but less frequently than
the relations of kinship. Many different kinds of divinities
are addressed by primitive peoples as — "Lord," "Ruler,"
"Chief." The warlike Omaha Indians call the thunder,
"Leader," "Commander." "Thy slave has come to thank
thee" is said in a prayer of the Ewe people to a *tro*. Among
the Greeks "King" and "Queen" are ancient modes of
address in prayer to divine beings. The Roman goddesses
are called "Lady" and "Queen." But nowhere does the relation subject to a lord play a more significant rôle than in the
Semitic religions, although even in them the original relation
was that of a child to his father. The relation of servant to
God is really an essential peculiarity of Semitic in contrast to
Indo-Germanic religion. The names for God among the
western Semites (Baal, Adon, Melech, Rabbat) throw light
upon man's relation to the divinity. The worship of God is
for the ancient Semites a slavish service.[11] As a slave is bound

[11] As the Roman speaks of a *colere* and the Greek of a θεραπεύειν, so
the Hebrew describes worship as an *âbad*, "to be a slave," "to perform a

to his master, so is man bound to his god, subject to his sovereign will. The pious Israelite regards himself in prayer as a slave, the pious Israelitess as a maidservant.

The relation of man to God which always resembles a social relation of men to one another, is in prayer one of dependence or subordination. In vows, on the contrary, a change of relation is usually effected. God and man stand on the same level, like two men who propose an exchange. Man promises God a service, and asks from Him a service in return: *do ut des*. The consciousness of dependence is here not obliterated but man does not feel himself " merely " dependent. The relation of dependence is rather a double-sided one. Each of the two participating parties is dependent on the other; each of the two, God as well as man, is at the same time giver and receiver. Here there is a co-ordination instead of a subordination of God and man. But even here is reflected an earthly social relation; not child and parent, not slave and master, not vassal and chief stand face to face, but two who close a bargain, who transact a matter of business.

The nature of the social relation to God is expressed unmistakably in the *mood* of prayer. Vows are those that are most devoid of a spiritual tone. Reverence, humility, trust fall into the background, man thinks only of his own interest, bargains and haggles. The devotional temper of prayer to the *Lord* is quite different. Humility and fear fill him who prays. He is penetrated with the greatness and power of the Lord, crushed with a feeling of absolute dependence. He shows himself courteous, submissive, devout; sometimes he even falls into fawning servility. Trust and confidence are not absent, but they are submerged by fear and feeling of inferiority. In this way the ancient Semites prayed, and in this way they still pray in the East to-day. Thus also do the peasants of our own day pray to God. According to the testimony of Pastor Gebhard who knows the people well, " God to the countryman in general

---

slave's service." In Arabic this same root *âbada* means "to adore." In prayer God is addressed as "Lord" (Babylonian, *bêlu*, Hebrew, *Adonai*), the goddess as "Lady" (*bêltu*); the Babylonian address, "my lord," "lady" (beltîa = Madonna) expresses the close connection of the individual person with God. The religious relation is here individualized.

is a master to be feared, ruler and judge of the world." " God is for him his gracious Master, who, like other gracious masters, can at times be quite ungracious." " The fear of God is and remains for the peasant the most suitable description of religiousness." The mood of prayer is again different when the suppliant's mind is filled only with the greatness and sublimity of his God, when the fear of a slave is as far from him as the heartfelt trust of a child. Such prayer is full of a ceremonial gravity, a dignified formality, devoid of all emotional extravagance. Again there is a different devotional mood wherever the relation to the divinity is conceived as that of a child. It is true that the name " father " in many primitive prayers is merely a polite phrase, not the expression of a real filial feeling; frequently the pleasing manner and cordiality in prayer are only half genuine, determined by the selfish effort to prevail upon God. But in many primitive prayers the names " father " and " mother " spring from the depths of the soul. In many prayers to ancestors, to the life-bestowing goddess, and to the exalted Supreme Father, we find the language of fervour and affection which springs from a real filial relation to the divinity. We must lay aside the modern prejudice that, as Alfred Maury said, " fear is the father of religion and love its late-born daughter." The real primitive man is no " savage," no " uncivilized creature," no half-brute whose only psychical springs of action are fear and self-seeking; " he is an unspoiled product of Nature of a lovable character." The attitude which primitive man takes up toward those people whose goodness he knows by experience is the same attitude which he assumes in communicating with supernatural beings. The same affection and trustfulness which he shows toward parents and relations he reveals also in prayer to those exalted beings who are to him as father or mother, grandfather or grandmother. He speaks as a child to his parents. In perfect candour he expresses himself frankly, he " pours out his heart " in simple confidence — God is no stranger, he knows Him well; with unaffected sincerity he loves Him because he has often experienced His goodness; with heartfelt confidence he trusts in Him, he relies on His power and kindness.

The kind of social relation in which the suppliant believes

himself to stand to the divinity gives to the devotional mood a quite definite colour. The choice of words, the sound of the voice, the play of facial features, the bodily attitude and gestures vary according to the devotional mood caused by the particular relation to the divinity. To grasp these fine variations psychologically is not possible, since the results of observation do not exist. It is enough to be able to affirm that the social relation to God may alter the devotional mood and the entire method of expression.

CHAPTER II

RITUAL PRAYER

PRAYER is at first a spontaneous emotional discharge, a free outpouring of the heart. In the course of development it becomes a fixed formula which people recite without feeling or mood of devotion, untouched both in heart and mind. At first prayer is an intimate intercourse with God, but gradually it becomes hard, impersonal, ceremonial, a rite consecrated by ancestral custom. Originally it springs directly out of the soul's deepest need or highest bliss; later its use is limited to definite, regularly recurring occasions. Originally it is the informal utterance of a depressed or happy soul, accompanied at the most by a simple gift; later it becomes an inseparable part of a complicated ritual of purifications, sacrifices, processions, dances, and consecrations. Originally it is the personal utterance of an individual or of the chief of a group; later it becomes the impersonal, professional business of the priests. Even among primitive peoples this process of petrification and mechanization takes place which transforms free prayer into precise and rigid formulas. At the festival of First Fruits the Bushman chief utters a prayer which is repeated every year in the same form. The Ceylonese Weddas have numerous devotional formulas which the Shaman recites and which his pupils learn by heart. Le Roy reports that the Bantu and Negrillo tribes have, together with free prayers, fixed forms " which are consecrated by use and which the officiants recite on definite occasions." Junod, writing about the Baronga tribes, says that " most of their prayers are wholly liturgical in character. The personal element is almost entirely lacking." In the worship of the peoples of antiquity formal prayers occupy an even more important place, especially in the Veda-Brahmanic religion which has the largest of all books of ritual, the Yajur-Veda, in the Egyptian religion where the ancient formulas of prayer have become magical charms, and in the Roman religion where the formal fixation of prayer is carried out in the strictest way.

How is it that from being a free outflow of the heart, prayer becomes an unchangeable, hard-and-fast form? As has already been remarked, the course of development was not direct but through an intermediate stage. The flexible, elastic outline, which in a free way was adapted to the concrete needs of the moment, is the link between spontaneous, formless emotional utterance and the precise and fixed formula which is transmitted as a traditional possession. The factors conditioning or favourable to this process of petrifaction are the frequent recurrence of the occasions for prayer as well as their close connection. with definite ritual acts. Acts of worship harden with amazing swiftness into sacred rites. As secondary factors may be considered a growing feeling of uncertainty in regard to the divinity, a feeling which is set to rest only by fixed formulas, as well as the inability for independent expression which compels the use of formularies.

The occasions for formal prayer are for the most part regular; it is especially on great festivals that the ritually fixed forms of prayer are used. But such are also employed in extraordinary circumstances, in particular needs and concerns. Devotional formulas serve mostly as an accompaniment of an offering, or an act of purification or consecration. In addition there are also independent formulas unconnected with sacrificial or lustral ceremonies, as, for example, morning and evening prayer which the individual regularly observes.

The prayer formula is stereotyped and strictly obligatory; the wording is inviolable, sacrosanct; no worshipper may dare to alter the words in the slightest degree, any more than he would think of making a change in the ritual acts of sacrifice, expiation, or consecration. The Romans gave heed with painful solicitude to the correct recitation of formulas of prayer. In order that the officiant might speak every word in its right place and might not put one word for another, the pontifex or another functionary read aloud to him the traditional formula. A deviation from the wording invalidated the prayer and the entire ritual action. According to Cicero, the Roman axiom runs thus: " If the aedile shall make a mistake even in one word or form of sacrifice, the sacred games are not duly performed."

The ritual formula possesses extraordinary stability. It is handed down unchanged through the centuries. The Egyptian books of worship of the Graeco-Roman epoch reproduce faithfully the ancient ritual texts which once were written on the walls of the pyramids. As Cumont says: " Under the Caesars were still performed with meticulous care the ancient ceremonies which had their origin in the beginnings of Egyptian history, and whose smallest word and most insignificant gesture were deemed important." Ancient and sacred formulas of prayer are still in use long after a complete change in religious conceptions — nay, the prayers continue to be recited even though their language has ceased to be understood. In the time of the Roman Empire old Latin prayers were still spoken which were completely unintelligible even to the priests. Sometimes such ancient formulas were transplanted even to countries where a foreign tongue was spoken. In the Hellenistic mysteries of Isis, the priest in the holiest act, that of opening the tabernacle, made use of the Egyptian language. The verbal persistence of the ancient formulas, in spite of the developments of the language or their adoption by peoples speaking other tongues, brings about the rise of languages wholly ritual in character. The most ancient ceremonial speech is the Sumerian which was always regarded as sacred by the Semitic Assyrians and Babylonians.

We find that besides these formulas which grew out of free prayers and then were perpetuated unaltered, there were some which were newly made for definite purposes. These are not, however, free prayers, inspired by the feelings of the moment; they are intentionally composed or thought out according to the pattern of other formularies. They are mostly the conscious elaboration of priests or officials. The framing of such prayers must satisfy stringent requirements. The officiant of the Batak tribes must employ the choicest expressions. In China, at solemn sacrificial ceremonies, the prayers were written down and recited. The Roman formulas had to be fixed in writing and were delivered in verbal agreement with the written form; the words of the prayer must possess an official solemnity, and even the composition of the special content of the individual prayer demands particular care; where especially the rule is to be observed: " In prayers there should be no ambiguity." [1]

Hence it is that wishes expressed at first under the most diverse circumstances attain at length to a formal character, and that new formulas are composed to fit other occasions till gradually there arises a complete system of devotional formularies from which a selection can be made to suit the case. The great sacerdotal religions of antiquity have a special ritual of sacrifice and a special form of prayer for all needs and necessities. The most comprehensive collection of such devotional and sacrificial forms is to be seen in the Indian Yajur-Veda; it contains, however, numerous other formulas which we must assign to the sphere of magic.

Not only the words but also the form of utterance of the prayer is strictly prescribed. Among the ceremonial prayers of the Batak people, no word may be incorrectly pronounced or wrongly emphasized. The Roman formulas had to be recited clearly and expressively. Every mistake or halt in delivery made the prayer valueless.

Solemn recitation is the form in which the prayer formula is usually given. But besides this there is also the singing of prayer. Le Roy says that the Bantu and Negrillo tribesmen partly say and partly sing their prayers. The form of singing always presupposes a fixed text. There is also evidence for the murmuring of the formula. Thus the sacrificial formula in the Veda-Brahmanic religion is murmured by the priest. It would seem this method was carried over from the magical to the prayer formulas.

The ceremonial character of the ritual act demands that the official who prays and offers sacrifices should not appear before the god in everyday dress but in festive garb or even in a distinctive ritual costume. At the greater sacrifices of the Batak people, the leader in prayer and the offerers of sacrifice put on festive dress and ornaments. (This is not necessary on unimportant domestic occasions.) The solemn

---

[1] *In precibus nihil esse ambiguum debet.*

Batak sacrifices are surrounded not only by rigid ceremonial but by a complicated ritual of *tabu*. An enormous number of sacred prescriptions must be observed if all is not to be in vain. The person who presents the offering must not come in contact with the shadow of a human being or of an object. His dress must be clean, his face washed and his hair brushed. During the celebration he must not yawn nor spit, and his dress must not be in disorder. No one may touch him or speak to him or name his name. On the day of sacrifice no one may do rough work. For eight days after the sacrifice the offerer and the priest must refrain from all cursing. Surrounded by an endless number of such sacred interdictions prayer must necessarily lose its native character as speech with God and degenerate into a magically operative rite similar to many others.

The *content* of ritual prayer is fundamentally the same as that of primitive, free prayer, of which it is really a fixed form. The core of it also is the petition for earthly blessings, the invitation to the act of sacrifice or the vow. But the invocation is much richer in expression, homage and praise are prominent, and naïve efforts at persuasion are much less frequent. Special value is attributed to the naming of the right name or title of honour. In China, every higher being must be named with his correct title by the official leader of prayer; Heaven is " Exalted Heaven," " High Lord "; ancestor, " Exalted Ancestor "; the earth, " Princely Earth," and so forth. At Rome when one was uncertain about the correct name and title of the divinity the prudent addendum was made to the invocation: " whether thou art a god or goddess," and the enumerated names and attributes closed with the sentence: " or by whatsoever name thou wilt be called." [2]

Characteristic of composed, ritual prayers is the invocation of one or two or even of many higher beings. We see this already among primitive peoples, especially in the prayers of the Baronga and Batak tribes, which exhibit the transition from the primitive and free to fixed and ritual prayer. When after the invocation of each divinity the same stereotyped formula is repeated, we call it a litany. The Cora Indians

[2] *Seu quo nomine vis appellari.*

recite such litanies every year at the harvest festival. They are especially frequent in the penitential Babylonian rituals.

Such litanies are generally the prayers of a group, a tribe, a city, or a people, uttered by the mouth of priestly representatives. Then there are similar formal prayers offered by a priest at the special behest of an individual. There are, indeed, formulas which laymen utter, as, for example, the daily prayers in the morning and evening and at meals or the regular prayers in connection with the sacrifices which the head of every household offers to his ancestors. But ritual prayers, properly so called, with which the ritual acts are accompanied are recited only by the priest or by the sovereign or official acting as priest. The formal prayers among the Batak people are spoken by the magician or sacrificing priest, sometimes also by the chief. In China (as in the ancient Greek city) where there is no priestly class in the strict sense, the ritual prayers are said at festivals or on extraordinary occasions by the state officials. The Chinese distinguish · between two classes of prayer-officials, the " great leaders " and the " small leaders " who officiate respectively at the " great " and " small " sacrificial ceremonies.

These liturgical functions were from ancient times transferred so as to become a part of the duties of certain officers of state. In ancient Rome, the ritual prayers were in part the work of the priestly college, in part that of aediles or consuls. In ancient India the Brahmans were " the possessors of the right art of prayer and sacrifice." When later the ritual system became more and more complicated the sacrificial prayer was the task of the *adhvaryu;* he performed the entire sacrificial act and murmured the sacrificial formula. The Brahman, on the other hand, as high priest superintended the correct performance of the whole sacred ceremony. Thus prayer becomes an insipid, professional matter, the business of the priests.

In origin prayer is a direct communion, fellowship, commerce of man with God. But when petrified into a ritual formula, the consciousness of God's presence and of immediate contact with Him threatens to disappear. Where strong excitations of feeling are no longer operative, vital interest

vanishes. The prayers are recited either with ceremonial
stiffness and frigid officialism or they are gabbled in a purely
mechanical manner. The leader, who utters the formula, concentrates his attention anxiously on the task of avoiding mis-
takes, leaving nothing out, and emphasizing correctly every
syllable. The multitude looking on is filled with pious dread
in the presence of the unintelligible and mysterious, but often
ignores the cultual act in an irreverent manner. "The attention of the listeners," says Warneck speaking of the Batak
sacrifices, "leaves much to be desired. Reverent devotion is
not necessary for the efficacy of the sacrificial prayers."
Gilhodes relates of the Katchin: "The priest who utters the
liturgical prayers is indeed the only person who pays a little
attention to what he says. Those present are occupied with
something else. The children amuse themselves, the grown-up
people drink beer, smoke opium, and talk together." And the
Baronga are reported to behave in the same way.

At first, prayer, like sacrifice, is man's means of influencing
God and of inducing Him to grant his wishes. By ritualizing
and mechanizing it, it becomes a formula which is valuable
and efficacious. It is the form, *not* the content of the prayer,
which brings about the answer. The suppliant has only to
give his attention to the correct repetition of the formula and
he may be sure that his desires will be granted. Inner sympathy with the language of the prayer, the mood of reverence,
the feeling of dependence, of trustful confidence, in short, all
psychic experience is subsidiary and negligible. Formal exactness is the sole and indispensable prerequisite to the efficacy of prayer.

Primitive prayer expresses always a vital, mutual relation
between God and man, especially a relation of kinship. But
when prayer becomes formally constrained and a part of a
hard-and-fast cultual system, coldness and estrangement un-
avoidably enter in. Instead of free and frank communion with
the divinity, there is a stiff ceremonial formalism. Warneck
writes of the sacrificial cult of the Batak people: "The varied
and rich ceremonial moves in forms which the people observe
among one another in ordinary daily life. For by tradition
and custom the polite laws of fashion are rigidly fixed even

to details. Observance of custom is much more important
than any free, spontaneous outpouring of the heart." Still
more rigid is the juridical relation to the divinity which is so
exactly expressed in the prayers of the Romans. Man stands
to God in a legal relation in which every act performed and
every service in return are precisely measured. Prayer is a
legal statement of facts concerning the ritual act which with
the objectivity, conciseness, and dryness of the law is drawn
up, written down, and read aloud by an official person. " It is,"
as Wissowa well says, " the necessary oral explanation of
the ritual act which on the mortal's side completes the legal
business, and when given in correct form at the same time
compels the divinity to take his part in this juridical relation." This prayer restricted by ceremonial stiffness or
legal formalism is a real prayer for all that; it reflects the
forms of intercourse in earthly society. In conformity with
earthly analogies, man seeks by means of a courtly ceremonial,
or by a legal agreement, to move higher beings and to compel
them to gratify his wishes. But the answer to the prayer,
even according to the Roman idea, lies within the free will of
the divinity: " If the augur performing the ritual act applies
the correct formula and makes no blunder in enunciating
it, the divinity — in case it wills to give it at all — is bound to
grant the request in the form prayed for and not in any
other." The binding of the divinity effected by the formula
is relative, not absolute. But here already the transition from
the prayer formula to the genuine magic formula takes place.
The prayer formula completely loses its character as prayer
and is degraded to become a magic spell when there is ascribed
to the words of the prayer an *unfailing,* immanent, and magical
power which, either by an absolute compulsion exercised on
higher beings, or by excluding entirely all activity on their
part, directly and automatically realizes the wish of the
reciter of the prayer.

Wherever ritualism and formalism gain the upper hand, the
free, spontaneous prayer of the individual is more and more
obscured. Man believes that he had done enough when he
performs the traditional rites, observes the prescriptions of
tabu, and recites industriously the sacred formulas. Should

anyone be particularly distressed or have at heart some special concern, he goes to the priest or the magician that he may select a suitable efficacious formula out of his rich treasury, and, in his stead, recite it with the accompanying gift. The religious life in its immediate power and freedom is thus arrested and stifled. The spontaneous expressions of the religious consciousness are reduced to a minimum. But free prayer can never die because the primal religious feelings can never die. Deep necessities and vehement desires ever give to the individual the power to forget all rites and formulas and, by one passionate cry, make a direct path to God.

CHAPTER III

PRAYER IN THE RELIGION OF GREEK CIVILIZATION

GREEK religion, like the prophetic religion of Israel, occupies a special place among the religions of the world. Whilst the great ritual religions of antiquity rose above primitive religion only by a blending of different ideas and by the external splendour of their sacerdotal system, in Greece, the primitive tribal and city cults developed spontaneously into a purer, freer, and deeper type of religion without any violent breach with the past, and without the conscious intervention of a philosophical or religious reformer. The Homeric poems, the *Iliad* and the *Odyssey*, form the first stage in this religious progress. Here the robust, artless religion of the Ionic knighthood finds expression in the joy of life. It is indeed still within the sphere of primitive eudaemonism; but there is a very great difference between this free-minded knightly religion and the primitive folk-religion which maintained itself in Greece through all the centuries. The gods are set free from their original restrictions of nature or of place, they are strongly individualized, they are personal figures with sharply defined features. The Olympic Zeus with his retinue of gods is the reflection of an Ionic prince surrounded by his captains. Prayer and sacrifice are the only forms of worship in which the Homeric heroes hold intercourse with their gods. All the rites of divination, purification, and magic, which form an essential part of the popular religion and even of official worship, here take a secondary place. The heroes of Homer are lifted above the fear of the eerie spirits of the dead which is active in every folk-religion. As in Israel, faith in the sole might of Jahve, so in Ionia, an enlightened free-mindedness, reduced the dead to ineffectual subterranean shadows.

The Homeric religion found its consummation and deepening in the full blaze of Greek civilization in the fifth century before Christ. Aeschylus, Sophocles, Pindar, Xenophon, and Plato are the spokesmen of the spiritualized piety which in the classical period penetrated the cultured circles of the Greek people. As the poets of the Homeric songs had broadened and purified the folk-religion by creating a common Hellenic pantheon and freeing religious worship from its entanglement with magic, so these great writers deepened and moralized it. The close relationship with the ceremonial system of the State was the guarantee that this spiritualization of the traditional religion did not result in emptying it of its real meaning.

The feeling of absolute dependence on higher powers is operative in every religion. But in no religion, except Judaism and Christianity, is this fundamental feeling so dominant in life and thought as in the religion of Greece. The Chorus in Aeschylus's *Suppliants* prays:

" Without Thee what can mortals attain? "

" The Greek felt in his deepest soul," says Rohde, " how soon he reached the limits of his power on all sides, how narrow was the circle in which his conscious will and designing intelligence could effectively rule. Everything which lies beyond this circle, everything which comes to man without his co-operation, or even apart from his forethought, he owes to the divine powers. But that is the greatest part, almost the entire content of life."

The great breadth of this feeling of dependence implies that the gods are not only powers of fate, but also represent the ideals of civilization, above all, ethical ideals. Like the prophetic religion of Israel the Greek religion of the fifth century B.C. is avowedly ethical. Whilst we can detect in Homer scarcely a tendency towards the moralizing of religion, by the fifth century ethical ideals thoroughly determined the character of religious belief and reverence. Of course, in many primitive religions the gods, especially the divine progenitors of the tribe, appear as moral law-givers and guardians; but in Greece under the influence of the advancing autonomous feeling for ethical values, " the gods themselves were moralized," as Rohde says; moral thought and action became a service of God; piety and temperance [1] coincide. This moralizing of religion, however, did not proceed from a conscious philosophical criticism and reform of the folk-religion but from a spontaneous refinement and intensification of the sense of moral and religious values. But it is not ethical values alone that find a place in Greek religion; the entire compass of cultural values, everything that belongs to the ideal (beauty as well as goodness) receives a religious consecration — social life, artistic creation, scientific knowledge, even whole-hearted enjoyment of life.

The Hellenic religion is the *religion of civilization* in general. It possessed the power to combine itself with all the values of civilization and thus to penetrate the entire social and intellectual life. " The Greek," says Dr. Farnell, " tended always to find a place in his religion for whatever he felt passionately about; and that is why Greek religion reflects so vividly the emotions and sentiments of the individual."

Greek religion unites with this many-sidedness an extraordinary clearness and harmony, a symmetry of psychic powers. It knows no syncretistic confusion, no showy splendour like the oriental ritual religions, no suppression of healthy emotions, no ascetic contempt of the world as in the Indian religions of redemption, no passionate urge, no consuming zeal for God's holy will as in the prophetic religion of Israel, no boundless yearning for the Kingdom of God as in the primitive Church. *Genuine* Greek religion knows also no mystical striving after a blessed union with God in ecstasy, after an abolition of the limits of individuality in a realm beyond the conscious life. Proportion and temperance [2] are its ideals. Emotionalism and absence of emotion, prophetic austerity and mystical indifference are alike foreign to it. In distinction from the religion of revelation, and from the mystical religion of redemption, it is a " natural " religion; not, of course, a religion of reason created by philosophical criticism, but an artless, primitive religion, ethically deepened and aesthetically clarified.

The peculiar quality of Greek religion is revealed nowhere

---

[1] εὐσέβεια — σωφροσύνη.   [2] μέτρον — σωφροσύνη.

so clearly as in prayer. The universal feeling of dependence which animates the Greek of the classical era is expressed most clearly by the fact that at every opportunity he appeals to the gods by prayer and sacrifice. " The offering of sacrifice and prayer pervades all the relations of the Greek people to a remarkable extent," writes Nägelsbach. " No religious doctrine is more universally valid for the control of public and private life alike than this, that everything must be begun with the divinity, that is, with prayer and sacrifice." Xenophon puts into the mouth of Christobulos these words: " An excellent word thou speakest, O Socrates, when thou recommendest that every work should begin with the gods, for the gods are lords over all the works of war and peace." And the Platonic Timaeus says: " Truly, O Socrates, all who possess even a modicum of wisdom, everywhere and always, at the beginning of every work, important or unimportant, call upon God." Prayer opens all public proceedings, popular assemblies, festivals, judicial processes, covenants, treaties, and wars. The Attic orators begin their speeches by an invocation of the gods; the Athenian senators prayed at the entrance of the senate-house in which were to be found the chapels of Zeus and Athene. On joyful political occasions, as also in success in war, festivals of thanksgiving were instituted, and connected with these were sacrifices, prayers, and songs. Prayer had a no less important place in private life. Every professional class called, at the beginning of its activity, on its guardian divinities. The most insignificant and common actions acquired by prayer and sacrifice a religious consecration. Isomachus, the leading character in Xenophon's *Economics*, begins the instruction of his wife in the art of housekeeping only after he has prayed that his teaching and her learning may prove profitable to both. The Athenians prayed even at the opening of a wine-cask and the testing of the wine that the noble drink might be for their good. The primitive custom of regular morning and evening prayers and grace before meat is the standing usage of Greek piety. Hesiod speaks of daily morning and evening sacrifice. In Plato's *Symposium*, Socrates in the morning addresses a prayer to the sun. Plato in the tenth book of the *Laws* testifies that the Greeks, like other nations,

show their devotional reverence at the rising and the setting of
sun and moon. A prayer preceded or followed a meal; and as
with uncivilized peoples the blessing on the food was generally
accompanied by a libation.

The vitality and inwardness of the Greek religion made impossible the stiffening of prayer into a ritualistic formula.
There were, of course, fixed forms of prayer in Greece which
were used in public worship, but in distinction from the Roman
religion the answer to prayer was never bound up with a
punctilious adherence to the letter. As O. Gruppe says, " the
thought of a definite arrangement of the words as of decisive
importance for the fulfilment of the prayer was quite alien to
the public worship of the Greeks and contrary to its nature."
The personal character of the Greek religion did not tolerate
the stunting of the living word of prayer into the dead, impersonal formulas of magic. The religion of Greece, in contrast
to the great oriental religions, did not expand into a complicated system of ritual; hence the prayer of worship kept its
simple, original character. Whilst the official prayer in public worship exhibits a certain inner and necessary constraint,
the private prayer of individuals in intellectual circles seems
to have risen above all formalism. So far as we can infer from
the scanty literary documents at our disposal, prayerful devotion was as free and spontaneous among cultivated Greeks as
among the great personalities of Israel and of the Christian
religion. Marcus Aurelius' description of Athenian prayer as
" simple and free " [3] is equally applicable to Greek prayer in
general. The language of the prayer is the direct expression
of the moods, the wishes, and the consciousness of value experienced by him who prays.

The variety of the objects for which the Greek supplicates
in prayer corresponds to the richness of his religious experience. Everything which he feels to be valuable and ideal
he expresses in prayer before his gods. Primitive man prays
only for the good things of this world; prayer for moral
values is alien to his thought. All ancient religions — the
Chinese, Vedic, Babylonian, Egyptian, old Roman, old
American, and the Homeric — are still within the realm

[3] ἁπλῶς καὶ ἐλευθέρως.

of purely eudaemonistic prayer; the feeling for ethical values seldom attains sufficient power to serve as a motive of prayer, on a par with the primitive feeling of life. When Greek civilization was at its height, religion, as with the prophets of Israel, achieved a comprehensive moralizing of religious experience; petition for moral values was made the centre of prayer. Callimachus puts at the beginning of his prayer a petition for moral excellence: " Give me virtue and riches; give me virtue and prosperity." Hesiod sees the best prayer in a request for abiding inner loyalty to the moral ideal. In the contest of song between him and Homer he puts this question to Homer: " What is the best thing for which one ought to ask the gods? " Homer answers: " To be always in harmony with the law in one's heart." Religious and moral ideals are comprehended by the Greek in the words " temperance " and " piety "; both form an important theme of prayer. In the *Choephoroe* of Aeschylus, Electra prays to her dead father: " Grant that I may be a more temperate and a more pious wife than was my mother." " Let there be granted to me temperance, fairest gift of the gods," prays the Chorus in the *Medea* of Euripides. In the *Phaedrus* the ideal of a moral personality becomes for Socrates a matter of prayer. The ripest prayer of the Greek spirit is his when he says: " Beloved Pan and all ye other gods that haunt this place, grant that I may become inwardly beautiful." The Spartan shows his hard, purposeful strength when, as Plutarch relates, he prays for power to bear wrong with manly steadfastness. The Greek knows nothing of that deep feeling of moral weakness and sinfulness which led the greatest men of Christian genius to sigh for grace and forgiveness. But when he is aware of a definite act of transgression or of neglect of duty or when he fears that he has, by a thoughtless word, offended the gods, he cries to them for pardon. Simonides prays to Zeus: " If I am bold in my prayer and demand justice for us, forgive me." As the Socrates of Xenophon exhorts: " If you are wise, my son, you will supplicate the gods to forgive you in case you have not honoured your mother enough." No religion more than the Greek has honoured and sanctified the forms of social life. The social feeling of the Greeks breathes in their prayers of interces-

sion. The prayer in which the dying Alcestis commits her
children to Hestia, the goddess of the domestic hearth, is among
the finest of Greek prayers:

> " Queen, for I pass beneath the earth, I fall
> Before thee now, and nevermore, and pray:
> Be mother to my orphans: mate with him
> A loving wife, with her, a noble husband.
> Nor, as their mother dieth, so may they,
> My children, die untimely, but with weal
> In the homeland fill up a life of bliss." [4]

A Greek educationist of Cos prays in a second century inscrip-
tion for " the health and virtuous behaviour of boys." The
high valuation put upon the city and the city government is
expressed in the intercessions which the individual citizen
makes for his city. Two prayers of Athenaeus have come
down to us, one to Athene, the other to Demeter and Persephone, in which the table-companions supplicate welfare and
blessing for their home town: " O Pallas Athene, sea-born
Queen, keep this city and its citizens from discord and from
all calamities and also from untimely death, thou and thy
father."

" To Demeter do I sing a song at the feast:
  Olympian Mother of the great goddess of the dead; be thou in-
    voked with her,
  O Persephone, daughter of Zeus! Protect ye this city! "

In yet another way is the social character of the Greek
religion revealed. Kindly feeling among friends is an important topic of prayer. But even prayer for personal moral good
shows a social strain. Pindar calls on Zeus to lead him in the
path of goodness so that he may leave a good name to his
children. Ethical and social values are pre-eminent in Greek
prayer; but it is not limited to those values, it embraces all
ideals and goods. Plutarch expresses still the thought of the
classical age when he says: " For *all* goods must those who
understand entreat the gods." It is the surest sign of the simplicity of Greek religion that in prayer, next to moral values,

---

[4] Euripides, *Alcestis* (Lines 163 seq.), translated by A. S. Way.

are those material values for which primitive man prays. Isomachus in the *Economics* of Xenophon reckons among subjects of prayer: " health, bodily strength, good repute in the city, kindly relation with friends, safety in war, increase of wealth." A good reputation would seem to have been to the Greeks of especial value since they pray especially for it. Solon prays to the Muses: " Let me at all times obtain good fortune from the blessed gods and enjoy honourable repute in the throng of mortals." Even a potter from Mesopotamia in the fifth century prays " that he may be of good repute among men." Material wealth also is considered by the Greek sage as worth struggling for. The Platonic Socrates prays for abundance of gold, of course with a qualification: " May my share of gold be such as none but the temperate can carry." The youthful freshness and beauty of the body is to the Greek a great blessing, therefore he supplicates the goddess of youthful beauty for a postponement of old age. " Put off old age, thou beautiful Aphrodite " — is a prayer recorded by Plutarch. Even the honourable enjoyment of love becomes an object of prayer. Xenophon exhorts men to pray to Aphrodite that " she may suggest lovable words and deeds."

The *naïveté* of the Greek religion meets us most openly in prayers of cursing and vengeance. Stereotyped formulas arise out of the folk-religion of later times in which black magic grew ever more and more luxuriantly, and these curse-formulas, graven on stone and lead, were sunk deep in the soil of the earth. But even in the official worship as in the private religion of the classical period the curse occupies a large space. For the Greek, as Leopold Schmidt says, " the exercise of righteousness was so much the most prominent side of the divine government that an effort after harmony with the divine will, which would have left untouched its penal activity, would have seemed unintelligible to him. . . . Hence the frequent prayers for the destruction of evil-doers which we are accustomed to describe as curses whilst the Greek included the two notions ' prayer ' and ' curse ' in one expression." The tragic poets afford us examples of the Greek prayer for vengeance. Sophocles makes Philoctetes pray:

> " But, O my fatherland
> And all ye Gods who look on me, avenge,
> Avenge me on them all in time to come,
> If ye have pity on me." [5]

The difference between classic Greek piety and the two purest expressions of the higher religious spirit, the religion of Jesus and the Buddha's doctrine of deliverance, leaps to the eye with special clearness. The Buddhist beggar-monk who undertakes the practice of " right willing " extends even to his enemies the wish: " May all higher beings be happy, free from care, disease, and pain." Jesus boldly demands from His disciples something apparently impossible of fulfilment: " Bless them that curse you, pray for them that despitefully use you." The Greek calls down upon his enemies the vengeance of God, in full assurance that the punitive righteousness of God will accomplish the curse. " Right against the unrighteous I demand, suffering to the wrong doers! " cries Electra in the *Choephoroe*. The Greek frankly expresses his wish for the destruction of his enemy. The Buddha and Jesus demand that not only should we suppress the natural feeling but even rise to the opposite wish, that we should bless, not curse. Faith in a religious ideal — in Buddhism freedom from feeling, in Christianity universal love of our neighbour — has destroyed in both the native simplicity of the desire for revenge, which is still alive in Greek religion, and in its place has set up a paradoxical disposition of mind.

Just as among even nature-peoples we meet with petitionary prayers of a general kind, so in Greek prayers the petition is couched frequently in general terms. An anonymous poet cries to Zeus thus:

> " King Zeus, give what is good, even if not prayed for,
> But keep far from us evil, though we ask for it."

Here the general petition comprehends superpersonal ethical values, and " worldly " personal values. Still there is a preponderance of the ethical and aesthetic element.[6]

All authentic Greek prayers reveal that clearness, harmony,

---

[5] Plumptre's translation.   [6] τὰ ἀγαθά, τὰ καλά τὰ ἐσθλά.

and inner sense of proportion which belongs to the essence of the Greek spirit. The passion of the great men of prayer in Israel is unknown to the Greek; prayer is no impulsive " outpouring of the soul " as the Old Testament phrase has it, no crying to God " out of the depths." Even in prayer man must moderate his emotions, he must hold back the turbulent impulse. " Speak now thy prayer in moderation " — says the one half-Chorus to the other in *The Suppliants* of Aeschylus, since the latter in its uncontrolled passion threatens to injure reverence for the divinity. Few words characterize so well as these the peculiar note in the spirit of Greek prayer.

As among primitive peoples, so among the Greeks there are many divinities to whom man can turn in prayer. Like the religion of the Orient, Greek religion also possesses a varied, richly organized pantheon. In its classical period no monotheistic tendencies are active; no creative deed of a religious genius put the one God of Heaven and earth in place of the " gods many and lords many " of Greek worship. The Greek prays, therefore, to the greatest variety of higher beings, divinities of nature, gods of various activities, local and guardian divinities. Advancing cultural development has indeed fused the innumerable spirits and gods of individual cities, districts, and islands into great national gods. But the blending of the divine powers in Greek religion cannot be compared with the gods of the Orient; its original, peculiar quality shines through it at all points.

Even the Hellenic gods are not universal divinities, but are limited in their influence to a specific province of nature or of human activity. Therefore the Greek turns, just as primitive man turned, not to a beloved divinity but to those divinities in whose power lies the fulfilment of the wish or to whose dwelling-place he is near. " Penelope supplicates Artemis," says L. Schmidt, " the sender of the quickly killing arrow, for death; the heroes despatched by Agamemnon, while advancing to the seashore, pray the god Poseidon that they may succeed in reconciling the defiant Achilles; and his attention being called to the near-by grotto of the nymphs, Ulysses, on his arrival at his native island, addresses his prayer to them."

Above the numberless individual gods stands Zeus, father

of gods and men, the god of heaven and the disposer of fate, the guardian of oaths, the protector of suppliants. He resembles the Vedic Varuna and the Chinese Hoang-tien-schang-ti, a primitive " divine progenitor " and " god of heaven." Whilst one turns to the other gods only on definite occasions, one calls on him under the most varied circumstances. Prayers for things of moral worth seem to have been preferably addressed to him. The appeal to several or to all divinities, as we frequently find in the poets, originally took place indeed in solemn cultual worship, and later penetrated into private prayer.

The gods to whom the Greeks pray bear the same anthropomorphic features as the higher beings to whom primitive man prays; they are described in Herodotus and Aristotle as " formed like man " and " similar to man." To be sure, the mature religious spirit of the classical period sets aside the frivolous, fantastic features in the Homeric divinities. But the gods remain always personal, thinking, willing, and feeling beings, who, though they excel men in power and blessedness, are like them in their spiritual life. They are never dissolved into non-personal natural forces. Man can enter into personal relations with the gods because they are like man. In prayer, an intimate fellowship with a present God takes place. Nowhere is this underlying thought in Greek prayer more finely expressed than in the *Hippolytus* of Euripides when the praying hero speaks to Artemis:

> For to me, sole of men, this grace is given
> That I be with thee, converse hold with thee
> Hearing thy voice yet seeing not thy face.[7]

The same thought recurs in the Platonic *Banquet* where Eryximachus defines worship, consisting of prayer, sacrifice, and divination, as " the mutual fellowship of gods and men." An earthly social relation is always reflected in man's relation to his god. Only the relation of servanthood is not possible to the feeling of the Greek as he prays, for the free Hellene bows not like the Semite as a serf before his divinity, nor does he stand in the loving relation of sonship, as the Christian does to God the Father. The Greek attitude to God is rather that

[7] A. S. Way's translation (Lines 85 seq.).

of a friend. The Greeks had a genius for friendship; and this peculiar characteristic of their social life is reflected in their intercourse with higher powers. He who prays and offers sacrifices does so with a frank, manly bearing. A measured dignity, a proud self-consciousness is coupled with respect and reverence. This is expressed in the physical attitude. The Greek neither kneels nor lies prostrate; he stands and lifts his hands to the gods he has invoked. Even in communion with them proportion is to be observed, extremes are to be shunned. Servility, humiliating flattery, importunate petition — these the Greek despises as barbarian. But there must be moderation even in conscious worth: self-exaltation is the worst crime against the gods; it is the sin of sins. Woe to him who strives after equality with God! [8]

The prayer of the Greeks is naïve and primitive. All the peculiar qualities of primitive prayer are here repeated: the blunt, vigorous eudaemonism, the appeal to a variety of gods, the realism of the idea of the divine and of communion with the divine. Nevertheless, Greek prayer stands incalculably higher than the prayer of primitive man, for it reveals a world of higher values.

Even the realization of the ideals of civilized life is dependent on the power of the gods; therefore, the Greek prays to them for everything that is " good and beautiful." The Greek enthusiasm for a cultured life pours itself forth in this prayer. This intimate bond between religion and civilized life is the great excellence of Greek religion; it is at the same time its fatality. For with the downfall of the civilization of which it was a part, it was bound also to perish. Only in the religion of the Renaissance had it a weak second blossoming. It flickered up once more in the revival of classical learning; in the devotional life of the creative minds of the Renaissance the naïve prayer of the Greeks came to life again. But its disappearance was inevitable. Greek religion died, as all the great ritual religions of the East had to die, though it excelled these in depth and purity. Only those religions which rise above nations and civilizations, the mystical religions of redemption and the prophetic religions of revelation, attain to historical

[8] μὴ μάτευε Ζεὺς γενέσθαι.

permanence. Wherever religion arrives at full development its inexorable demand by an inner vital necessity is for primacy in the spiritual life. The entanglement of religion in the general interests of civilized life is peculiar to the primitive stage of religious development. The great men of genius in religion are raised above primitive religion by the fact that they set religion free from bondage to civilization and lift it to a higher realm. Hellenic religion is, therefore, primitive religion, though, of course, in its noblest and purest form; but in dying it gave birth to a religion above all nations and civilizations, the mystical neo-Platonic religion of redemption.

CHAPTER IV

CRITIQUE AND IDEAL OF PRAYER IN PHILOSOPHICAL THOUGHT

It is in the field of primitive forms of religious worship that the negative criticism of religion finds its material. Philosophical thought, be it metaphysical or anti-metaphysical, ethical or theoretic and intellectualistic, idealistic or materialistic, theistic or deistic, pantheistic or atheistic in its tendency, is always in inner opposition to the naïve piety of primitive man. That natural eudaemonism which is so characteristic of primitive religion, like the anthropomorphic realism that dominates the savage's idea of God, arouses philosophical criticism by an inner necessity.

Such criticism it is true rarely goes so far as a complete denial of religion. Only consistent materialism and positivism repudiate as a matter of course all religion as delusion and deception, yet they usually seek to support such reflection by a clumsy psychological explanation, after the manner of the Sophists, Hume, and Feuerbach. Idealistic philosophy on the other hand, whether its idealism is a metaphysical, an epistemological, or an ethical one, despite all contrary tenets, has something in common with religion, even in its primitive form — belief in a world of the supersensuous behind the world of appearances, a world of higher good above the world of everyday interests.

It is this divided attitude, partly rejecting and partly approving of religion, which encourages idealistic philosophy to seek to transform empiric religion into ideal religion. Philosophic thought tries to make ethical and rational the traditional, cultural religion by excluding eudaemonism from piety, purifying the conception of God from all anthropomorphic features, and putting in place of acts of prescribed worship the realization of moral values in the individual and social life. This ethical, rational, ideal religion is not naïve religion, but a reformed religion, born of conscious criticism of naïve piety; not pure religion, but a philosophical religion, in Kantian phrase a " religion within the bounds of pure reason." The relation of this philosophical religion to vital religion is now close, now loose. The reverence of a Confucius for the religious tradition and the power of accommodation to the popular religion shown by Stoicism stand contrasted with the uncompromising rejection of naïve piety by Xenophanes and Fichte. How different the religious warmth and prophetic impressiveness of a Socrates from the abstract and jejune ideal of religion proclaimed by a Seneca or a Kant! But all these thinkers have this in common, that in place of the existing religion they have constructed an ideal religion, which they hold to be true, pure, genuine, and universally valid.

The native eudaemonism and powerful realism of primitive religion is nowhere seen so clearly as in sacrifice and prayer. For this very reason the philosophical criticism of religion is apt to be directed against primitive prayer and sacrifice. Prayer constituted a serious problem even for ancient philosophy. Whether one was to pray; and to whom, had been debated since the days of Xenophanes and was never settled. The question of the philosophical justification of prayer occupied the Greek fathers as it did the Pythagoreans and Psalmists. Even by the philosophy of the Enlightenment and by Kant attention is bestowed upon the problem of prayer. Yet philosophical criticism hardly ever ends in a radical rejection of prayer in general, rather does there grow out of it a positive ideal of prayer. A standard of prayer is set up from the point of view of ethical values and a metaphysical theory of knowledge. The true and perfect prayer of the philosophers is contrasted with primitive and spontaneous prayer as well as with the ritually ordered worship of the people and its priests. In the words of Hierocles, the wise man " is the only priest, the only lover of God, the only one who knows how to pray."

I. Content of Philosophical Prayer

Primitive man prays for life and health, for food, sunshine and rain, for possessions and many children, for honour and reputation, for victory and the destruction of his enemies. This hale, vigorous eudaemonism is branded by the philosophers as irreligious and immoral. Von Hartmann says: "From the point of view of a higher religious consciousness the eudaemonistic aims of ordinary religion must appear to be irreligious." To the strongly ethical temper prayer seems weakness. Seneca has described it as the "consolation of a sick soul." "For what purpose do you need prayer? Make your own happiness!"

It seems petty, repellent, and unmanly for a man not to reconcile himself to his fate, but defiantly to pray for the fulfilment of his momentary wishes and cravings. In the judgement of Kant "it is at once an absurd and presumptuous delusion to try by the insistent importunity of prayer, whether God might not be deflected from the plan of His wisdom to provide some momentary advantage for us." The good things for which the ordinary man prays are not real values. The Cynic Diogenes reproached the populace with praying to the gods, not for true, but for only seeming goods. Socrates explained that those who prayed for gold, silver, power, and such like, acted as if they prayed for success in a game of dice or in a battle or in anything else the outcome of which was uncertain.

Prayer for transitory worldly goods is held to be unworthy by the philosopher who is straining after the moral ideal. Only for abiding ethical values ought man to pray. The philosophical ideal limits the subjects of prayer to the circle of moral and spiritual values. No one has so enthusiastically presented this ethical Gospel as the Stoic Epictetus. "Ask from the gods," he says, "not what you crave, but that you may be free from all craving. The gods will hear you when you pray not for what is pleasant, but for what is morally good. And they will give you what is morally good, if you rejoice not in pleasure but in virtue. Remember to pray to the Great for what is great for they will not give you what is little. Nothing is greater and more exalted than God; when, therefore, you pray to the gods, pray for that which is godlike for that which is unstained by any earthly passion." Clement of Alexandria in his *Stromata* says similarly of the Christian gnostic: " He prays that there may be given and preserved to him the really good things that belong to the soul."

The philosophers pray, first of all, for the realization of moral values in the individual life. Xenophanes asks for " power to do righteous things." Apollonius of Tyana prays for " freedom from possessions and from need." Epictetus maintains that one should ask for " sobriety of soul." Maximus of Tyre names as the objects of prayer, " a virtuous soul, a quiet life, a blameless walk, a hopeful death — those wonderful gifts bestowed by the gods." Clement of Alexandria writes: " The perfect gnostic prays for the growth and preservation of spiritual insight just as the ordinary man prays for unbroken health." Seneca exhorts: " Ask for a right spirit, for health of soul." Juvenal gives in the tenth *Satire* the truly Stoic rule of prayer: " You should pray for a sound mind in a sound body; for a stout heart that has no fear of death, and deems length of days the least of Nature's gifts; that can endure any kind of toil, that knows neither anger nor desire."

The ethical ideals which to the philosophic eye are the only subjects of prayer are, nevertheless, not limited to the individual life, but comprehend the life of all men. Pythagoras desires that wise men should " pray for fools that they may receive what is good, since these people do not know what is really good." In Voltaire's prayers there speaks the cosmopolitan, humanitarian ideal of the French Enlightenment: " Thou hast not given us a heart that we may hate one another, nor hands that we may strangle one another, but that we may help each other to bear the burden of a wearisome and transitory life; that the small distinctions in the dress which covers our weak bodies, in our inadequate languages, in our absurd usages, in all our imperfect laws, in all our senseless opinions, in all our social grades, which to our eyes are so different and to Thine so alike, that all the fine shades which differentiate the atoms called ' men,' may not be occasions for hate and persecution." The general prayer of intercession of the Christian Church is in a shadowy way hinted at in these ancient and modern philosophical prayers.

In all these instances the ethical petition is framed in a concrete way: the wise man prays for moral values more or less exactly outlined. But frequently the prayer is formulated in an abstract and general fashion, corresponding to the absence of definite motives of prayer. The general form of petition is found already among primitive people: but while these pray for " happiness," and " divine favour," the philosopher prays exclusively for " the good ": in the former, prayer has a materialistic, in the latter, a purely ethical character. Pythagoras said that we should pray for only that which is good, and warned against the particular naming of concrete wishes. Socrates merely prayed for gods " to give whatever is good, since they know best what *is* good."

The leaving of all personal wishes to God leads to that form of philosophical prayer which reaches its perfection in Stoicism: the expressions of complete absence of desire, absolute indifference, unreserved surrender to the hands of Fate.

The wise man prays but he does not ask; he does not so much as pray for the attainment of moral good; he only confesses his absolute dependence, renounces his own will and wish and is ready for any fate, life or death, happiness or unhappiness, honour or shame, without opposition or contradiction. " Lead me, O Zeus," cries Cleanthes, " and thou O mighty Fate, whithersoever I am appointed by you. I follow without hesitation, and even if I will not in my foolishness, yet must I follow." Seneca has translated this prayer into Latin. He has also preserved for us the solemn renunciation of Demetrius in which he hands over to the gods, body and soul, goods and children. " Will ye take my children? From you I have received them. Will ye take a part of my body? Take it, I give away nothing great, since I must soon leave behind me my entire body. Will ye take my soul? Why should I hinder you from taking back that which ye have given me? "

A notable spirit of manly freedom and resolution breathes in the prayer which Epictetus commends to his disciples: " Lift up thy head as one freed from bondage, and dare to look up to Heaven and to say: ' Use me then for what Thou wilt. I am of one mind with Thee, I am Thine. I appeal not against Thy decrees, lead me whither Thou wilt, put on me what dress Thou wilt. Wilt Thou that I am in public office or in private life, that I stay here or flee, that I am poor or rich — for all that I will defend Thee before men: I will reveal the nature of each thing what it is.' "

The Stoic ideal of prayer, that is, the perfect surrender of the human will to the divine, the bowing before the eternal decrees of fate, was also highly prized by the men of the French Enlightenment. Rousseau believed that " the most perfect prayer is entire resignation to the decisions of the will of God. Not what I will, but what Thou wilt. Thy will be done! Every other prayer is superfluous and contradicts this one." Diderot cried out at the end of his *Interprétations de la Nature:* " O God, I ask nothing from Thee, for if Thou art not, the course of nature is an inner necessity, and if Thou art, it is Thy command." Voltaire prayed: " O God of all worlds and of all beings, the only prayer which is befitting to Thee is submission, for why pray to Him who has ordered all things, foreseen all things and linked together all things in a chain from the very beginning? " Voltaire's prayers were therefore conditional, laden with the unreserved acknowledgement of the eternal ordinances of God.

In the expression of resignation and surrender the Stoic ideal of prayer has a point of contact with the prayer of mystical religion. The " Suscipe " of Loyola, many prayers of à Kempis, St. Teresa and Madame Guyon agree verbally with the prayers of Demetrius and Epictetus. Epictetus's words: " Do with me what Thou wilt, Thy will is my will, I am Thine," are repeated by the mystics times without number. And yet behind the same words are dispositions of soul which are fundamentally different. In spite of all their solemnity and sublimity, and of their deep moral earnestness, Stoic prayers reveal a certain coldness and impersonality. They lack that inwardness and warmth, that touch of rapture which is peculiar to the prayers of Christian, Sûfi and Hindu mystics. The prayer of the Stoics and the *illuminati* is just an ethical ideal; that of the mystics springs from the depths of *religious* experience. The resignation of the Stoics is the fruit of a strong moral will which with courage and resolution bows before inevitable destiny, whereas the submission of the mystic is rooted in the perfect surrender of the self to the Highest Good in love to God. The Stoic ideal is much more closely related to the absorption of the Buddhist than to the prayer of the mystic. Yet the Stoic, like the mystical prayer of submission, is distinguished from the Buddhist mood of indifference, for in the latter there is wanting any direct turning towards a supreme metaphysical reality.

Another form of mystical prayer and meditation which is hinted at in the philosophical ideal of prayer is solemn contemplation, adoration and praise of the divine majesty and glory as revealed in all things, great and small. Epictetus says: " What word suffices to praise and glorify the works of Providence? Had we insight could we do anything else than collectively and individually praise God and glorify Him and give thanks to Him? . . . If I were a nightingale I would sing like a nightingale. If I were a swan like a swan. But I am a being gifted with understanding, so I must praise God. This is my task, I fulfil it, and I shall not abandon this my post so long as it is decreed for me; and I ask you to join with me in this song of praise." Even Kant seems to have experienced something of the wonderful power of silent mystic contemplation. In his critical discussions about prayer, he writes: " The divine creation, its profound wisdom in the smallest things, and its majesty in great things, has been contemplated by man from the remotest ages, but in modern times its wonder has been greatly enlarged. It has power to transport the mind not only into the mood which annihilates man in his own eyes, but exalts his soul with such a sense of his own destiny, that words, even those of a kingly man like David, fade into nothingness because the feeling inspired by such a view of the work of God is inexpressible."

The similarity of philosophical adoration, and of mystical contemplation is unmistakable. Of course there is an immense difference in the intensity of feeling: with the philosopher a solemn mood, a quiet feeling of exaltation; with the mystic a blessed intoxication, an emotional rapture which rises to the disappearance of self-consciousness in ecstasy; with the one there is a sense of infinite distance between him and God, with the other a blessed at-one-ment with Him in love.

The content of philosophical prayer, therefore, is threefold: petition for moral good, submission to destiny, adoration of the divine greatness — a lofty ideal, indeed, and one born out of a spirit at once deep and pure. And yet, for the philosopher this prayer is not a necessity as it is for the religious man who cannot live without it: it is something that can be dispensed with. The moral ideal can be realized without supplicating for the help of divine grace. Says Seneca: " How foolish to pray for a good spirit since you can win that of yourself! " Maximus of Tyre and Clement of Alexandria stress the idea that the wise man who prays for moral blessings wins them not by the help of divine grace but by his own strenuous efforts. So too Rousseau, who says: " It is not God who changes, but we who change ourselves by lifting ourselves up to Him. *All for which we ask Him, as we should, we give to ourselves.*" In the moral philosopher there lives the unshakable belief in man's native moral power whilst the noblest religious spirits are penetrated with the deep feeling of man's moral helplessness. The emphasis is laid not on the prayer for what is good, but exclusively on the moral disposition and moral act. As Seneca says: " He who imitates the gods honours them sufficiently." " If we do our duty to God, if we worship Him, if we are righteous — that is our true prayer and praise," so writes Voltaire. Guyau the eloquent champion of an ethico-social religion of the future, asserts that: " If love is the essential factor in true prayer, the mouth may not only speak of it, heart and hand must practise it, that is, there ensues *the substitution of moral action for prayer.* Moral action is the most disinterested, the divinest and the most human of prayers." True prayer, therefore, is not prayer for the attainment of the ideal, but for the will to do good. This true prayer is bound to no occasions, to no moods, to no appeal to God; it is prayer without ceasing. Kant writes in " Religion within the Limits of Pure Reason ": " A heartfelt wish to be pleasing to God in all our action, that is, the disposition to transact all our business as though done in God's service, is the spirit of prayer which ' without ceasing ' can and ought to be in us." Kant's penetrating mind has laid bare the implications of the ideal of prayer of philosophical ethics. Whenever prayer is transferred to the inner moral disposition, real prayer, which is the turning of the soul to God, the supplication for moral power, and the utterance of a resigned spirit, becomes nothing but a mere expedient of ethical training. Prayer is thus stripped of its religious character, robbed of its independent value. The " spirit of prayer " ceases to be prayer and becomes a mere moral substitute.

II. The Philosophical Criticism of Prayer and the Philosophical Ideal of Prayer

Primitive man finds no problem in prayer; for the pious man it is the most obvious expression of the religious life. As Matthias Claudius humorously puts it: " To ask whether man may pray is like asking whether man may have a nose." But for philosophical reflection, on the contrary, prayer is an imperative problem. " Whether one may pray " — this question which Maximus of Tyre chose as the title of a philosophical discourse has repeatedly struck the minds of philosophers. It lies unexpressed at the bottom of all religio-philosophical discussions about prayer. Now what makes prayer a philosophical problem is not chiefly the contradiction between the materialism of primitive prayer and the idealism of philosophical ethics, for we can get rid of this contradiction by the exclusion from prayer of all earthly petitions and the limitation of petitional prayer to moral values. A much deeper antagonism separates the religious ideas and notions underlying prayer as ordinarily understood, and the rational philosophical concept of God.

1. All simple prayer presupposes faith in the real existence and anthropomorphic character of the God to whom prayer is made. God for the philosopher is something quite different from what He is for the ordinary religious individual. He may be conceived as " personal," " non-personal " or " super-personal," but never is He a man-like Being who feels and thinks

as a dweller upon earth. God is " Being," the " Absolute," the " World-Ground," the " World-Principle," the " World-Soul," the " Idea of the True, the Beautiful and the Good," or even only a " postulate of the reason," but He is not " Lord " and " Father," whose nearness to him who prays is an immediate and undoubted certainty. A theistic just as much as a pantheistic metaphysic banishes all anthropomorphism from the conception of God. This contradiction makes intelligible the severe judgements which many philosophers pronounce on prayer. Voltaire says: " We address prayer to God only because we have created Him in our image — we treat Him as a Pasha, as a Sultan whom we may irritate or soothe." Schopenhauer writes still more pungently: " If we make an idol of wood, stone, or metal, or put it together out of abstract conceptions, it is all one. It remains *idolatry* as soon as we have before us a personal Being to whom we sacrifice, on whom we call and to whom we give thanks. At bottom, it matters not at all, whether we sacrifice our sheep or our inclinations; every rite or prayer testifies unquestionably to idolatry."

All prayer — that of primitive man as well as that of the great men of religious genius — presupposes faith in the real presence of God. Long ago Heraclitus criticized this faith in the nearness of the God addressed in prayer. " You pray to these idols as if someone dwelt in the temple," he said. Seneca opposes the primitive conception of the restriction of the Deity to a given place. " We ought not to raise our hands to Heaven," he says, " nor beg the temple-keeper to let us approach the ear of a god's statue, as if we could be heard better thereby. God is near thee, with thee, in thee." Kant sees in this realistic belief in the divine presence, " a slight attack of madness."

Primitive prayer is a real communion of man with God; it rests on the belief that man can influence God, can win Him over to his side, can change His will. But to philosophical thought the conviction is essential that the events of the world are ruled by an unbroken conformity to law, whether this be conceived as an inviolable causal necessity or a realization of the divine plan of the world. Primitive prayer presupposes belief in the changeableness of God, whereas the unchangeableness of the Absolute belongs to the elements of metaphysics. It seems to the philosopher as an intellectual limitation and childish defiance of fate to wish to move the infinite God to abolish the strictness of natural law, or to prevail upon Him to change His eternal world-order.

Natural science in our own time has strengthened belief in the immutability of natural law and has borne this belief far and wide. Traditional prayer, therefore, has been to a great extent abandoned both in intellectual circles and among the masses of our great cities. As Paulsen says: " It is scarcely open to doubt that faith in the wonder-working power of prayer is in a condition of rapid decay. This is to be observed among European peoples since the beginning of the era of modern scientific inquiry. In proportion as meteorology has explained atmospheric events, and in proportion as physiology and pathology have explained the facts of bodily life, in like proportion have natural safeguards and remedies displaced supernatural ones. . . . We have become more and more familiar with the presupposition of an unbroken causal connection in Nature." All original, direct prayer, that of primitive man as that of the greatest saints, is a trustful intercourse with God, a personal relation to Him, in which are always reflected earthly relationships, those of subject, family, friend, lover. But a pantheistic Deity, immanent in the happenings of the world, excludes such a relation of prayer as much as the God of Deism who stands apart from the world and has no interest in it. Man can as little enter into a relation of prayer to the " First Unmoved Mover "[1] of Aristotle or to the *anima mundi* of the Stoics: to the *deus sive natura sive substantia sive universum* of Spinoza as to the *grand être* of Auguste Comte. Paulsen writes: " A personal relation is a relation such as exists between man and man, in which there is a mutual exchange of thoughts, feeling, services. That just this same relation is possible between man and God even the boldest anthropomorphism finds it dubious to maintain, or has anyone the courage to say that precisely the same relation exists as between parents and children, friends and neighbours? " The greatest spirits in the realm of religion have had this courage.

[1] πρῶτον κινοῦν ἀκίνητον.

Not only have they said that there is a personal relation between God and man, but they have lived in such a relation. They have stood in innermost communion, in abiding fellowship with their God. God was to them a real Father or Lord or Friend or Bridegroom.

2. Rational philosophical thought destroys the essential presuppositions of a simple prayer. These are: faith in the anthropomorphic character of God, in His real presence, in His changeability, in the reality of personal communion with Him. The strict logical consequence would be a radical rejection of prayer. This, however, is seldom achieved except in avowed materialism and naturalism. It is as if philosophical thinkers had an instinctive presentiment of the richness of the soul's life, unveiled in the prayers of great men of genius, and of the power which religious man experiences in believing prayer: for they have not maintained unconditionally the rejection of prayer and have sought to adjust prayer to their philosophical system. Even Auguste Comte, though he denies all belief in a super-sensible world, recommends in his *Positivist Catechism* a daily prayer. The forms in which prayer has been reinterpreted are various.

(a) Respect for tradition sometimes leads to a retention in an external way of ritual prayer and sacrifice. Confucius took part in the rites in which Heaven, earth, gods, spirits and ancestors were adored. He did not desire that men should make too much of them or make any additions to them, but he insisted on their correct observance. Seneca and Epictetus piously adhered to the traditional ceremonies. Seneca believed that " religious usages should be observed not as pleasing to the gods, but as commanded by the laws." Epictetus requires " the giving and sacrifice of the first fruits according to ancestral customs."

(b) Sometimes we meet with an illogical wavering between a rejection of prayer in general and an appreciation of a refined form of prayer. Seneca and Voltaire illustrate typically the indecision and uncertainty of philosophers in their judgement of prayer and of religion as a whole. In them the most contradictory currents of thought cross each other. Also the discussions of prayer by Maximus of Tyre and of Clement of

Alexandria show a wavering attitude. Even Spinoza, pene-trating and stringently logical thinker as he was, does not hold fast to the rejection of prayer demanded by his metaphysic unconditionally or without explanations. "I do not deny," he says, "that prayer may be very useful to us, for my under-standing is too weak to be able to determine all the means which are at God's disposal to lead men to the love of Him, that is, to salvation."

Diderot's absolute scepticism is expressed in the prayer with which he concludes the "*Interprétations de la Nature.*" "O God," he prays, "I know not whether Thou art, but I will think as though Thou didst look into my soul, I will ask as though I stood in Thy presence. . . . If I am good and kind, what does it matter to my fellow creatures whether I am such because of a happy constitution, or by the free act of my own will or by the help of Thy grace?"

The prayer of this son of the Enlightenment ends with a query which is only the cheerless expression of a restless spirit that ever questions but never affirms!

(c) Another reinterpretation is frequently given to prayer by making it a mere recollection of God or the symbol of a pious disposition, a humble and grateful mood, a trusting and loving heart. The element in prayer which is objectionable to the philosopher, the thought of an influence brought to bear on God is accordingly set aside, the objective, metaphysical character of prayer is obliterated, and the significance which is admitted is purely subjective and psychological. A Pytha-gorean philosopher, Diotegenes, calls grace before meat a beautiful custom; it serves by the thought of God to put our-selves in a lofty frame of mind. Guyau attempts a reconstruc-tion of the Christian idea of intercessory prayer. "If prayer is to find an answer in itself," he says, "it ought not to be addressed to a Being outside us, it must be a spiritual act of love, a deed of love to one's neighbour. This lovely feature of prayer has a beauty that will not perish with the supersti-tious notions which will be gradually detached from the cus-tom." "Prayer" writes Dürr the psychologist, "is for the pious man of the new faith, but the expression of trust in the unalterably fixed direction of the course of the world and life."

(d) Most re-interpreters resolve prayer into contemplation. The turning of the mind to God which is essential to simple prayer forms only its outer dress or even wholly disappears; the dialogue becomes a monologue, and instead of living intercourse and fellowship with God we have a mere thinking of and about God; instead of an appeal to God we have meditation on the riddles of existence or on the moral values and aims of life. The ideal prayer of the Christian gnostic which Clement inserts in his *Stromata* is purely contemplative; it contains no petition but only the contemplation of the divine world-order and the expression of moral resolution. "I would deliver myself from craving that I may unite myself to Thee. Truly admirable is the created order, everything is rightly linked together, nothing happens without a cause. I would be free from desire, striving after Thy righteous election which divides the good from the others." Toland, the English philosopher of the Enlightenment, addresses his prayer not to a living supernatural Power, but to an abstract conception. "O philosophy, thou guide of life, thou seekest for justice and expellest vice. What would we have been, nay, what would life in general have been, without thee? . . . Whose help would we rather use than thine? Thou hast bestowed upon us the true peace of life and hast abolished the fear of death." The dialogue form of this prayer cannot disguise its character as a monologue. Kant says that prayer is strictly a soliloquy. This thought is defended by modern philosophers of religion, such as A. Dorner, Guyau, and von Hartmann.

(e) Whilst thus soliloquizing contemplation is held up as the ideal of prayer, prayer in the proper sense of the word, the turning to God and speaking with Him, is considered a means of training which may indeed be dispensed with, but which nevertheless is useful for the cultivation of "the religion of the spirit." "In public popular addresses," writes Kant, "prayer may and must be retained because it can exercise great influence and can make a great impression." A. Dorner regards the address to God in prayer as "the imaginative form for setting forth the contents of prayer."

(f) A philosophy with theistic or theological interests does not concern itself with the shallow analysis which empties prayer of its real meaning, but seeks for a rational justification of its metaphysical presuppositions and of the faith in its answer. Origen was the first to attempt a really profound defence of prayer. He formulates the problem with great precision: " If everything happens in accordance with the will of God and His decrees stand fast, and nothing of what He wills can be reversed, then prayer is absurd." His solution of the problem would, on the one side, leave intact the unchangeableness of God while, on the other hand, it seeks to maintain the real influence on God which lies at the basis of naïve prayer. God sees from all eternity what the individual man will freely choose, and accordingly frames His now unchangeable decrees in view of the free decisions of the will and the freely willed actions of men, and especially in view of their prayers. God thinks: " this man who will be instant in prayer, I will grant for the prayer's sake that for which he prays; that man, I shall not answer because he will not be worthy of being answered." This speculative attempt to prove the metaphysical possibility of an answer to prayer, recurs repeatedly in Christian theology in a similar form. It is found in a fine setting in Eckhart. " In His first eternal view God saw how all things were to happen. He saw even the least prayer, the least good deed which anyone was to do and considered which prayer and which act of devotion He should hear. He saw that thou wilt to-morrow call upon Him with zeal and beseech Him earnestly, and that invocation and prayer of thine God will not answer to-morrow, for He has heard it in His eternity before thou becamest a human being. But if thy prayer is dishonest and insincere, God will not deny it to thee, *now*, for it is from all Eternity that He has denied it. So then, God in His first eternal view, looked upon all things and does nothing incidentally, for everything is a thing done before."

Every hypothesis of this sort is simply a supplementary attempt to effect a compromise between the demands of rational thought and the essential presuppositions of genuine prayer. To the man of simple piety — to primitive man as to the religious genius — " this dialectic, partly intellectual and partly mystical, which crushes out the primary fact of the religious life," is superfluous and unintelligible. His assurance of being in direct communion with God cannot be destroyed by any philosophical criticism; it is in need of no philosophical help or justification. Even the great theologians who as *thinkers* wrestled with the problem of prayer and only too often (one thinks of Schleiermacher) surrendered to an intellectualistic and anti-supernatural metaphysic, as *men of prayer* were raised above it; they did not question nor indulge in subtle inquiries, but lifted themselves up to God, and poured out before Him their need and their joy.

Rational philosophical thought means the disintegration and dissolution of prayer. Prayer, the spontaneous and direct expression of religious experience, is subjected to an alien authority when forced into the categories of philosophical ethics and metaphysical theories of knowledge. Where these categories are accepted prayer ceases to be a " pouring out of the heart," a direct expression of religious feelings, moods and emotions. The praying man may not speak to God from the bottom of his heart, may not reveal his wretchedness and necessity; his innermost yearning and craving, his hope and trust must remain dumb. Only petition for " the good," perfect resignation, contemplative adoration may form the content of prayer. The positive ideal of prayer which philosophic criticism sets over against living prayer seems to the religious man as to the psychologist of religion a cold product of abstraction, a miserable substitute for the real thing. Even the purest type and most beautiful flower of philosophical prayer, Epictetus's prayer and hymn of submission, is in spite of its sound, as compared with the mystic's devotion, but the shadow of true prayer. The prayer of the philosopher is no real communion as between persons, no intercourse with God, no personal relation, no vital communion with Him.

The abstract ethical and rational law of prayer is only a halting-place on the road to the dissolution of prayer. Prayer, the heart and soul of religion, sinks to a mere instrument in the service of morality and reason, it is pushed from the centre to the mere periphery of religion. It is degraded to an educational expedient which the mature man no longer needs, is only a crutch which the morally strong man throws away. " He who has made progress in the good life ceases to pray, for can-

dor is one of its first maxims." This honest word of Kant sets
in the clearest light the disintegrating tendency of the philosopher's critical standard of prayer.

Prayer is, as we saw in the introduction, " the essential and
characteristic expression of the religious consciousness." The
peculiarity of the reconstructed religion of philosophy is nowhere so clearly and unambiguously revealed as in its attitude
to prayer; here it betrays the fact that it is not a religion.
Auguste Sabatier admirably says: " Natural religion is no
genuine religion. It robs man of prayer: it keeps God and
man far apart from each other. . . . At bottom this religion
is only philosophy. It has never been anything but an abstraction."

The philosophical ideal of prayer has become practical only
within the narrow limits of a philosophical school; it has never
touched the outer circles of ordinary men and women. It
possesses no constructive energy; it can produce only dissolving and destroying effects. But as little as rites and incantations could stifle simple prayer, so little can philosophical criticism kill it. Life in its irrational defiance shows itself stronger
than thought in its uncompromising logicality. There arises
an inner necessity for man to pray: " to be a human being —
that means to pray." The distresses of life are too heavy,
the will to live too strong, the liberating and consoling power
of prayer too wonderful for man to be able to satisfy himself
with the chill prayer of a philosophical ideal. Natural prayer
is indestructible. By its power and passion it lives in all lands
and times; still more wonderfully and more powerfully it lives
in the devotional life of great religious personalities. The
delineation of their life of prayer only reveals the philosophical ideal of prayer in all its coldness, its lack of life and
substance.

CHAPTER V

PRAYER IN THE EXPERIENCE OF GREAT
RELIGIOUS PERSONALITIES

PHILOSOPHICAL thinking undermines the power of natural, primitive prayer by subjecting it to non-religious tests of validity. Philosophical criticism and philosophical ideals of prayers rob it of its elemental strength. Simple, natural prayer in its native realism, its direct force and its dramatic energy springs up in the creative, devotional life of great religious personalities, and this is the type of prayer which philosophy subjects to criticism and idealization. The features of primitive prayer appear most clearly in the prophetic type of piety. But even in the prayer of the mystics the distinctive quality of genuine prayer is unmistakable. It is only in certain forms and states of mysticism that prayer is fully transformed and dissolved, and here this comes about from other motives than those which are at work in philosophic criticism. The differences between prophetic and mystical prayer demand a special exposition. We must, however, give a preliminary sketch of the elements common to these two types of prayer.

Prayer is the free, spontaneous expression of experiences which emerge on the heights of the devotional life and which deeply stir the soul. It is not subject to any religious and philosophical criticism, is burdened with no intellectual problems and is not bound up with traditional rules and formulas. Its deepest motive is the burning desire of the heart which finds its rest in blissful union with God or in assured trust in Him. It is fundamentally the same motive infinitely purified, refined and enlightened, which gives birth to all the manifestations of primitive religion, the desire for power, peace, and blessedness.

Like primitive prayer the prayer of the religious expert

manifests the realism untroubled by rational thinking which challenges philosophical criticism. To the mind of him who prays God has the distinct features of a human personality: He thinks, wills, feels, is self-conscious. Only the contemplative prayer of the mystic, now in a weaker, now in a stronger degree, has a tendency to de-personalize the idea of God. The primitive belief in the real and immediate presence of God is essential to all personal experience of prayer. To be sure, God does not dwell as primitive man imagined, in a perceptible, natural object; rather does He abide invisibly as the unseen Guest, *dulcis hospes animae*, in the inmost soul of him who prays. As in primitive religion, prayer is no mere monologue but an immediate contact with a living and a present God, a real communion with Him, which is never limited onesidedly to man but always implies mutual intercourse. And as in primitive religion, the relation to God expressed in prayer is the reflection of a social relation, whether of subject or servant or friend or bride or child. In this social relation are rooted those states of soul which appear still more strongly than in primitive prayer, frankness, warmth of feeling, and trustfulness in God.

The essential features of primitive prayer stand forth with self-evident clearness in the devotions of great saints and prophets. Nevertheless, personal prayer is something absolutely new when contrasted with primitive prayer, or the ancient song of praise, or even with the prayer of Greek religion in the classical period.

1. The first fundamental distinction lies in *the separation of prayer from sacrifice*. Among primitive and ancient peoples prayer is nearly always accompanied by sacrificial offerings. Even in Greek religion, prayer and sacrifice go side by side. Plato speaks of them as two things that are inseparably linked together. In personal religion the separation is effected. Lao-tzse's mysticism, Plotinus's striving for redemption, the Buddhist's absorption — all these have broken with every kind of sacrifice. In Israel it was the great prophetic achievement of Moses to have made personal communion with Jahve independent of all sacrificial rites. It is true that the Israelite of a later age gave a large place to sacrifice; but the prayer of the

great prophets and psalmists was fellowship with God apart from any connection with sacrifice. The liberation of the devotional life of the Christian from all sacrifice is the legacy of the Old Testament prophets. But the prayer of personal religion has not only freed itself from the traditional net-work of sacrificial ritual, it has set it aside and has taken its place. The devotional life of prayer excludes every material offering because prayer itself is seen to be the purest and most perfect offering. Both in Hellenistic mysticism and in the prophetic religion of Israel there arose the sublime thought that prayer is the true sacrifice and the only one worthy of God. Porphyry says " We must present to God our reverent meditation as a holy offering. This sacrifice consists in freedom from passion and in contemplating God." In Israel it was the prophet Hosea who was the first to designate prayer as the " offering of our lips." We repeatedly come across this identification of prayer with sacrifice in the psalmists. " Let my prayer be set forth as incense before Thee; the lifting up of my hands as the evening sacrifice." The author of the Epistle to the Hebrews writes: " Through Him then let us offer up a sacrifice of praise to God continually, that is, the fruit of the lips." Justin Martyr writes: "I also say (as do the Jews of the Dispersion) that prayers and thanksgivings which are offered by righteous men are the only perfect and well-pleasing sacrifices to God." Clement of Alexandria says: " We honour God by prayer and send up in righteousness this best and holiest sacrifice." " Prayer," says Rothe, " is essentially sacrifice. On the one side, the only prayer is a sacrificial prayer and on the other, the only sacrifice is a sacrifice of prayer."

2. In primitive religion man comes to his god in prayer only at certain times, under special circumstances or on the regular occasions of public worship; only under the urgency of need or the pressure of desire, or the prescription of custom does he call upon higher powers. But in the personal religion of great saints prayer is not limited to certain occasions; it accompanies all thought and action; it becomes a *life of prayer*, a continuous hourly and daily intercourse with God. Tendencies in the direction of a continuous devotional life already

appear in primitive and ancient cultural religion. For example, in the South African Baronga tribe, an epileptic who has been freed from his disorder, erects in his hut an altar to the spirits of disease. As often as he enters it he makes an offering of tobacco to them. If he goes on a journey he takes leave of them; when he returns he salutes them. Among primitive and ancient peoples we find a preintimation of continuous relation in prayer in the intercourse of the professional priests with the gods to whose service they had dedicated themselves. Their piety penetrated their whole life and governed all their interests. One might say that they always lived in the presence of the gods.

But this cultural communion with the divinity is only a poor hint of that living communion with their God which the great religious personalities enjoyed as they prayed. Mohammed in his early prophetic enthusiasm spent many nights with his disciples in prayer. Jesus passed whole nights in prayer. Catherine of Siena prayed through the night until the convent clock called her to mass. Luther prayed at least three hours a day, Ignatius Loyola seven hours a day. Of Francis, his biographer has said that " it was not merely that he prayed so much, it was rather that *he became prayer.*" The challenge of the Apostle to his young churches: " Pray without ceasing; for this is the will of God in Christ Jesus to you-ward " — has been uttered again and again by the great spirits in the realm of Christian piety. Bernard of Clairvaux exhorts: " Pray in tears without ceasing. Pray continually, entreat God day and night." Tersteegen says: " Let your constant business from morning till night be prayer." " Your vocation is to commune with God day and night in your heart by the practice of true prayer."

Thus do men of religious genius remain in continuous contact with God through prayer. In moments of great inner excitement spontaneous outbursts of prayer rise only as peaks out of the level of their ordinary life of devotion. This abiding communion with God in prayer produces the consciousness of ever being in the divine presence, a sense which is diffused over their every thought and act. The nearness of God is to them always so certain, so self-evident, that they cannot recall their past experiences or reflect upon their present state without invoking Him and speaking to Him. This permanent experience of the immediate presence of God is the type of prayer characteristic of the great religious autobiographies. Even when they do not in so many words pray, these great men are in an attitude of prayer. Their entire life is for them, as Origen finely remarks, "one great continuous prayer." [1] As Augustine says: "There is an interior prayer without ceasing." "Yearning prays continually, even though the tongue is silent." "The goal of all perfection is this that the spirit is freed from all carnal inclinations and is lifted up into the spiritual until every word and every volition becomes one continuous prayer." So writes the author of *De adhaerendo Deo*. Sebastian Frank remarks: "The introspective, spiritually-minded who live and move in God, often pray when they do not open the mouth, and do not even know that they pray."

3. But there is a still deeper difference between the prayer of primitive man and that of higher religion. The natural man regards prayer as his own achievement. Like his religion as a whole, his prayer is a bargain between himself and God; a human activity met by a corresponding activity on the part of God. He prays in order to win God over to his purposes, to change His mind, so that He may no longer be angry and punish but may give and help.

The truly and deeply religious man, on the contrary, who prays and struggles for God Himself, feels that his praying is not his own work, his own achievement, that it does not rise up out of his own heart but comes down from above, streams out of the plenitude and power of God. He feels instinctively that he could not pray unless God Himself put into his heart the thoughts and feelings and laid upon his lips the words and sighs of prayer. The mysterious impulse which drives him to prayer is the revelation of the indwelling God at work in the deepest places of his soul. Prayer which thus springs out of fathomless depths is at the same time the divine gift of grace; it is breathed upon or poured upon the devout soul as a charism from on high. The great men of prayer testify in

---

[1] μία συναπτομένη μεγάλη εὐχή.

countless places to the miracle of this inspiration. " That we pray is a divine gift," says Augustine. Thomas à Kempis prays: " Thou hast first stirred me up that I might seek thee." Says Luther: " Wherever a Christian is there is truly the Holy Spirit who does nothing except pray always." " Prayer," says Arndt, " come from God and goes to God." In a similar vein Bunyan writes: " Only the Spirit can lift up the soul to God in prayer. If the Spirit comes into the heart, then it is indeed prayer, otherwise it is not." So also writes Spurgeon: " Only the prayer that comes from God rises to God." Nor is this miracle of God-inspired prayer confined to Christians; it has been experienced by non-Christian mystics, as is illustrated in the *Masnavi* of *Jalâl-ed-dîn-Rûmî.*

The passionate yearning which is poured forth in prayer does not spring from man's narrow heart but from God's eternal love to allure and to draw man upwards towards itself. It is only to outward seeming that man's cry for help echoes in an infinite void, only to outward seeming does the answer fail to come. In reality the answer is already implied in the prayer. Wherever prayer lifts up its voice God is present, and though man may not behold His countenance nor hear His voice, God dwells near him invisibly, and guides him though he does not suspect it. " Thou wouldst not seek Me, if thou hadst not already found Me " — is the word of God to Pascal. Savonarola also received this comforting message when in his painful imprisonment he was in danger of losing his faith in prayer. Divine " Hope " appeared to him in outstreaming glory and said: " Tell me, who has lifted up from the earth thy heart to God? Who has led thee to prayer? . . . Was it not the Lord who works all in all? And if He continually gives thee such gifts, why then does sadness ask: ' Where are thy prayers! ' " A wonderful paradox is displayed in the religion of prayer: " Prayer is a divine deed in the human soul," writes Girgensohn. " Through prayer God enters the soul, imparting to it His powers and forming it according to His will — this is the last and deepest meaning of prayer." Whenever man prays straight from the heart this prayer is God's speech to man awakening in him and bestowing upon him that very desire and understanding which is the soul of the prayer.

" Christian prayer is, therefore, a spiritual echo: it is God's voice sounding in the human heart and resounding up to the Heaven whence it comes," as A. Stolz remarks. In the deepest sense, therefore, the prayer of the devout soul is God's own prayer; it is the great God praying through the small heart and weak mouth of man. " The tongue itself," says Mânikha Vâçagar, " which cries to Thee, nay all the powers of my being which cry to Thee — all are Thine."

The great Christian men of prayer have had recourse again and again to the pregnant confession of the apostle in the eighth chapter of the Epistle to the Romans in order to express the wonder of the God-inspired prayer from the heart: religion is the work not of man but of God, not man's discovery but God's revelation, not man's achievement but God's free gift.

Since prayer is the undeserved gift of God, devout souls pray with passionate yearning for the power to be able to pray aright. " Enlighten, inflame me, teach me what I ought to pray," cries Savonarola. " Grant that I may not pray alone with the mouth," supplicates Luther; " help me that I may pray from the depths of my heart." " Do Thou continually pray in me," is a petition of Tersteegen.

Deep and fervent prayer is no art of man or of human wisdom but the free gift of God which must be sought in all humility and sincerity. The secret will always remain hidden from the mass of men. Enlightened and clever people will smile at this paradoxical marvel. But religious persons in the great moments of their spiritual experience will grasp this profound mystery that it is not poor, miserable man who prays but the infinite God who has chosen him as His vessel to contain the heavenly treasure.

4. Real prayer, then, is for the great religious souls a free gift, but this gift is not to be passively waited for and passively received; it is to be consciously and intentionally sought, cultivated, practised. It is true that in the supreme moments of religious experience prayer breaks forth unconsciously and involuntarily out of deep, inner excitation. But the great men of prayer have betaken themselves to prayer not only under the compulsion of an overwhelming experience of God; they

have also in hours of spiritual "dryness" deliberately collected their thoughts in devotion, they have meditated about religious truths and pondered on significant forms of prayer, and by these arts have called forth the mood of prayer. All deep religious natures have persistently performed exercises in prayer. The majority of mystics have methodically and systematically frequented the school of prayer, and some of them have worked out a refined technique and in their discourses on the subject have given a psychological formula for training in the art. This conscious and continuous cultivation of prayer is an important distinction between primitive and personal religion.

5. In primitive religion prayer serves for the attainment of earthly aims, deliverance from danger, freedom from distress, acquisition of riches, injury to one's enemies. But what the great masters of prayer sought was not earthly happiness; it was God and spiritual salvation. "Say to my soul, 'I am thy salvation'" — in these words of the psalmist, Augustine summarized all the desires he expressed in prayer. Pascal will pray for nothing but God himself: "All that is not God cannot satisfy my yearning. It is God Himself for whom I pray and whom I seek." Luther admirably paraphrases in mystical phraseology this contrast between the lower and the higher form of piety: "He who thinks only of using God without enjoying Him, knows nothing of the joy which Christ promises to him who prays." The ordinary commonplace person rejoices in the good things of life and tries, therefore, to gain these things by calling on God to help him, whereas he who truly prays, as Herrmann says, "has joy in God himself." He cultivates prayer for its own sake. He seeks in it living nearness, and immediate touch, familiar intercourse and heartfelt communion with the Eternal. He longs for those wonderful effects which are vouchsafed to the pious soul in believing prayer, for inner unity and peace, spiritual freedom and strength, for confidence, hope, steadfastness, illumination, inspiration, and ecstasy. Again and again we find in the writings of the great masters of prayer the enumeration of the blessed effects of living prayer. Mechthild of Magdeburg has in very powerful language described these effects. "This

prayer has great power. It makes a sour heart sweet, a sad heart joyful, a poor heart rich, a foolish heart wise, a faint heart bold, a sick heart well, a blind heart able to see, and a cold heart full of fire." He who has once felt this wonderful power will be irresistibly and ever anew driven back to prayer. Prayer which heretofore was a mere instrument in the service of life has now a value in and for itself; it is an end in itself; it separates itself from all merely relative matters and becomes something absolute, for its object is absolute, that is, God and His complete sovereignty over the world and the soul.

6. Since the prayer of personal religion does not serve for the mere attainment of help and gifts, the chief element in it is not, as in primitive prayer, petition and persuasion. Rather is prayer the expression of all that stirs in the soul of the religious man: emotions pleasurable and painful, all moods and feelings of value, spiritual need, yearning for redemption, consciousness of sin, feelings of insignificance, the struggle for moral purity and power, but also adoring reverence, wonder, ecstasy, yearning, desire, surrender, love, confidence, trust, resolve, resignation, serenity. While philosophy is apt to regard prayer as merely petition for moral good and resignation, in reality the prayer of religious genius is as deep, broad, and rich as the human soul. The entire range of feelings, moods, emotions, volitions, and judgements of value reappears in it.

7. Primitive man prays at the place where the god dwells. If the god sojourns afar, the worshipper will at least direct hands and eyes towards his dwelling-place. The prayer of the great men of religion is, on the contrary, a praying " in spirit and in truth " free from all limitations of place; for it is certainly not in natural objects or in temples built by human hands that God dwells, but in the inmost soul of him who prays. But only in the still silence of the heart, far from the hurly-burly of the outer world, does the devout man experience the presence of God in the fulness of power awakening awe and blessedness. Hence when he feels the impulse to pray he hurries to some lonely spot, there to be alone with his God and to pour out his heart before Him. Among the Omaha Indians, when a young man arrives at a marriageable age he goes to a solitary place to pray to Wakanda. In another Indian tribe,

the Osages, the man who would pray withdraws from the camp
or from his companions. What among primitive peoples is
exceptional becomes the rule in personal religion. " We can
pray," says Plotinus, " only when we come alone to the
Alone." [2] John of Damascus calls solitude " the mother of
prayer." All great men of prayer, mystics, and prophets, seek
for solitude in prayer, whether it be in the distant mountains
or the dark forest, in the quiet chamber or the dead of night.
The individual nature of the prayer of great religious souls
expresses itself in this solitariness. In the deep quiet of Nature
or in the closed chamber, the devout soul can open up converse
with the Infinite and can pour out to Him all its happiness and
woe. But in the solitude of prayer not only does man speak
to God, God answers the call of man, in silent yet none the
less intelligible speech. " The revelation given in prayer becomes clearer as one progresses in prayer," as A. Sabatier says.
" Out of a revelation inherent in a first prayer, springs forth
a purer prayer, and from this prayer a higher revelation."

The longer a devout man continues in sincere supplication,
and the more deeply he penetrates into the mysterious world
of prayer, the more distinctly is the Invisible and the Eternal
revealed to him. In prayer the vital feeling of the awful nearness of God is intensified until it issues in a spiritual vision of
the Infinite, in an inner hearing of His word which summons,
awakes, warns, and consoles. In the mystic's life of prayer
the prevailing mood is wondering and trembling contemplation of God, in that of prophetic spirits it is the reverent
hearkening to His voice. This *inner* perception of God in
prayer which takes the form now of hearing, now of seeing,
is sometimes so powerful that it carries all before it and calls
forth pseudo-hallucinatory sensations. The spiritual experience of direct intercourse with God is accompanied by
stimulation of the visual or auditory organs of sense. The
confessions of the Old Testament prophets as well as of the
great Christian and non-Christian mystics are full of such
marvellous visions and auditions in which God reveals Himself. We find them also, though much less frequently, in the
great men of the New Testament. Sometimes these experi-

[2] μόνους πρὸς μόνον.

ences appear very suddenly and unexpectedly in the consciousness of the religious man; generally, however, they arise out of
prolonged prayer, forming its crown and culmination. But
besides these irregular, forceful expressions of divine self-
revealing in prayer, there is the more usual still, small voice
of God in converse with him who prays. When the devout
man has poured forth to God all his heart, his misery and
distress, he inwardly pauses with the petition: " Speak, Lord,
for thy servant heareth." And God speaks to the silent and
attentive soul, He reveals to it His will, answers its questions,
resolves its doubts, stills its longing, and soothes its pain. The
extraordinary dialogues between God and man with which religious literature from the Pentateuch to the works of Western mystics is crowded, are not merely the poetic and artistic
clothing of deep religious thoughts; they are the reflection of
this mysterious commerce of the praying soul with the God
to whom it prays. The divine answer is not the echo of the human appeal; on the contrary, it is a divine self-manifestation
and self-revelation. In the devotional life of men who are
highly gifted religiously, the speech of man to God and God's
speech to man are inseparably connected; but this second part
of the drama of prayer excels the first in wonder-working
power and glory. As Luther excellently remarks about the
relation of both parts: " To speak to God means to pray; this
is indeed a great glory that the high Majesty of heaven should
stoop to us poor worms and permit us to open our mouths to
Him. . . . But it is still more glorious and more precious that
He should speak to us and that we should hear Him. Both are
great and good blessings from God since the scripture calls
these two the spirit of grace and the spirit of prayer. For He is
the source of both; He allows us to speak to Him (through
prayer) and He also speaks to us (through the Spirit of grace).
But His speech is more comforting than ours."

Since it is to him who prays in solitude that God reveals His
nature and will, every new creation in the sphere of religion
has its origin in solitary prayer. The great truths of revelation
are ripened in the quiet of prayer and meditation; and here
also great religious resolutions are taken. The solitude of
prayer and of absorption is that which makes possible mys-

terious visions, ecstasies, and states of bliss, nay, it is the birth-place of world-religions and the source from which have sprung great religious reformations. In the lonely mountain of Sinai Jahve revealed Himself to Moses as the God of Israel; in secret fellowship with God the Spirit of Jahve seized the awe-struck prophets and made them His messengers to proclaim His holy will to the people of Israel; in the stillness of prayer, at the baptism by the Jordan, this same Spirit came also upon Jesus of Nazareth and revealed to Him the profound secret of His divine sonship and Messianic task; in the lonely sojourn in the desert the Paul who had been laid hold of by Christ at Damascus won the power to become an Apostle to the Gen-tiles; on a solitary mount near Mecca Mohammed was called to be the messenger of Allah; in the remote crags of the high-lands of Alverno, Francis of Assisi, as he prayed and medi-tated, was made one with his crucified Saviour and received the marks of His wounds; in private struggles in prayer Luther won at Worms that unshakable strength, assurance, and con-fidence with which he was able to defy a world of enemies, and as a man of prayer he became the great Reformer, the inaugurator of a new era in the history of Christianity. And even the gentle and self-renouncing sage of India, whose mes-sage of salvation to Asia became a world-religion, has become through the " silent prayer " of absorption, the founder of a religion. When in loneliness by the river Nerânjâra he had passed through the four stages of *dhyâna* (contemplation, ab-sorption) he grasped by " intuitive knowledge " the secret of the world and redemption, the four sacred truths of suffering, the cause of suffering, its destruction and the way to its destruction. Everything that is great, new, and creative in the history of religion rises up out of the unfathomable depths of prayer.

8. All great men of prayer discern in the manner and method of their own praying, or in the direction in which their devo-tional life runs, the ideal form of prayer, true, genuine prayer, in opposition to which the prayer of the ordinary man appears as false, or as, at most, a preliminary stage of ideal prayer. The standard of prayer which the great prophets and saints have proclaimed is not, like the philosophical standard of

prayer, subject to an alien principle, that is, it does not originate in a sphere of ethical and metaphysical values foreign to
the religious life; it is ruled by its own law, purely religious; it
grows directly out of its own vital experience of prayer. We
are indebted to nearly all creative religious personalities for
instructions in prayer by which they would draw others up to
the heights of their own devotional life. Among prophetic personalities, advocacy of their own ideal of prayer frequently
becomes a severe polemic against those forms of prayer which
contradict this ideal, such as the materialistic, mechanical, and
magical prayer of the mass of men.

9. The life of prayer as lived by the great religious souls
of the world has a connected historical relationship. There
is no such connection either in primitive or in ancient religion;
for the mechanical transmission of formulas of prayer or the
composition of devotional hymns in accordance with older
models cannot be considered an inner historical connection.
This historical continuity is characteristic of all productive
spiritual life. The great experts in prayer, just like the creative artists and the philosophical thinkers, stand in a mighty
stream of historical development. Prophetic religion is fully
conscious of this historical continuity, for in its view the revelation of God being accomplished in history, that is to say,
expressed psychologically, in the religious experience of certain
historical personalities, is the starting point and guiding principle of the religious life. This connection exists, indeed, in
mysticism, but owing to the timeless and non-historical character of the mystical experience, it is never fully recognizable
in that experience, and even where it comes to consciousness
it is considered not as an authentic connection but only as a
matter of literary dependence.

The history of religion knows only three great independent
currents of development which possibly may go back to two.
There runs an unbroken chain from the Atman-Brahman
mysticism of the Vedic Upanishads to the Vedanta of Sankara
on the one side and on the other through the mystical technique
of the Yoga system to the Buddhist doctrine of salvation.
Another line of development equally continuous leads from
the Orphic-Dionysiac mysticism through Plato, Philo, and the

later Hellenistic mystery cults to the neo-Platonic mysticism of the Infinite of Plotinus, which in turn is the source of the " mystical theology " of the pseudo-Dionysius the Areopagite. His writings became a great storehouse from which, as von Hügel says, all later Christian mystics " took over much of their literary material." Rightly has he been called " the father of Christian mysticism." Dionysius nurtures the entire mysticism of the Eastern Church; mediated by Scotus Erigena and the Victorines of the Western Church, he exercises a decisive influence both on its religion and its theology. Nay, he has even had a lasting effect on the mysticism of Islam. Perhaps this second chain is only an offshoot from the first, since the Eleatic speculation and the Orphic doctrine of redemption have possibly borrowed essential elements from early Indian mysticism. The prophetic religion of the Bible, which is poles asunder from mysticism, manifests the same continuity; starting from Moses — perhaps from Abraham — it runs through the prophets and psalmists to its culmination in Jesus and is perpetuated by Paul and John. This line continues in the succeeding Christian centuries, though it becomes weaker under the influence of mysticism and of a syncretistic ecclesiasticism, until it again finds its pristine strength in the biblical Christianity of the Reformers.

New forms of religion of an especial cast arise in virtue of the intermingling of mysticism with the prophetic religion or with popular piety. In the Hellenistic mysteries of the Orient the spiritual yearning for redemption is bound up with very ancient sensuous, cultual rites; and in the Hindu Bhakti mysticism are fused the Atman-Brahman wisdom of the Upanishads, the acosmic speculation of the Vedantas, the dualistic philosophy of Samkhya, the technique of the Yoga system with the popular cults of Vishnu-Bhagavan-Krishna-Râma and of Siva. In Philo of Alexandria the prophetic religion of the Old Testament is united to the mysticism of Plato and is at the same time influenced by the Egypto-Hellenistic mysticism of Hermes. The prophetic religion of revelation and the mystical religion of redemption is fused to a still greater extent in the history of Islam and Christianity. In the Arabo-Persian Sûfism Mohammed's prophetic faith in

God is bound up with Hellenistic Gnosis and neo-Platonic ecstasy and speculation, yet also with the Vedanta wisdom and the mystical meditation and Nirvana of Buddhism. In its earliest creative period mysticism has already penetrated into Christianity. In Paul's experience of Christ the two opposed types of religion meet each other in forceful energy; their inner contradictions remain unreconciled. In the Fourth Gospel, which is under the influence of Hermetic mysticism and Philo, their union is already accomplished; a gentle divinely intimate mysticism speaks in all the words of the Johannine Christ. Still, within the limits of the New Testament, we can speak only of a "relative reception" of Hellenistic mysticism, preparatory to a later full reception. The religion of Paul and John is prophetic yet with a powerful mystical strain. In after centuries, however, this ancient mysticism flowed into Christianity in ever wider furrows and created a Christian mysticism which is mysticism in the full sense of the word but which shows nevertheless strong traces of the religious spirit of the Bible. In Gnosis, its earliest form, this Christian mysticism is overburdened with mythological speculations, but in Clement and Origen it is clarified by the power of philosophical thought. Augustine unites in remarkable harmony the neo-Platonic mysticism with the Biblical religion of revelation. The entire Middle Ages in their devotional life are nurtured by his spirit, but the writings of the Areopagite also afford the same nutriment. In Anselm, Bernard of Clairvaux, Albertus Magnus, Thomas à Kempis, Francis of Assisi, Bonaventura, Thomas Aquinas, the Augustinian idea of religion predominates, while in Eckhart, Tauler, and Catherine of Genoa, the prevailing thought of God is that of the Areopagite. Mediaeval mysticism as determined by Augustine attains a new and original apprehension in the great Spanish saint, Teresa. The great Quietist mystics, Francis of Sales, Molinos, Madame Guyon, whose influence extended to the Lutheran and more especially to the reformed type of religion, drew out of their deep life in God. Lutheran mysticism which fuses the Biblical religion of Luther with Bernard's Jesus mysticism and Tauler's mysticism of the infinite, finds classical expression in Johann Arndt, whereas the reformed mysticism in which Hispano-French quietism meets mediaeval and reformed ideas, possesses in Tersteegen its most highly gifted representative. Thus the two great lines of development, mysticism and the religion of revelation, constantly cross, separate, and unite in the history of the Christian religion.

Their place in a comprehensive course of historical development determines the religion of the great religious personalities. Prayer is, of course, the most spontaneous and the most personal expression of religion; the independent creative power of men of pre-eminent religious genius is revealed in prayer with especial clearness. Nevertheless, the continuity of their inner life with that of their predecessors is distinctly recognizable in their prayers. The Buddha's method of contemplation is dependent on the Yoga technique of meditation; the spirit of prayer in the Old Testament prophets and psalmists continues to energize in the communion of Jesus with His Father; the devotional life of the early fathers and reformers is governed by the prayers of the devout men of the Bible; the praying of the great mediaeval saints is deeply affected by Augustine's devotional experience. In spite of all individual peculiarities the praying of the greatest men of religion shows an inner dependence on the devotional life of their forerunners.

10. In the exposition of prayer in personal religion it is almost exclusively Biblical and Christian personalities that have to be taken into account. Christianity, including the prophetic religion of the Old Testament, is "the peculiar home of personal prayer," as Söderblom remarks, or it is, as Bousset says, simply, "the religion of prayer," that is, the religion in which prayer is the focus of personal piety. To be a Christian means to be one who prays. "Thou then art not a Christian that art not a praying person" — such is the judgment of Bunyan. Luther remarks in his homely way: "As a shoemaker makes a shoe, and a tailor makes a coat, so ought a Christian to pray. Prayer is the daily business of a Christian." To be sure, prayer is the essential utterance of all the religions of the world; it is not an exclusively Christian but a universally human phenomenon. But the personal *life of prayer*, free and living intercourse with God, has its native abode in Christianity as it has nowhere else in the entire history of religion.

In this sense Luther's remark is sound: " To pray is a strange work which no one but the Christian performs and yet it has been very common in the world." What the non-Christian religions exhibit in the life of personal devotion is infinitely meagre in comparison with the richness and variety of the spiritual life revealed in the prayers of men of genius in Christianity. The religion of the literary hymn-writers in India, Babylonia, Egypt, and Peru, like the religion of cultivated Greeks, never rises to the heights of a personal life of prayer. The Greek philosopher's ideal of prayer is a pale abstraction, the mere shadow of real prayer. The cold deistic rationalism and moralism of Confucius has no room for the passion of prayer. The contemplative inwardness with which Lao-tsze meditates on the *Tao* never rises into the direct address of prayer. Genuine prayer is alien to the pantheistic mysticism of the infinite in the Upanishads and Vedantas, the mystical psychic technique of the Yoga system, and the Buddhist struggle for redemption. The absorption which takes its place is not prayer in the strict sense of the word, though it touches closely the mental prayer of many a Christian mystic. Even Plotinus, " prince of the non-Christian mystics," as von Hügel calls him, is always limited to " silent prayer " and never rises to a personal appeal to the Infinite. Even the deftly graded prayer of his later disciples lacks every breath of such intimacy with and surrender to God as moves through the prayers of Christian mystics. In the great religions of law, originating in a prophetic reform, Talmudic Judaism, Persian Mazdaism, and Orthodox Islam, the fiery lava of prophetic experience is hardened into cultual and ethical law; they offer no soil for the development of free, spontaneous prayer. Formal obligatory prayer is demanded by legalistic strict Judaism rather than any informal expression of prayer; official Islam subordinates free prayer (*du'a*) to prescribed prayer (*salât*); in Mazdaism the unrestricted prayer of the heart is even tabooed. The Mahayana development of Buddhism, Bhakti mysticism, primitive Islam, and the Arabo-Persian Sûfism are the only currents of non-Christian religious development in which we find a tender and fervent, a passionate and vigorous life of prayer. Mohammed, the Islamic mystics Bayazid, Ferîd-ed-dîn-Attâr, and Jalâl-ed-dîn-Rûmî, the Indian Mystics Mânikha Vâçagar, Yâmuna Muni, Tulsi Dâs, and Nanak, are non-Christian personalities worthy to be placed beside the men of genius in Israel and Christendom as great men of prayer. Nevertheless, the records of their prayers can be regarded only as parallels alongside the incomparably richer testimonies of Western personalities.

The variety of forms revealed in the Christian life of prayer results from two facts: first, that the religion of the Old and New Testaments is a *personal* religion which makes possible a free unfolding of the emotional and volitional life, whilst the negative religions of redemption in India seek for salvation in a non-emotional state of the soul; and secondly that through the connection of Biblical Christianity with Hellenistic mysticism, rich possibilities of fruitful syntheses come into existence. The history of the Christian life of piety is the most striking proof of the uniqueness and absoluteness of Christianity among the religions of the earth. Compare Christian with non-Christian prayer and you will be compelled to agree with Harnack when he says: " Christianity is not one religion among many; it is religion. He who does not know this religion, knows none, and he who knows it and its history knows all."

Out of a crowded multitude of praying Christians a few of eminent greatness stand forth, those who are peculiarly the creators of the Christian life of prayer, and those who, standing on their shoulders and perpetuating or renewing in creative fashion their type of piety, have influenced most enduringly the devotional life of after-times. The ultimate roots of Christian prayer go back to the prophetic mediation of Moses between Jahve and Israel. He is the great man of prayer who intercedes for his people with Jahve; none of his contemporaries stand in such immediate relation to Jahve as he. He " sees Jahve's face." He " communes with Jahve face to face." He " speaks with Him mouth to mouth." The tremendous dramatic realism which is peculiar to the prayer of the great Christian personalities, is the creation of Moses. The prayer-life of the older leaders and prophets of Israel, of a Joshua, a Samuel, an Elijah, and an Amos, moves within the forms of the Mosaic intercessorship; they stand to Jahve " in a direct relation, not for their own advantage but for the good of the community; they pray for their people and in the name of their people." In Jeremiah this prophetic intercessorship becomes *a personal relation in prayer*. He has been rightly described by Cornill as " the first man of prayer known to the history of religion." Another has called him " the father of true prayer."

The Psalms of the Old Testament are in their inmost essence nothing else than the prayer-life of Jeremiah transformed into poetry. In these devotional songs the deeply depressed community of exilic and post-exilic times pours out its unspeakable sufferings as well as its indestructible trust. Like Jeremiah, whose book of prophecies was their Gospel, they struggled in prayer out of the anguish and despair of the present into a victorious confidence and hope in the future. The most profound word in the Psalter: " Whom have I in heaven but Thee; and there is none upon earth that I desire beside Thee. My flesh and my heart faileth but God is the strength of my heart and my portion forever " — this word Jeremiah first experiences; he won this confidence first for himself, and then for all the children of God after him. One hears the music of these Hebrew Psalms through all the Christian centuries; the Psalter became " the peculiar prayer-book of the primitive church "; and to this day it is the prayer-book of all monastic communities who daily praise and supplicate the Eternal in the words of the Singers of Israel; and evangelical piety also draws from it faith and power.

But the psalms of the Exile and of the Maccabean period are only the first fruits of the spirit of Jeremiah's prayer. To him also is due the *individualism* of prayer which after the captivity became the common possession of the Jewish people. " The later Judaism," writes Bousset, " did indeed liberate prayer from rite and cult for wider circles; it has worked prayer into the very substance of the devotional life of the laity; and it has created manifold forms of prayer." These prayers of post-exilic Judaism exercised an influence as great as the older psalms on the private and congregational prayer of the early church. Even the holiest prayer of Christendom, the Lord's Prayer, is closely related to these prayers of later Judaism. So also is the prayer of Mohammed completely filled with the spirit of Jewish piety.

Accordingly, " since the days of the psalmists Israel has taught the peoples to pray." Nevertheless, we would be wrong should we agree with Rabbi Perles, who makes this statement, that Jewish prayer is the highest form of all prayer and believe that the finest Christian prayers from the Lord's prayer to the hymns of the Church are *only* " an echo of Jewish prayers." Rather does the inwardness of prayer enter on a new epoch with Jesus; nay, we may even say with Söderblom, that " the inwardness of prayer in the strictly personal sense has been created by Him." Mysticism which practises religious inwardness with astonishing mastery, knows as long as it remains logical, only an *impersonal* inwardness. The inwardness of the great men of prayer in Israel, however deep and powerful it may be, remains *superpersonal;* the praying " I " of the old prophets and psalmists is never the religious personality in its individual separateness, but always the people of God, the holy congregation in its collective aspect. Only Jeremiah, the tragic failure of whose prophetic calling made him a solitary pray-er, is an exception. The intercourse of Jesus with God is through and through a personal heartfelt fellowship with the Father. Though He had passed through the school of the psalmists and prophets He rises head and shoulders above them when He prays; He is the perfection of their piety, " the most powerful man of prayer in history " — as Wernle has said. The most primitive phenomenon of prayer, the relation of man as child to his Father-God, shines through His prayer in its greatest purity and power. Jeremiah and the psalmists of the Exile struggled in anguish of soul for unconquerable trust in Jahve; the prayer of Jesus in the hour of His death-agony is not only an utterance of trust but of surrender as well: " Not my will but Thine be done! " " This prayer on the Mount of Olives is the highest moment in the history of prayer, the most profound word in religion that has ever been uttered," as the philosopher Höffding has described it. In this and in other brief ejaculatory prayers faithfully transmitted by His disciples, in His short exhortations to sincerity and confidence in prayer and in His own model prayer the devotional life of Apostles and Church fathers, monks and mystics, reformers and theologians, has been ever kindled afresh. His prayer in Gethsemane has been repeated after Him by millions of the children of men: countless multitudes have been led up by the Lord's Prayer to the spiritual height of His life of prayer; His parabolic words about persevering, vehement prayer have awakened unbounded confidence in the hearts of the devout. The confession of the Fourth Gospel, " Out of His fulness have all we received and grace for grace," has been nowhere so abundantly verified as in the prayer of pious Christians. The measureless and far-reaching influence that goes forth from Jesus' prayer-life is the most convincing proof of the uniqueness, the creative power of His personality. Such prayer could well up only from depths at once human and divine.

Like His good news of God, the gracious Father, and of the coming Kingdom, the prayer of Jesus is something creatively new; but this new thing is still interwoven with the old forms of piety and the religious conceptions of the Jewish people. Its liberation from these bonds is the achievement of the Apostle Paul. It was he who broke through the national limits of the Gospel. Out of the preaching of the Kingdom delivered to the Jewish people he made Christianity a world-religion. It was he also who on the foundation-stone laid by Jesus reared the cathedral of the Christian life of prayer. He is the creator of Christian congregational prayer. It is true that he has by no means given to the young Church hard and fast formulas of prayer, but relying on the devotional terminology of the Jewish synagogue, he has created a powerful and resonant language of prayer for public worship which the Christian Church has preserved through all the centuries as a precious heritage. Still more: Paul has put intercessory prayer at the very centre of the devotional life of the Christian. He himself, the great missionary and pastor, was a master of the art of intercessory prayer. He prays unceasingly for the salvation and spiritual growth of his churches, and exhorts them unceasingly to pray for themselves and for their brethren. The most significant influence of the Apostle upon Christian prayer, however, lies in the fact that through him it comes about that all communion with God has an immediate relation to Jesus Christ. As Paul knows no other God than the God revealed in Christ, so he knows no other prayer than prayer to the " Father of our Lord Jesus Christ," prayer in and through Christ. And this prayer " in the name of the Lord Jesus " comes of itself to be a direct prayer to Him. Paul has an especial significance for the devotional life of the Christian in that through prayer he entered into a personal and intimate relation to the glorified Jesus. Already in the primitive community of Palestine the believer had sent up a wistful prayer to the Lord enthroned at the Father's right hand — " Come, Lord Jesus! " — which found its way very soon into the public liturgy. But the human lineaments of Jesus had been too deeply engraved on the memory of the primitive disciples for tnem to be able to commune in the same way with the Risen One as with the Father in Heaven. Paul, on the contrary, who was not one of the original disciples and to whom the glorified Christ appeared first on the way to Damascus, would " no longer know Jesus according to the flesh," that is, the human and historical Jesus, but only the Son of God exalted to the glory of the Father. His entire thought, will, and feeling were so possessed by love to his heavenly Lord and Saviour that he could say: " It is no longer I that live but Christ liveth in me "; he had but one longing — to depart and to be with Christ. This enthusiastic love of Christ must necessarily issue in personal communion with Him, in an abiding fellowship in prayer. And yet this religious communion is entirely a personal relation of the Apostle to his Lord. In the primitive Church as in early Christianity the ceremonial prayers spoken by the congregation at the celebration of the Eucharist — apart from the formulas of the *Maranatha* and the *Kyrie Eleison* — were not addressed to Christ directly but through Him and in His name to God the Father. When Origen advocates prayer in the name of Jesus and rejects direct address to Jesus and when Augustine knows only prayer to God through Christ not to Christ Himself — they are in harmony with the earliest liturgical tradition. On the other hand, popular religion used the direct appeal to Christ in prayer from the earliest times. This popular custom made its way first into responses and hymnal poetry, and much later into strict liturgical prayer. In the personal religion of Western nations prayer to Christ first wins a prominent place in the early Middle Ages. Doubtless it was contact with the Pauline spirit which led Anselm and especially Bernard of Clairvaux into loving communion in prayer with the Lord Jesus. Paul is, therefore, the creator of Christ-mysticism, that is, of personal relation through prayer to the heavenly Christ as Lord and Saviour of the individual soul. Although this influence of the Apostle on the devotional life made itself felt only after centuries, it has no small meaning for the history of individual Christian prayer. Through Bernard, Paul has powerfully affected the method of prayer in mediaeval and modern mysticism.

The practice of Christian prayer has been affected almost more profoundly by Augustine than by Paul. After Jesus and Paul no personality has exercised such a lasting influence on the Christian religion as this man, the greatest of the Church Fathers. His religious thought and experience shows the most splendid synthesis of the Hellenistic concentration on the mystic search for the infinite and the biblical prophetic religion of revelation. In his praying are united the most profound contemplation and the most energetic strength of will, the passionate power of the biblical psalms and the serene depth of neo-Platonic absorption, Paul's faith in forgiving grace struggling out of a deep sense of guilt and the mystical Eros of Plato and Plotinus hastening heavenwards; the unconquerable trust in the divine will revealed in the Bible and the blissful contemplation of the neo-Platonic *summum bonum*. His praying is the expression both of the deep woe and weal of the heart and of the elevation of the mind to the Highest Good, of the humble cry to God " out of the depths " and of the experience of essential oneness with God in his inmost soul. Nevertheless, in this peculiar fusion of the two opposed types of religion neo-Platonic mysticism has the precedence. The goal of all prayer for Augustine is the return to the infinite One, the essential unity with the Highest Good. " Neither in the thought nor in the feeling of Augustine," says Scheel, " is the first place assigned to specifically Christian ideas. The genuine Augustine is the neo-Platonic Augustine." This spirit of mystical prayer of the Bishop of Hippo was to live and energize through the Christian centuries. The spiritual legacy of Augustine nourished both the subtle dogmatics and simple piety of the Middle Ages. Anselm and Aquinas, Francis of Assisi, Gertrude of Helfta, Bonaventura, Thomas à Kempis are dependent wholly on Augustinian mysticism in their contemplative devotional life. But his influence reaches far beyond the limits of the Catholic Church and penetrates deeply into evangelical religion. " The religious language we use," says Harnack, " which is familiar to us from hymns, prayers, and books of devotion, bears the stamp of his mind. Without being aware of it, we still speak with his words, and he has been the first to teach us how to express the deepest feelings, and to find words for the dialectic of the heart."

The devotional religion of the Middle Ages is Augustinian; but its two component elements, the Pauline prayer for pardon and the neo-Platonic ascent to the supreme Light, characterize respectively the two main periods of mediaeval religion. In the first half of the Middle Ages a stern, harsh mood of penitence rules the entire religious life; the feeling of guilt disturbs the soul to its depths; sinful man shudders before the awful might of the great God, he trembles before the majesty of the Eternal Judge, he quivers in anguish as he faces his last hour. In his distress and dread he begs for mercy, for forgiveness of sins, for aid and protection against the assaults of Satan, and for a happy death. The atoning act of Jesus on the Cross, and the merits of the saints are the foundation of his trust. The grandly terrible *Dies irae* of Thomas of Celano is the most eloquent expression of this devotional mood which thrills the soul of the early Middle Ages. In the second mediaeval period another spirit of prayer prevails: it is the spirit of the neo-Platonic Augustine. The most serious themes, guilt, grace, and sin, never wholly cease to sound, but they are overborne by the mystical yearning for a blessed union with the infinite God. " Perfect love casteth out fear." The first traces of this mystical love to God and vision of Him are found in the prayers of Anselm; but Bernard of Clairvaux forms the turning point at which penitential dread passes into the disposition of love and at which the Pauline mysticism centring in Christ is wedded to the neo-Platonic, Augustinian mysticism centring in the Infinite. He is the father of the mysticism at the heart of which is Jesus as Sufferer and Bridegroom. In the religion before his day we find only tendencies towards these motives of mystical piety. In Bernard the Pauline " imitation " of the suffering and dying Christ becomes a tenderly sad and profoundly sympathetic absorption in the sorrows of the Crucified. Paul's communion in prayer with the exalted Lord passes into a sweet and gentle fellowship of love with the Heavenly Bridegroom which borrows from the Song of Songs its imaginative images and transparent symbolism. The mystical life in the privacy of Catholic monasteries as well as the extravagant love of Jesus in evangelical pietism, are alike nourished on the Saviour-mysticism of Bernard.

Next to Bernard two solitary *religieuses* of the thirteenth century have mightily influenced the mystical life of aftertimes. The beguine Mechthild of Magdeburg has put the bridal love of the soul for the Saviour-Christ into even more fervent and vigorous language than that of the great Cistercian. Gertrude of Helfta was her disciple. Her devotional language, indeed, is inferior in religious freshness and artistic originality to the poetic speech of Mechthild, yet it became the normal language of the praying mystic in succeeding centuries.

From Francis, the most lovable of all the Catholic saints, there went forth an abiding influence on mediaeval prayer. Something of that childlike and joyous confidence which lived in the prayers of Jesus awoke in the " little poor man " of Assisi whose entire endeavour was directed to the imitation of the poor and humble life of his Lord and Master. Yet at heart his pure and intimate prayer-life was not evangelical but mystical. Of course, this mysticism is not reflective, like the neo-Platonic. It avoids all that harsh hostility to the world which cleaves to the piety of most Western and Eastern mystics. His mysticism is rather a childlike, naïve enthusiasm which is kindled anew at the sight of every creature and which pours itself forth in rapturous devotion, jubilant praises, and joyful thanksgiving. " He did not cease," says his biographer, " in all elements and creatures to praise and glorify the

Creator and Disposer of all." The *Canticle of the Sun* is the permanent expression of this enthusiastic spirit of devotion. But Francis unites with this joy in nature and in God a mystically ecstatic love of Jesus which in inwardness and power is no whit inferior to that of Bernard and the saintly *religieuses*. The wonderful stigmatization in the grotto of la Verna is but the physical manifestation of that mystical union with Christ which crowned his life of prayer. Through the instrumentality of his great Order his prayerful and happy love of God and of Jesus became the common possession of many.

In contrast to this emotional ideal of mystical prayer, Eckhart and Tauler proclaim the ideal of a silent prayer of the heart to which the glow of religious passion and yearning is alien. In Suso's prayer, on the contrary, the childlike, loving joyousness of the poor man of Assisi comes to life again as well as the nuptial love of Bernard of Clairvaux. In the piety of Thomas à Kempis, author of the unique *Imitation of Christ*, the varied tones of prayer of the great mediaeval men of religion are united in a wonderful harmony. This unpretentious devotional booklet has naturalized in the widest circles, even outside Catholicism, the spirit of prayer as seen in Augustine, Bernard, and Francis. A peculiar significance for post-Reformation mysticism in the Catholic Church belongs to the Spanish Carmelite, St. Teresa. She is probably the greatest woman mystic in the history of religion. No mediaeval female saint and mystic is her equal in depth of soul. As Edward Lehmann has said: " In her, mysticism was not only an impelling power, it was personal genius. And just in this inner creative power lies the greatness of Teresa. She was not satisfied merely with realizing in feeling what the men of her time produced in thought, like the German *religieuses*. No, the thoughts conceived by men first received perspective and living expression by passing through this feminine brain. She speaks much of the watering of gardens; she herself has richly irrigated the garden of the mystics. Everything which in men's systems was dry and wooden, blooms and blossoms under her influence." The ideal of " interior prayer," the " prayer of the heart " which she extolled, rules the entire devotional life of Catholicism in the seventeenth century. She is also the creator of that psychologizing tendency in mysticism which has seriously sought to perfect the observation, description, and analysis of mystical states and experiences. She has created that singular ladder of prayer which leads up from the contemplation of the great truths of redemption to the blissful God-intoxicated state of ecstasy. Mystical prayer becomes with Teresa a fine art of prayer. Herein lies the greatness of her genius, that in her the liveliness and originality of mystic devotion are not weakened or disturbed by the artistic practice of prayer, and the penetrating, religious exploration of the soul. All the great mystic lovers and teachers of prayer in the sixteenth and seventeenth centuries, John of the Cross, Francis of Sales, Fénelon, Tersteegen, Madame Chantal, and Madame Guyon have learned from this Spanish nun.

Luther's vigorous, healthy, and cheerful type of devotion forms the opposite pole to Teresa's art of mystical prayer; it is the most important contribution made to the subject in the entire history of Christian prayer. After Jeremiah, Jesus, and Paul, the German reformer is indeed the most powerful among the eminent men who had a genius for prayer. His freedom from mediaeval mysticism springing out of neo-Platonism, and his exclusive relationship to biblical religion, gave rise to a creative renewal of the prophetic and primitively Christian type of prayer. Luther's praying is not a contemplative absorption in God as the infinite One and " Highest Good," but an emotional expression of the deep necessities of heart and conscience, which ends in the joyful utterance of trust and surrender.

The central prayer of primitive Christians for the coming of the Kingdom of God rings out from Luther's mouth with its ancient mighty sound. The simple-minded realistic faith in the power of persevering prayer is proclaimed by none of the great men of the Christian religion so energetically and powerfully as by Luther in connection with the parables of Jesus. Luther's devotional life is rooted wholly in the prayer of the biblical personalities. He is not, like Augustine and Bernard, the creator of an original mode of prayer; his praying is the echo of those prayers which came from the lips of Jeremiah, the psalmists, Jesus, and Paul. His ideal of prayer is a copy of the biblical model. Luther, with an assurance and boldness possible only to a man of unique religious genius, has eliminated the neo-Platonic element which had penetrated into Christian prayer and thereby restored the prophetic type of prayer to its religious purity. And yet this restoration was no mere mechanical rejuvenescence and imitation but a creative and original renewal. Here is the wonderful thing in Luther's religion, that he who had passed through the school of mediaeval mysticism, and had taken up into his devotional life its most precious qualities, its grand individualism, its heartfelt intimacy with God, and its gentle love of Christ, was able to enrich with a mystical element the simple and vigorous devotional religion of the Bible without dimming or distorting its purity. Luther's prayer is genuine prophetic prayer, but shows a distinctly mystical element which in his early reforming period is stronger than at a later time, but which never wholly disappears.

Luther's ideal of prayer exercised a quite astonishing influence on the devotional life of his time. Not only the teaching about prayer of the spiritually allied reformers, Melanchthon, Calvin, and Zwingli, but also the books of prayers and the devotional literature of the first decades of the century of the Reformation were determined by Luther's biblical standard of prayer. A deep influence on the devotional life of the reformed churches went forth from Calvin's personality. His congregational prayers show, it is true, a thorough-going dependence on Luther; his teaching about prayer in the *Institutes* agrees with Luther's even to the wording. And yet Calvin's spirit of prayer in its characteristic creative power is strikingly different from that of Luther. A childlike simplicity and affectionateness speaks in Luther's prayer, whereas in Calvin's is revealed a masculine gravity and a stern, penitential tone. From Luther's prayer there streams a joyful religious trust and surrender to God; from Calvin's a sacrificial, world-regenerating moral energy. In Luther's prayer the deep impulsion and hot passion of the heart are poured forth without reserve; in Calvin's the ardour of religious emotion is controlled by the dread thought of the unapproachable and holy majesty of God. Luther's prayer is the simple expression of the needs of heart and conscience and the fervent entreaty for comfort, help, and grace; Calvin's prayer constantly circles round the grand purpose of salvation, that is, the glory of God. "We pray," he says, "to the glory of God. We ask first for what only serves His glory, and then for whatever serves our well-being."

This clear and strong spirit of prayer which in greatness rises above Luther's childlike piety, but remains far below it in intimacy with God, lives again in the Baptist preacher, John Bunyan, England's greatest religious genius, and in the lonely pious thinker, Blaise Pascal, who overcame all the doubts of the understanding by the irrational boldness of his strong faith in God.

Luther's and Calvin's influence on evangelical piety was very soon flung back by the incoming tide of mediaeval mysticism. About 1550 the mystical method of prayer began to enter into Lutheran books of devotion from the Catholic literature of prayer, and by the end of the sixteenth century it had won uncontested precedence in all German books of prayer. The connection between Catholic mysticism as represented by Bernard and Tauler, and Lutheranism as represented by Melanchthon reached its height in Johann Arndt. The Lutheran prayer for divine grace is fused with the mystical yearning for blissful oneness with God in the depths of the soul. But in this union of biblical and mystical prayer, as with all the great men of religion in the Middle Ages, the mystical element preponderates and the specifically evangelical elements are constantly coloured and altered. Arndt's influence on Lutheran piety reaches as far as the period of the rationalism which cut the ground from beneath all mystical tendencies. The religious revival of the nineteenth century brought with the reawakening spirit of Lutheran piety a renewed appreciation of evangelical mysticism as understood by Arndt.

For the reformed devotional life Tersteegen became specially important, and his influence extended even into Lutheranism. He is the most eminent mystic on evangelical ground, nay, speaking generally, one of the greatest writers of mystical

prayers and hymns. His devotional hymns, of which many
to this day are sung in evangelical services, reveal an unspeakable nearness to God, a soft tenderness of soul, and a quiet
peace of heart. The reverential trembling and silence of the
soul before the mystery of the divine presence, the dumb contemplation and speechless adoration of the Infinite present in
the depths of the soul, are seldom so simply yet so eloquently
sung as by this divinely gifted artisan. Tauler's deep and
quiet mysticism of the Infinite forms the underlying tone of
his particular type of piety; but in addition all the various
motives of Christian mysticism, the deeply sympathetic contemplation of Christ's passion, the love of Jesus as Bridegroom,
inner yearning for the Saviour in the Sacrament, quietist calm,
and, in addition, Luther's heartfelt trust in the giving and forgiving God, form with that underlying tone a religious symphony of great solemnity and beauty. As à Kempis in his little
book of devotion, so Tersteegen in his hymns has bound together into a unity the manifold forms of mystical prayer.

The personal religion of the Christian East remains inferior
to the Christian West in richness, variety, and extent. It is
confined to world-abandoning anchorites and monks. Out
of the multitude of solitary contemplatives three great men
of prayer stand forth who have exercised a determining influence on the devotional life of contemporaries and successors. Macarius of Egypt who first proclaimed quiet interior
prayer as the true ideal of prayer; Nilus of Sinai who has
given guidance in prayer to anchorites seeking after God in
the wilderness; and lastly, Symeon " the new theologian," the
classical representative of Byzantine mysticism. In contrast
to the monotony which cleaves to the prayer-life of Eastern
monasticism Symeon's melodious hymns reveal an astonishing
wealth of religious experience. Harsh contempt of the world
side by side with rapturous delight in God, passionate yearning
for God together with gentle and quiet intimacy with Him,
admiring contemplation of the infinite Light and humble surrender to the grace and redemption of Christ the Saviour,
a spiritual and loving desire for the fulness of the divine life
together with inner absorption in the mystery of the Eucharist
in which the non-sensuous God, outside time and space, draws

near to the devout soul in lowly, sensuous guise — in the harmonious fusion of these varied mystical moods and ideals lies that unique power of enchantment which streams forth in Symeon's book.

From the countless choir of Christian men and women who have prayed, the clear voices of these great lovers of God ring out distinctly and powerfully. They are pioneers in prayer and hymn, after whom other devout spirits have prayed and sung; they are teachers and guides who showed to others the path of prayer to God. To him who heeds their exhortation to pray and follows their guidance, who listens with reverence to them as they pray and humbly and reverently repeats their words, to him as to them will be revealed the unfathomable mystery of the divine, the power and glory of the Infinite.

CHAPTER VI

GENERAL CHARACTERISTICS OF MYSTICISM AND PROPHETIC RELIGION

In the personal piety of great religious spirits two main types stand forth with distinct prominence. Nevertheless, the psychology and philosophy of religion have not quite accurately characterized them. James opposes the religion of "healthy-mindedness" to that of the "sick soul." Translating these terms into ordinary language we should speak of a joyous optimism or of a gloomy pessimism as the fundamental aspect of a man's religious life. James also distinguishes from another point of view the religion of the "once-born" and that of the "twice-born"; with the first, religion is a harmonious development, with the second, it is marked by a decisive conversion followed by a new birth. Söderblom was the first to distinguish clearly and decisively between these two chief tendencies in religious experience. He describes them as "personality-denying" and "personality-asserting" mysticism, "mysticism of the absolute" and "personal mysticism," "mysticism of feeling" and "mysticism of will," "acosmic religion of redemption" and "prophetic religion" or "religion of revelation."[1] Similarly Seeberg distinguishes between a "speculatively-contemplative" and a "voluntaristic" mysticism. Here the word "mysticism" is understood in a wider sense than communion with God taking place in the depths of the soul; it means "an assurance which has not passed through the usual paths of the senses and reflection." But this wide application of the term, embracing as it does all higher religion, does not commend itself, because it covers phenomena

---

[1] The term "religion of revelation" does not imply here any religio-metaphysical valuation, but simply an historical and psychological characterization.

that are too diverse and therefore contradicts the etymology and traditional linguistic usage of the word.

Mysticism is that form of intercourse with God in which the world and self are absolutely denied, in which human personality is dissolved, disappears and is absorbed in the infinite unity of the Godhead. The lofty type of religion, standing at the opposite pole from mysticism, does not come under this definition. It is, therefore, better treated not as a special form of mysticism but as something quite different and independent. A simple, unambiguous description of this type in which its essential nature is clearly outlined is difficult. It is best characterized by the terms used by Söderblom, " prophetic religion " and " religion of revelation " whereby, of course, light is thrown on only one aspect of the problem; by the first term on the activity of the religious vocation, by the second on the peculiarity of the idea of God. Since this type of piety is especially represented by the Old and New Testaments and receives in the Gospel of Jesus its classical form, it can also be called simply " biblical " or " evangelical " religion.

Seldom only has mysticism been carried out to its strict logical consequences, as in the Upanishads, in the Vedanta of Sankara, in the Hinayana school of Buddhism, Plotinus, the Areopagite, Eckhart, Tauler, Angelus Silesius, and Molinos. It loses for the most part, under the influence of the prophetic experience or of the popular religion, its non-personal character and takes on a more personal colouring. The Tao mysticism of Lao-tsze, the Hindu Bhakti mysticism (as it appears in the *Bhagavadgîta*, and still more clearly in Râmânuja, Tulsi Dâs, and the Tamil mystics), the cultual mysticism of the Hellenistic mystery-religions, the mystical piety of Philo the Jew, the Sûfist mysticism of Islam, the Christian God-mysticism, show through all the centuries personal warmth and fervour, enthusiastic power and devotion, as opposed to the sobriety, coldness, and monotony of pure mysticism. Nevertheless, even this more personal mysticism in its inner structure is clearly separate from purely prophetic religion and agrees with logical mysticism in the goal of all its efforts after salvation. The structural difference of the two types must be, in the first place, worked out so that the diversity of prophetic and mystical prayer may be better understood. And here also it is necessary to make clear the definite, fundamental religious conceptions which always recur in our exposition of prophetic and mystical prayer, as for example, faith, love, ecstasy, sin, salvation, and so forth.

Mysticism arose within the great religions of ancient civilizations in Greece (Orphism), India (Upanishads), China (Taoism) and in Egypt; yet only Greek and Indian mysticism have had a great historical development. Mysticism exhibits in its rise a negative reaction against the developed religion of civilization. The prophetic religions of Zoroaster, Moses, and in a certain sense also, Mohammed, grew directly out of the but little developed primitive religions of nomadic tribes. By creative experiences in which these prophetic personalities were overpowered by the self-revealing God, primitive religion sprang up to the height of a personal monotheistic faith. It is only from the Mosaic revelation that a long process of development results, whilst Zoroastrianism, like Islam, soon hardened into a constricted, legalistic religion.

1. *The Fundamental Psychic Experience in Mysticism*

In times when a highly developed civilization is in a state of decay, as in ancient India, the Graeco-Roman world, mediaeval Germany, and France of the sixteenth and seventeenth centuries, the feeling of life and self, the healthy will to live is weakened in gifted and noble-minded persons, and joyous faith in the future, in the concrete values, aims, and tasks of life, collapses. A vehement dislike of the world and civilization seizes them, a burning desire for an infinite Good gives them no rest and violently urges them to free themselves from the world, civilization and society.

The pious man, dissatisfied with the world and its glory feels himself a stranger on the earth, he is conscious that he is dreadfully fettered by the body, he sees in it a wretched prison, a dark grave. The thought of the ancient Orphic play on the Greek word for " body," (sōma-sēma) " body-prison," which Plato has appropriated, runs through the mystical literature of all the Christian centuries. The fettered soul yearns for freedom from the bonds of the physical organism, in order to soar to heavenly heights, to return to the infinite and the divine from which it sprang. It is only through man's inner being that the way to redemption is to be found. This means to tear oneself forcibly from all the ensnaring charms of the outer world, to close the gates of the senses,[2] to turn wholly inwardly, " to withdraw oneself into oneself," as Albertus Magnus puts it, to plunge into the lowest deeps of the soul.[3]

But it does not suffice that the pious man hungering for redemption is freed from the outer world of things, he must rather escape from his own ego, from all selfish wishes and desires. He must stifle the natural psychic impulses which call forth disquietude in man, especially the clamant and importunate tendencies of the will. He must drive out of the soul the creations of the imagination which perpetually rise up out of the depths of the emotional life; nay, he must even be free of concern about and appreciation of all worldly objects. The entire natural life of the soul is consciously and intentionally hemmed in, cut off from the outer world, all vital inner life and endeavour " done away," " brought to rest," " killed "; " the senses must be blinded," " man must sink away from himself and all things," as Suso phrases it.

Thus in the mystic's soul is achieved a great negative process, " a systematic letting die of all the propensities of life." Plato designates this process by the old Orphic term " purification," the neo-Platonists call it " simplification,"[4] an expression which passed into the language of the Christian mystics. Eckhart in a remarkable linguistic creation of his own characterizes it as an *entwerden*, " a ceasing to be "; Suso names it a " ceasing to be a creature "; the Indian, like the western mystics, describe it bluntly as " annihilation," " the becoming nothing." This negative process carries the mystic out of the customary state of mind into a supernormal state of intense concentration, to complete " withdrawal " and " inwardness,"

---

[2] μύειν.

[3] [The real author of *De adhaerendo Deo* from which the phrase in the text is taken is now believed to be not Albertus Magnus but Jean de Kastl.]

[4] κάθαρσις — ἄπλωσις — *simplificatio*.

to deep peace, blessed quiet and passive " not doing," to complete *abandon*, painless and joyless indifference.

This complete emptying and denudation of the psychic life, this stripping off to the uttermost of everything earthly and human, this introversion or perfect turning in upon oneself is only a preparation for exclusive concentration on the infinite, the divine, the eternal. " The entire soul," says the author of *De adhaerendo Deo*, " with all its powers and potencies is gathered up into God so that it becomes one spirit with Him, and thinks, feels, and knows nothing but God." All suppressed passion and yearning is directed towards this supreme Value, the inner concentration becomes a flight to the highest Spiritual Reality; renunciatory calm, an unreserved surrender to the Highest Good, deep, heartfelt peace, a blessed rest in God, quiet, inner bliss, an ardent " beholding " of the eternal Beauty. Every type of mysticism knows this upward struggle of the purified soul, to the Highest Good. But among many mystics of the East and the West, this spiritual experience of values and mystical yearning for God is intensified into a burning and consuming religious passion which the mystics of all times and lands call " love." And since this mystical experience of God is ineffable blessedness and bliss, the mystics like to speak of the " enjoyment of God." [5] Thorough-going, impersonal mysticism, on the contrary, exalts above the emotional impulsion towards the Infinite, the non-emotional solitariness, stillness, and unity of the soul. " I praise seclusion in preference to all love," says Eckhart.

Mystical love is a straining and striving after the Highest but it is not yet its possession; it is only a movement toward the lofty goal but it is not yet the goal itself. Mystical love is perfected in ecstasy; it is, as it were, " the mother of ecstasy," as Dionysius the Areopagite says. But even the chill, non-emotional mysticism to which the glow of mystical passion is quite foreign, knows an exaltation akin to ecstasy, that is, *Nirvana*. *Ecstasy* and *Nirvana* are two inexpressible mystical secrets. In psychological language both are supernormal states of the soul which presuppose a perfect cessation of the

---

[5] ἀπόλαυσις θεοῦ — *fruitio Dei*. The Indian word *bhakti* includes the idea of enjoyment.

normal conscious life; both occur relatively seldom in mystical experience. Both exhibit an experience of unity and value of such a height, purity, and blessedness as would be impossible in the normal life of the soul. But in spite of the similarity of their inner structure they stand at opposite poles from each other. Ecstasy is boiling point, Nirvana is freezing point, ecstasy is a positive height, Nirvana is a negative height (and yet as " height " something positive); ecstasy is infinite fulness, Nirvana is infinite emptiness. Ecstasy is the highest pitch of emotion. Although the suppression of the normal emotional life is its presupposition, it even possesses an emotional character and has an emotional history; it shares with the normal emotional experience the element of spontaneity, passivity, involuntariness, impersonality, brevity, and lasting effect. It is generally pictured as a being " seized," " overmastered," " submerged," " swallowed up," " possessed," " filled full." Nirvana, on the contrary, is complete disappearance of emotion, a continuous, permanent state of profound quiet and perfect solitariness, a blessedness without excitement, transport, or storm, not a being possessed, but a being utterly self-absorbed.

The physiological characteristic of ecstasy as of Nirvana is cataleptic rigidity and complete anaesthesia, which are frequently accompanied by levitation or the moving of the human body in the air without support. Ecstasy is psychologically characterized — the description by Plotinus is most admirable — as the experience of the unreserved psychic unity and simplicity, the experience of the pure " I." As Angelus Silesius says, " in ecstasy the unity swallows up the otherness." The ecstatic " gazes on himself," " beholds his I " face to face, " tastes his own substance." This naked, abstract, emptied " I " which is unveiled when all concrete, psychic contents are removed and when all the unified psychic powers are manifest in concentrated might is nevertheless experienced not as one's own but as a foreign " I." " He has become another and is no longer himself," says Plotinus. " He beholds in himself his naked heart and this heart is not his heart," says a Taoist mystic. The experience of the pure " I " has the quality of the experience of a religious value. That " I " wears the features of " the holy "; it seems to the ecstatic, in the pregnant terms of Rudolf Otto, as the *numinous*, exciting fear and dread, as a " tremendous mystery," but also as an attractive and alluring *fascinosum*. Indeed, this latter element in the experience of the " holy " preponderates in the feeling of the ecstatic. Confessions of ecstatics agree in describing ecstasy as unspeakable bliss, as overwhelming happiness, " eternal blessedness," " deathless joy." This ecstatic experience is, nevertheless, distinguished from the normal experience of religious values just as much as the experience of the pure " I " is distinguished from normal self-consciousness. In contrast to the usual voluntary experience of values it is unrelated, wholly enclosed in itself. If it were related to an objective vehicle of value (and were this the " I " itself), there would arise the contrast of subject and object which rules the soul's normal life and which is dissolved in the experience of the pure " I."

The ecstatic experience is for him who has been awakened from ecstasy incomprehensible and indescribable. The ordinary conscious life was broken in upon and therefore the mystic, having returned to this life, is not able to declare and explain what he really experienced. But the marvellous power and greatness of his experiences constrain him to interpret it. The strange, limitless, supreme, holy thing that he has experienced must have been a divine thing with which his soul has been united in an inconceivable and ineffable fashion. For Lao-tsze this highest experience of the mystic is the *tao*, the eternal world-order; for the men of the Upanishads it is *Brahma*, the universal divinity; for Plotinus, it is the One, the Illimitable,[6] from which streams forth all the diversity of existence; for the theistic mystic of the East and the West it is the divine Lord and Saviour who condescends to the devout soul. The incomprehensible paradox that the small human " I " has become an infinite " I " the mystic can understand only as meaning that he himself has become God. As Plotinus says, the ecstatic " has become God, nay, rather he is God." Catherine of Genoa declares joyfully: " My ' I ' is God, and I know no other ' I ' but this my God." And Madame Guyon expresses herself in a similar fashion. Other mystics do not

---

[6] τὸ ἕν — τὸ ἄπειρον.

venture to speak of the soul's identity in essence with God, but content themselves with speaking of the indwelling of God in the soul. Plato expressly emphasizes the fact that the soul is not God but only in the image of God, or " related to God " or the " divine." [7] Many Christian mystics in their humility describe the ecstatic union with God not as a union of essence, but as a union of married love; the soul does not disappear in God but fuses with Him in deepest unity. " God is in me and I am in Him. He is mine and I am His." So writes Elsa of Neustadt. But in spite of this milder and weaker formula which is in harmony with personal theism, the fundamental psychological character of the ecstatic experience is the same in the one as the other. " The mystic's soul turned inwards experiences God in itself in its innermost essence and deepest ground," as Koepp remarks. God and the soul are bound together in indissoluble unity.

2. *The Fundamental Psychic Experience in Prophetic Religion*

The fundamental psychic experience in *mysticism* is the denial of the impulse of life, a denial born of weariness of life, the unreserved surrender to the Infinite, the crown and culmination of which is ecstasy. The fundamental psychic experience in *prophetic* religion is an uncontrollable will to live, a constant impulse to the assertion, strengthening, and enhancement of the feeling of life, a being overmastered by values and tasks, a passionate endeavour to realize these ideals and aims. Paul, for example, speaks of " being led by the Spirit," of being " fervent in spirit," of the " power of the Spirit." Mysticism is passive, quietist, resigned, contemplative; the prophetic religion is active, challenging, desiring, ethical. The mystic aims at the extinction of the emotional and volitional life, for the delight of ecstasy can be purchased only at the price of killing the will to live. In prophetic experience the emotions blaze up, the will to live asserts itself, triumphs in external defeat, and defies death and annihilation. Born of a tenacious will to live, faith, immovable confidence, reliance and trust firm as a rock, bold, adventurous hope break forth at last out of the bosom of

[7] θεοειδής — ξυγγενὴς τῷ θείῳ.

tribulation and despair. The mystic is one who renounces, resigns, is at peace; the prophet is a fighter who ever struggles upwards from doubt to assurance, from tormenting uncertainty to absolute security of life, from despondency to fresh courage of soul, from fear to hope, from a depressing consciousness of guilt to the blessed experience of grace and salvation. He is no happy possessor but must ever establish his confidence in life in a creative act, in a free, moral deed, " in hope believing against all hope," " rousing himself against despair," as Luther says. No one has expressed in such pithy words as Paul the continuous emergence of trust and power out of anxiety and distress. " As dying and behold we live," he writes; " as chastened and not killed; as sorrowful yet always rejoicing." The feeling of absolute security in spite of all external uncertainty, to which the pious man struggles, has been described by the psalmist in a very remarkable way. " Yea, though I walk through the valley of the shadow of death I will fear no evil; for Thou art with me."

Thus faith is the basic experience of prophetic piety, of course not in the intellectualist sense of mere assent to truth, but in the sense of a fundamental feeling of confidence in life. Hence it is no mere hoping and seeking but an immovable having and possessing. *" Ut credo, ita habeo,"* says Luther. Nay, in the midst of time and mortality, it bestows already eternal life and everlasting blessedness. But, this confidence of faith awakening life and bestowing blessedness cannot be attained by any efforts of our own will. All ethical or ascetic achievements, even the highest moral perfection, cannot avail to create this purely religious assurance. It must rather well up with original freshness and vigour from the depths of the soul; it is a miracle, nothing but the grace of God, " a divine work in us," a deed of the Spirit of God in the human soul. This confidence of faith is experienced not as the ecstatic bliss of the mystic in a supernormal state. It does not presuppose an emptying and sublimation of the normal life of the soul; it is rather always experienced, even in the rush of daily life, without any artificial heightening of the emotional life.

" Faith," " trust," " confidence " — that is the *leitmotif* which sounds through the entire literature of the Old and New

Testaments and resounds anew in the writings of the reformers. If " love " and " union " are the central conceptions of mysticism, " faith " is the watchword of prophetic religion. Faith is that religious power which the oldest historical books of Israel report in praise of the patriarchs. " And Abraham believed Jahve and it was counted to him for righteousness." The great men of God in Israel again and again demand from their people a trusting faith in Jahve. Isaiah is pre-eminently the prophet of faith. " In quietness and confidence shall be your strength," is his exhortation to his people. Daring trust is that lofty mood of the soul which the adepts of prayer — Jeremiah and the exilic and post-exilic psalmists — won in a hard inner conflict. It is Jesus who has spoken the most powerful and the most paradoxical words about faith: " All things are possible to him that believeth." Simple trust in God is here raised to the boldest miracle-working faith. In trustful faith in God the Father, who for Jesus' sake bestows grace, salvation, forgiveness, Paul found rest for his soul tormented by sin and thirsting for redemption. " The righteousness which is from faith " is, therefore, the central idea round which circles the entire thought and feeling of the Apostle. In faith in Christ the fourth evangelist lays hold on eternal light and life. " He that believeth hath eternal life " — this word, not the Philonic idea of the Logos, is the leading motive of the fourth Gospel. In joyful faith in God's sin-forgiving grace Luther found peace for his heart after he had wrestled in vain for long years to find salvation by the works of the law. The reformed doctrine of *sola fides* is only the clearest and most logical formulation of the basic feeling of the entire religion of the Bible.

The contrast between this prophetic vital feeling and the mystical is as sharp as possible. Mysticism flees from and denies the natural life and the relish of life in order to experience an infinite life beyond it; prophetic piety, on the contrary, believes in life and affirms it, throws itself resolutely and joyfully into the arms of life. On the one side we have an uncompromising denial of life, on the other an unconquerable belief in life.

Additional Psychological Characteristics

(a) The devotional life of the mystic comes to a climax in extraordinary experiences which happen in a state of supernormal consciousness: ecstasies, besides visions and auditions of an ecstatic character, in which excitations of the senses are bound up with purely spiritual experiences. Even in prophetic experience, decisive events such as the prophetic call and revelation are frequently accompanied by raptures, visions and auditions, but these appear much less frequently than among the mystics, or are entirely absent. Only two visionary states are recorded by Jesus. In contrast to mysticism, all extraordinary ecstatic experiences have no significance for the life of piety, properly so-called, which lives in communion with God by prayer, faith and moral action. Paul has marked as the highest gifts not the ecstatic speaking with tongues, but faith, hope, and love. Luther shows even a strong disdain of everything visionary. "If it were within my power," he says, "that God should speak to me from Heaven or appear to me, I would not wish it."

(b) Mystical experience is never wholly naïve, but is always bound up with a tendency to reflective thought; among some, to metaphysical speculation as in the Upanishads, Plotinus, and Eckhart; among others, to careful psychological self-analysis as in Yoga, Buddhism, Teresa, and the Quietists of the seventeenth century. The experience of prophetic personalities, on the contrary, is perfectly simple and unreflective, lifted above speculative thought, and free from all psychologizing. Here there is just as little subtle meditation on the nature of God as meticulous self-analysis and self-exploration; here is only faith, hope, and love.

(c) Mysticism shows a conscious intention; only in this way does it succeed in mortifying the natural emotional and volitional life. It has devised refined methods of asceticism and meditation in order to induce or to facilitate the occurrences of mystical states. The perpetual struggle for an artificial "simplification" of the natural psychic life brings about a uniformity of experience, a constriction of what is individual, personal, spontaneous. Mysticism, therefore, reveals a certain uniformity and monotony. Fundamentally all mystics say the same thing. It is only contact with prophetic piety which gives to Christian and Sûfi the stamp of individuality. No-where does the uniformity of mysticism appear more strongly than in the conceptual schemes of the Buddhist canon or than in the writings of the Quietist mystics of the seventeenth century. In contrast with this, prophetic piety is marked by lack of intention, unconscious spontaneity, free unfolding of individual aptitudes. It scorns all system and method, all psychical technique, all " training of soul." Thus the result is the startling fact that the inner religious life of prophetic spirits is richer, more multiform, and more diverse than that of the mystics who nevertheless are entirely absorbed in their inner world.

(d) Mysticism is the religion of feminine natures. Enthusiastic surrender, a delicate capacity for feeling, soft passiveness are its characteristics. Mysticism has numberless pre-eminent representatives among women, such as Râbia, Mechthild, Gertrude, Catherine of Genoa, Catherine of Siena and Madame Guyon. The mystical soul plays the woman's rôle in converse with God. " Wife " is in Eckhart's judgement, the noblest name for the soul. Prophetic religion, on the contrary, has an unmistakeably masculine character, ethical severity, bold resoluteness and disregard of consequence, energetic activity. As St. Paul says: " Stand fast in the faith, quit you like men, be strong." " God asks from us very bold and manly things," writes Zwingli, " that we may cleave to Him alone and find in Him our only consolation and hearken only to his will."

3. The Idea of God in Mysticism

The idea of God in the extreme mysticism of the Absolute is merely the speculative interpretation, the metaphysical projection of the experience of ecstasy. In ecstasy the mystic experiences himself as a complete unity; so also the God of mysticism is an undifferentiated unity, the " Simple," the " most simple," the " One without a second," the " only, pure, clear One, free from all duality." In ecstasy all the variety of psychic experience as also of the external world ceases. For the mystic who awakens out of the bliss of ecstasy, out of the experience of unity to the normal, conscious life, the objective world in its diversity is deception and illusion, *mâyâ* or at least the dim emanation or dark shadow of the only genuine reality. Ecstasy is the final stage in the depersonalizing achieved in the mystical life; the God of the speculative mystic is non-personal, wholly devoid of anthropomorphic features. Thought, will, and self-consciousness are extinguished in ecstasy; likewise " the One " neither thinks nor wills nor is self-conscious. The ecstatic condition is perfectly empty of all concrete content, " perfect emptiness," " unconditioned negation." The absolute Unity is also completely without any quality; one can assert nothing of it; it is the " No, No," as it is called in the Upanishads, " exalted above being," [8] as Plotinus says. Ecstasy is a hidden, incomprehensible mystery. It can never be grasped in thought and described in words, since it is beyond conscious experience. The divine likewise is exalted above all speech, unnameable and inexpressible, the " Abyss," the " Silence " as the Gnostics say. " It is," says Lao-tsze, " something hidden, with no name to describe it, an Unfathomable, nay, the absolutely Incomprehensible." The ecstatic stands in solitary quiet and unmoving fixity, having come, as it were, to a standstill; the God of the mystic is also at a standstill, " actionless," " beyond activity," the " unchanging Light," as Augustine says, " tranquil and tranquillizing all things," as Bernard has it.

The mystical conception of God is, therefore, thoroughly static. He who is sunk in ecstasy is beyond all values; in the words of Plotinus, " he has left behind him the beautiful as he has passed beyond the circle of virtues." The God of extreme mysticism possesses neither ethical nor aesthetic predicates; He is " higher than virtue, higher than goodness, higher than beauty," says Philo; or as Plotinus puts it, He is the " super-good," the " super-beautiful." [9] The ecstatic experiences an infinite Value, the Supreme Blessedness; the God of the mystic is, therefore, the Highest Good, the *Summum Bonum*, a term which was coined by Plotinus following Plato and which, through Augustine, became most frequently used as descriptive of God. It meets us also in the Song of Songs

[8] ἐπέκεινα τοῦ ὄντος. [9] ὑπεράγαθος — ὑπέρκαλος.

of Indian mysticism, the *Bhagavadgîta,* nay, even in the *Tao-teh-King* of Lao-tsze.

Clearer and more concrete is the idea of God in personal mysticism which interprets ecstatic experience in mysticism not speculatively but in a simple, imaginative fashion. God is not the non-personal, unqualified Unity beyond reality and values, but the highest Value conceived as a personality. He is the living Lord, the lovable Saviour who stoops to man's petty soul in order to raise it up to Himself. The Infinite assumes an earthly form, the *summum bonum* becomes a human Redeemer-God, the Vishnu-Krishna-Râma in the Indian Bhakti religion, Jesus Christ in western mysticism, especially since Bernard of Clairvaux. Nay, so deep is the condescension of the heavenly Saviour-God, that He as a living bridegroom draws near to the yearning soul, woos it with His love, and with a tender embrace unites Himself with it. Since here the personal features of the naïve idea of God are living we call this mysticism by a term coined by Rudolf Otto, "mysticism of personal theism" in contrast to "mysticism of the Absolute." But even in this personal mysticism God is not the living, active Will, but the changeless, still Majesty, the statically conceived perfect Ideal, "the eternal Rest of the Saints," as à Kempis writes.

4. *The Idea of God in Prophetic Religion*

As the idea of God in mysticism exhibits the hypostatizing of ecstasy, so the idea of God in prophetic religion is the reflex of the dominance of the will in the experience of faith. " Faith is the creator of the Deity," says Luther in a paradoxical but striking phrase. God is not the immobile, infinite Unity, but the living, energizing Will, not the quiet Stillness but the active Energy, not always at rest but ever in action, not the highest Being but the supreme Life, — so run the contrasting terms of Augustine. " My Father worketh hitherto," says the Johannine Christ. The experience of the mighty power of God becomes in prophetic spirits an anxious dread before the inescapable wrath of the living God. " Jahve is the true God; He is the living God and an everlasting King: at His wrath the earth trembleth " is the word of Jeremiah. On the power of the living God prophetic spirits feel themselves absolutely dependent; in His hands are weal and woe, blessing and cursing, life and death. " No sparrow falls to the ground without your Father." But trustful faith, immovable confidence, produces the wonderful paradox that the angry, jealous, and judging God is at the same time the giving and forgiving God, the Helper and Deliverer, that the Almighty Power in its inmost essence is nothing but wisdom, compassion and goodness. God is " the Father of mercies and God of all comfort." " God is love."

The mystic experiences in absolute silence the presence of the Infinite and draws into his deepest being the gentle breath of divine peace. The prophetic feeling of God's presence is an experience of the activity of God and possesses a far greater dynamic; everywhere and always he traces His living nearness and consuming power; not even in the underworld can he escape it.

Extreme mysticism strips the idea of God of all personal attributes until it arrives at the " bare," " pure " Infinite. The God of prophetic spirits, on the contrary, has unmistakably the features of a human personality, in whom primitive anthropomorphism lives on, spiritualized indeed, but in all its original power. God is Lord, King, Judge, and when trust has cast out all fear, He is Father.

5. The Valuation of History

(a) In Mysticism. The static God with whom the mystic in his ecstasy becomes wholly one is outside time and space, without any vital relation to the world and history. The idea of a revelation of God in history is quite foreign to mysticism; it is a purely super-historical religion. Christian mysticism was therefore obliged, like the mysticism of Philo and of Islamic Sûfism, to re-interpret the biblical faith in the historical revelation of God and to lower the history of redemption to a mere means of preparation for mystical experiences. The historical facts of biblical history fade into transparent symbols of super-temporal truths; they become mental states, are transferred from the external course of the world to the depths of the devout soul. As Augustine says in his Enchiridion, " Whatever took place on the Cross of Christ, in the grave, in the Resurrection on the third day, in the session at the right hand of God that by these things the Christian life might be figuratively set forth not in mystical words but in dramatic deeds — all that is here accomplished." Mediaeval mysticism, indeed, moved by the thoughts of Augustine, allowed to ripen a gentle, refined Saviour-mysticism, the thoughts and moods of which continually circle round the biblical pictures of the incarnate Son of God, His birth and childhood, His suffering and death. The human image of Jesus mystically re-touched becomes the model for the mystical imitation of Him. The poverty-stricken life of Jesus, His quietist, passive virtues of humility, love and obedience are to be realized by the mystic in his own life. But this imitation of Christ which from the time of Bernard lends its characteristic features to the mediaeval, especially the Franciscan ideal of piety, is fundamentally only the representation of the mystical process of salvation, a counterpart of the mystical process of " ceasing to be " in biblical pictures. It is only something preliminary, the way of purification which is followed by the higher stages of the path of salvation. But the New Testament picture of Jesus moulded anew by mysticism has a still further value as the material of mystical meditation with which the next stage of the perfect life commences. The mystical life of devotion is nourished by the powerful emotional stimuli which radiate from this picture; from them it draws in its power and fervour. But on the summits of the mystical life the devout soul must renounce all these highly emotional images of the Saviour and His passion, he must, as the German mystics say, " get away from images." At the moment of the soul's highest vision of the Highest Good and of its perfect union with it, all thoughts of the human and historical Christ have completely vanished. Augustine's axiom, going back to the Alexandrian Theology, " through the man Christ you reach the God Christ," recurs repeatedly in the mediaeval mystics. Hence the incarnate Son of God and Redeemer is not the historical revealer of the eternal will of God, but the sensuous symbol of the spaceless, timeless, and infinite Deity. If the devout man would attain to this he must advance beyond the historical Christ;

he must rid himself of His image as of the image of every creature.

(b) *In Prophetic Religion*. For mysticism God is He who is at rest in Himself, who is sufficient to Himself, the Silent One, the *deus absconditus*. For prophetic religion God is the Creator and Worker, the Speaker, the *deus revelatus* who manifests His will in Nature, as in the course of individual and national destiny. History is the peculiar province of His revelation, it forms the basis of fellowship with Him, the firm foundation of all faith. The emigration of the children of Terah from Chaldea, the Exodus of Israel from Egypt, the wanderings in the wilderness and the conquest of Canaan, the victory over the neighbouring tribes are the will and work of Jahve to which the prophetic preaching constantly refers. The Exodus, the giving of the law and the making of the covenant at Sinai, are, for Old Testament religion, *redemptive deeds* to which all faith and hope for the future cling in times of humiliation. But the Old Testament prophets struggled to a still deeper apprehension of history from a religious point of view. Not only in conquests and victories, but also in the suffering and tribulation of the people, did they learn the will and word of God. Israel's humiliation is Jahve's judicial punishment; foreign kings are His instruments. Nay, in the song of the Righteous Servant of the second Isaiah, faith in history as revelation soars up to the daring conviction that Israel sacrifices itself in vicarious suffering for the peoples. In the primitive Christian experience, instead of external historical events and prophetic leaders, there comes a particular historical personality, the Son of God as the highest revelation. " When the fulness of the times came, God sent forth His Son." The personal God thinks, speaks and acts in and through Christ; the Christian experience of God is indissolubly bound up with the historical personality of Jesus. The New Testament religion is strongly Christocentric. It knows no communion of man with God except in and through the Lord Jesus Christ, the Revealer and Mediator; it knows no prayer except in the name of Jesus, to the Father of our Lord Jesus Christ. The incarnation, sacrificial death, and resurrection of the Son of God are the great Christian deeds of redemption on which is sustained the consoling faith in God's redeeming and sin-forgiving grace. This Christian faith in the historical ground-work of salvation has its most powerful expression in the Apostles' Creed where the entire drama of redemption is comprehended in concise brevity. Mysticism, aiming at the super-temporal and the infinite has abandoned this historical, Christocentric form of the experience of God or has, at least, completely transformed it. The revival of the prophetic and evangelical religion by the reformers brought about a renewal of the idea of historical revelation. "God is not an uncertain God," writes Luther, "but a God who has revealed Himself at a certain place, and has portrayed Himself by His word and by certain signs and miracles."

"The Absolute," says Kierkegaard, "is revealed in history and indeed in such a scandal-provoking form as that of the Crucified." The contrast of the prophetic religion to mysticism appears nowhere so clearly as in the value set upon history. In mysticism there is the passing beyond space and time into the divine infinite beyond, in prophetism there is the firm adherence to the revelation of God given in space and time; in mysticism there is absolute freedom from all the objective facts of history, in prophetism there is the stringent connection of the experience of salvation with objective history; in the former, a direct and essential union with God, in the latter, fellowship with God, in and through Christ, "pan-Christism," to use von Hügel's phrase.

6. Attitude Toward Authority

The relation to religious authority is closely connected with the relation to history. To be sure, the mystics speak of revelations of God in the sense of mystical inspirations, visions, ecstasies; yet these are not the prerogatives of divinely commissioned men, they may be vouchsafed in principle to every pious man who enters upon the mystical path of redemption. Moreover, they have significance only for the personal experience of devout persons who have been favoured with them, but they possess no binding authority for all men. Mysticism knows only a subjective inner revelation. Not from the outside as an objective, historical fact does revelation come to man; it is not teachable and communicable. God must rather communicate Himself to him in the depths of his soul. Here is the reason why mysticism ultimately is exalted above all religious authority. Even Christian mysticism, despite its sincere subjection to religious tradition, ecclesiastical dogma and discipline, shows a sovereign inner freedom from all dogmatic authorities and ecclesiastical conventions. Even the personality of Jesus possesses no authoritative significance for mystical piety. The picture of Jesus in the Bible retouched by mysticism, which is for the mystic the object of imitation, has no authority from a moral point of view. That mystics, nevertheless, willingly obey Church authority is accounted for by the passive, quietist character of all mystics. Mysticism needs the protection of the Church in order that it may lead undisturbed its calm contemplative life; it needs the hard crusts and husks of ecclesiasticism in order that its tender and sensitive heart-piety may suffer no harm. All the great Catholic mystics were strongly ecclesiastical, so loyal and devoted to the Church that they even offered the sacrifice of the intellect without a murmur. Teresa confessed repeatedly on her deathbed: " I am a daughter of the Church." Eckhart and Madame Guyon, when opposed by the authorities of the Church, have strenuously protested their loyalty to the Church and their orthodoxy, although in their mystical experience of God they were far removed from Church dogma. Molinos even solemnly forswore his quietist mysticism. And they could do so with a good conscience, for this renunciation of personal freedom, this humble obedience to authority, is for them only a piece of the mystical " ceasing to be," of ascetic self-mortification and self-denial. On the solitary heights of the vision of and union with God the mystic is indeed perfectly free of all ecclesiastical authority, all dogmatic obligation, as from all historical revelation, for he has himself become God.

The personal contact and union of the mystic with the divine is not a " revelation " of God, in the strict sense of the term, for " revelation " is peculiar to *prophetic* religion. Here revelation is an objective, historical fact, a universally binding communication of the divine will. The bearers of this revelation are few in number, " sanctified from the mother's

womb," specially equipped personalities. The experience of
salvation rests on the proclamation of divine revelation. " Belief cometh of hearing and hearing by the word of Christ."
The idea of authority is rooted in prophetic religion as revelation. God communicates His will in the creative experiences
of the prophets; He speaks through their mouths; their word
is therefore binding upon contemporaries and upon posterity.
The high esteem and reverence which the great mystics enjoy
in the circle of their disciples are not to be compared to the
central position and personal authority which Moses and the
prophets possess for the religion of Israel, Mohammed for
Islam, Jesus and Paul for primitive Christianity and for the
Reformation. Here we are concerned not with a mere state of
being attracted to and stimulated by great and congenial personalities as in mysticism, but with an entire determination
of one's experience by that of creative personalities. This
authority is, however, not impersonal and objective like the
teaching office of the Church, to which the mystics subject
themselves, but living, religious, personal. Even behind the
written Word by which Luther swears there stands the personal authority of the biblical men of genius who are the
bearers of God's historical revelation. Since the prophetic and
evangelical religion bows before no institutional, ecclesiastical authority, but only before the personal authority of pre-
eminent men of God, it knows no mere assent to legalized and
authoritatively communicated doctrines, but only the free,
creative appropriation of the deepest religious experience
which floods the souls of those great men of religion. Whilst,
therefore, in mysticism the most profound obedience to and
the completest emancipation from authority stand independently side by side, in prophetic religion, submission to the
authority of the self-revealing God is united in perfect harmony with the most personal and vital freedom.

7. Sin and Salvation

Sin is, in the thought of mysticism, not the negation of
ethical values and standards, but the unrestrained indulgence
in the natural emotions and impulses, the naïve assertion of
life, delight in life and in the world, and the perseverance in

the spiritual isolation of the individual existence which these involve. Sin is for the Buddhist " thirst for life " (*bhava-tanha*), for Augustine, " concupiscence," the uncontrolled desire of life, for the author of *Theologia Germanica*, " self-will." Since this vital impulse and this strong desire for existence are nourished by the impressions of the sensuous world and the constitution of the human body, mysticism identifies " sensuousness," " the world," " the flesh," with sin. Just because sinfulness is viewed as something external, natural, it is for the mystic only a metaphysical fatality, which does not touch the core of man's being, the ground of his soul. Sin is, therefore, a " not-being," [10] as the Areopagite says, " an estrangement from God," as Augustine has it, a " privation," a " defect," an " absence," as Eckhart expresses it.

For prophetic religion, on the contrary, sin lies in a breach of the God-ordained order of moral values, in a revolt against God's holy will. The psalmist cries: " Against Thee, Thee only, have I sinned." The feeling of sin consists in the condemnation of the self as laden with a religious and moral unworthiness, in the feeling of utter wickedness, in the experience of a chasm between the ethical ideal willed by God and our own moral weakness. The distance between man and God is not metaphysical but moral. Sin and grace, guilt and justification, condemnation and forgiveness — that is the great problem of biblical religion which permeates the entire Old and New Testaments, which is never forgotten in the history of Christianity but which comes to fresh life in its original strength only in the Reformers. The feeling of guilt attains in prophetic religion a crushing force quite alien to mysticism in the strict sense. Sin is the most frightful reality, so frightful and monstrous that it is intelligible only as the efflux of an anti-divine power, Satan.

Mysticism seeks salvation in liberation from the world and creaturely existence, from all " non-being," and would in this way come to the only true being. Man should deny being and thus cast aside the veils of mortality and remove the difference between finite and infinite. Then he becomes one with the Divine. This ecstatic union with God is the peculiar ideal of

[10] μὴ ὄν.

mysticism. The way to this sublime goal of redemption is however very hard and steep; only by degrees can the man, hungering for salvation, approach the infinite ideal; step by step must he climb up the ladder of redemption which ascends to the dizzy height of ecstatic union with God. The most important stages of this path are, according to the neo-Platonic formula which, through Dionysius, has become the universal property of Christian mystics, Purification, Illumination, and Union.[11] The Buddhist way of salvation coincides with these mystical steps: Asceticism or morality — meditation — knowledge;.only the Buddhists add a fourth stage, deliverance, that is, *Nirvana*. This process of redemption is a painful endeavour to ascend to a higher sphere, but the sustaining grace of God must be united to the putting forth of one's utmost effort if the devout soul is to gain the goal. The path to the higher mystical states oan indeed be prepared by continual toilsome effort but their appearance in the soul is not man's work but God's. Even Buddhism, which, in thorough-going fashion, carries through its principle of self-redemption, views the liberating " illumination " and the redeeming Nirvana, as something marvellous and gracious, as " a divine gift without a Giver."

In contrast to the complicated mystical way of salvation is the prophetic experience of salvation as something infinitely simple. "To come to the Father" is not as with the mystics, " to ascend as on wings to heaven, but with heartfelt confidence to commit oneself to Him as to a gracious Father " — so writes Luther. Salvation is the restoration of communion with God which has been lost by sin; it is the bridging of the gulf between the unworthiness of the self and the worthiness willed by God, and this can be achieved only by God in " salvation," " forgiveness," " justification." Man cannot achieve redemption by his own efforts, not even by the greatest works of asceticism. Rather is redemption a free act of divine grace. The man who has inwardly condemned himself, experiences his own unworthiness, is not able, as Luther says, to win or to revive by his own power a joyful conscience, a vital feeling of

---

[11] κάθαρσις — ἐλλαμψις — ἕνωσις; *via purgativa — via illuminativa — via unitiva*.

assurance. It must spontaneously well up within the soul. On man's side is needed first the moral act of a change of mind, a revolution in the soul, self-condemnation, a radical breach with the past, and then, a trustful turning to God, a simple, childlike, humble, joyful confidence in His grace and mercy. A " return to Jahve " is what the prophets of Israel demand from sinful Israel. By the simple confession: " Father, I have sinned, I am not worthy to be called Thy son," the prodigal son in the parable wins forgiveness and restoration to the father's house; by the humble entreaty, " God be merciful to me a sinner! " forgiveness and justification are bestowed upon the publican. According to Paul, salvation and forgiveness are only to be found in faith in the all-gracious Father-God. Luther revived this biblical idea of salvation to which Augustine, the former neo-Platonist, could never quite advance. It is faith which bestows salvation and redemption and faith alone, *sola fides*. Man can do and effect nothing for his salvation, he can only believe and trust, receive and return thanks. Paul, Luther and all the great men of religion who have fought through the battle between the consciousness of sin and the longing for God, cling fast in their faith and in the consolation of forgiveness to an historical redemptive deed, the atoning death of Jesus on the Cross, which offers them an objective guarantee of the forgiving and justifying grace of God. The psychological peculiarity of the experience of salvation is not changed by this objective support. There is always the inner disagreement between the loftiness of the moral ideal and our own moral unworthiness and weakness which is overcome by a creative act of trust.

The difference between the mystical and prophetic doctrine of salvation is as clear as possible. In the former we have a complicated way of redemption, a difficult ascent, leading to dizzying heights; in the latter a spontaneous religious and ethical act of self-condemnation, of the will to good, of trust, which bestows freedom, power and blessedness.

8. *Relation to Ethics*

Mysticism does not value moral action as a thing good in itself, an absolute aim, that is, as the realization of values in personal and social life, but as a means to deaden the senses and suppress the emotions. Asceticism is the morality of the mystic, the purification of the soul's life. It has a negative, non-ethical significance as the more remote, yet, of course, indispensable preparation for union with God, while the proximate preparation consists of contemplation, prayer, and absorption. Even the splendid heroism and self-sacrificing charity of many a Christian mystic, such as Catherine of Genoa, serve only for purification, self-surrender, and self-mortification, and are intended to make smooth the path to ecstatic union with God. As in the path of redemption of neo-Platonic and Christian mysticism, so in Buddhism the lowest rung of the ladder is moral action, a mere preliminary stage to " absorption " and " knowledge." Morality is significant in the first place for the mystical life inasmuch as it is the psychological preparation for the higher mystical experiences. In the second place it is significant as a criterion of the soundness of the mystical and ecstatic phenomena. In Teresa's judgment, it is " not the soul which feeds most on spiritual sweetmeats and comforts that is perfect in the love of God, but the soul which is most firmly resolved to fulfil God's will and never again to offend Him."

This more definite appreciation of morality which we find in many Christian mystics rests on biblical and evangelical foundations. Thorough-going mysticism, on the contrary, attributes to ethics only a provisory and disciplinary significance. Inasmuch as it conceives morality only as something preliminary and preparatory, the religious man struggling to gain the highest must leave the kingdom of moral ideals behind him; he must discard the will directed towards concrete moral tasks and values, as well as instinctive tendencies; he must abandon the holy works of self-discipline and the love of his neighbour as well as all his daily duties. As Yâjnavalkya says: " Beyond good and evil action the immortal passes on," a sentence which is repeated in the *Dhammapada* and the *Bhagavadgîta*. Plotinus has a similar judgment: " the soul must not have either good or evil traits in order that as an ' alone ' it may receive the Alone." Works of charity must be discarded for fear they might disturb the inner isolation and unity. At the apex of the experience of mystical isolation and in the vision of God, the kingdom of moral values has ceased to have any significance. The perfected soul is " beyond good and evil." As Ferîd-ed-dîn-Attâr says: " Where love is, good and evil have disappeared."

In prophetic religion the moral will and deed are not provisional, not a mere preparation for union with God, but " a doing of God's will," as Jesus repeatedly asserts. Morality is not cut off from religion, nor is religion dissolved away in morality, as in the reconstructed religion of the philosophers, but is in vital, organic connection with it. This binding together of religion and ethics was the achievement of the two founders of revealed religions, Moses and Zoroaster, an achievement brought to perfection by the prophets and by Jesus. God is not " the more than good "; He is the substance and source of all moral goods, the holy Will, the sovereign Legislator and Judge who demands and commands, avenges and condemns. The fulfilment of His moral requirements in the individual and social life, in purity of heart and self-discipline, in brotherly love and self-sacrifice, is just as much the service of God and intercourse with Him as faith and love and prayer. " Right " and " righteousness " in the Old Testament constitute the essence of practical religion. Paul places active love above all miraculous gifts, nay, even above faith and hope. Vital spiritual experience spontaneously urges to moral activity, joyous faith in God cannot but reveal itself in moral deeds. " Faith worketh by love."

Thus while moral activity in mysticism is only a preliminary stage on the way to union with God, in prophetic piety, on the contrary, it is itself communion with Him. Mystical morality has a purely negative significance; it would remove an obstacle to salvation; it would repress the natural, emotional life. But in prophetic religion morality has a positive value. It seeks to realize God-ordained ideals which have an intrinsic value, not merely a value in view of a religious ideal. Mystical ethics is thoroughly individualistic and non-social. By unwearied striving after personal perfection the individual is to attain an inner emotionless unity. Prophetic religion strives to realize as much a personal as a social ideal. It demands purity

and truth as much as it demands giving and forgiving love;
it knows no morality which is not at the same time social; nay,
the social aspect of moral activity is in its view more important
than the personal.   For Paul and John, " the love of the
brethren " is just Christian morality.   For Luther, the service
of God issuing from the power and blessedness of faith is the
service of our neighbour.   " God does not need our work and
kindness," he says, " but we are to do to our neighbour what
we would do to Him."

9. *Mysticism and Social Fellowship*

(a) Pure mysticism is extremely individualistic, non-social;
it is concerned with nothing except " God and the soul," as
Augustine says.   " The devout soul," says the author of *De
adhaerendo Deo*, " must be so unified with God that it is as
though there were nothing else than God and the soul itself."
To flee from the social order, and take up the solitary life is
the presupposition of the mystical experience of salvation.   In
absolute loneliness isolated from all other human beings, the
mystic stands face to face with himself and with God.   The
self-consciousness, the feeling of values peculiar to all creative
personalities, whether religious, or philosophical, or artistic,
is in the mystic without any mingling of the social element;
it consists in the assurance of being individually chosen, par-
doned, illumined, blessed, deified.   When this self-consciousness would express itself in sensuous symbols, there comes in
the mystical idea of spiritual nuptials.   The fervent soul
knows itself as the chosen bride of God, made happy by the
tender love of the heavenly Bridegroom.   The extreme individualism of the mystical life is limited to the times of most
intimate and personal communion with God, to the contemplative life in the narrowest sense of the term.   But an expansion of the mystical into the social consciousness takes
place in the contemplative life, and indeed in the form of
intercession, which finally issues in active benevolence.

Prophetic religion, on the contrary, is out and out *social*.
" We, who are many, are one body," says Paul.   To be sure
the prophet also stands in the presence of God as an individual,
but he is never isolated from other men.   The distress which

vexes him is not his own only, it is that of his brethren as well; the redemption for which he longs is also the redemption of his people, his fellow believers, nay, entire humanity; the values, standards and tasks, which he in his own emotional experience learns to recognize as an inescapable necessity, are seen to be duties not for him only but for all men. Hence the self-consciousness of the prophet has an active and social quality which is lacking in that of the mystic. Moreover, the great prophetic leaders know themselves to be chosen by God, not, however, to the ecstatic enjoyment of Him and to the bliss of divine love, but to concrete, positive duties, to the proclamation of the will of God, to work for the Kingdom of God. The Old Testament prophets know that they are messengers of God called to preach judgement and redemption to their people. Jesus knows Himself as " sent " to herald the approaching Kingdom; but His vocation is not only prophetic, it is also eschatological. As Messiah and God's Son, it is His mission to break the tyranny of Satan in the world, to judge Israel and to set up on earth the kingdom of righteousness and blessedness. Paul knows himself " separated from his mother's womb " and " called to be the Apostle of the Gentiles," set apart to preach the Gospel of God. Mohammed calls himself proudly " the ambassador of God." The prophetic self-consciousness is therefore the consciousness of a vocation and a mission in contrast to the mystical consciousness of being the recipient of divine favour.

(b) The mystical experience consumes the devout man, holds him prisoner within his own soul; hence he has no impulse to preach, to carry on a missionary propaganda, or to effect a reformation of men and their surroundings. Mysticism, as the term implies, is an *esoteric* religion, fit only for a few gifted persons who journey to God aside from the broad highway on a solitary path of their own. Mystics do not go into the streets to show the crowd their precious treasure which they have found after long seeking and struggling; they do not preach to the masses and they make no converts. " The soul which is ' initiated ' [12] into the holy scenes cannot lightly declare to anyone the divine mysteries, but must guard them,

[12] μύστις.

keep them secret, and shield them in their ineffableness." So writes Philo. Only to a few like-minded persons athirst for redemption do the mystics tell of the mysteries revealed to them in secret. They describe their experiences to intimates; they compose guides to the spiritual life for their unknown and scattered spiritual kindred. Mystical interchange of thought takes the form of personal oral instruction imparted to a striver after perfection by an initiate, a master, the *guru* in India, the *seich* in Sûfism, the " spiritual father " in the monasticism of the Eastern Church. But then ensues the introduction to the secrets of the inner life in the form of confessions, of epistolary spiritual direction, and of guidance to salvation by means of literature. Literary creation is a characteristic of all mystics. Celebrated male and female mystics stand related to one another in a relation of trustful friendship as, for example, Hildegarde of Bingen and Bernard of Clairvaux, Margaret Ebner and Henry of Nördlingen, Elizabeth Stagel and Suso, Catherine of Genoa and Marabotto, Teresa and John of the Cross, Madame Chantal and Francis of Sales, Madame Guyon and Père Lacombe. But even widely celebrated books of mystical devotion are not intended for all men universally but only for individuals or small groups. The word " upanishad " means " confidential communication," the *Imitation of Christ* is a book of meditations for the cloistral cell; Madame Guyon explained to Bossuet that she had written her mystical books only for a few souls who practised mentally " interior prayer."

Prophetic personalities also know the blessedness which loving intercourse with God bestows in the loneliness of prayer; but they do not remain there; the divine commission which they have received drives them forth into the world. The prophet must speak, the " power of God " compels him also to preach God's Word to all the world, even if he is conscious of inward repugnance. The prophet must preach and threaten, comfort and punish, confess and exhort, fight and arouse. He addresses himself not to individuals but to the great public, the masses. Jeremiah says: " And Jahve said unto me: ' Proclaim all these words in the cities of Judah and in the streets of Jerusalem.' " " Woe is me," cries Paul. " if I preach not the Gospel." A will to conquer that cannot be bound, a passionate desire for the conversion and sanctification of men energizes in apostles, prophets, missionaries, and reformers. The great missionary world-religions, the Jewish Dispersion, Islam, and Christianity, are the product of this universal prophetic impulse. Even in the missionary preaching of the Buddha and his mendicant monks there lives something of the power of prophetic religion; here the motive of compassion transcends the governing principle of mysticism.

(c) The knowledge that not all are called to " the spiritual life," to " perfection," makes mystics tolerant towards alien religions as also towards the traditional worship and religion of the people. The mystic sees even in the rudest cultual act a presentiment of sublime mystical experiences. He makes room for forms of religion originating in a lower stage of development, as a valuable disciplinary help on the way to salvation. Over against the " esoteric," profound religion of which only a few elect and gifted souls are capable, he sets the " exoteric " religion in which the deep secrets of mysticism are offered to the average religious man under rude veils and external symbols. In its tolerance and flexibility mysticism has no strength to take up the fight against the traditional religion which it has inwardly overcome. It clings to this religion, however great the inward cleft may be which separates the one from the other. In soft, passive pliancy Sûfi mysticism has been able to adapt itself to the stiff, legalistic religion of Islam, just as mediaeval and quietist mysticism was able to come to terms with the narrow and hard hierarchical Church.

In contrast to mysticism, prophetic religion is essentially intolerant. The absoluteness of the standard, the validity of the religious and moral ideal admits of no compromise. Prophetic movements always exhibit an unrelenting opposition to the popular religion; they are against all the objects of worship and devotion that are on a lower level than the prophetic ideal. Prophetic religion has a strong tendency to a decisive breach with the traditional and conventional faith; it is *revolutionary*. The great upheavals in the history of religion are born of prophetic experiences. The prophets are always reformers, creators, heralds of a purer and nobler religion. Prophetic preaching is characterized by bluntness, sternness, severity, and moral firmness. This is seen in Mazdaism and in Islam. The Old Testament prophets are jealous for Jahve. They lead a merciless fight against the polytheistic tendencies of the Canaanitish folk-religion, a fight for the ethical worship of God against the sacrificial cultus. Jesus calls down a terrible woe upon the cities of Israel which had not obeyed the preaching of the kingdom and had not repented, and upon the Pharisees who by the externalism and legalism of their religion were putting obstacles in the road of the kingdom. The stern polemic and the intrepid battling of the Old Testament prophets is continued in the entire public activity of Jesus. " Think not," He says, " that I came to send peace upon the earth; I came not to send peace but a sword." This passionate intolerance of the prophetic spirit is no less observable in Paul. " If any man loveth not the Lord, let him be anathema." The same revolutionary fighting spirit flames up in the Reformers, especially in Luther.

(d) Mysticism has no power to build up a spiritual fellowship. Hardly ever do mystical personalities form the centre of an energetic communal life as happens within religious sects and confraternities. When a mystic thinks of a religious fellowship, it is only an invisible Church, a purely spiritual communion of all minds living inwardly with God which extends beyond space and time, beyond all distinctions of race and creed. Even Buddhism is no argument against the non-social character of mysticism. The illogical resolution which the Buddha formed at the moment of his enlightenment to preach the deep secret doctrine of salvation to all the world accounts for the fact that Buddhism grew out of a sublime mystical doctrine of redemption into a comprehensive world-religion with widespread congregations. But this transition led to a religious syncretism and therewith a transformation and degeneration of the original Nirvana mysticism of the Buddha.

As contrasted with mysticism, prophetic activity is inwardly linked to a religious fellowship. The Old Testament prophets and Jesus work within the religious community of their people. But in the main, the prophetic personality reacts against the traditional faith, and becomes the centre of a new association, whether smaller or larger than the parent body. *The great prophetic leaders have power to build up a body of believers.* The disciples of Jesus gradually became independent in their conflict with the synagogue. Paul is the great organizer of churches, the creator of the Christian Church. The Reformers gave impulse to the creation of great religious communions which, being separated from the main body of the Catholic Church, united themselves closely with the national states and yet did not assume the firm structure and close compactness of the sects. Calvin's theocracy alone kept the form of a sect.

10. *Relation to the World and Civilization*

Thorough-going mysticism is indifferent to all the values of civilized life; it can live only in isolation from civilized activities and occupations, it does not tolerate contact with the world and matter; like moral action, work is, for it, simply ascetic discipline. No doubt sometimes powerful cultural movements have gone forth from mysticism as from Buddhism and mediaeval mysticism. Plastic art has received valuable impulses from mystical piety. The mystics have even created in the literary and poetic realm things of high aesthetic value, as, for example, the religious poetry of the Buddhists, the poetry of the Persian Sûfi and of Christian mystics. Not a few mystics are to be counted among the greatest of philosophers. And yet artistic and scientific research are fundamentally as foreign to mysticism as is the political and social order. All civilization and all work in it belongs to the " world " and is dangerous to the salvation, isolation, and unity of the soul. The pious man must, therefore, die to civilization as to his own emotions and impulses. Logical mysticism is indifferent, nay, hostile to all civilization. To him who has tasted the happiness of ecstasy all the values of life seem empty. Therefore all great mystics preach contempt of the world and flight from it. " We must hasten to get away from this world," says Plotinus, " we must feel sad that we are still fettered to something that is alien to us." And the exhortation of à Kempis' *Imitation of Christ* is, " This is sovereign wisdom to strive after the Kingdom of Heaven by despising the world."

The real ideal of the mystical life is that of the monk and the hermit. But this monastic mysticism, in India as in the Christian West, is met by a freer mysticism. In India it is the *Bhagavadgîta*, in Christendom it is German mediaeval and French quietist mysticism, which rejects an external flight from the world, but all the more decisively demands an inner withdrawal and freedom from it. The pious man should be in the world but not of it, should live in the world a hidden life with God. A positive appreciation of the ideals of civilization is as much excluded in this world-affirming mysticism as in the radical world-denying type. The attitude of mystical piety towards the world and society is seen with especial clearness in its valuation of marriage and the family. The celibate life is for the mystic an intrinsically necessary condition of the higher religious life. Marriage is a fetter which hinders the unreserved surrender to the one Highest Good.

Prophetic religion is not at all hostile to civilized life (except when it is compelled to lead a sectarian existence and so, of necessity, is forced to take up a certain attitude of exclusiveness towards the world). There is befitting it rather an appreciation of civilized life, either open or silent, or at least the capacity for harmonizing the possession of religious values with the ideals of civilization. The thought of civilization has received special emphasis in the Mazdaism of Zoroaster: the Zoroastrian religion, in spite of its emphasis on the end of the world, is the religion of the optimism of civilization. Zoroaster took up even scientific reforms into his prophetic programme. Indeed, in the Gathas of the Avesta the skilful cattle-breeder, the industrious farmer, the just landlord, and the truly pious man are one and the same. He who does not zealously till the soil and expand the realm of Mazda by the claims of the settled life is no true worshipper of his. In the prophetic religion of Israel the absence of all thought of the life beyond and the intimate relation between the religion and the national destiny excluded all hostility to the world and civilization.

11. *The Hope of Immortality*

The most intimate spiritual experience in every type of religion is reflected in its expectation of a future life as well as in its idea of God. The goal of all ardent hope of immortality is indeed nothing else than the sublime ideal of redemption which already is sought and striven for in this present mortal life. This world and the next are not opposed to each other in higher religion but are bound together in a vital experience of God. What the believer experiences in the great moments of his inner life forms the content of the life beyond which awaits him after bodily death. The God who lays hold of him and blesses him in the deepest places of his soul is also the God of eternal life, nay, " He is eternal life," [18] as Augustine says. As Feuerbach puts it: " God and immortality are identical; the concept of God is in itself the concept of immortality."

In its conception of the life beyond, mysticism reveals its individualistic, non-social character. Eternal redemption and blessedness is for mysticism only the everlasting permanence of that highest experience for which it longs and to which it strains in this world, the ecstatic vision of and union with God, the Nirvana which sets free and makes blessed. Liberated forever by death from the oppressive fetters of the body, the soul living inwardly with God is able to abide in that supreme mystical condition. It sinks down into everlasting rest and uttermost peace, or it beholds in glowing ecstasy the ineffable Beauty, the " Highest Good," and unites itself with the infinite Unity in boundless bliss. The state of perfection in the world beyond is essentially identical with the experience of God here and now; it is, therefore, like this experience, interpreted by the mystics by means of the same images and ideas. The " eternal life " of mysticism is the " eternal vision of God and of union with God," abiding ecstasy. In the non-personal mysticism of India " perfect Nirvana," ecstasy and Nirvana, here and now, are but an anticipation, a " foretaste," of the heavenly ecstasy and of Nirvana in the world beyond.

The hope of future blessedness in prophetic religion as dis-

---

[18] *Deus ipse vita eterna est.*

tinguished from the same hope in mysticism is at once individual and super-individual. As the mystics sought for " eternal life " in ecstatic bliss, prophetic spirits sought for it in the blessed state of being hidden in and guarded by the protecting hand of God. The pious man who with immovable, resolute, and joyous confidence trusts in and relies on the God of help and salvation and is in intimate, vital communion with Him, has already overcome death and annihilation; his fellowship with God lasts forever.

Close on this assurance of personal eternal life rising out of the prophetic fundamental experience of faith, we find in the revealed religion of the Bible, a super-personal, eschatological hope. This prophetic faith in the future is concerned not with the blessedness of the individual soul but with " the end of the world," the coming of the great day of God, the advent of the Kingdom of God. The individual's longing for blessedness is subsidiary to the hope of the final victory of goodness. This earth on which sin and suffering, death and the Devil reign, will perish amid appalling catastrophes and in its place will come a new world in which all the powers of evil are brought to nought, " a new heaven and a new earth wherein dwelleth righteousness." The divine drama of salvation will be gloriously consummated, and sin and evil exterminated, all tears wiped away, and the hunger of every soul appeased. God will triumph over all His enemies, He alone will rule as King, " all and in all."

But the faith of later Judaism and primitive Christianity expected the dawn of the Kingdom not in the remote but in the near future: " The Kingdom of God is at hand." Jesus, the primitive community, and Paul were firmly convinced that very soon this world would pass away and the everlasting reign of God begin. This faith in the realization of the ideal, in the triumph of divine over demoniacal powers, in the victory of goodness over evil is so strong and vehement that it wings its way over centuries and millenniums and sees as very close at hand what later Christianity expected only at a far-off end of the world. But again and again there appeared in the history of the Christian religion men and communities who with enthusiasm expected and proclaimed the nearness of the end of the world and the coming of the Divine Kingdom. Moreover, even non-Christian prophets like Mohammed were filled with faith in the near dawn of the close of all things. And yet for all men of prophetic genius the Kingdom of God is not a thing exclusively of the future, it is already a present fact. Here and now it begins. In preaching, in miracles and deeds of power, in charismatic enthusiasm, in faith in the redemption which has appeared in Christ as also in the moral life, the Kingdom begins to be realized. " God's Kingdom," says Luther, " has begun here and ever grows, but in that other life it is perfected."

12. *Monism of Mysticism and Dualism of Prophetic Religion*

Mystical experience consists in the unification and simplification of all psychic activity, and this is rendered possible by isolation from the objective world and the suppression of the emotional life. The barriers between God and man disappear in the ecstatic experience; man vanishes in God, fuses with Him in perfect unity. Every contrast, every difference, every dualism, disappears in the mystical experience. " All twofoldness is past," says Ferîd-ed-dîn-Attâr. The distinction between God and the world, this world and the next, present and future exists no longer; all differences in being and value are abolished; the opposition of good and evil is alien to the ecstatic. The philosophical monism of Sankara and of Eckhart is only the logical, metaphysical interpretation of the ecstatic experience which is without any dualistic tension or sense of contrast.

The *prophetic* experience, on the other hand, reveals an antagonism of opposites; of dramatic strain, dualistic energy. Fear and hope, distress and trust, doubt and faith, struggle with one another; the contrast of moral worthiness and unworthiness is always alive in the prophetic consciousness. This great dualism runs through the entire world of ideas in prophetic religion. God and man are never mingled. The primitive belief in the distance between God and man continues here, only ethically deepened. " God is in heaven and thou art upon the earth." Full of humility the sinner draws near the holy God. Even the childlike trust of Jesus in God

His Father remains always a personal fellowship, it never goes as far as a mystical " union." The cosmic dualism of flesh and spirit, body and soul, multiplicity and unity, plays a part also in mysticism. But the prophetic dualism is experienced as something universal, ethical, personal, uninfluenced by any speculation. Jahve and the Baalim, Ahura Mazda and Angra Mainyu, God and Satan, angel and devil, good and evil, light and darkness, sin and grace, life and death, heaven and hell — the whole treasury of prophetic ideas reveals in antithetical pairs the vital dualism of this type of religion. " God's kingdom fights without ceasing with the Devil's kingdom," says Luther.

13. *Final Characterization*

Mysticism is neither a Christian inheritance nor a peculiarity of the Christian religion, although in this religion it has assumed its finest and most beautiful form. It has penetrated into Christianity (as also into Judaism and Islam) from the outside, from the syncretist mystery religions, later religious philosophy, especially from neo-Platonism. The Gnostics and the Alexandrians, but above all Augustine and the Areopagite, were the gates by which it entered. Mysticism has indeed lost in purity and logical quality, but has gained in depth and warmth, fervour and power, from an intermingling with prophetic religion. It is important however in an age when the value of mysticism is discovered afresh and when it is regarded as the essence of Christianity, to distinguish clearly and sharply these two great powers of the religious life, mysticism and prophetic, biblical religion. Certainly the ultimate psychological root and ideal conception common to the two types is the struggle for a pure life, love and blessedness, and faith in a supreme, absolute, and transcendent Being in whom this yearning is satisfied. Certainly the innumerable contrasts between these two types have been lessened and bridged over in history, most splendidly in Augustine and Francis, but they cannot be wholly ignored. " Personality-affirming " and " personality-denying " religion, the experience of God which values history and that which ignores it, revelation and ecstasy, prophetism and monasticism, transformation of the world and flight from the world, preaching of the Gospel and contemplation — these contradictions are too great to give us the right to assert an essential identity of both types. Mysticism and the religion of revelation are the two opposite tendencies of the higher piety which in history ever repel, yet ever attract each other.

CHAPTER VII

PRAYER IN MYSTICISM

IT IS very difficult to present clearly the mystical type of prayer, as it is generally found in close connection with simple popular religion or with prayer of the prophetic type. With the Christian mystic and the Mohammedan Sûfi the prophetic mode of prayer more or less predominates. The Christian mystics like to use a biblical vocabulary and a devotional terminology which spring from a diametrically opposed type of piety. Mystical thoughts are veiled in a foreign garb. But prayer is not only expressed but also experienced by the Christian and Islamic mystics in its prophetic form; states of mind which are peculiarly mystical such as inner unity and peace, serenity, love, yearning for the Highest, are mingled with convictions of faith, trust, confidence, and consolation, so that prophetic passion breathes warmth and strength into the quietude of the mystic's heart. But a fine ear will always detect the mystical undertone.

Closely connected with this first difficulty there is another. The intermingling of mystical religion with the popular and prophetic types, gives rise to a great variety of mystical tendencies which are directly recognizable in the method of prayer. We have a mysticism marked by ecstasy and visions (Upanishads, Yoga, Plotinus, Suso, Catherine of Genoa, Teresa, Bernard, Francis of Assisi), while Augustine, Thomas Aquinas, Eckhart, Tauler, the *Imitation of Christ*, and the Quietists represent a mystical harmony from which all irregular experiences are absent. There is a warm emotional mysticism (the Indian Bhaktas, the Sûfis, Plotinus, Augustine, most of the mediaeval mystics, and the Pietists), and the cool, unemotional type Upanishads, Buddhism, Eckhart, and the Quietists. There is a simple and fanciful mysticism (Sûfis, Mânikha Vâçagar, Bernard, Francis of Assisi, Suso, Symeon,

" the new theologian "), and a reflective, rational, and theoretic mysticism which seeks to understand and control the mystical experience either by philosophic speculation in the case of the Upanishads, Sankara, Plotinus, Augustine, the pseudo-Dionysius and Eckhart, or by psychological analysis as with Yoga, Teresa, Angelus Silesius, and the Quietists. Then we have a fervent, erotic mysticism (the Indian Krishna mysticism, Bernard, the mystical *religieuses*, the Herrnhuter Pietists) and a purified mysticism which is remote from all erotic tendencies (Augustine, Thomas Aquinas, Francis, Tauler, Tersteegen) ; a mysticism of personal theism in which the devout believer enters into loving fellowship with God (the Indian Bhaktas and the majority of Christian mystics), and a mysticism of an impersonal and monistic character in which the individual soul is lost in the infinite, non-personal divinity (Upanishads, Sankara, Plotinus, Dionysius, Angelus Silesius) ; an intimate devotional mysticism of prayer in which the act of communion with God is usually consummated in the simple language of prayer (the Bhaktas and the majority of Christian mystics), and a mysticism of pure absorption, to which the lively realism of the life of prayer is quite foreign (Upanishads, Yoga, Buddhism, Plotinus, Tauler, Angelus Silesius) ; a cultual mysticism whose rapt contemplation is kindled by an external object of worship (Bhakti mysticism, Mystery Religions, Eucharistic mysticism of the Middle Ages) ; a non-cultual, non-sensuous mysticism in which the mystic vision of God dispenses with all external supports (Upanishads, Plotinus, Augustine, the evangelical spiritualists, Quietists). Manifold as are the forms, there is an element common to all, and the type thus resulting is clearly distinguishable from that of prophetic religion.

I. Motive and Aim of Mystical Prayer

The goal to which mysticism aspires is the isolation and the unification of the inner life, by detachment from the world, and union with God. Asceticism conduces to the renunciation of the world of sense. This is the *via purgativa* whereby moral and ascetic practices kill the sensuous life. The unification of the soul is accomplished in prayer, and in the contemplation which begets and nourishes prayer (*via illuminativa*). Thus prayer is the first step towards that perfect unity of soul which is experienced as union with God (*via unitiva*). Asceticism is the more remote means, prayer or absorption the nearer, for the attainment of this goal. As Bonaventura says: " The aim of prayer is union with God." Eckhart says: " We ought to pray so fervently that all our organs and powers, both eyes and ears, heart, mouth, and all our senses are absorbed in it, and we should not cease till we discover that we desire to be united to Him whom we have present and to whom we pray, that is, God."

Like asceticism and good works, mystical prayer is only preliminary and preparatory, a means to the end of union with God, not an end in itself; it is only " a golden ladder which touches the skies and on which one climbs up to God." The crown of prayer is that ecstatic union in which the soul is lost in the boundless fulness of God. The mystics love to speak of this culminating point in the experience as prayer at its highest. Antony, the father of monasticism, believed that prayer was not perfect so long as the monk was still conscious of himself and of the subject of his prayer. A similar judgment is that of Peter of Alcantara: " Silent prayer is only perfect, when he who prays is no longer conscious that he stands in silent prayer before God." Angelus Silesius sings:

> " The noblest prayer is when one evermore
> Grows inly liker that he kneels before."

This ecstatic union with God can only be called prayer by the use of an inaccurate metaphor. In these cases of ecstasy there is no such consciousness of the difference between " I " and " Thou " as is essential to all prayer. Under such conditions an actual prayer, even though it be only an act of silent adoration, is impossible. " All things pray except the First " is a significant saying of Theodore the neo-Platonist quoted by Proclus. But when the soul has become one with this " First " it also ceases to pray.

The mystic's longing for perfect simplicity and unity of soul is the deepest motive of all mystical prayer and absorption. In the mysticism of personal theism this tendency is enriched by emotional warmth and power. The struggle for union with the Infinite becomes here a passionate love of God, a consuming thirst for the Highest Good, which rises to an entrancing vision and blessed enjoyment. Frequently the overpowering emotion must have relief in speech. "My soul is wounded," confesses Symeon, "the new theologian." "My heart is on fire, I long to speak with Thee, O my God." The mystic ravished by God's infinite beauty, pours out before God in loud cries or in quiet, devotional speech his love and yearning, his rapture and surrender, his happiness and bliss. This unrestrained speech and ejaculation welling out of the heart's passion is quite alien to pure, impersonal mysticism where prayer is only a silent, emotionless sinking into the immeasurable flood of the One, the Divine.

The passion of the theistic mystic expressed in prayer wells up spontaneously at times from the subconscious depths, but generally it derives its emotional strength and fervour from religious meditation. Even the deep absorption of the pantheistic mystic cannot dispense with preparatory contemplation. All mystical prayer and contemplation is nourished by meditation, purposely cultivated and practised. This consists in "recollection," that is, tense concentration of attention on one object, then in the careful pondering and contemplation of a religious idea which is generally stimulated by the reading of an edifying text or the recitation of a devotional formula. It is religious ideas which form the subject of the meditation, ideas productive of strong emotional stimuli such as the frightfulness of sin, the shortness, uncertainty, and misery of life, death, the Last Judgment, the punishments of hell and the glories of Heaven, the greatness, goodness, and beauty of God. Mediaeval mysticism, centred in Jesus, adds to these an abundance of new themes — the life, suffering, and death of the Saviour, His meekness and the various incidents of His betrayal and death. Tense preoccupation with ideas coloured with emotion, such as these, releases in the soul of the contemplator moods which not infrequently reach intense emotional heights, trembling anxiety, harsh contempt of the world and oneself, bitter remorse, mournful sympathy, a bitter-sweet emotion, joyful gratitude, fervent longing, and the melting surrender of love. These various moods and feelings are expressed by him who meditates in words of prayer. " Never canst thou pray devoutly and fervently," says Johann Arndt, " except thou settest before thine eyes the mirror of the meek and humble life of Christ, His poverty, humiliation, sorrow, and ignominious death." Mystical meditation is accordingly nothing else but the methodical preparation for prayer. The technical character of this preparation is admirably described by the expression " spiritual exercise " (*exercitia spiritualia*), which we find for the first time in Albertus Magnus and Gertrude of Helfta. The systematic schemes of meditation of a Bonaventura or an Ignatius Loyola agree in this that they let the devotional thoughts pass into pious outpourings of the heart, in loving colloquies of prayer and in the prayers of thanksgiving and petition, and sacrifice.

II. Form of Mystical Prayer

Whether he is consciously concentrating on God or expressing spontaneously the sense of being laid hold of by God, the. mystic's prayer is frequently free, unrestricted speech with God; the choice of words is the work of the moment. Where prayer is consciously and intentionally employed as a means to recollection and contemplation, the attentive and sympathetic utterance of a definite formula of prayer is customary. Suso used a variety of existing prayers and hymns such as *O crux ave spes unica*, or the *Salve regina*. Short formal prayers repeated over and over again during contemplation and in everyday life, called by Augustine " ejaculatory prayers," are much used by the mystics. Among the monks of Mt. Athos a prayer is constantly repeated with auto-hypnotic effect: " O Lord Jesus Christ, Thou Son of God, have pity upon us! " The Mohammedan Sûfi attain the same end by constant repetition of the formulas: " Allah! Allah! " " Glory be to Allah! " " There is no God but Allah! " But this formalized, oral prayer is only a preparatory discipline to the prayer which is peculiarly mystical. As Tauler says: " Every oral prayer helps true prayer, but it is not true prayer." David of Augs-

burg advises that as " he who would eat honey must take it out
of the wax, so must we draw out of the words the divine and
honied sweetness of grace."

Mysticism shuts man off from the outer world and forces
him back on the world within. It paralyzes the bodily means
of expression so that the soul remains turned inward upon
itself and preserves its own isolation and spirituality. Words
disturb the peace and unity within; utterance implies a coming forth out of deep abstraction. " Where the abstraction
is deep," says Teresa, " speech becomes difficult." All mystical prayer, therefore, tends to pass from prayer in words (either
spoken aloud or inwardly framed) to wordless prayer, from
speech with God to silent contemplation of God. As Plotinus
puts it: " We ought to call upon God not with loud cries, but
with the soul by raising ourselves to Him in prayer." The
old Greek monastic mystics, especially Macarius, never tire of
recommending to their disciples inner prayer without words
and without images. John Cassian speaks of " that higher
state of prayer, that glowing, nay, inexpressible prayer which
surpasses all human understanding, which has nothing to do
with the sound of the voice or the movement of the tongue or
even with any inner silent form of speech. It is this which the
spirit, illumined by the inpouring of heavenly light, expresses
not in the narrow forms of human language, but pours forth as
from a welling spring, since in a very brief moment it grasps
more than can be measured either by utterance or thought."
This wordless prayer is a *state of prayer,* not an act of prayer.
" The prayer of the heart," says Madame Guyon, " is not a
single act or series of acts which the soul undertakes, but the
essential state in which the soul lives."

The mystics express the higher value of silent prayer by
contrasting " inner " or " contemplative " with " oral " or
" outer " prayer. Wordless prayer is the *oratio interior* of
Augustine, the *oratio mentalis* of Teresa, " the prayer of the
mind and the heart " of Francis of Sales. The thought comes
to us from very ancient times that silence may be true prayer,
the genuine Divine service. This idea is found in later Egyptian religion and in the syncretist mysteries, and attains great
significance in neo-Pythagorean thought and neo-Platonism.

It repeatedly recurs in Christian and Mohammedan mysticism. Tersteegen thus finely and fervently describes the inexpressible prayer of silence:

> " When inmost cloud and darkness brood
> I kneel in depths of quietude
> O adoration holy!
> Better than best that ear hath heard
> Is uttered now without a word
> To loving heart and lowly."

Francis of Sales describes mystical prayer as the " colloquy of silence," for it takes place in wholly secret " aspirations " and " inspirations." " Eyes talk with eyes, heart with heart, and none except the holy lovers themselves understand." Silent prayer is also readily pictured by the image of breathing. The writer just quoted speaks of mystical prayer, using a play on words: " *Nous aspirons à lui et respirons en lui.*" Madame Chantal defines prayer as " a wordless breathing of love in the immediate presence of God."

The contrast which exists between mystical prayer and spontaneous primitive prayer is here manifest. Spontaneous prayer is simply speaking and crying out from the fulness of the heart; the inner prayer of the mystic sunk in the depth of his heart is a silence, a breath, a vision. In the former we have a violent outburst of emotion, in the latter all the energies of the soul are in subjection.

III. Nature and Content of Mystical Prayer

In naïve prayer the essential content is the expression of need and desire, but this is not true of mystical prayer, although the outer form is often one of petition. " God and the soul " — God, the highest and only Value, and the particular " I " in all its lack of value — that is the kernel of the mystic's prayer. According to the classic mystical definition, " Prayer is the ascent of the mind to God." Already Origen hints at this definition when in explaining the words of the psalmist, " Unto Thee have I lifted up my soul," he describes prayer as " the lifting up of the soul." In a sermon ascribed to Augustine it is said: " Prayer is an ascent of the soul from the earthly to the heavenly, a striving to that which is above, a yearning for the Invisible." Nilus of Sinai and John of Damascus define prayer as the " anabasis of the mind to God." [1] This definition has become the normal definition of Catholic theology. It is true, however, that the more non-personal type of mysticism, the goal of which is the dissolution of the individual in God, uses this definition with a slightly different shade of meaning when it describes prayer as less an ascent to the God *above* the soul, than an entering into God who is present *in* the soul, less an attempt to elevate oneself up to God than a willingness to sink down into Him. Thus Tauler defines prayer as " the direct entrance of the spirit into God; an absorption of the spirit in the Spirit of God."

But as a matter of fact the theological formula, " the elevation of the mind to God," states admirably the peculiar quality of mystical prayer. The mystic's prayer is just the turning of the mind to the one Highest Good. This can happen either with or without emotion: it can be touched with a painful or pleasurable mood or with both at the same time; it can be experienced as a flight to the highest peak or as a submergence in the deepest abyss; it can assume the outer forms of contemplation, petition, adoration, or resignation. In spite of all diversity in experience, feeling, and form, there is only one theme in mystical prayer: God the Supreme Good and the soul which is meant to attain the vision of God and union with Him. Hence mystical prayer seems monotonous when compared with the rich variety of form in simple and primitive prayer. Nevertheless, the content of mystical prayer implies an inner progress. The term " elevation " of the soul to God indicates that in mystical prayer there is an immanent movement. The worshipper advances from concentration to contemplation, from the ardent longing for God to the blessed possession and enjoyment of God. In concentration the experience of the Highest Good has the quality of tension, in contemplation that of relaxation.

[1] ἀνάβασις νοῦ πρὸς θεόν.

A. *Concentration*

The praying mystic turns away from external reality, suppresses by force of will all ideas and emotions directed towards it and focuses his whole attention on the highest spiritual Reality, that is, on God. As Tauler says: " Turn thyself in truth from thyself and from all created things and centre thy mind wholly upon God." Macarius exhorts: " God is the Highest Good; thou must concentrate all thy thoughts upon Him, only upon Him must thou wait, and only Him must thou behold. . . . With attentive mind must thou tarry the Lord's leisure until He visit thy soul." The concentration expresses itself sometimes in the form of petition, less frequently in the form of earnest complaint and question; yet contemplation continually breaks in upon the petition or the question. The salvation of the soul is the subject of the petition. The mystic supplicates God for the state of mind at which he aims, namely, the isolation of the soul from the objective world, the suppression of all emotions and instinctive movements of the will, inner peace and unity, enthusiastic surrender to the Highest Good, ecstasy. The entire gradation in the stages of the mystical process of salvation from the " purgative " to the " illuminative " and from the " illuminative " to the " unitive " way is reflected in the content of mystical prayer.

The *purgative way* means (a) detachment from the world. " Plant fear of Thee in my heart," prays Symeon, " the new theologian," " that I may flee from the world to Thy commandments and separate myself wisely from it." So, too, Margaret Ebner: " I pray Thee to give us a true separation from all this world and an entire renunciation of ourselves." " Grant to me," says Thomas à Kempis, " that I may die to all things that are in the world, that for Thy sake I may be willing to be despised and ignored in this age. Turn for me all earthly things into bitterness, all lower and created things into contempt and oblivion." " Empty me," says Arndt, " of all sinful love of the creature." It means also (b) detachment from the feelings and desires of the self. " If in me," writes Augustine, " there dwells a desire for anything superfluous,

do Thou purify me, and make me capable of beholding Thee! "
" Grant that we deny ourselves daily, die to our sinful thirst
for glory and in our whole life let Thy glory be the sole aim
of all our actions," is the prayer of Arndt. À Kempis writes:
" Deliver me from evil passions and heal my soul of inordi-
nate affections, that being inwardly healed and thoroughly
cleansed, I may be fit to love, strong to endure, and resolute
to persevere." J. H. Newman prays: " Cleanse my heart from
all that is worldly, proud, and sensual, from all perversity, all
disorder, and all harshness of temper." Finally, it implies
(c) the spirit and sorrow of repentance. " Grant me," says
Symeon, " tears of penitence, tears of yearning, tears of salvation, tears which purify the very dregs of my soul and make
me wholly pure." Mechthild of Magdeburg prays: " Cleanse,
O Lord, my heart to-day from all earthly love and pour down
Thy heavenly water into my thirsty soul that I may weep for
Thy humiliation and the pitifulness of my sins."

The *illuminative way* implies (a) rest and peace in
God. À Kempis writes: " Grant to me above all things that I
can desire, to rest in Thee and in Thee to have my heart at
peace." " Thou art the true peace of the heart; Thou art its
only rest." " My heart cannot truly rest nor be fully content
unless it rest in Thee and rise above all Thy gifts and every
creature." Pusey offers the same prayer: " Let me not seek
out of Thee what I can find only in Thee, O Lord, peace and
rest and joy and bliss which abide only in Thine abiding joy.
Lift up my soul above the weary round of harassing thoughts
to Thy eternal presence. Lift up my soul to the pure, bright,
serene atmosphere of Thy presence that there I may breathe
freely, there repose in Thy love, there be at rest from myself,
and from all things that weary me; and thence return, amazed
with Thy peace, to do and bear what shall please Thee."
(b) Identification of one's own will with God's will. Bonaventura prays: " This I would, this I desire, this I long for
from the depths of my heart, that in me, by me, and through
me, not my will but Thine be done." Similarly à Kempis:
" Grant me always to do Thy will and to desire what is most
acceptable to Thee and what pleases Thee best. Let Thy will
be my will and let my will ever follow Thy will and agree with

it wholly." "Give what Thou commandest, and command what Thou wilt!" cries Augustine. (c) Exclusive turning to the Highest Good. Thus Anselm: "May nothing, I pray Thee, be sweet to me without Thee, nothing pleasing, nothing dear; apart from Thee let nothing beautiful smile upon me." À Kempis prays: "Grant me, O Lord, heavenly wisdom that I may learn to seek and find *Thee above all things,* to know and love Thee above all things." "For Thee," cries Bonaventura, "may my soul long, for Thee may it always hunger and thirst, to Thee may it ever strive, Thee may it seek and find, to Thee may it hasten and Thee attain, may it think of Thee, speak of Thee, and do everything to the honour and glory of thy name." (d) Faith, hope, and love. Augustine: "If by faith they find Thee who take refuge in Thee, grant them faith; if by virtue, virtue; if by knowledge, knowledge. Increase in me faith, hope, and love." "Grant that I may believe in Thee more, set my hope on Thee, love Thee " — so prays Thomas Aquinas. "Lord, in asking for fervour," prays Newman, " I am asking for faith, hope, and charity." (e) Fervent love to God. " O love that ever burnest and is never consumed! " exclaims Augustine. " O love, my God, kindle me! " Similarly Newman: " Breathe on me with that breath which infuses energy and kindles fervour. . . . In asking for fervour I am asking for Thyself, for nothing short of Thee, O my God." Anselm cries: " I love Thee, my God, with a great love and I desire to love Thee more! " À Kempis writes: " Enlarge me in love that I may learn, with the interior palate of the heart, to taste how sweet it is to love and to bathe and to be dissolved in love. May I be held fast by love, going beyond myself through excess of personal ecstasy. Let me sing the hymn of love, let me follow Thee, my Beloved, let my soul be lost in Thy praise, jubilant in love." Tersteegen prays: " Draw our love and heart's devotion wholly to Thee that we, in all places, at all times, and in all things, may see only Thee and love only Thee." " Come into my heart and fill it with fervent zeal by filling it with Thyself."

The *unitive way* is experienced in (a) the consciousness of the presence and vision of God. " Set up Thy tabernacle in me," prays Symeon, " dwell there and abide there unceasingly." Similarly, Peter of Alcantara: "Prepare for Thyself in me, O God, a splendid chamber, that Thou, according to Thy promise, mayst dwell in me and there establish for Thyself a place." "Oh, that Thou wouldst enter into my heart," cries Augustine, "and inebriate it that I may forget my ills and embrace Thee, my only Good!" "On earth, in Heaven, or when all this has passed away — when shall I behold Thy countenance?" asks Mânikha Vâçagar. "Shew to me clearly," beseeches Symeon, "the face of Thy Godhead and appear to me in a way wholly apart from the senses." "Come, Oh come; for without Thee I shall have no joyful hour or day; for Thou art my joy and without Thee my mind is empty. I am miserable and in a manner imprisoned until Thou dost refresh me with the light of Thy presence and show me a gracious countenance." So À Kempis invokes the divine presence. "Show me Thy countenance," says Gertrude of Helfta, "and let me see Thy form." (b) Ecstatic union with God. Pseudo-Eckhart prays: "Eternal Father, I pray Thee from the bottom of my heart and with all the power of my soul that Thou wouldest give me in the innermost and most sacred depths of Thy fatherly heart an ever indwelling nature, life, vision, speech, and activity, that I at all times may be shut up in Thee and abide in Thee." David of Augsburg: "Sink Thyself in me, change me into Thyself, else I will never be satisfied." À Kempis writes: "Oh, when shall it be fully granted me to see how sweet Thou art, my Lord God? When shall I fully gather up myself in Thee that by reason of my love to Thee I may not feel myself but Thee alone, above all sense and measure." Similarly writes Peter of Alcantara: "When shall I be Thine? When shall I cease to be mine? When wilt Thou unite me wholly to Thee, take me up and transform me into Thyself?" (c) Eternal vision of God and union with Him in the world beyond. "O Love, Love!" cries Gertrude, "when wilt Thou lead my soul out of prison? Oh, when wilt Thou deliver it, the solitary one, from the fetters of the body? When wilt Thou lead me into the chamber of my Bridegroom that I may be united to Him in everlasting enjoyment? O Love, hasten my nuptials for I would die a thousand deaths to taste such bliss." "When shall I rejoice in Thee?" questions

À Kempis. " When shall there be settled peace, peace sure and undisturbed, peace within and without? " " O merciful Jesus, when shall I stand to behold Thee? When shall I contemplate the glory of Thy Kingdom? When wilt Thou be to me all in all? Oh, when shall I be with Thee in Thy Kingdom which Thou hast prepared from eternity for those that love Thee? . . . . Come, Lord Jesus, and take me from a foreign country, recall Thy exiled one to the fatherland. Come, gracious Redeemer, make me to share in Thy eternal glory."

B. *Contemplation*

In the mystic's prayer to God there is an onward movement from longing to possession. At first his ardent longing is to be purified from all feelings and wishes and to be entirely ruled by his experience of the Supreme Good; but now he is taken possession of by this one infinite Good. He no longer asks for anything nor does he concentrate his energies; he only contemplates the infinite goodness, greatness, and beauty of God. As Plotinus says: " The spirit remains immovably sunken in contemplation; it gazes on nothing else but Absolute Beauty, it turns itself wholly to it and concentrates on it, and at last is as it were filled with power." Dread, reverence, wonder, astonishment, rapture seize him; an infinite bliss pours through him. In matchless words Plotinus has described this wonderful experience of mystical contemplation: " And one that shall know this vision (the Highest Good) — with what passion of love shall he not be seized, with what pang of desire, what longing to be molten into one with This, what wondering delight! If he that has never seen this Being must hunger for It as for all his welfare, he that has known must love and reverence It as the very beauty; he will be flooded with awe and gladness, stricken by a solitary terror; he loves with a veritable love, with sharp desire; all other loves than this he must despise, and disdain all that once seemed fair. This indeed, is the mood even of those who, having witnessed the manifestation of Gods or Supernals, can never again feel the old delight in the comeliness of material forms; what then are we to think of one that contemplates Absolute Beauty in its essential integrity, no accumulation of flesh and matter, no dweller on

earth or in the heavens — so perfect its purity — far above all
such things in that they are non-essential, composite, not
primal but descending from this? " ² Contemplative meditation is for the most part silent; the rapturous vision of the
summum bonum is speechless. But sometimes the emotion
accompanying the wonderful experience is so overpowering
that it breaks out into language. Then the contemplative
mystic ejaculates rhythmically brief cries of prayer.

(a) *Purely aesthetic contemplation.* The mystic contemplates God as the only, highest, and infinite Good, as the source
of all values intellectual, ethical, and aesthetic, as the
cause of bliss and blessedness, as the single highest goal of all
human striving. " Thou art the highest good," writes Augustine. " Highest, best, most mighty, most pitiful and most
just, most beautiful and most strong! God above whom is
nothing, outside whom is nothing, without whom is nothing.
God under whom is everything, in whom is everything, with
whom is everything." Anselm exclaims: " Most sweet, most
kind, most loving, most dear, most powerful, most to be desired, most precious, most lovely, most beautiful, Thou art
sweeter than honey, whiter than milk or snow, more delightful
than nectar, more precious than jewels and gold, and dearer to
me than all the riches and honours of the world." Francis of
Assisi, after he had received *stigmata,* broke out into a
cry of joy: " Thou art alone the holy Lord God who doest
wonders. Thou art mighty, Thou are great. Thou art most
exalted. Thou art almighty King, holy Father, King of
heaven and earth. Thou art good, all good, the highest good,
the living and true Lord God. Thou art love. Thou art patience. Thou art humility. Thou art security. Thou art joy
and delight. Thou art justice and temperance." Gertrude of
Helfta prays: " Thou art my true and perfect love. Thou
art my truest well-being. Thou art my entire hope and joy.
Thou art the *highest and best good.* Thou art the thirst of
my heart. Thou art the entire pleasure of my spirit. Thou
art the life of my soul. Thou art the beginning and end of all
good." À Kempis writes: " Thou, O Lord my God, art best
above all things. Thou alone art most high, Thou alone art

most powerful, Thou alone most sufficient and most full, Thou alone most sweet and most consoling; Thou alone art most beautiful and most glorious above all things in whom all things are found at once good and perfect and always have been and always will be." In a hymn of Mânikha Vâçagar we read: " O unstained brightness, gleam of a flower in full blossom, O teacher, honey-sweet food of the gods, thou highly honoured, guardian, loosener of chains, great stream of boundless tenderness! " " O highest Lord," ejaculates Teresa, " O Thou my King, O exalted might, infinite goodness, eternal wisdom, without beginning and without end, fathomless depth of wonder, source of all power and beauty! "

Sometimes the contemplation of the divine infinitude and fulness of being becomes in brilliant paradoxes a contemplation of God as the union of opposites. Augustine exclaims: " Most merciful yet most just, most hidden yet most present, most beautiful yet most strong, stable yet incomprehensible, unchangeable yet all-changing, never new never old, ever working yet ever at rest." So too, Symeon, " the new theologian ": " Thou art wholly immovable, yet ever moving; Thou art wholly outside all creatures yet in all creatures; Thou fillest the universe, yet art Thou wholly outside the universe." David of Augsburg cries: " Thou art in all things, on all sides at all times. Thou art over all things with kingly power and with Thy native dignity. Thou art under all things: all things are founded on Thee."

The contemplation of the opposites included in the being of God may at times rise to the pantheistic thought of the " One and All." A Prayer of the Maitrayana-Upanishad begins with the words: " Thou art Brahma, Vishnu, Rudra, Prajapati, Agni, Varuna, Vayu, Thou art Indra, Thou art the light of the night, Thou art the spirit of food, Thou art death, the earth, the All: in its manifoldness all that is rests in Thee." Mânikha Vâçagar exclaims: " Thou art the Heaven, Thou art the earth, Thou art the wind, Thou art the light, Thou art the body and the soul, being and not-being."

This is pure, fully selfless, free from all desire, aesthetic contemplation of the *summum bonum*, the One and All, and it is this adoring absorption in the being and plenitude of God which forms the chief part of mystical prayer. Though it again and again slips into petition and resignation, yet at its highest it is distinct from all other forms of prayer.

(b) *Praise and Thanksgiving.* The contemplation of the greatness, goodness, holiness, and beauty of God passes over frequently into a rapturous rejoicing and giving of praise and thanks. " Let my soul praise Thee that it may love Thee; and let it confess to Thee Thy mercies that it may praise Thee. Thy entire creation ceases not nor is silent in praising Thee. Neither the spirit of man, with voice directed unto Thee, nor creation animate or inanimate, by the voice of those who contemplate it, that so our souls may rise out of their weariness to Thee, leaning on the things which Thou hast made, and making them stepping-stones to Thee " (Augustine). " Almighty, all-holy, most exalted and supreme, wholly good, who alone art good, unto Thee do we render all praise, all glory, all thanks, all honour, all blessing, all good. So be it, so be it! Amen " (Francis of Assisi). " Let Thy name be praised, not mine; let thy work be glorified, not mine; let Thy holy name be blessed, let no praise of man be ascribed to me. Thou art my glory, the joy of my heart. In Thee shall I glory and rejoice all the day long " (A Kempis). Or take this from Teresa: " O Lord of the universe, all creatures would praise Thee! Who can proclaim loudly enough how faithful Thou art to Thy friends? Would that I had understanding and knowledge and words wholly new that I might glorify the wonders of Thy love as my soul feels it."

(c) *Surrender and Resignation.* The praying mystic knows no other good than the Infinite, and in splendid heroism he renounces all self-will and gives himself wholly to God. The perfect surrender of love follows the contemplation. Augustine says: " Not with doubting but with assured consciousness do I love Thee, Lord. Thou hast stricken my heart with Thy word and I loved Thee." " Lord," says Francis, " I neither have, nor love, nor desire anything but Thee." Love to God brings about a perfect denial of all self-will, an unreserved surrender to the Highest Good, a heroic submission to the sovereign will of God. " Take away my entire liberty," prays Ignatius Loyola. " Take away memory, understanding, and all my will.

What I have Thou hast given me: I give it all back to Thee
for Thy governance. Only give to me Thy love with Thy
grace and I am rich enough and ask for nothing more." " Here
is my life, my will, my honour," writes St. Teresa, " all is Thine,
I give all to Thee, do with it according to Thy good pleasure."
Newman prays: " Lord, I give myself to Thee, I trust Thee
wholly. Fulfil Thy high purposes in me whatever they be —
work in me and through me. Let me be Thy blind instrument.
I ask not to see — not to know — I ask simply to be used."
This surrender of the human will to the divine, the mystic
describes as " an offering." " I bring to Thee Thyself in me
and myself in Thee as an offering of praise," says Gertrude.
" I have nothing more; what I am and experience in Thee —
all that I give to Thee." " I desire," writes À Kempis, " to
offer myself unto Thee, a free-will oblation, and to remain
Thine forever." The expression of the mystical prayer of
resignation agrees in various ways with the prayer of Epictetus.
In spite of the striking similarity no literary connection between the Christian mystic and the Stoic philosopher is conceivable. The words of prayer which are identical are the
expression of fundamentally different psychic moods. The
Stoic prayer of resignation is the expression of a courageous
moral will which is determined to bear every fate, while the
mystical prayer of resignation issues from the enthusiastic
surrender of love to the Highest Good whereby every personal
wish and will is renounced.

(d) *Contemplation of One's Own Unworthiness and of the
Divine Miracle of Grace.* The contemplation of one's own unworthiness is often connected with the contemplation of God
as the only Good. Says an unknown Dominican mystic: " The
human creature sinks into his own littleness and nothingness;
the clearer and the more distinctly the greatness of God shines
upon him, the more he realizes his own littleness." Symeon,
" the new theologian," confesses: " All the organs of my body
and soul I have stained with sin from my birth onwards; I am
wholly sin." Similar confessions of sin and words of extreme
self-contempt may be read in countless writings of the mystics.
For there is here a strangely paradoxical experience. The
inner eye of him who prays is directed towards a double object,

God's infinitude, holiness, beauty, and love, and the meanness, sinfulness, and corruption of the self. All these contrary emotions and judgements pass into a harmony which is yet a contrast, an overwhelming experience which breaks out into prayer. " I am poor and needy," writes Augustine, " but Thou art rich to all those that call upon Thee . . . But now when my groaning is a witness that I am displeased with myself, Thou shinest out and art pleasing and art loved and art desired that I may be ashamed of myself and renounce myself and choose Thee, and may please neither Thee nor myself, otherwise than in Thee." À Kempis speaks to God: " O Lord, my God, Thou art to me whatsoever is good. And who am I that I should dare to speak to Thee? I am Thy poorest, meanest servant, and a most vile worm, much more poor and contemptible than I can or dare express. Yet do Thou remember, O Lord, that I am nothing, have nothing, and can do nothing. Thou alone are good, just, and holy, Thou canst do all things, Thou accomplishest all things and fillest all things."

The paradoxical character of the mystical experience is increased by the thought that the infinite God stoops to insignificant sinful man, communicates Himself to him, and unites Himself to him. The mystic glories in this incomprehensible miracle of grace; he scarcely dares to look up, he trembles, he thrills with ecstatic bliss. " How can I, stained in body and in soul, appear before Thee? " asks Symeon. " How can I, a wretch, stand before Thy face? How must I not flee from Thy glory and the flashing light of Thy Holy Spirit? " ".My God, that I love Thee is not astonishing," Bayâzîd confesses, " for I am Thy servant, weak, impotent, needy, but it is strange that Thou lovest me, Thou, the King of Kings."

The contemplation of the Highest Good and of one's own nothingness passes over into the contemplation of the divine miracle of mystical union. Frequently the prayer is only astonishment at the great, the incomprehensible thing which has transpired in the divinely favoured soul. As Gertrude says: " Who is like Thee who hast founded heaven and earth, to whom thrones and dominions do service and yet who seekest Thy bliss among the children of men? How great art Thou,

King of Kings, and Lord of Lords, who rulest the stars and givest Thy heart to men! "

C. *Ecstasy*

The highest and holiest prayer of the mystic is the ecstatic " prayer " which is no longer prayer in the ordinary sense. In the ravishing vision of God, there is a decisive distinction between the soul and God, between the finite creature and the infinite Spirit; but in the ecstatic union with God, all distinctions are abolished, the praying soul and the Being prayed to, the " I " and the " Thou " are mingled together in indissoluble unity. Every word of prayer, nay, every prayerful attitude of mind has ceased; there are no longer two, but one; the finite is swallowed up by the infinite. This ecstatic " union of substance " is inexpressible because it is accomplished in a realm beyond ordinary consciousness. But when the mystic awakes from the ecstatic, God-intoxicated state, he tries to express the inexpressible in stammering words. He can only make known his happiness in the formula: " I am Thou and Thou art I." This prayer is found on the lips of Indian, Persian, Greek, and Christian mystics. " I am Thou " and " Thou art I," this formula of identity we meet most frequently among the Persian Sûfis. Jalâl-ed-dîn-Rûmî cries in rapture: " I am Thou and Thou art I! " And in a longer prayer he says: " There is no longer ' I ' and ' Thou ' between us. I am not I, Thou art not Thou nor art Thou I. I am in perplexity as to whether I am Thou or Thou art I." Nay, even from the lips of Christian mystics we hear this exclamation. Angela of Foligno prays: " Thou art I and I am Thou."

More frequently the Christian mystic substitutes this " formula of *immanence* " for the formula of identity:

> " I sink myself in Thee,
> I in Thee, Thou in me " —

so sings Tersteegen. Only when the mystic can utter such a prayer has he found God completely and abides at one with Him eternally. Jalâl-ed-dîn-Rûmî, the classic writer of Islamic mysticism, has veiled this thought in a striking parable: " A lover came once by night before the door of his

beloved and knocked. Then she cried: 'Who knocks there?'
And he answered: 'It is I.' She did not open the door, but
said harshly: 'Away with you!' Then the young man went
abroad and wandered through the world until love with its irresistible strength drove him back to the abode of his beloved.
And he knocked again, gently and softly, in shy hope. And
again the question of his beloved rang out: 'Who knocks
there?' And he answered: 'It is thou who standest once
again before the door.' Then the one whom he adored opened
to him with the words: 'Enter, Beloved; my little chamber
is not large enough for two, but since thou art nought but I,
there is room in the chamber and at the table.'"

The fundamental thought of mysticism is clearly expressed
in this story, the identity of the human and the divine.
Throughout the mystical literature of the East and the West
there sounds this *leitmotif*, this formula of ecstatic identity.
The mystics form an invisible brotherhood scattered through
all lands and times; though separated by space and time they
reach hands to each other and agree in saying that God and
man are separated only in outer appearance, both are indissolubly one. In spiritual transport they utter the great mystical prayer: " I am Thou and Thou art I."

D. *The Refusal to Pray for Earthly Goods*

Naïve requests for external things are irreconcilable with
the fundamental strain of mysticism. When they do occur
among mystics, chiefly as petitions for others, they play an
altogether secondary rôle, independent of mystical prayer
which is centred on God and salvation. The genuine mystic,
like the philosophical critic, rejects prayer for earthly things
as irreligious. The subject of prayer is exclusively, " God and
the Soul," God the Highest Good, and the salvation and
blessedness of the soul in the Highest Good. As Augustine
says: " Ask nothing from God except God Himself." " Ask
for the blessed life " — and for him the blessed life is the
eternal life, the contemplation of the divine blessedness forever. He looks upon prayer for material goods as " carnal
prayer "; to the spiritually twice-born only " spiritual prayer "
is seemly. With the same argument Saadi the Persian mystic

rejects prayer for external gifts: " A true servant of his Lord is only he who does not forget his Lord on account of his Lord's gifts, but he works faithfully on God's path who has begged from God as a gift God Himself." Prayer for the fulfilment of self-seeking wishes contradicts the mystical ideal of absolute identity with the will of god. " To pray ' Ah Lord, turn from me this fate,' is verily sin against Him who gave it " (Jalâl-ed-dîn-Rûmî).

Finally, the nothingness and worthlessness of everything earthly makes prayer for the things that pass away mere folly. Eckhart sets forth the repudiation of all self-seeking, materialistic prayer in a charming parable: " A sick man was asked why it was he did not pray to God to make him well. The man said that he did not like to do so for three reasons. One was that he wanted to be sure of this, that the loving God would never allow him to be sick unless it were for his own best good. Another was that if a man is good he will desire what God wills, and not that God should will what he desires. And therefore He wills that I should be sick, for if He did not will it I would not be sick. And so I ought not to wish to be well. . . . The third reason why I do not ask God to make me well is this: I will not, and I ought not to pray the rich and loving God for such trifles. Supposing that I should come one or two hundred miles to the good Pope and should say to him, ' O Lord, Holy Father, I have come a hard road, two hundred miles at great expense, and this is why I have come: I beg you to give me a bean.' Truly he himself and whoever else heard it, would say that I was a great fool. Now this one thing is certain truth, that every good compared with God is less than a bean. Therefore, if I am a wise and good man, I should refuse with scorn to ask God to make me well."

Logical mysticism rejects not only petition for earthly things but petition in general. Petition is the expression of wish and will; the mystical ideal, on the contrary, is complete absence of wish and will, freedom from desire, and absolute abandon. Hence Eckhart, Catherine of Genoa, as well as the quietists of the seventeenth century go so far as to reject all petition, even petition for religious and moral blessings, and limit prayer to the expression of this mood of " indifference." Catherine of Genoa receives this exhortation from Christ: " Never say ' I will ' or ' I will not.' Never say ' my ' but always ' our.' When thou prayest the Lord's Prayer take as the foundation of it ' Thy will be done,' that is, Thy will be done in all things, in soul and in body, in children, in relatives, in friends, in goods and chattels, and in every other thing which meets thee, either for weal or woe." In her later years she could pray: " Never, O my God, for about thirty-five years have I asked anything for myself."

E. *The Psychological Stages in Mystical Prayer*

Mystical concentration on the Highest Good can consist either in a conscious and deliberate turning of oneself to God or in a condition of being unconsciously, involuntarily, ecstatically captured and carried away by God. The state of contemplation comes into being spontaneously for the most part during times of voluntary meditation and concentration, or as a result of a deliberate concentrated effort to produce anew by intentional concentration a devotional mood formerly experienced in spontaneous adoration. Concentration, the act whereby the gaze is fixed upon a single object, is the condition which produces a unification of the entire inner life, and absorption of all ideas and volitional impulses directed towards other objects, as well as the suppression of ordinary emotions. This self-composure and contemplation in prayer produce of themselves the condition of consciousness sought by the mystics, namely, peace and rapture, sometimes even to a loss of consciousness in ecstasy. These two factors — the difference between spontaneous and deliberate prayer, and the approach of ecstasy — necessitate a classification of the stages of prayer from the standpoint of the growing simplification of the psychic state, the lessening of the field of consciousness and the increase of its intensity. The neo-Platonic mystics speak of " ideas " or " conceptions " of prayer. Christian mystics speak of " stages " or " steps of a ladder." An Islamic mystic, Algazâlî, speaks very finely of the " veils of prayer " where the progress is to be conceived, not from below upwards, but

from without inwards. In all such classifications, " prayer "
does not mean ordinary prayer, which finds its deepest expression in words and ideas, but the mystical " state of prayer "
(*état d'oraison*). Francis of Sales says: " Prayer and mystical
theology are one and the same thing."

The construction of a " ladder of prayer " leading to ecstasy
presupposes a high gift of psychological analysis. Its aim is
threefold: (1) Axiological: the value of the individual psychic
states is estimated from the standpoint of the completed mystical experience, that is, ecstasy. (2) Psychological: by the
description and analysis of the prayer-states the mystic seeks
to come to a clear understanding of his own experience. (3)
Pedagogical: the detailed description of the psychic experiences should make it possible for other men to have these
experiences and by these steps of prayer to attain to perfect
union with God.

Although the descriptions of the stages of prayer, their number and their characteristics, vary, yet there is no essential
difference between the neo-Platonic, Sûfi, Hindu, and Christian
mystics; their basic psychological character is identical even
with the stages of absorption in the Yoga and in Buddhism,
though in the latter every notion of prayer, that is, communion with God, is excluded. The finest psychological training is evident in the stages of prayer described by Teresa and
in the stages of absorption of Buddhism. The description
of the individual stages of prayer is for the most part a
characterization of the psychic experience or state: recollection, meditation, contemplation, rest, union, ecstasy. The
ladder of prayer of the Hindu mystics describes very happily
the psychic mood of the particular states of prayer by the
various social relations. The pious soul rises from that of
slave to that of friend with the divinity, then filial love, and
finally arrives at the transport of love in the nuptial relation.
We meet with the same gradation of stages in Western mysticism as represented by Bernard of Clairvaux, Thomas of
Celano, and Angelus Silesius. Yet this ladder of the spiritual
life does not describe the facts with psychological exactness.

(a) The ladder of prayer strictly so-called begins with the
conscious and deliberate concentration of the attention on

God or a religious idea. At this first stage, in the view of Teresa and other mystics, man himself is active, whilst the psychic states of higher prayer arise spontaneously and are not directly produced by conscious concentration and meditation, but can only be prepared for and encouraged. They are, accordingly, a work of divine grace. The praying man seeks for solitude. He turns his attention, by an act of the will, from the outer world, he " collects the mind," " draws it away from all hearing and seeing," as Madame Guyon says; he frees himself from the scattered multiplicity of the soul's contents. He concentrates his attention deliberately on a definite religious idea. The liberation from external things accomplished by tense concentration and the restraint of all vehement desires and emotions effects a deep feeling of complete solitariness and inner freedom. The concentrated contemplation of ideas with a feeling-tone produces a lasting mood suffused with tender delight. " The work of prayer," says David of Augsburg, " is turned into the sweet joy of devotion." In this soft and affecting mood the Christian mystic experiences the direct presence of God. Madame Guyon speaks of a *goût expérimental de la présence de Dieu*, which the soul gains by meditation.

(b) In the second stage of prayer the deliberate strain on the attention characteristic of the first stage disappears; the activity of discursive thought is paralysed; a complete stillness reigns in the soul of him who contemplates. The uplifting and liberating meditation yields to the lofty state of inner unity, blessed peace, blissful rest, entrancing clearness. " The soul," says Teresa, " rests profoundly satisfied in God." John of the Cross says: " The soul ceases to think of anything and establishes peace in God." Among Christian mystics this mood of blissful peace is not altogether without an object, but is sustained by the love of God, by the pure and spiritual experience of the Highest Good, by " an act of the will," as John of the Cross puts it in his scholastic terminology. " The soul wholly filled with love rests in God," he says, " and is united most delightfully to Him in blissful wonder." Similarly Teresa says of this stage of prayer: " The soul enjoys its highest good." David of Augsburg, John of the Cross, Teresa, Al-

phonso de Liguori call this stage " the prayer of quiet " and
this is a very admirable description of it.

(c) The third stage (as also the fourth where five or more
steps are distinguished) implies no essential distinction from
but only an intensification of the preceding stage. The dimin-
ishing and restraining of the normal life of the soul advances
further. Teresa calls this state a " slumber of the powers of
the soul." The intensity of the rapture is heightened. " The
soul as it contemplates," says Teresa, " loses itself in perfect
passivity in its Highest Good. It only desires God, belongs
not to itself any longer but only to Him." The expression
" contemplation " best does justice to the psychological
peculiarity of this stage.

In Buddhistic mysticism and among Christian Quietists
rapturous contemplation does not follow on the mood of peaceful blessedness but the " holy indifference," the still serenity,
the cold unemotional state. The third Buddhistic *jhânam*
forms the transition from deep blessedness to sheer indifference. The intensity of the blissful feeling grows less and less,
the mood of delight fades, the feeling of blessedness passes
over into unruffled serenity. Like the Buddhist ladder of
absorption, the ladder of prayer of Christian Quietists leads
also from the blessed mood springing from meditation to the
extreme mood of indifference. Francis of Sales denotes
quietude and *union* as the lower, *submission* and *conformity*
as the higher stages of the contemplation which succeeds
meditation. Madame Guyon regards the mood of indifference
as belonging to the second rung of the ladder. The stages of
prayer described as *oraison de simplicité, oraison de simple
présence de Dieu, oraison infuse,* are distinguished only by the
degree and purity of the indifference. The character of this
mood of *sainte indifférence* of the Christian Quietists is quite
the equivalent of the *upekkhâ* of the Buddhist beggar-monk.
And yet there is a fundamental inner distinction. The mood
of indifference of the Christian mystic is sustained and penetrated by surrender to God as the Highest Good. The indifference to pleasure and pain, the renunciation of all one's
wish and will becomes here the unreserved submission to the
sovereign will of God. The object of the monk's knowledge

and valuation is not a highest value but a supreme lack of value, not the infinite God to whom he unconditionally surrenders himself, but the impersonal causal connection, the sorrowful circle of births from which he has escaped.

(d) The last and highest rung of the ladder is denoted mostly by the term *union*. David of Augsburg says: " Man becomes with God one thing." The Buddhist ladder of absorption culminates not in the storm and transport of ecstasy, of possession by God, but in the unemotional stillness of Nirvana, in the extinction and death of every vital movement, in the state of annihilation (*nirodha*) of the ordinary life of the soul. From painless and joyless serenity, the saint rises to the sublime freedom, peace, and blessedness of Nirvana. The state of Nirvana growing out of the fundamental mood of indifference has been also experienced by Christian Quietists: Madame Guyon, with that sureness of psychological touch peculiar to her, describes it thus: " The understanding is obscured, the will loses all elasticity, the slightest vital movement of the selfhood is dead. Wish, inclination, desire, aversion, antipathy — all are gone. The soul enters into the dark and awful state of mystical death since it has passed over into a state of complete absence of feeling. It has become utterly indifferent to the world, to itself, and to God. It neither loves nor hates any more; it neither suffers nor rejoices; it does nothing good and nothing evil, it does nothing at all. The soul has nothing, wills nothing, is nothing; it is in the state of nothingness." As in the Buddhist Nirvana, the thought of God, as well as consciousness, are absent in the " mystical death " of the Christian Quietists. The Buddhist Nirvana is the final, supreme goal of all striving for salvation, it is redemption. The " mystical death " of the Christian mystic is not a final fact, it is only a stage of transition. Resurrection comes after death, blessed union with God after annihilation.

F. *The Idea of God Underlying Mystical Prayer*

The God whom the mystic adores is conceived as absolutely static. The spiritual Reality in which he by contemplation sinks himself, is a static ideal; the object of contemplation can be only an Ultimate, a Final. The idea of God lying at the root of primitive prayer, as an energizing power controlling destiny, is almost wholly absent from the mystic's devotional experience. The God of mystical contemplation does not possess the strongly marked feature of personality which is peculiar to the idea of God in primitive prayer. It is significant that in mystical prayers God is so often addressed by such a neutral expression as *summum bonum*. A complete de-personalizing of God, such as is achieved in the speculations of a Plotinus, an Eckhart, a Sankara, is really not possible so long as the speech of devotion or even the inner gesture of prayer to God exists. The majority of mystics do address God in the anthropomorphic language of primitive prayer. But wherever aesthetic intuition and solemn adoration of the Highest Good take the place of loving intercourse with God, there the features of the divine personality begin to fade. " I am in love and I know not with whom," says the Sûfi Ferîd-ed-dîn-Attâr.

Naïve mysticism, in which the lovers' analogy plays so great a part, is less affected by this tendency to deprive the image of God of its human features. In it prayer is not exclusively contemplation and concentration, but a heartfelt love-discourse and a trustful intimate fellowship between the soul and God. Here God is condescending in love to man, the beloved Friend, the passionate Bridegroom and Lover. The prayer of mystic love in its native power and perspicuity reveals the human idea of God underlying the naïve prayer of primitive man. The prayers of the Christian " nuptial " mystics are directed less seldom to the infinite God than to " sweetest Jesus," whose human character lends liveliness and material distinctness to the mystical conception of God as the *summum bonum*. As Suso excellently observes: " Since the soul, owing to the weakness of the body, cannot all the time cleave nakedly to sheer goodness without the help of images, it must have something figurative which may lead it inwards. And the best thing for that purpose is the lovable picture of Jesus Christ, for man finds there life, that is, the highest reward and the greatest gain."

G. *The Experience of the Presence of God in Prayer*

All mystical praying is penetrated by the undoubting assurance of the real, immediate presence of God. In prayer " one has God in front of him," says Eckhart. To pray means for Teresa " to remain in the presence of God." Madame Guyon says: " God is more in us than we are in ourselves: we have Him and taste Him." In that state of unity and quiet, freed from all emotions, in those deep and blissful moods, the praying man believes he can trace the presence of the Infinite: for God dwells, as Augustine says, " in the secret places of the rational soul which are called the inner man "; or as Tauler remarks, " in the innermost recess where alone is true unity." The object of conscious meditation and concentration is to make it possible for one to realize divine presence, by the creation of a unified state of the soul. According to Teresa, contemplation has in the first stage of prayer to transport itself into the presence of God and to remain there. Madame Guyon says: " The chief exercise [of meditation] must be the presence of God." The experience of the presence of God in contemplation of the *summum bonum* has a quite different psychological character. What the praying individual experiences here is not a feeling of softly gliding onwards but an emotional excitement that carries one away. The experience of God's presence is not inwardly but outwardly concentrated; there is no inner " perceiving " or " tasting," but a spiritual vision of God.[3]

The consciousness of the presence of God belongs to the essence of prayer; it is a sure criterion in deciding whether the mystical contemplation and absorption may be described as prayer. In the Buddhistic absorption this experience is wholly lacking. The " abiding," as the technical term is, does not mean " abiding " in the presence of God, but a remaining with and in oneself.

---

[3] ὁρᾷ αὐτὸν νοεροῖς ὀφθαλμοῖς, as Symeon, "the new theologian," says.

H. *The Relation of God and Man as Expressed in Mystical Prayer*

The mystic's prayer is no mere thinking about God, not the thoughtful realization to oneself of a metaphysical reality into which philosophical criticism mostly dissolves it, but a real contact, a genuine communion and converse with a God experienced as present, a fellowship which in the end leads to perfect union with Him, to the submergence and disappearance of the soul in Him. Proclus defines prayer as " the drawing together and binding of souls to the gods." According to the pseudo-Jamblichus, prayer makes us " companions of God." Proclus also describes prayer as an " association with God." This neo-Platonic characterization of prayer recurs again and again in Christian mysticism. Nilus of Sinai defines prayer as " the converse of the mind with God." Symeon, " the new theologian," says of him who prays: " He converses with God face to face." The *Imitation of Christ* speaks frequently of " talking familiarly with Jesus," Teresa of " inner intercourse," " intimate communion," and of the " holy society of the Lord." St. Francis of Sales defines prayer as " the discourse and conversation of the soul with God," Tersteegen as " familiar intercourse with God." In solitariness, set free from all the world and all creatures, the praying man speaks to his God, " the alone with the Alone." This neo-Platonic description also appears again in Christian mysticism. To pray means to be an individual alone with God, to stay in His society as a solitary.

The self-abandoning surrender to God as the only and highest Good excludes the primitive thought of a real effect on God to be aimed at in prayer, of a change in His will. The exclusive concentration on God and the complete absence of desire conditioned thereby makes impossible a primitive will to influence God in the interest of one's own wishes. Belief in a real communion with God is for mysticism not identical with an actual influence on God. Man prays to God, as Augustine says, " that he himself may be constructed, not that God may be instructed.[4] Prayer is not ordained to move God to fulfil

---

[4] *Ut ipse construatur, non ut Deus instruatur.*

our wishes, but to awaken in us a longing for God and to raise us up to God. "He who stands in a boat," says the pseudo-Dionysius, "and seizes a rope flung to him from a rock and pulls it in, does not draw the rock to himself but he brings himself and the boat nearer the rock."

Intercourse with God in prayer in purely contemplative mysticism has no counterpart in the social relations of humanity. God, the *summum bonum*, is too great, too spiritual, too holy for man to commune with Him in all fervour, love, and rapture, as he can commune with his fellows. Only in primitive imaginative mysticism, untouched by philosophical theory, is the relation of the pious man to God a clear reflex of the relations of the social order, the relations of servant, friend, child, bride. These relations are, nevertheless, not considered of equal value; they are arranged in an ascending scale — a truly mystical proceeding. In the Hindu Vishnu cult, "love is revealed in the relation of a servant to his master, of a friend to his friend, of a child to his parents, and of a wife to her husband." The communion of the soul with God in prayer is mirrored in simple mysticism mainly under the forms and symbols of the marriage relation, as is manifest even in the mode of address used in prayer. "You may, if you will," says Angelus Silesius, "confess God as your Master, but I will give Him no other name than Bridegroom."

I. *Direction in Mystical Prayer*

The mystics address their teaching in prayer to the few mystically endowed souls who strive after perfection. Typical examples are the *Golden Little Book of Contemplation* by Peter of Alcantara, and the *Moyen court et très facile de faire oraison* of Madame Guyon. The mystical guide to prayer is a psychological prescription. It consists of the description and analysis of experiences which are vouchsafed the praying mystic at different stages of the spiritual life. It gives detailed, sometimes ingeniously refined methods and rules in accordance with which concentration and meditation should be carried out, and by the application of which the disposition for higher states of prayer may be created. But mystical teaching gives its experience not only of the methods but of the material for meditation. Such methodical instruction has been given, among others, by Bonaventura, Teresa, Peter of Alcantara. The *Spiritual Exercises* of Loyola gives us the most compact and systematic arrangement and the most logical completeness in detail. From the concise and methodical rules for meditation given by the great saint has come forth a flood of books on religious contemplation which, put in the hands of the average man, complete themes for meditation and prayer. The introduction to prayer given us by the mystics is not limited to the conscious and deliberate practice of meditation; hints are given how he who prays is to conduct himself when he passively experiences states of prayer, recognized as being outpourings of supernatural grace, in order not to let them dissolve away, but to increase their intensity.

The mystical teaching in prayer does not indulge in dogmatic criticism of the moral standards of other forms of prayer, such as is found in expositions of the prophetic and philosophical ideals of prayer. The mystic, to be sure, values differently the various kinds of prayer, but he does not condemn, nor does he oppose those forms of prayer which lie below the level of the mystical ideal. The mystical training in prayer never becomes a polemic; it considers formal praying in words as a preliminary stage to interior prayer, not as a contradiction of it.

CHAPTER VIII

THE VARIANTS OF MYSTICAL PRAYER

. THE character of all forms of mystical prayer is uniformly similar; yet it varies in accordance with the manner in which certain particular elements inherent, under some aspect or another, in all mystical prayer, are thrown into relief. Often the different variants combine. Thus the mysticism of the *Imitation of Christ* harmoniously unites the cultual motive with the nuptial and quietist motives. Sometimes, however, one of these motives predominates, with the result that an entirely independent line of thought, in conflict with the others, is created. The mysticism of syncretistic mystery religions is purely cultual, that of Lao-tsze and the Indian Atman prophets a mysticism of the Infinite; the mysticism of Molinos and Madame Guyon is wholly quietistic and that of Mechthild of Magdeburg and other nuns a purely nuptial mysticism.

I. SACRAMENTAL AND CULTURAL MYSTICISM

The ground in which all mystical prayer and self-absorption are rooted and from which they draw their nourishment and strength, is meditation. This meditation always has its source in the concrete, mostly in a creation of the imagination, but often in a tangible perceptible object. Thus the Buddhist mendicant monks meditate on the transitoriness of all earthly things while contemplating a flowing river or even a putrefying corpse. When Christian mystics meditate on the nothingness of life, they sometimes contemplate a human skull. When they lament their misery caused by their sins or when they ponder upon the great secret of redemption, they steep themselves in the image of the crucified Redeemer.

Apart from profane things and representations of religious

art, " holy " objects or such as belong specifically to a cult form the mainstay of meditation and prayer in non-Christian and Christian mysticism. But the holy object means more to the mystic than a mere incitement to pious thoughts and emotions. By looking at it he is even inspired to see and experience the real presence of God. The Lord abides in a mysterious, sensuous, and yet supersensuous way in the cultual object. It is true that the God of the mystics is spiritual, and infinite; He is not open to the senses, Heaven and earth cannot contain Him, much less a small material object. And yet, the presence of God within the holy object is a certainty beyond all doubt, as well for the mystic as for primitive man. Certainly to the former the sensuous and the material are not identical with the metaphysical and the spiritual: the visible and the tangible are but a sign and a pledge of the invisible and divine, yet still not only a mere shadow of a higher reality, but a reality in itself. Symbolism and realism, sensuousness and spirituality, the natural and the supernatural are united in perfect harmony.

In almost all mysticism there is a certain connection with worship. Even in Plotinus, one of the greatest mystics of the infinite, traces of sacramental mysticism are found; the strange rites of the mystery cults are visible pictures and symbols of sublime mystical experiences. The Upanishads of the Veda are the direct outgrowth of the elaborate character of Vedic rites. According to a very recent interpretation *upanishad* originally meant nothing more than the contemplative adoration of a holy object. Ancient Buddhism alone, which, with its peculiar radicalism, developed mystical thought into its ultimate form, condemns any connection of mystical self-absorption with worship.

In Hindu Bhakti mysticism the motive of worship is an important factor: tender mystical piety and the popular cult of the gods merge into each other. The mystical adoration of the divine Lord (*îsvara*) and Saviour, of Vishnu or Siva, is inspired by the God's image, the " *arcâ.*" In the statue that has been consecrated by a special ceremony (*avâhanam*) the god is really and personally present; his image is an " *avatâra,*" i.e., a personification and incarnation of the god beyond time and space. When the devotee sees the statue of his god, illumined by the dim gleam of flickering lamps and veiled in clouds of incense, he sinks down in rapturous amazement and adores in profound devotion the greatness, beauty, and love of his god who is so present to him. The fervent and impassioned psalms of the great Tamil mystic, Mânikha Vâçagar, which were all written or conceived in the temples of Siva, were produced by the contemplation of the god's sacred image. In the temple they are to this day recited daily by the faithful in the presence of the statue.

All the mystery cults of oriental Hellenistic syncretism have a fundamental mystical tendency. The words " mysticism " and " mystery " have not been derived without reason from the same root.[1] Very ancient barbaric rites, pomp and ceremony, mysterious consecrations take their part in the service of the mystic desire for redemption; they are to lead the mystic on a sensuous, supersensuous, and magic way unto salvation and blessed union. Dieterich says of the celebrated liturgy of Mithras, " Union with God is the aim of the whole action, everything is directed towards this end." This union with the divinity will be accomplished most directly and most fervently by partaking of the divine food and drinking the divine drink. Another way to ecstatic union, an outstanding example of which is found in the Egypto-Hellenistic mystery cult, is the contemplative adoration of divine images. According to the testimony of Porphyry, Egyptian priests passed their whole lives in gazing on and contemplating the gods.[2] As Cumont says: " Egypt is the country from which contemplative piety passed into Europe." In the Roman worship of Isis the images of the gods were " exposed " — to adopt the word of the Roman Catholic liturgy — from early morning till the late afternoon for quiet adoration by the initiated. Apuleius speaks of the ineffable delight that possessed him when he gazed on the image of a god. A mystical prayer contained in the Mimaut papyrus gives us the words of thanksgiving and supplication of a mystic whose blessed portion it had been to look upon the image of a god: " We rejoice that thou hast revealed thyself to us; we rejoice that thou hast made us holy by thy revela-

---

[1] μύειν.   [2] τῇ τῶν θεῶν θεωρίᾳ καὶ θεάσει.

tion, while we are still in the flesh. Mankind thanks thee for having experienced thy Majesty. We have experienced thee, thou Life of men's lives, experienced thee, thou Light of all experience, experienced thee, thou Mother pregnant with the seed of the Father, thou sanctuary of the germ of life. While, thus, we pray to thee we make no other petition than that thou wilt graciously remember us."

The cultural mysticism of the Hindu sects and of the syncretistic mysteries, in spite of all their fervour and their aesthetic charms, is in the grip of primitive idolatry. Christian mysticism, on the contrary, became united with worship, without its spirituality and purity having been corrupted by base conceptions and images. Neither a fetish nor an idol, but the eucharistic mystery, the body of the Lord contained under the sensuous veil of bread, is for the Christian mystic the outward sign of God's direct and real presence. Since the earliest Christian times the Eucharist has had a mystical character and a mystical signification just like the rites and sacraments of syncretist holy fellowships. By partaking of the sacred elements the Christian community entered into fervent fellowship with the exalted Lord and received divine life and strength. With the progressive penetration into the Christian Church of mystical motives during the later years of ancient times, the fundamental principles of mystical union and deification united more and more with the primitive Christian conception of the Eucharist. However, it is only in the zenith of Christian mysticism, that is, in the mediaeval mysticism of the Eastern and Western Churches that we can speak of a eucharistic mysticism in the proper sense of the word. Thomas Aquinas, à Kempis, and Symeon, " the new theologian," are the classic examples of Christian sacramental mysticism. Mediaeval mysticism has individualized to an astonishing extent the primitive conception of the Sacrament of Sacraments and, thereby, deepened and intensified it. In early Christianity the Eucharist is a common meal — " the Lord's Supper " it is called by the Apostle — a meal which unites around one table the company of believers with the exalted Lord. For mysticism the reception of the Eucharist is the union of the individual soul with its heavenly Lord and Redeemer. For the ancient Church the partaking of the holy bread and the drinking from the chalice meant a communion with Christ; for mystics the receiving of the Eucharist is a mysterious union with their heavenly and beloved Redeemer. Countless times they experienced ecstasy or an emotion akin to ecstasy at the altar. Mechthild of Magdeburg says: " When we receive the body of God the divinity unites with our innocent souls, and God as a human being is mingled with our bodies." The value set upon the frequent receiving of the sacrament by mystical piety has its origin in this experience.

The spread of the cult of the Eucharist, which began in Western Christendom in the thirteenth century, brought about a development of sacramental mysticism which extended far beyond the eucharistic liturgy of the primitive Church. Not only in the Mass and in Communion, but also beyond them, mystical piety and prayer concentrated more and more on the eucharistic Redeemer. On the lighted altar or in the hand of the priest the congregation of prayerful believers was permitted to see the presence of the Redeemer in the substance of the bread, unconcealed in the splendid " monstrance." On less solemn occasions the faithful could contemplate Him in the pyx or ciborium. And also outside the general service the devout hurried to the tabernacle where the sacramental Redeemer abode. For primitive Christian mysticism the closed monk's cell was the principal place for quiet prayer and meditation; in the newer Western Catholic mysticism churches and chapels with the tabernacle become the main place for mystical prayer. Magdalena of Pazzi says: " Pray rather before the holy sacrament than in any other place, for as the abode of God is in heaven, so His earthly dwelling-place is in the tabernacle." One might even speak of a mysticism of the tabernacle. With the intense idea of the faith that God is " truly, really, and bodily " present in the sacrament of the Altar, very strong aesthetic charms are blended: the stillness of the silence, the sunlight filtering through multi-coloured stained glass windows, or nocturnal darkness, the " constantly burning light " before the tabernacle, restlessly flickering and glimmering, the fragrant perfume permeating God's habitation, all these aesthetic sensations unite in producing a peculiar, languorous, and voluptuous mood that gives an emotional depth and warmth to the belief in God's sensuous presence. The mysticism of the tabernacle belongs to the most wonderful phenomena known in the history of religions: it is one of the hidden, inexhaustible sources of Catholic piety.

Mystical prayer is not changed in its substance and character by the sacramental motive. In it special reference is only made to the presence of the Lord in the Eucharist and to the mystical union at its partaking. Precisely for that reason mystical prayers used at the communion service assume a peculiar character. The most finished and most fervent of all eucharistic prayers is the anthem *Adoro te devote* of Thomas Aquinas, one of the most beautiful mystical hymns that have ever been composed. The usage of mystical prayer as a communion prayer has been extended far and wide. It was especially communion prayer originating in mediaeval mysticism that gave a very strong mystical character to ordinary Catholic piety. Also the substance of eucharistic prayer reveals the peculiar progress of mystical prayer. In prayers before the Communion supplication and longing predominate, in prayers after it meditation, praise, and thanksgiving, but there is no strict dividing line between these two forms of prayer.

A. *Concentration*

(a) *The Way of Purgation.* David of Augsburg prays for purification from passion and sin: " Beloved Lord Jesus Christ, make warm and fervent my heart's longing for Thee with Thy love-giving blood, that flowed from Thy burning heart when Thou wast exalted on the cross. . . . O intensely loved Lord, now pour Thy love-giving blood over my barren heart, so that it may become fertile with virtue and quicken and warm my dying desire, and heal and give peace to my wounded soul and to my mortal pains, that it may partake of the balm of Thy healing power and experience its sweetness, and irrigate and nourish my barren heart with Thyself, O life-giving Food, that I by hastening to Thee in all the trials and troubles of this mortal life may gain courage and strength and power, until I arrive where Thou goest and where Thou art in peace on the right hand of the Father where Thou waitest for us."

(b) *The Way of Illumination.* À Kempis prays for enlightenment: " Illumine mine eyes to behold this great mystery, and strengthen me to believe it with undoubting faith. Illumine my blindness with the clearness of Thy presence . . ."; for faith, hope, and love: " Grant to Thy poor beggar to feel a little of that fervent love for Thee in the holy communion, that my faith may grow stronger, and my hope more perfect in Thy goodness . . ."; for fervour of love and yearning: " Thou wilt, therefore, that I should receive Thee and join myself to Thee in love . . . O my God, eternal love, my perfect good, I desire to receive Thee with as strong a wish and as profound reverence as ever any one of Thy saints has ever felt."

(c) *The Way of Union.* À Kempis prays for union with God in the reception of the sacrament: " My soul desires Thy body, my heart desires to be united only with Thee. Give Thyself unto me and it suffices, for without Thee there is no consolation." Thomas Aquinas prays for the vision of God in the world beyond: " I pray Thee that Thou wouldst condescend to lead me a sinner to that unspeakable joy where Thou art to Thy saints true light, full satisfaction, perpetual joy, consummate gladness, and perfect bliss."

B. *Contemplation*

(a) *The Presence of God.* À Kempis contemplates the infinite presence of God: " Behold Thou art present here with me on this altar, Thou, my God, Holy of Holies, Creator of men, and Lord of angels "; the Highest Good: " Thou alone art my food and drink, my love and my joy, my delight and my perfect good . . . Behold in Thee is all that I can and ought to desire." He praises and gives thanks to God: " O God, invisible Creator of the world, how marvellously dost Thou deal with us, how sweetly and graciously dost Thou deal with them who purpose to receive Thyself in this blessed sacrament." He surrenders himself: " Receive me unto the praise of Thy name that hast made ready thy precious body and blood for my food and drink."

Thus also the prayer of cultual sacramental mysticism is mystical prayer throughout in its structure, its wording, its thoughts, and feelings. The difference from pure mysticism lies only in this, that it has in all stages from meditation to the consummation of the mystical union an inward connection with a visible object of worship, and that the sublime mystical experiences and states (with the exception of ecstasy itself which stifles the normal consciousness) are in close contact with outward perception. The experience in prayer of the presence of God depends on the belief that God is embodied in a sensuous object, the experience of mystical union is based on the sensuous enjoyment of food and drink by which the devout worshipper believes he appropriates God Himself. Both ideas, the notion of the sensuous presence of God as well as the idea of the partaking of God by eating the holy meal, are very ancient; they originate in primitive religion. By uniting the mystical central ideas with these primitive conceptions the mystical experience in its purity and tenderness is not endangered and weakened, it even gains strength and fervour, warmth and passion. The cultual sacramental mysticism is the most striking example of the fact that in piety sensuousness and spirituality do not exclude each other, nay, even can be united in a higher synthesis. Even religious genius is able to draw nourishment and strength for its deepest and most spiritual experiences from insignificant external observances of worship.

(b) *Nuptial Mysticism.* Naïve, loving, visionary mysticism is usually found in the symbol of the bride. The relation of the soul to God is conceived as a relation of love or betrothal, the ecstatic union with God as the union of love, the mystical delight as the joy of love. The idea of sexual union of human beings with God is, however, no original creation of mysticism but belongs to the primitive sphere of religion.

The nuptial idea, however, only assumed a predominant position in mediaeval mysticism, so that the numerous traces of the bridal motive in the ancient Church appear to be merely beginnings. In the days of the Minnesingers and the knightly worship of women the flourishing mysticism which centred in Christ fused with the tender eroticism of the Germano-Roman peoples. The religious nuptial motive which, long before, had been introduced into the piety of the churches became now the *leitmotif* of the mysticism of convents secluded from the world. The father of Christian nuptial mysticism is Bernard of Clairvaux. He was the first to consider the fervent love poetry of the *Song of Songs* as a symbol of the changeable experiences of an emotional mysticism. But what used to be with Bernard merely an exegetic interpretation and a theological theory, became a fervent emotion and an ardent passion in the lonely souls of the nuns. The piety of the God-fearing nuns and other women has henceforth been dominated by the bridal motive. The most fervent and tender sounds of womanly bridal mysticism are heard by us in the booklet of *The Flowing Light of the Godhead* of which Mechthild of Magdeburg was the author: here we find all life, love, passion, and poetry, untroubled by any shadow of reflection. She has given utterance to her deepest experiences and emotions not in the ceremonial language of churches and theology, but in her sonorous native tongue which she handles with masterly poetical power. But, not only pious nuns and women but also monks and other men considered, after Bernard's explanation of the *Song of Songs*, the divine Lord and Redeemer as the Beloved and Bridegroom of their souls. Only those personalities whose piety finds its bearings in the classical mysticism of God of Augustine (Thomas Aquinas, Bonaventura), or in the mysticism of the Infinite of the Areopagites (Eckhart, Tauler), are further removed from nuptial mysticism. The two principal representatives of mediaeval nuptial mysticism are Suso and Jacopone da Todi. Also the tender, sweet piety of the author of *The Imitation* shows an outstanding erotic strain. In the same way mysticism in the days subsequent to the Reformation is mainly marked by the nuptial motive. John of the Cross and Teresa are the most prominent nuptial mystics; even in the case of Angelus Silesius, the dispassionate mystic of the infinite, the nuptial idea is strongly marked. Pietistic religion in the Netherlands and in Germany often displays an intensely erotic character. Zinzendorf has worked out the erotic motive in the most decisive way. But also outside Christianity the bridal idea plays an important part in mystical experience. In Persian Sûfism the mystical relationship with the divinity is considered as a delightful and soothing relation of love, or as an enthusiastic erotically tinged friendship. In India a sweet and passionate eroticism is attached to the mystical veneration of the Redeemer-God Krishna or Râma, an incarnation of Vishnu. The erotic Krishna songs are exactly similar to the hymns of love about Jesus in the West. Also Kâbir, the founder of the mixed Hindu-Islamic sect of the Sikhs, describes the intercourse with God as a fervent nuptial relationship.

The religious relation of the soul to God has been represented in the nuptial mysticism of both East and West as a tender erotic intercourse. The whole poetical vocabulary of this mysticism is erotic: the glance of love and the word of love, the chamber of love and the bed of love, the bliss of love and the pain of love, the play of love and the jests of love, embracings and huggings, resting on the bosom and pressing to the heart, fondling and kissing, the giving of self, the undressing and the wedlock — all the individual concrete images of love poetry are repeated in the confessions and spiritual songs of nuptial mystics. As in primitive sexual rites, so also in the sublime love mysticism, the soul has always been considered as the female and God as the male part of the love relation. The passionate surrender of self to the Heavenly Bridegroom often unites with the tender motherly love to the Child of God. Languorous nuns who imagine they are playing the rôle of the Mother of God, speak of pregnancy and childbirth, of the fondling and nourishing of the babe Jesus. Even in the case of Angelus Silesius, who is free of all sentimental exaggeration, we meet these strange pictures. The Indian Krishna and the Persian Sûfi mysticisms contain the affectionate motherly fondling of the divine Bambino.

For the passionate intoxication of mystical eroticism two explanations are ready to hand. Religious eroticism is explained as a sublimation of physical eroticism. Psychoanalytical research has confirmed this explanation; in mystical love-passion the controlled, inhibited sexual impulse thus prevented from natural functioning, finds an artificial relief, an unnatural satisfaction in the life of fantasy. This psycho-pathological explanation corresponds fundamentally with the historical theory that sees in mystical eroticism only a survival of primitive sexual rites. Coarse dramatic poems on sexual union with God became more and more refined, in the course of historical development, into fragrant poetry on bridal mysticism; the bodily function has been replaced by multi-coloured pictures of fantasy. Both theories are, in a measure, right, for there is no doubt that in the mysticism of love the natural sexual impulse plays a part; there is just as little doubt that the idea of community of nature of Man and God has been inherited from primitive religion. In Hellenistic as in Gnostic mysticism, perhaps, too, in Indian Krishna mysticism, the connections of mystical bridal symbolism with the primitive cult of sex are very direct. Both explanations, however, are unsatisfactory; they miss the kernel of the matter psychologically. Erotic symbolism has to be understood from the psychological character of this special type of mystical experience. This mystical experience compels the pious to interpret, to fashion, and to develop it, by erotic images.

Ecstasy (or the state nearest akin to ecstasy) is experienced by the mystic as an incomprehensible miracle that needs to be explained and illustrated. The unsophisticated who are not able to master this experience in the language of speculative metaphysics use analogies from ordinary human experience. The complete surrender of self to the highest Good, the experience of the complete union of the " I " with the " Thou " and the rapture resulting therefrom, has an analogy to the union of two human beings in love. Even the mysticism of the infinite which has a philosophical tendency and which is free of any erotic strain uses sexual love as a symbol of ecstatic experiences. The Brhad-âranyaka-Upanishad says: " As one in the embrace of a beloved wife is unconscious of internal or external occurrences, so the spirit who is in the embrace of the primal Self is unconscious of internal or external occurrences." Plotinus says of ecstatic union: " There is no space between the Soul and the highest Good; there are no longer two, but both are united in one; they cannot be separated from each other so long as one is there. This union is imitated in this world by lovers and loved when they wish to unite in one being." If the greatest and most spiritual of all mystics saw the profoundest symbol of mystical union in the sexual union, how much more must simple-minded nuns, to whom speculative and philosophical reflection is as unknown as psycho-analysis, explain to themselves the miracle of ecstatic delight as a tender voluptuous bliss.

The experience of a highest Good, the complete surrender to it by which self-consciousness is annihilated, is in itself a purely spiritual action; but in actual psychical life, as with all experiences of value, it is supported by, accompanied by, and wrapped up in feelings, emotions, moods, and instinctive impulses. In this psychic law we find the reason for the fact that purely spiritual experience of the highest Good has the tendency to unite with sexual impulses and desires. Herein originates the double meaning of the word " love," which personal theistic mysticism has chosen as its central idea at all times. Sometimes it means the instinctive sexual inclination, desire, and passion for sensual sexual union, and this meaning is philologically the original meaning, as the Indian word *bhakti* (" enjoyment of love ") especially shows. It also means purely psychical love, the immaculate, spiritual, contemplative experience of the highest Good, which is free from egoistic aims. In spiritualistic mysticism, in which strong philosophical motives are at work, the pure experience of the *summum bonum*, the God-love, remains free from all sexual impulses and inclinations; on the contrary, in naïve mysticism, where mystical experience is neither limited nor regulated by any philosophical ideas, the sentimental, instinctive sexual love-experience associates itself with the sublime mystical love-experience and with mystical eroticism. But here, too, the fundamental experience is no emotional phenomenon, but the pure spiritual act of valuation which aims at a metaphysical object. The centre of nuptial mysticism is the specifically mystical element; the sexual element belongs to the circumference.

Nuptial mysticism is marked by a strong emotionalism. The desire to obtain a constant and utmost supply of emotional effects is to some extent pathological. According to a psychological law, however, active emotions of great intensity evaporate rapidly, though the emotional experiences of these mystics have a longer life than normal psychical experiences owing to an irregular or pathological increase of the whole emotional life. On the other hand, strong emotions are followed by an exhaustion of the emotional life, and the reaction is all the greater; the highest activity of the feelings is followed by complete apathy, a deadening of the emotions, from which, however, suddenly and involuntarily a new emotional experience supervenes. Nevertheless, on the one hand by an effort of will directed to recover it, on the other by complete resignation, this change can be induced and hastened. Mystics, yearning to experience emotions, again and again complain of their emotional wells being dried up; they characterize these spiritual conditions as *siccitas*, drought, dryness, cold, darkness, emptiness, and thirst. It is this polarity of emotional life that creates the criterion of the presence of God. In the highest bliss the pious feel the nearness of God, in despair His remoteness. This swinging between the heights of joy and the depths of despair, between the nearness and remoteness of God is explained by the vivid fantasy of simple mystics as an animated love drama, as depicted in the love poetry of the Jewish *Song of Songs* or in the Indian *Gitagovinda* in most vivid colours. The heavenly Bridegroom unites secretly with the loving soul; He embraces, kisses, and cherishes it with unutterable tenderness. But the sweet delight of the joy of love does not last long. " It cannot endure for long when two lovers unite secretly," says Mechthild of Magdeburg. The lover flees from the arms of the bride and abides for some time far away to try her faithfulness; she, desperately unhappy about her isolation, mourns and sighs for the lost one, until finally he returns and the joys of love are renewed. This lawful change in the emotional life is illustrated by simple mystics in the same way as is ecstasy by pictures of fantasy in love poetry, but the union of these erotic pictures of fantasy with the moods, emotions, and experiences of worth veiled by them are not subsequent and conscious, but unconscious in the centre of the experience itself.

So erotic symbolism has its origin inwardly in the experi-

ences of the simple, emotional, imaginative mysticism. The
erotic tendencies immanent in mystical experiences are often
increased by real, genuine, natural sexual emotions, the normal
function of which has been inhibited owing to a delayed pu-
berty or to a compulsory celibacy and which seeks a psychical
and imaginative satisfaction in meditation and prayer. There
is something true in the hard and cynical words of Nietzsche:
" The envious look of the bitch of sensuality darts from all
their actions. Right up to the heights of their virtue, right
down to the depths of their chilled spirits this beast and its
malevolence pursues them." Very distinctly one can notice
the fervent impulse and passion of the natural sexual instinct
in the case of those languorous nuns with whom the spiritual
imaginative intercourse with the Bridegroom and the divine
Bambino takes the form of sexual pathological fetishism.
However, everybody who knows the whole pious life of female
mystics in its deepest spirituality and divine fervour, will
comprehend that the natural sexual emotion is only a secondary consideration. Sexual eroticism belongs to the periphery
of mystical experience, it does not stand in the centre.

The prayer of nuptial mystics is in its fundamental principles the same as the normal type of mystical prayer. The
ascent from concentration to contemplation can clearly be
observed in both cases. The difference is found in the method
of prayer: the prayer of love mysticism has a much more personal and human character than spiritualistic mysticism. In
the former the elevation of the soul to the highest Good becomes
a languorous, intoxicated love conversation with the heavenly
Bridegroom. Concentration by will-power on the highest becomes a consuming love longing, the blissful contemplation of
the *summum bonum* becomes a voluptuous love delight, and
intimate love conversation a flirting love game which takes
place in stammering language or images of fantasy without
words. In prayer tenderly intimate intercourse of love of mystical souls with the heavenly Bridegroom is held. " Prayer,"
says Mechthild of Magdeburg, " brings together the two lovers,
God and the Soul, in a place of delight where they speak freely
of their love."

1. *The Introductory Words of the Prayer*. Even the in-

troductory words of the prayer show the erotic character of this mysticism. The following expressions are just as strange to spiritualistic mysticism as to primitive religion and to prophetic piety. À Kempis exclaims: " O most sweet and most beloved Jesus! " " *O dolce e amoroso cavaliere*," cries Catherine of Siena. " O, beloved of my heart, O darling little Jesu! " is the invocation of Margaret Ebner.

2. *The Longing for Love.* The supplication for the mystical enjoyment of God becomes in nuptial mysticism a supplication for the delight of love in the arms of the heavenly Bridegroom. Thus Suso prays: " The bedchamber is closed on our intimacy, our love couch is bedecked with flowers. Come, O my beloved! Nothing remains now but for you to take me in the arms of Thy boundless love to let me fall into a blissful sleep." Mechthild prays: " O Lord, love me much, love me often, love me long. The oftener Thou lovest me, the purer I shall be; the more lustily Thou lovest me, the more beauteous I shall be; the longer Thou lovest me, the holier I shall be here on earth."

In the state of *siccitas*, of emotional aridity, in which all tender moods are dried up, the longing for God's delight becomes a heart rending complaint of love. The despairing soul, pining for love, complains of her terrible need and isolation and sighs intensely and fervently for its remote and hidden Bridegroom. " Thou hast wounded my inmost heart," cries Gertrude of Helfta, " by thy form and beauty. If I am not united to Thee, I shall be forever unhappy."

3. *Love-delight.* When the chaste state of emotional indifference has been replaced by the lustful heat of a love emotion, then the heart's rapture overflows in a stream of sweet and intimate love talk. " Now I begin," Suso avows, " to speak freely. I wish to talk with my Lord, with my husband, nobody can prevent me, I will fondle my beloved. That is what I long for with all my heart." The emotion is often so intense that the man, filled with the grace of God, loses power of speech and can only mumble incoherently. " These are words of love," Teresa teaches us, " in its sweet delight, the soul no longer knows the difference between God and itself. The love which it received from Him produces the result that

it finds itself again in Him, forgetting itself, as if it were his own; in intoxicated bliss it can only stammer." Sometimes, however, the bliss of love remains entirely mute; the love prayer is then ðnly a speechless rapture and enjoyment, fondling and embracing. " O my Beloved," says Suso, " O fulfilment of all my desires, what shall I say, O Beloved Lord, as my love has taken away my speech? My heart is full of love words, if only my tongue could utter them. My emotion is unfathomable, my love is boundless and therefore I have no words for what is in my mind and heart! " The poetical love prayers of the nuptial mystics only give us a feeble illustration of the intoxicated love stammering and the delicious dalliance in these gracious hours. Suso's words are an illustration: " Thou art the All-highest to my eyes; the All-sweetest to my mouth; the most tender to my touch and the most Beloved of my heart." " Thou art my King, Thou art my Lord, Thou art my Love, Thou art my Joy, Thou art my Happy Hour and my Joyful Day, Thou art All that creates a joyous love in my heart. And therefore, O my Beloved, what is the use of uttering words? Thou art mine and I am Thine, and thus it must ever remain."

The prayer of nuptial mysticism, of all forms of mystical prayer, is the most closely related to simple supplicatory prayer. In it there lives something of the simple eudaemonism and egoism of the naïve suppliant: it unites to the exclusive address to God the desire for pleasurable moods and emotions, behind which a certain egoism and a secret joy in pleasure is hidden. The idea of God underlying this prayer shows the same concrete anthropomorphism as underlies all primitive prayer. God is not the completely spiritual, the infinite *summum bonum*, but the sweet, loving, and tender Bridegroom, who thinks and feels as humanly as the pious soul and who is as full of warm love passion as this soul which is consuming itself in its love for Him. The prayer of erotic mysticism further shows much more distinctly than purely contemplative mystical prayer the primitive realism of direct intercourse with God. The relationship with God is, as in simple prayer, the distinct reflex of a sociological connection, viz., the earthly nuptial and love relationship. Just as in an intimate relation of love, shyness, veneration, and a feeling of dependence are suppressed in the prayer. Mechthild has been asked by the Lord " to rid herself of fear and bashfulness." Teresa tells us that in her intoxication of love, " she speaks with God boldly." Katherine of Emmerich reports: " When sometimes, at night, I was overwhelmed by love and compassion, and in my intoxication talked with Him intimately, as I have done since my childhood, and when I was watched I was accused of brazen audacity towards Him." The distinction between Man and God disappears: the lover and the Beloved are placed on the same level. " Thou art mine and I am Thine," cries the soul that has been united with the heavenly Bridegroom, and these words of prayer resound in the divine echo. " Thou art mine and I am thine," answers Christ to Teresa. " Thou art my love as I am Thine," says the Redeemer to Margaret Ebner. The consciousness of the distance between Man and God which characterizes primitive prayer and which finds a very striking expression in the pure mystical contemplation of the *summum bonum,* has been extinguished in the love bliss of nuptial mysticism.

All these elements — the tender and passionate eroticism, the simple longing for delight, strong anthropomorphism, the reflex of earthly social conditions, the absence of the difference between Man and God — distinguish the prayer of nuptial mysticism clearly from that of purely spiritual mysticism. Nevertheless, compared with the latter, it is not an independent type of prayer, but merely a variant. The very fact that in the piety of nuptial mystics one finds spiritual contemplative prayers side by side with simple erotically tinged ones, and that the two kinds mingle, proves that they are not contraries. In the sweet nuptial love conversation the mystical concentration and contemplation of the *summum bonum* takes only an unpretentious, unsophisticated, and human form. The turning towards the Highest, the submergence in the Infinite loses its abstract character and assumes a vivid appearance, a concrete colouring. Nuptial mysticism has therefore one thing in common with cultual mysticism in that both, contrary to purely spiritual mysticism, have something sensuous in them. Cultual mysticism draws its fervour and warmth from gazing at a tangible, visible object of worship; nuptial mysticism inflames its passion and tenderness by erotic images and fantastic highly coloured imaginings. Yet both, in their divine love and rapture, are real mysticism.

(c) *Quietist Mysticism.* One can understand the quietist mysticism by considering it as the very contrary of emotional nuptial mysticism. Quietism tries to overcome by radical resignation and indifference the various states produced by the exhaustion of the emotion such as the deadening of feeling, " coldness," " aridity," and desolation. One first finds quietist thought in the case of the mediaeval nuptial mystics (Mechthild of Magdeburg, Suso, à Kempis); it is more strongly developed with Teresa; here it always subordinates itself to the nuptial motive. In the case of Francis of Sales, the quietist idea predominates over the nuptial motive. In the Roman Catholic mysticism of the seventeenth century quietism eventually gained an absolute mastery and resulted in a type of mystical experience that threatened the heart of Christian piety. With sound instinct the Church at last refused to allow any radical development of quietism. The older quietists, Francis of Sales, Madame Chantal, Brother Lawrence, Bishop Petrucci, Cardinal Bona, were as yet unmolested. Only later when through the writings of Madame Guyon and, even more so, through the *Guida Spiritale* of Molinos, quietist piety had gripped the whole of Roman Catholicism, was it stigmatized as heretical. Molinos had to retract, Fénelon had to withdraw his statements, Père Lacombe and Madame Guyon were persecuted. Expelled from the Catholic Church, quietism was welcomed by the Protestants (Arnold, Tersteegen). A parallel to quietist thought in Western mysticism is the kind of Indian Bhakti mysticism that extols *tyâga* (devotion) and *prapatti* (apathy) as religious ideals.

Quietist mysticism is unemotional. It aims at complete apathy, lack of will, vacancy of mind; the harsh mortification of sensuous emotions and natural feelings develops in the case of Madame Guyon into a pathological self-torment. Consistent quietist mysticism renounces all ecstatic and visionary experiences. Neither the extraordinary mystical experience nor the tender pleasurable emotions and melting moods of delight are the criterion of the gracious presence of God. Quietist mysticism is unimaginative in opposition to the wealth of imaginative pictures contained in bridal mysticism and cultual mysticism. The soul yearning for completion must, as Cardinal Bona says, " become more and more free from imaginations and pictures, faith must become naked faith through which it addresses itself directly and only to God." Quietist mysticism condemns as secret egoism the erotic desire of nuptial mystics for " sweet feelings and tender consolations " (Teresa), for the " *être caressé* " (Guyon). " Piety," says Francis of Sales, " is not this mild mood, not this tangible consolation nor the sweet tenderness of the heart, which produces tears and sighs. The really devout man has to accept from the hand of God pleasurable and painful moods alike: light and darkness, lightness and sterility, strength and weakness, temptation, endeavour, dulness, and uncertainty." The state of " dryness," of complete inner despair and isolation, is meant to be a spiritual martyrdom, as the imitation of the crucified Redeemer through which the soul acquires perfection. " *Qui n'a pas le goût de la croix, n'a pas le goût de Dieu*," says Madame Guyon.

The religious ideal of quietist mysticism is the " holy indifference," the absolute resignation, the complete conformity of human will with that of God, the selfless love of God (*amour désinteressé*). Quietist prayer, therefore, can be nothing else than the realization of the " holy indifference." " Prayer and resignation are one and the same thing," so runs an axiom of Molinos. This quietist indifference is a vague, gentle mood, devoid of any emotionalism, therefore it does not express itself by spoken prayers or ejaculations. In deepest rest and in complete silence reposes the soul that has killed all its desires and aspirations. Molinos and Brother Lawrence did not utter a word while praying, they were incapable even of saying the Lord's Prayer. Madame Guyon says of the soul that is in the state of indifference: " It is not capable of a verbal prayer. . . . A simple Lord's Prayer would take an hour." However, not only free of words, but free of all concrete imaginings must the praying person keep himself. Bishop Pietro Petrucci says: " The inward prayer of the heart which the soul utters without words in the peace and stillness it has in God, is the expression of a pure, simple, naked, and mystical faith that has been freed from all support of knowledge, from all feeling and all imaginations and pictures — it is the expression of a pure free love, free from the desire for reward." One of the forbidden phrases of Molinos reads: " When praying, one has to persevere with a dim and general belief in peace and one has to free oneself from any other concrete thought of the attributes of God." The extinction in the soul of all imaginative, emotional, and volitional life sometimes involves a dimming consciousness. Hence Madame Guyon's maxim: " This prayer needs no words, nay, the praying person need not even once be conscious of his praying."

The whole contents of quietist prayer consists in the surrender of the will to God, the absolute submission to His will, the sacrifice of the ego. A Spanish mystic, Gregor Lopey, prayed for three years in no other words than these: " Thy will be done on earth, as it is in Heaven. Amen. Jesus!" Madame Chantal prays in a state of profound despair: " Yea, O Lord, do what pleases Thee. I desire it. Destroy me, I am content. Crush me, it is my will. Rend in pieces, break and burn everything according to Thy desire. I belong wholly to Thee." The same self-disdain and self-sacrifice have been expressed in one of Madame Guyon's prayers: " O Thou Will of God, Thou wouldst be my paradise in hell! O my God, destroy my will and there shall be nothing I love more than my destruction! O Thou, Will of my God, Thou art the Paradise of Paradises, the God of my God!"

Quietist indifference excludes all supplication from prayer, for supplication is a result of desire, longing, and aspirations, which the quietist mystic must destroy. " The soul," says Francis of Sales, " has no other attitude towards God than that of waiting, which excludes fear and hope as symptoms of egoism." As our own desires and self-will have to be destroyed, supplication for spiritual gifts and mercies is just as much prohibited as that for life and health.

Madame Guyon assured Bossuet that she was incapable of asking God for anything in prayer. A condemned phrase of Molinos says: " To him who has entrusted himself to God's

will, it is not becoming to ask God for anything, for supplication as an act of one's own will and one's own choice is an
imperfection and a desire that God's will should be conformed
to ours and not ours to His." Moreover, the prayers of thanksgiving and of praise are rejected. Just as these souls are not
allowed to ask God for anything, so they may not thank Him
for anything, as both are acts of one's own will.

As a pure prayer of surrender the prayer of quietist mysticism has a certain passive character; the praying person
neither demands nor entreats, he submits himself without reserve to the sovereign will of God. Therefore quietists like
to speak of " passive prayer " or " passive prayer of the heart "
as the only true and complete prayer. They compare the
quiet, God-surrendered soul with wax that can be pressed and
moulded to God's liking, with a lifeless statue which its owner
can place and replace whenever he likes. Francis of Sales
says: " If one has entered into the presence of God, one always
remains therein. One does not look at Him, nor does one
speak of Him, one simply remains where one has been placed
by God like a statue in a recess. Were you to ask a statue:
' Why art thou here? ' it would reply: ' Because the sculptor
placed me here.'

' Why dost thou not move? '

' Because he wishes that I remain at rest here.'

' But wouldst thou not like to have the strength to move in
order to go nearer to him? '

' No, not unless he should command it.'

' Hast thou then no desires at all? '

' No, for I am there where my Master placed me. His
wishes are the only satisfaction of my being.' "

But this passivity and lack of will is but the outer side of
quietist devotional prayer; behind it is hidden a living activity
and volitional power. According to Madame Guyon the quiet
passive prayer of the heart is not a dull brooding without life,
but a free lively adherence to God. The unconditional and
complete self-surrender to God, the radical sacrifice of will, is
an act of volition; it is only possible under a high tension of
spiritual activity and is not consistent with the quenching of
an illumined consciousness. Only when this tension of will

has become impaired, consciousness begins to be troubled, the mystical soul passes from the state of prayer, of indifference, into a Nirvana-like state of "mystical death," of "annihilation."

Quietist praying is sustained and permeated by the mysterious experience of the presence of God in the deepest places of the soul, which is characteristic of all mystical prayer. In tranquil silence and in peaceful indifference the quietist feels the gentle breathing of God. To this extremely vague, indefinite mood of indifference is attached the experience of the presence of the Infinite. For some quietist mystics devotional prayer is reduced to a mere experience of the presence of God. Brother Lawrence, in whose life quietist piety appears in perfected form, says his prayers are nothing but " the practice of the presence of God."

Quietist prayer is the most radical form that praying can assume. Quietist mysticism dispels natural simple prayer just as does cold philosophical criticism. The thought of God's presence is all that finally remains of real prayer. Herein lies the only difference between quietist prayer and the Buddhist renunciation of self, between the " holy indifference " of Christian Quietists and the painless and joyless *upekkhâ* of the Buddhist mendicant monks. They were really Buddhist moods and thoughts that dominated the quietist mysticism of the seventeenth century and wasted the very marrow of Christian piety.

(d) *Absorption in Buddhism.* " What prayer is to other religions, the devotion of absorption is to Buddhism." This judgement of Oldenberg is very much the same as that of another very fine interpreter of Buddhist mysticism, Hermann Beckh. " One can understand the nature of Buddhism as a religion and at the same time its difference from other religions only by accentuating the importance of meditation and comparing it with the part prayer plays in other religions. If in the latter prayer means the nerve of the religious life, this nerve is in Buddhism meditation and meditative absorption in the spiritual or metaphysical." This self-abnegation, indeed, plays the same part in Buddhism as does meditative and contemplative prayer in neo-Platonic, Sûfistic,

Hindu, and Christian mysticism. It is true that, at first sight, the Buddhist meditation appears completely different from mystical prayer. All the characteristics of mystical prayer are missing: the turning to God as the Highest Good, the experience of His presence in the depths of the soul, the living contact and " intercourse " with the Divine. Yet, however different the phenomenological structure of mystical prayer seems to be from that of Buddhist meditative absorption their psychological relationship is just as evident. The very comparison of the four stages of *Jhâna* with the stages of prayer of Christian and neo-Platonic mystics shows very strikingly that the psychical proceedings are analogous in both cases. But it is not only a psychologically similar, but ultimately a phenomenological relationship. Even Buddhist meditation is in its way an ascent to the *summum bonum,* certainly not in a positive sense, not the vital turning to a supreme Divine Reality, but in a negative sense, an emptying of self and a giving-up of self, that finds its culminating point in Nirvana. As Nirvana is nothing else than the *summum bonum* of mysticism, only in its most negative form, the self-abnegation that aims at Nirvana is nothing but an ascent to the Highest and the Last, as in a mystical prayer. Buddhistic meditation has only rejected all those elements which make mystical prayer to be prayer in the original sense of the word. Buddhistic absorption is mystical " prayer " in the very sense in which Buddhism is a mystical " religion." [3]

SUMMARY OF THE CHARACTERISTICS OF MYSTICAL PRAYER

Mystical prayer is, in its most classical form, the sublimest kind of prayer. It is free from egoism, eudaemonism, and the anthropomorphism of primitive prayers, and yet it is real, living prayer, no pallid product of abstraction as is the philosophical ideal of prayer that has been born out of rational and ethical criticism. The serene and sublime contemplation of the *summum bonum* in which the devout person surrenders

[3] As I have treated Buddhistic meditation in a special monograph (Munich 1918, second edition 1920) this reference to it here may suffice.

himself to the infinite God, appears to many as the purest and
most tender, the most fervent and profoundest form of all
prayers. Many people are inclined to call the mystical prayer,
i.e., the ascent of the soul to the Highest Good, the most complete form of prayer. For even the prophetic type of prayer
of the Bible, to which our inquiry now turns, does not show
that refinement, tenderness, and world-denying spirituality
characteristic of the Augustinian type of mystical prayer. The
devotional religion of both the Old and New Testaments and
of the Reformation has not the impressive movement of mystical prayer. Nevertheless, the prayer of the Bible and the
Reformation in its unpretentious simplicity and childlike sincerity of heart, in its healthy passion and original, native
power stands incomparably nearer to genuinely human feelings than contemplative, mystical devotion in its calm renunciation and majestic solemnity, its melting tenderness and
consuming, passionate surrender.

CHAPTER IX

PRAYER IN PROPHETIC RELIGION

As with mystical prayer, there are considerable difficulties incident to the study of prayer as it occurs in the scriptures of prophetic religion. Furthermore, there are relatively few individuals who are perfectly clear examples of this type of personal religion. The devotional life of by far the larger number of religious geniuses represents in varying degrees a mixture of the mystical and prophetic. We know but little of the prayer of the truly creative personalities of prophetic religion; too little, at least, for any exhaustive psychological examination.

We have no direct evidence of the nature of the devotional life of Moses and Zoroaster, the fathers of the two religions of revelation. The prayers preserved in the Pentateuch of Moses (Jahvist and Elohist) and the Gathas of Zoroaster are in their present form compositions of their disciples. Yet they give a convincing picture of the forceful, dramatic realism which distinguishes the devotional intercourse of these men with God. We possess very valuable authentic testimony about the prayer life of the Old Testament prophets, of Jesus, and of Paul; unfortunately, however, but few actual prayers — none of Paul's in exact wording.

In order to understand and fill out these sporadic and fragmentary reports it is necessary for us to turn to the prayers of those who, while retaining their own spontaneity, independence, and individuality, have been inspired by these biblical characters. These are the anonymous Hebrew writers of the Psalms, who gave poetic form to prophetic prayer, and those personalities of the Reformation and of modern times whose devotional life is inspired throughout by that of the personalities of Scripture, particularly by that of Jesus. Luther, Zwingli, Calvin, Fox, Bunyan, Pascal, Kierkegaard are among these. The evidences of their lives of prayer are incomparably richer and more detailed than those of the men of the Bible, the most abundant material being contained in Luther's writings. Investigation of the devotional life of such individuals, who are clearly of the prophetic type, permits the discovery of prophetic elements appearing in the prayers of such personalities as are to be reckoned among the mystics: Augustine, Francis, Ignatius, and the Indian Bhaktas.

I. Occasion and Motive of Prayer

The mystic tends to resolve prayer into contemplation and absorption; in prophetic devotion the naïve prayer of primitive man resumes its realistic power and vitality. A fresh and original creation of prayer takes place on the summit of the religious experience of these great prophetic personalities. Usually, as with primitive man, it is the concrete need of the moment which gives occasion for the prayer. It is when the healthy love of life, the elemental, vital sense is menaced, or when a conflict arises between a value experienced and the actual reality which threatens it, that the motives arise for calling upon God in prayer.

The prophet Amos, fearfully apprehensive of the calamity coming upon Israel, cries out: " O Lord Jahve forgive! O Lord Jahve cease! " When Jahve summons Jeremiah to preach as a prophet, he recoils before the difficulties of the prophetic calling. A mournful entreaty is born of the inner division between the realized task and the natural feeling of weakness: " Ah, Lord Jahve! behold, I know not how to speak: for I am a child." This man's prophetic activity was unsuccessful; it only involved him in ignominy and persecution. The dreadful humiliation of his prophetic self-respect, the grief because of the shipwreck of his life-work which he had received at Jahve's hands drove him to pour out in prayer before God all his dire need and despair.

Jesus, who in His resolve " to give His life for many," had come to Jerusalem, when He felt Himself in the hand of His enemies began in Gethsemane to be " greatly amazed and sore troubled." Overcome by the horror of death He uttered a threefold agonized cry for help to His Father: "Father, if it be possible let this cup pass away from me." Upon the cross, forsaken by all His disciples, viewing the external collapse of His life-work and feeling the darkness of death closing over the glory of His Messianic future, He breaks out in passionate lament: "My God, my God, why hast thou forsaken me?" a cry of fear from one sunk in the depths of despair. Paul, suffering severely the "thorn in the flesh, a messenger of Satan to buffet me," cries to the Lord thrice for deliverance from it. When in prison Savonarola faced execution he gave vent to his deep anguish in a powerful prayer: "Let me not be put in shame, dear Jesus, for in Thee only do I hope; there is no deliverance for me except in Thee, O Lord. All have forsaken me; for my spiritual brothers and sons have rejected me, my spiritual children abhor me. Cast me not away from Thy presence." Luther stood before the Imperial Diet at Worms in a decisive hour. The conflict between his faith in the righteousness of the cause for which he fought and the anxious fear of a threatened catastrophe found expression in a vehement prayer: "Ah God! Ah God! O Thou my God, O Thou my God, stand by me, against all the world, wisdom and reason; do Thou do it, Thou must do it, Thou alone. It is indeed not my cause, but Thine." John Bunyan fought a fearful battle for the assurance of his salvation; his torturing consciousness of sin left no room for a trustful feeling of life. He prays: "O Lord, I beseech Thee, show me that Thou hast loved me with everlasting love."

But it is not only one's own personal need which is the occasion of the prayer of these devout spirits, but also common need, even that of strangers. The prophets of the Old Testament, who feel and suffer with their brethren, are driven by the trouble and danger of their people to intercede ever and again with Jahve that he will consider and forgive faithless and wayward Israel. Jesus on the cross cries to His Father for pardon for His enemies. Paul never grows weary of supplicating divine grace for his brethren and his Churches.

Crises, temptations, and needs are the chief, but of course, not the only occasions for prayer. With prophetic personalities sometimes also ecstatic revelations, the dissolving of torturing doubts, blessed insight into God's plans and counsels, the sudden enjoyment of God's goodness, protection, and guidance are the determining experiences. Thus, as with primitive man, good fortune as well as dire need, even if much less frequently, is the cause of prayer. Among Jeremiah's outpourings there is but one prayer of adoration: " There is none like unto Thee, O Jahve; Thou art great and Thy name is great in might." Four prayers have come down to us from Jesus: an appeal for help, an intercession, a cry of fear, and only one outburst of joy. As all doubts of His being the Messiah cleared away and the profound mystery of His sonship to God broke upon Jesus, the certainty and blessedness of that mystery known only to the childlike and simple of heart streamed over Him and poured itself out in a prayer of joyful thanksgiving: " I thank Thee, O Father, Lord of heaven and earth, that Thou didst hide these things from the wise and understanding, and didst reveal them unto babes." Among the many prayers of Luther, we find a surprisingly small number of such as give praise and thanks. The contrast with mystical prayer could not be clearer. In mysticism, contemplative adoration forms the climax of all prayer and meditation; in prophetic religion, praise and thanksgiving are secondary to petition and intercession.

The experiences that form the motives of prayer are, therefore, the same as with primitive man, *emotions* of great intensity, which press for discharge, whose character is most frequently that of suffering, more rarely that of joy. But in contrast with those which drive primitive man to prayer, the emotions are almost always produced by experiences of spiritual value. These experiences, however, are not non-egoistic and wholly disinterested, like the experience of the highest good, which, in mystical meditation is the motive of prayer and the devotional state.

When he prays, the mystic, with concentrated gaze beholds undisturbed one supreme spiritual Reality, which for him is the embodiment of all values, and in this contemplation he forgets and loses himself. The emotions which move the prophetic genius to prayer possess a positive reference to a self; his own or another's ego has to him a worth, or a simultaneous worthiness and unworthiness. The emotions of terror, fear, shame, depression, grief, distress, remorse, or those of pride and delight, rapture and bliss, are related directly to the elementary feeling of self. In disagreeable emotions, one's own vital feeling, that is, the feeling of the value of one's existence and of life and the world in general threatens to diminish, while in agreeable emotions it is intensified. This is not, as with primitive man, a matter solely of physical being and its comforts, but of the meaning and worth of life, of life which is spiritual, personal, ideal.

The chief motive of prophetic prayer lies, therefore, in painful emotions. " In my distress I called upon Jahve, and cried unto my God." " My soul is cast down within me, therefore do I remember Thee." " When a Christian is in distress, anxiety and trouble," says Luther, " there is no other comfort or counsel except in holding fast by prayer and crying to God for help." And again, " No one prays for anything deeply who has not been deeply alarmed." " What kind of a prayer would it be if need were not there and did not so oppress us that we felt it? " Calvin says that " the best spur to calling upon God is for saints when they are caught in need and tortured by the greatest disquiet." Luther has illustrated the emotional character of the experiences giving rise to prayer with remarkable plasticity of language when he describes genuine prayer as " living," " strong," " powerful," " mighty," " earnest," " anxious," " troubled," " passionate," " vehement," " fervent," " ardent." He speaks of " calling upon God in heat." Bunyan exclaims: " O the heat, strength, life, vigour, and affection that is in right prayer! " The vital feeling touched by this painful emotion manifests itself in an intensive striving and longing to overcome the inhibitions and to maintain that which is so dear. Instinctive, unconscious effort to banish that which menaces the vital feeling is involuntarily associated with the emotion. The painful state of feeling is not merely a passive condition of stimulation and impression, but the psychic activity is ever roused to direct itself to the preservation of the spiritual personality. " Trouble," in the words of Luther, " touches the heart and wakens ardent longing for God's help." Luther characterizes this element in the experience which produces prayer as "inward, earnest, fervent desire," as "heartfelt longing and yearning," "sighing and craving from the bottom of the heart." He speaks also of "bold" and "thirsting" prayer. Bunyan calls the striving urged on by the emotion, "hunger." Speaking of his prayer for the assurance of salvation, he says: "I cannot express with what yearning and longing I cried to Christ."

The consciousness of complete dependence upon a higher will, which primitive man feels only in definite experiences, such as need, desire, and reverence for that which is sacred, is the sum and substance of the whole religious life of prophetic individuals. Everywhere and always, the pious man traces the guiding hand of God. In all things great and small, in happiness and unhappiness, in the ways of common life and in the sanctuary, he realizes his complete dependence upon Him who is Lord of all, whose will determines everything which happens. It is this vital feeling of the nearness of God and dependence upon Him which causes in the moment of strong, inner excitement the explicit turning to God and calling upon Him. The prayer may be a despairing lament, but usually the consciousness of dependence, on the one hand, and the powerful will to live and instinct of self-preservation on the other, give rise to confidence and trust; God can and will save me. Hope is the real motive from which prayer proceeds, while painful emotion is its compelling, driving power. Luther says: "The first stone in prayer is confidence." "He who would pray must first believe." "The best thing of all in prayer is faith." "Right prayer must flow from such faith and trust." "The real and actual cause, the *efficiens causa* of prayer is faith." Bunyan writes: "The Spirit helps the soul to turn the face to God by putting a soft feeling of grace in the heart in order to encourage it to go to God." Calvin, in his theological discussion of prayer, holds that "right prayer goes forth in the first place from the experience of need, then from trust in the promise." "From both emotions, fear and hope, should prayer issue from pious souls."

The emotional intensity of sympathy, the feeling of oneself in another's distress, bodily or mental, urges to prayer, as does the sense of one's own need. The threatened good represented in another human personality is felt as if embodied in one's own ego. With pity always comes the effort to help. But the work of succour is not enough; the consciousness of the entire dependence of all that happens upon God and the expectation of His aid thus lead to intercession.

The joyful emotions giving rise to prayer may dispense with all reference to the ego, as is the rule in mystic devotion. Self-forgetful surrender to the highest good creates the prayer of praise or adoration. In the pure prophetic experience, the agreeable emotions are chiefly related to one's own ego and its good. Bunyan puts among the motives of prayer, " the sweet feeling of the grace received, encouraging, comforting, strengthening, enlivening, enlightening grace." The feeling of joy, satisfaction, assurance, which fills pious souls when the tension is relieved, painful inhibitions are overcome, and revelations flash in the mind, is linked up with the consciousness of dependence, and thereby creates a feeling of profound gratitude to God from Whom come all knowledge, assurance of salvation, and redeeming grace. Prayer here takes the form of *thanksgiving*.

Prophetic prayer is therefore a spontaneous manifestation of emotion, an involuntary discharge, the " outpouring of the heart," as the Old Testament by a striking figure of speech has expressed it. All great masters of prayer have appropriated this figure as their definition of prayer. Bunyan speaks of " the opening of the heart, an affectionate pouring out of the soul, the unbosoming of a man's self." Calvin and Luther use similar language. Spontaneity and involuntary activity are marks of the emotional life. The emotions cannot, like ideas, be produced by an effort of the will; their origin does not depend on us. They overpower man and lay hold of his entire means of expression: mimicry, gesture, and speech. Religious emotions in the pious man force their way unconsciously and unexpectedly, from evident and inner necessity, to expression in prayer. Prayer wells up from the subconscious life of the soul. The individual feels a compelling impulse, he cannot do otherwise than pray. " I was forced to pray," occurs again and again in the confessions of George Fox. When the inner impulse was wanting he was not in a position to utter a prayer. Thus he writes: " I could not pray at a man's command." " Truly blessed is that necessity," cries Savonarola, " which drives me to God, compels me to speak with Him, urges me to pray to Him." " Right prayer," says Bunyan, " gushes from the heart when it overflows with trouble and bitterness, as blood is pressed out of the flesh by a heavy burden resting on it."

All psychic experiences which cannot be voluntarily set in motion, all that suddenly breaks into consciousness from the sphere of the unconscious, above all, everything which comes as inspiration, revelation, ecstasy, is considered by the religious person as supernatural and sent from God. Mystics see in the devotional state of " quietude," " union," and " rapture " the gift of divine grace. The worshipper cannot bestow it upon himself but must take it humbly, in utter passivity. Prophetic piety, likewise, attributes spontaneous prayer to the mysterious working of God. As Bunyan says, " God put it into my heart to cry to Him." Prophetic natures, when they have in view experiences spontaneously welling up from the unconscious life of the soul, like to speak of the " working of the Spirit." The " Spirit of God " is that mysterious power which pierces into the depths of the soul and compels the devout person irresistibly to pray. In concise language Paul writes: " The Spirit also helpeth our infirmity; for we know not how to pray as we ought; but the Spirit Himself maketh intercession for us with groanings which cannot be uttered." Luther says: " When the Holy Spirit specially touches and stirs the heart, then prayer is wont to become very hot." Fox confesses: " We pray privately and publicly according as the Spirit inspires us." According to Bunyan, without the Spirit man cannot pray, " for it is impossible for the heart to pour itself out without the Spirit's help." " What a great task," he exclaims, " for a poor soul who feels sin and the wrath of God to say believingly this one word — ' Father '! Therefore the Spirit must be sent into the hearts of God's people that they can say, ' Father.' "

Neither one's own necessity nor that of one's fellow men limits itself to certain moments and concrete situations. The need for and dependence upon God is an abiding state; therefore, in the religious life of the prophetic type also there are regular, daily, as well as special, motives for prayer. The motives of regular daily prayer, however, are determined not so much by the emotions as by moods relatively lacking in intensity. A general feeling of unrest, insecurity, dissatisfaction, of inner disharmony, or even, on the contrary, of satisfaction, pleasure, confidence, urges to prayer. Frequently, indeed, even this desire to pray is absent, and yet in such cases the prayer will not be neglected. The pious man betakes himself then voluntarily, with full consciousness, to prayer, either through meditation upon a religious idea, or by means of a formula of prayer, the meaning of which he makes his own through repetition of the words. He usually attains thus to a devotional mood from which now his own spontaneous prayer freely flows. Luther practised both methods of voluntary recollection in prayer or devotion. "I am sometimes," he says, "so cold and cheerless that I cannot pray; then I close my ears and say, 'I know God is not far from me, therefore I must cry to Him and invoke Him.' I set before myself the ingratitude and ungodly nature of the Adversary, and thereupon I become warm and burn with anger and hate and then I say, 'O Lord, hallowed be Thy name, Thy Kingdom come, and so on.' Thus my prayer grows warm and fervent. An excellent help and expedient for awakening prayer is to read, sing and hear God's Word and read through the Psalms carefully or even attend the ordinary service of the Church. There the heart gradually becomes warm and the Spirit is kindled in us."

To be sure, there is here no systematic psychological technique aiming at perfection in the art, as is peculiar to mysticism. "Prophetic piety," as Söderblom says, "is not mechanism nor training, but music in the soul." Yet it nurtures and demands a daily schooling in prayer. Luther speaks of "doing and practising prayer." Calvin desires the careful observance of regular daily times of prayer, not as a legal duty of meritorious service, but as "a discipline for our weakness by which it may be exercised and continually stimulated."

II. Form of Prayer

Prayer that breaks forth vehemently out of emotion is almost always a *free* outpouring of the heart. The words of prayer that have been spoken in decisive moments by the great masters of prayer are improvised, an individual creation of the moment. The petitioner does not borrow words from a formula, nor does he seek new words; they come to him spontaneously. The emotion creates its own peculiar expression from its own productive energy. True, spontaneous prayer, in the words of Bunyan, " is not a premeditated, stinted form, but a prayer extempore, made on a sudden according to what he felt, thought, or understood of himself." " Right prayer must as well in the outward part of it, in the outward expression as in the inward intention, come from what the soul does apprehend in the light of the spirit." Luther did not keep to the biblical words when he used the Lord's Prayer. The actual words of the prayer, like the experience giving rise to it, the spontaneously rising emotion, is the work of the divine Spirit. " The Spirit inspires the words," says George Fox.

Yet, as with primitive man, the spontaneity, the effective force and ardour of the prayer do not exclude the adoption of a devotional formula. Brief, energetic, and passionate ejaculatory prayer and sighs are frequently bound together in a form. Luther, Bunyan, Pascal, at the height of their religious experience, make use of biblical words. Even Jesus Himself on the cross, when His own words were swallowed up in the death agony, gave voice to His despairing outcry in the opening words of one of the Psalms. And yet His prayer is spontaneous, in no sense restricted or formal. " He did not pick His words," says Söderblom, " He did not think but poured out His anguish." The borrowed words receive a totally new content.

The principle of spontaneity and freedom in prophetic worship was carried so far by George Fox and with such logical radicalism that he rejected all fixed prayer, all praying " according to repetition," as antichristian and as contempt for the apostolic rule. Others of the prophetic type, not so extremely radical, value the prayer that clings to a traditional formula, rich in content, as preparation and stimulus towards spontaneous devotion. It is just at such times, when productivity is at a halt through emotional and spiritual " dryness," an experience surely not peculiar to the mystic, that it is necessary to resort to classic models of prayer, and to reanimate one's own drooping religious feelings. Luther exhorts: " Thus if one would pray by himself alone in the church or at home and has no better words or form, let him recite the Lord's Prayer and rouse his own spirit of worship with these or similar words." " Oral prayer is not to be despised but it is necessary to rouse and kindle the prayer of the heart." But this restricted prayer has a merely disciplinary significance; it is only, in the words of Sabatier, a " prelude to genuine, free prayer," or as Rothe puts it, " a means of learning how to pray aright." A devotional writer of the Reformation era in the preface to his little book of prayers offers this advice: " Thou shouldest not limit thyself to words such as these, but thou shouldest let fall the ladder of words as soon as thou hast ascended and hast entered into the secret of the praying spirit."

The primal creative act or religion is re-enacted at the summit of experience of the great religious leaders; the earliest phenomena of religion appear again in the prophetic experience. The first prayer uttered by man upon earth was a short passionate cry to a higher being for help. The prayers of the great prophets, born of deepest inner agitation, are brief outcries, consisting sometimes in a single ejaculation, often repeated several times in the same, or with only slightly varied words. The publican in Jesus' parable was justified through this simple language: " God, be merciful to me a sinner." Moreover, the Lord's Prayer, intended as a guide to prayer, shows the same rich brevity and unadorned simplicity which are the marks of genuine prayer. In Gethsemane Jesus repeated the same words three times. Luther's rule, " the fewer the words, the better the prayer, the more words the worse prayer," " one should pray briefly but often and fervently," admirably emphasizes the psychological fact that the spontaneous, emotional prayer manifests on its formal side a condensed brevity. Breadth and elaboration of diction, rounded periods and fulness of imagery, are sure signs that the prayer is of a literary character.

Prayer which springs forth from emotion, at least when it does not become one and the same cry repeated without change, is rather abrupt, sometimes even disconnected and incoherent. This abruptness of the order of thought does not exclude a rhythm in the words, as for example in the prayers of Jeremiah, Francis of Assisi, and Luther. Of course the rhythm is not perfectly regular and artificial, but a natural rhythm in harmony with the rise and fall of the emotion.

An ardent prayer may be a silent one of the heart. Augustine writes: " My confession, O my God, is mine, in Thy sight silently and not silently: in sound it is silent, in affection it cries aloud." A Jewish Chassid says: " Man may pray in a whisper, while his heart cries in his breast." It is true, intensive emotion most often makes itself heard in audible ejaculation, as in the case of naïve man. " I cry unto Jehovah with my voice "; " nevertheless Thou heardest the voice of my supplications when I cried unto Thee," confesses the psalmist. Jesus cried from the cross with a loud voice, " *Eli, Eli, lama sabacthani*"; that is, " My God, my God, why hast Thou forsaken me? " Luther was accustomed to stand in the evening by the window praying aloud.

The intensity of the emotion that moves to prayer may be so great that human language no longer suffices to express the agitation of the soul. The emotion finds only incomplete discharge, not in intelligible words, but in disordered sighs and stammerings. Bunyan says that, " the best prayers have often more groans than words," " words cease because of the overwhelming anxiety of the heart." " Even a Christian's moan," says Luther, " is a prayer." Yet, there are emotions both of joy and sorrow, which never manifest themselves even in formless stammering and inarticulate mutterings. The psychic agitation is so powerful that it deprives us of speech; we would speak, to lament or rejoice, to pour ourselves forth in utterance, but we are inhibited within. It is as if the emotions had become choked and were unable to find discharge through the avenues of the body. Thus the raging excitement, the irresistible compulsion, the passionate yearning desire, terminate

in an unspoken prayer of the heart. Paul calls such prayer
" groanings which cannot be uttered," in which " the Spirit
himself maketh intercession for us."   In this Pauline self-
revelation Luther and Bunyan have found again their deepest
experience of prayer.   Thus Bunyan writes: " Then a man
desires indeed when his desires are so strong, many and mighty
that all the words, tears and groans that can come from the
heart cannot utter them. . . . A man that truly prays one
prayer, shall after that never be able to express with his mouth
or pen the unutterable desires, sense, affection, and longing,
that went to God in that prayer."

Despite the external similarity, this wordless groaning is
still quite different from the *oratio mentalis* of the mystic.
The mystic keeps silence because fixed concentration, meditation and contemplation, are disturbed by speech; the prophet
is silent because the emotion is so great that language fails
him. In the former, speech is absent by reason of the emotionless, inner peace, or because of the ecstatic vision of the
supreme good; in the latter, inability to speak is due to the
overmastering, compelling power of the emotion.

The stammering and muttering which attempt to express
the psychic emotion consist in disconnected and imperfectly
articulated fragments of sentences and words, yet they employ
the natural form of speech.   Emotional experiences of an
ecstatic nature, as with the early Christians and the Quakers,
are likely to manifest themselves in a completely new and
incomprehensible language, the " speaking with tongues."
Glossolalia, a form of devotional language peculiar to individual ecstasy, is very contagious. Paul speaks of praying in
a tongue, " my spirit prayeth, but my understanding is un-
fruitful. For he that speaketh in a tongue speaketh not
unto men, but unto God."

III. Content of Prayer

The essential nature of mystical prayer is concentration and
absorption, that of prophetic prayer is discharge of emotion.
In the former, there is silence undisturbed by emotion, or a
mind steeped in contemplation, in the latter, an " outpouring

of the soul," a " crying unto God out of the depths." Mystical
prayer, at least in its beginning, is conscious and voluntary
direction, prophetic prayer is thoroughly naïve, and involuntary, an expression of oneself through inner necessity. Simply
and without restraint, the petitioner unveils himself to God;
he confides to Him the agitation and tumult of his inmost soul,
his fears and troubles, his desires and hopes, even his doubts
and rebellion. The object of mystical prayer is exclusively
God, the only reality, the highest worth; the object of prophetic
prayer is the sorrow and the joy, the anxiety and fear which
belong peculiarly to man, but also his reliance and confidence.
The mystic is familiar with self-observation and self-contemplation to the point of psychological self-analysis; the
humbleness and nothingness of his own ego into which he
absorbs himself in his devotion are the dark background from
which the infinity of God exalts itself with paradoxical effect.
Prophetic worship, on the other hand, is not methodical self-
contemplation, but passionate self-manifestation.

The essential content of prophetic prayer is the unrestricted
expression of the compelling emotion. Calvin defines prayer
as " instituted in order that we may confess our needs to God
and bring Him our complaints as children bring their griev-
ances confidently to their parents." Many Christian mystics,
also, influenced by the spirit of prayer of the scriptures, express themselves thus naïvely in worship. Teresa was
accustomed in her " prayer of quiet " " to place her needs
quite simply before God."

(a) Complaint and Question

One's need may be expressed merely in the form of a complaint. In the prayers of biblical characters, questions constantly recur full of doubt and reproach. " From the depths
of the abyss," writes Calvin, " and from the jaws of death the
servants of God send up a cry to the Lord." Jeremiah cries:
" Why hast thou smitten us, and there is no healing for us? "
The Psalmist says: " Why hast thou forgotten me? Why go
I mourning because of the oppression of the enemy? " " O
Jahve, why castest Thou off my soul? Why hidest Thou Thy
face from me? " Jesus, in the agony of death, does not offer a

petition; He complains and questions with the opening words
of the twenty-second Psalm.

Sometimes anxious questioning passes over into bitter
reproach. In language audacious, almost blasphemous in
sound, Jeremiah, not knowing what to make of Jahve, cries
aloud: " Ah, Lord Jahve, surely Thou hast greatly deceived
this people and Jerusalem saying, Ye shall have peace;
whereas the sword reacheth unto the life." " Wilt Thou indeed
be unto me as a deceitful brook, as waters that fail? " Ha-
bakkuk utters a cry of reproach: " O Jahve, how long shall
I cry, and Thou wilt not hear? I cry out unto Thee of violence
and Thou wilt not save." The author of the Book of Lamentations complains in his despair: " See, O Jahve, and behold to
whom Thou hast done this! . . . Thou hast slain them in the
day of Thine anger; Thou hast slaughtered and not pitied."

The awful problem of God's justice in the face of evil
kindles in the soul of the pious man not a theoretical brooding,
but a passionate wrestling with God, manifested in accumu-
lated complaints, reproaches, and interrogations. Job is full
of such outcry: " Wherefore hidest Thou Thy face and holdest
me for Thine enemy? " " I cry unto Thee, and Thou dost not
answer me; I stand up and Thou gazest at me. Thou art
turned to be cruel to me." " Wilt Thou harass a driven leaf?
And wilt Thou pursue the dry stubble? For Thou writest
bitter things against me, and makest me to inherit the iniquities of my youth."

(b) *Petition*

The usual form in which need is expressed is petition, nega-
tively for deliverance, positively for aid and support. Prayer
is for Luther the coming of a beggar to God " who opens wide
his cloak in order to receive much." Prayer is defined by
Zwingli as " a begging for the necessaries of life; a calling
on God for help." " Man tells what he desires," says Luther;
" he desires to get out of his misery, to be free of the evil
thing; he begs for aid; he is not abashed before exalted Majesty but speaks outright, ' help me, dear God! ' ' O that I had
this or that! ' " The kernel of prophetic prayer is, like that
of primitive prayer, the simple request for deliverance from

an evil or for the granting of gifts and favour. The Lord's Prayer, the model prayer of Christianity, is exclusively petition. Its contrast with the mystic's prayer is evident, for in the latter the request is secondary; and if the prayer appears as a petition, this is for the most part a method of expressing mystical concentration and contemplation.

The object and " goal " of prophetic petition is the affirmation or realization of a good, whether a personal one — belonging to one's own or another's ego — or a super-personal one. The material values, which are the exclusive end of primitive prayer, are less significant than the spiritual ones, whether with an ethical colouring or genuinely ethical.

1. *Personal Religious Values.* The assertion of one's own worth is a most important petition with prophetic personalities, especially those of the Old Testament. The worshipper entreats that he may be saved from inner catastrophe, the breakdown of his self-respect: " not to be put to shame," as the Old Testament strikingly expresses it.

The assertion of one's worth has as its corollary the " putting to shame " of one's adversary. If one's worth is acknowledged, the unworthiness of the enemy must be made manifest. Thus the prayer for deliverance and justification passes over into a passionate cry for vengeance: " Let them be put to shame that persecute me," cries Jeremiah, " but let me not be put to shame; let them be dismayed, but let me not be dismayed; bring upon them the day of evil, and destroy them with double destruction." " Let me not be put to shame; let not mine enemies triumph over me," begs the Psalmist. " Let me not be put to shame," prays Luther, " nor become a scorn and laughing-stock to my enemies." Prayer is offered for security of life. " Keep me as the apple of the eye; hide me under the shadow of Thy wings, from the wicked that oppress me." " Teach me Thy way, O Jahve; and lead me in a plain path because of mine enemies," so pray the singers of Israel. Mohammed utters such a prayer: " O God, cover my defence-lessness and protect my spirit; save me from that which is before me and behind me; that which is at my right hand and at my left; that which is over me and under me; I take refuge in Thy strength."

Prayer is made also for light in inward perplexity. The singer prophets of the Gathas cry repeatedly, " This I ask Thee, tell me the right (the truth) Ahura! " And Bunyan, doubting whether the books of the Ranters were of God or contrary to the Divine will, prayed: " Lord, I am a fool, and not able to know the truth from error; Lord, leave me not to my own blindness, either to approve of or to condemn this doctrine. If it be of God, let me not despise it; if it be of the devil, let me not embrace it."

Petition for the forgiveness of sins occupies a central position in prophetic prayer, while in mysticism it belongs to the periphery of the devotional life. The devout person seeks to be delivered from the feeling of guilt which oppresses him, from the crushing sense of his nothingness and powerlessness, which prevents him from meeting life in confidence and hope. Nothing but divine grace, freely bestowed, can transform the bitter self-condemnation to firm self-confidence, the trembling fear to peace and trust. This inner change and renewal is readily conceived as healing: " Heal me, O Lord, and I shall be healed." " O Jahve, have mercy upon me; heal my soul, for I have sinned against Thee."

The fifty-first Psalm is a most affecting penitential prayer, in which the renewing grace of God is set forth in a wonderful imagery, taken in part from the formal language of ancient religious worship: " Purify me with hyssop and I shall be clean: wash me and I shall be whiter than snow."

Such a heartfelt prayer for pardon is familiar in other Psalms; together with a similar petition in the Lord's Prayer, it runs through the liturgy of the Christian Church, attaining peculiar force and depth in the early Middle Ages. Thomas of Celano has given imperishable expression to this oppressive penitential seriousness in the *Dies irae:*

> " King of Majesty tremendous
> Who dost free salvation send us,
> Fount of pity, then befriend us!
>
> Righteous Judge! for sin's pollution
> Grant Thy gift of absolution,
> Ere the day of retribution."

Savonarola prays in touching fashion: " O God, Thou who art Compassion, take from me my sins for they are my greatest misery! Lift me up, wretched as I am; show Thy work in me; manifest Thy power in me. The deep of misery calls to the deep of compassion. The abyss of sin calls to the abyss of grace. The depth of compassion is greater than the depth of wretchedness; let then the abyss of compassion swallow up the abyss of wretchedness." It forms the burden also of prayers of the Reformation and appears no less in evangelical hymns. Luther prays: " I beg that Thou have pity on my soul's need, have pity upon me and forgive my sin." The evangelical prayer for forgiveness is found likewise outside Christianity, although in isolated instances and showing less fervour. Mohammed prays: " O God, I have sinned much, and none beside Thee forgives me my sin, so pardon me and have mercy upon me, for Thou art He who grants forgiveness and mercy."

Assurance of pardon and hope of grace are genuine, deep, and strong, only where the consciousness of guilt and weakness have overwhelmed the penitent and crushed him to the ground. Absolute trust in God's gift of grace can rise only out of complete self-condemnation. For this reason, the great prophetic leaders implore the power of self-knowledge and self-judgement. Luther prays: " Dear God, rule Thou me that I with spiritual eyes may recognize and acknowledge my inherited disease and weakness and so be led to the right knowledge of Christ and be governed, purified, and sanctified, by Thy Holy Spirit." Pascal prays: " Grant that I may judge myself, that I may examine myself before Thou judgest me, so that I may find mercy in Thy presence. Touch my heart with repentance for my faults." The petition for power to judge oneself goes so far as the paradoxical petition for punishment of one's sinfulness. " O Jahve," cries Jeremiah, " correct me but in measure; not in Thine anger, lest Thou bring me to nothing." " Chastise us gently in Thy goodness," prays Calvin. " Grant, O my God," cries Pascal, " that Thy all-powerful grace may make Thy chastisements health-giving to me."

Invocation of " God's Spirit " is closely associated with prayer for pardon and inner renewal. The Spirit of God is in fact the marvellous power which recreates and renews man, the source of all divine joy and strength, the giver of life and love. A petition of the Lord's Prayer, according to a traditional version not to be found in the text of the Gospels but probably authentic, reads, " Let Thy Holy Spirit come upon us and cleanse us." The same prayer has its classic formulation in the familiar hymn, *Veni, creator spiritus.*

Salvation and redemption in biblical religion lie in trust in God as the merciful Father. Inasmuch as this faith is, however, the work of God within man, a free gift of divine grace, the evangelical petitioner makes supplication for it with the same yearning with which the mystic prays for blessed union with God. Luther's words are: " Teach us, dear Father, not to rely upon, or console ourselves with our good works or deserts, but firmly to trust and yield ourselves to Thy boundless mercy alone." " Grant that we with joy may know, name, love, and call upon Thee as Father in all our necessities."

2. *Personal Ethical Values.* Personal, purely ethical values do not occupy so large a place in prophetic prayer as they do in the rationalistic and ethical prayer which is the ideal of the philosophers. Despite the close relationship between religion and morality, prophetic and evangelical piety, which is in its very nature faith and trust, never resolves itself into morality. Petitions for moral good do not proceed, as in philosophical religion, from conscious insight into ethical standards, but well up spontaneously from a natural feeling of the value of moral tasks as willed by God. The psalmist prays that he may observe his moral duties:

> " Teach me, O Jahve, the way of Thy statutes;
> And I shall keep it unto the end."

> " Make me to go in the way of Thy commandments;
> For therein do I delight."

" Bring us not into temptation," becomes a prayer for strength to overcome the temptation.

" Give me not a proud look, and turn away vain hopes and concupiscence from me," is the prayer of Jesus the son of Sirach. " Be pleased to keep us upright," prays Calvin, " that we may not stumble through the weakness of our flesh, and since we of ourselves are too weak to be able to remain firm even for a moment, and are constantly surrounded and oppressed by so many enemies, since the world, the flesh, and the Devil do not cease to make war upon us, do Thou strengthen us with Thy Holy Spirit and arm us with Thy grace." Prayer is made also for the conquering of evil tendencies and natural selfishness. Luther prays: " Give us grace that we may subdue the lust of the flesh. . . . Help us that with Christ on the Cross we may slay and destroy its evil tendency to unchastity and all its desires and allurements, that we may yield to and follow none of its temptations."

Kierkegaard has this prayer: " Lord, make our heart Thy temple wherein Thou wilt dwell. Grant that every unclean thought and every earthly desire may, like the god Dagon, be broken in pieces every morning at the foot of The Ark of the Covenant. Teach us to rule our flesh and blood and let this be our bloody offering so that we can say with the Apostle, ' I die daily.' " Brotherly love, long-suffering, and submission are the graces sought in prayer. In the Jerusalem Talmud we read: " May it be Thy will that no heart nourish hatred against us, and that our hearts nourish hatred against no one." " Let no one among us," prays Luther, " seek his own things and forget before Thee those of others."

3. *Ethical and Social Values* (*Intercession*). Prophetic religion is thoroughly social; the individual lives with others and for others. The pious man never approaches God in that individual isolation practised by the mystic, but always in close association with the brethren. The Lord's Prayer is essentially not the prayer of the individual, but a common prayer. As Luther says, " It binds people together within one another, so that each prays for the other and with the other." Such common prayer naturally expands into a special petition for the brethren; especially for all those in personal relation to the intercessor. The object of prayer is not only one's own need, but that of the brethren, with special attention to the inner needs of the soul.

This intercession for others, coexistent with prayer for oneself, is surprisingly evident in the prayers of primitive man. The intercessions of the Old Testament prophets are largely vicarious mediation: Moses, Samuel, Jeremiah, pray in the name of the people and as commissioned by them; the object of the prayer is the common need of the entire nation, which the prophet shares with all other members of the social community.

A purer and more personal tone is characteristic of the intercession of Christian leaders. They seek exclusively the salvation of others — and not at the same time their own salvation as identified with that of the community. Jesus prays for Cephas, whom Satan has desired to have, that his faith fail not. Paul intercedes for the spiritual health of the Churches; he beseeches God to give them " a spirit of wisdom and revelation in the knowledge of Him "; that their " love may abound yet more and more in knowledge and all discernment." Polycarp prays for " all who at any time had come in his way, small and great, high and low." Luther and Calvin are masters of intercession. Almost every letter and the greater part of Luther's writings bear witness to his true and heartfelt prayer for others. Again and again he assures the recipient of his letters that he prays for him and desires the latter to pray also for him. Luther makes petition for his wife and children, his neighbours and associates, his friends and comrades in the faith. Calvin, too, was zealous in intercession for all dear to him. Thus he writes to Viret: " I ask God to keep you always in His care, to strengthen you by His Holy Spirit to resist all temptations and to make you grow in all things to His glory." And to the French Reformed Churches he writes: " I make petition to God that He may be pleased to increase in you the gifts of grace which He has bestowed upon you, to make you strong in true constancy, to protect you in the midst of wolves and to glorify Himself in you in every way." Spener included by name in his daily intercessions a large number of acquaintances, even resorting, in his pragmatic way, to formal lists, so that all should be in order and no one be forgotten.

The universality of Christian love deepens and broadens the naturally rich number of personal relationships; prayer includes all members of the Christian fellowship. Paul exhorts to persevering prayer for " all the saints," that is, for all Christians. Luther prays for the evangelical princes, for the emperor and the Imperial Diet, for government and clergy, for the German army in the field against the Turks, for martyrs in prison, for monks in temptation, for widows and children in affliction, for the sick and the dying. All-embracing, mediating love finds enduring expression in the liturgical prayers of the Christian Churches; secular authorities and spiritual guides, believers and unbelievers, sinners and saints, the sick and the well, even the heathen, Jews, and heretics, are remembered.

The universality of Christian intercession thus seeks to reach beyond the borders of the religious community. Jeremiah and Baruch bade the exiles in Babylon to pray for that city. The Jews of the Dispersion at Elephantine pray for the Persian king; the early Christian Church in Rome for the emperor. The author of the First Epistle to Timothy exhorts to prayer for all rulers and those in authority. Petition for those far remote from the body of Christians is an essential part of private as well as public Christian worship.

The idea of universal intercession reaches its culmination in the paradoxical exhortation of the Sermon on the Mount: " Pray for them that persecute you." The contrast between this utterance and the spirit of vengeance which speaks from the prayers of Jeremiah and many of the Psalms, is unmistakable. That a sincere, earnest, and spontaneous prayer for one's enemies is a psychological possibility, is evident from the cry of Jesus upon the cross: " Father forgive them; for they know not what they do," and in the echo of this prayer throughout the history of Christian martyrs from the time of Stephen to Hus and Heinrich of Zütphen.

4. *Super-Personal Religious and Ethical Values.* The manifold concrete values, individual or social, which constitute the " end " of prayer are comprised in the petition for the coming of the Kingdom of God in its fulness; that is, for the realization of the sum of all good, the transformation of all the actual into a perfect ideal reality. This is the supremely important petition of prophetic prayer, into which merge all other desires. Jesus' prayer is essentially eschatological, an earnest entreaty for the speedy coming of the " fulfilment."

" Thy Kingdom come," is the central petition of the Lord's Prayer, around which all the others are grouped. It is varied by the one that precedes it, " Hallowed be Thy name," and elucidated by the one that follows, " Thy will be done, as in heaven so on earth." It is repeated in negative fashion at the close, " Deliver us from the evil one." The petition concerning the Kingdom of God occurs in the *Didache* in the interesting variant — " Let grace come, and let this world pass away."

When Jesus urges to importunate prayer, the object of this passionate, yearning desire is the coming of the Kingdom and associated with it the vindication of the elect, for which the righteous cry day and night. " Maranatha," " Come Lord Jesus," is the continuous moan of the early Church directed toward the ascended Lord, a prayer which becomes the significant closing word of Revelation. Wherever in Christian sects the hope of a final millennium has burned brightly, this apocalyptic prayer has gone up incessantly from hearts burdened with longing. " Come, Lord Jesus, come quickly," is the cry of the English Independents. Luther's prayers, too, are full of this supplication for the final fulfilment. Here is an example: " Help, O Lord God, that the happy day of Thy holy future may soon come, that we may be saved from the deceitful and evil world, the Kingdom of the Devil, and set free from the dreadful torment which, inwardly and outwardly, we are compelled to suffer from evil people and from our own conscience." The following prayer of Savonarola also bears an eschatological character: " O Jesus Christ, my Lord and my God! Hasten to help Thy Church! Help Thou Thy whole Kingdom! Remove, O Lord, evil and its grievous influence. Arise in Thy wrath, O Lord, for no longer can we bear the wicked! "

Where faith in the nearness of the eschatological kingdom of God begins to wane, instead of this transcendental kingdom there appears a prayer for the sovereignty of God here in time, that is to say, the publishing abroad of His word and the extension of the Church, the victory of true morality and the glory of God. We have the following in a prayer of Calvin: " We pray Thee that Thou mayst exercise over us all

Thy lordship and power, that we may more and more learn to subordinate ourselves to Thy majesty, that Thou mayst in all things be King and Ruler, mayst guide Thy people by the sceptre of Thy word and the power of Thy Spirit, and mayst put to shame Thy enemies by the might of Thy truth and righteousness." Pascal prays with uncompromising spirituality: " I ask Thee for neither health nor sickness, neither life nor death, but that Thou mayst dispose of my health and sickness for Thy glory, for my salvation and *for the good of the Church,* and of Thy saints." According to Bunyan " we must pray for the glory of God and the advancement of Christ," " for abundance of grace for the Church, for help against its temptations, that God would let nothing be too hard for it, that all things might work together for its good."

5. *Eudaemonistic Values.* Mysticism must, if it is to remain true to itself, reject as unworthy of genuine piety naïve prayer for external good things, every petition not concerned with God Himself. The earthly is in fact an unreal, deceptive show, something which ought not to be, a worthless thing and therefore a menace to spiritual welfare, a hindrance to union with God. Emotions and desires which assert themselves ought not to find free expression in prayer, but must be stifled, mastered, killed. The foundation of pure mysticism is the asceticism that gradually deadens the cravings of the senses and the emotional life of the soul fed by them. The great prophetic personalities, on the contrary, were not ascetics. Nothing was further from them than the systematic mortification of the natural emotional and instinctive life. No trace of such disgust towards common daily occupations or the trivial pleasures of life can be found in them as we find in very many mystics. The innocent joy in life which Jesus manifested was a ground of offence even to the strict Pharisees, who were by no means mystics. The men of the Reformation, turning from the world-renouncing mysticism and reviving the prophetic piety of the Bible, definitely rejected all asceticism.

Due to this anti-ascetic spirit the prophetic leaders, in contrast with the mystics, make no distinction between prayer for heavenly and for earthly blessings, between spiritual and material values, although naturally preoccupation with interests of a moral and religious nature leaves only the lowest place for earthly wishes. It is a sign of his complete naïveté and healthy naturalness, as well as of his freedom from philosophical rationalism and mystic and ascetic pessimism, when the devout person can pray for life, food, and health, with the same conviction, fervour, and confidence as for pardon for his sins and the coming of the kingdom of God; for the least thing as for the greatest.

The prayers of the Old Testament prophets and of the Psalms reveal almost without exception some interweaving of eudaemonistic elements. Israel's national independence and greatness are the goal of their most impassioned expressions of desire. Daily bread is among the objects for which Jesus' disciples are to ask. Mystical and philosophical motives led in later Christianity to transforming the simple request for bread into a spiritual one, but the very words of the prayer permit no such transformation. Jesus unhesitatingly encourages his disciples to pray for a mitigation of the tribulation and terror of the approaching end. " Pray ye that it be not in the winter." He gives voice to genuinely human feeling, unconstrained by stoic or quietist indifference, when in the fear of death he prays earnestly that the cup may pass from him. Paul's exhortation to the Philippians: " In nothing be anxious, but in everything . . . let your requests be made known unto God," permits no limitation to prayer for spiritual blessings. His threefold entreaty to be delivered from the " thorn in the flesh " concerns his severe bodily illness, probably epilepsy. James exhorts to prayer for the sick: " Pray one for another, that ye may be healed." When Thomas Aquinas, following Augustine, laid down the principle, " It is permissible to pray for whatever it is permissible to desire," he only puts into a concise formula the biblical and early Christian belief that there is no difference between prayers for spiritual and prayers for material things. Luther speaks still more specifically: " We ought to bring before God all sorts of necessities; first, spiritual needs; after that, common temporal needs of this life on earth." In a period of great drought, he did not hesitate to pray to God for rain, as primitive peoples in tropical countries and pious peasants in Europe do: "How, wilt Thou not then give rain, inasmuch as we cry and beseech Thee so long?" Calvin prays for the wife of his friend Viret that she may have a safe confinement. Kierkegaard goes so far as to say: "Never has it occurred to me to have any hesitation in simply asking God whenever I wanted to enjoy myself, to help and grant me to enjoy myself rightly — which would be nonsense if God were a fanatical bugbear."

Mohammed instructs one of his followers: "Pray God for thy welfare in this world and the next." He himself was accustomed to offer morning and evening the following prayer: "O God, I pray Thee for well-being in Thy religion, in my existence, in life, health, and property." Modern evangelical theologians have decisively emphasized the biblical thought of the right to pray for what is earthly and temporal. Rothe says: "The subject of petitionary prayer may be in itself everything which can be the subject of a Christian's wish, whether it be a spiritual good or a so-called external one." Monrad believes that "everything which moves in our souls, great and small, we can take up into our prayer." W. Herrmann has found a most suggestive formulation of the biblical motives of simple petition: "Faith certainly does not so operate that the Christian shrinks from petition for natural things. This simplification of prayer would be an emptying of its meaning. Whatever really burdens the soul so that its peace is threatened thereby should be brought before God in prayer in the confidence that His love understands our anxious cleaving to earthly things. This attitude to the Father which meets us in Christ effects an inner strengthening against the things which captivate us. If we try to free ourselves from them and accordingly do not include them in our prayer, we injure ourselves in two ways: (1) Our prayer becomes thereby dead and unreal; it is then in truth not our own prayer but perhaps the possible prayer of a quite differently situated person. (2) We do not in it place ourselves really before God who would be sought as Helper and Deliverer. For in it we dream of a God who, to be sure, loves the ideal of man but does not sympathize with our need. If, on the contrary, we turn to God with what weighs heavily on us, the trust which He evokes in us brings about an unburdening of our inner life."

Mysticism and ethical philosophy stigmatize prayer for temporal blessings as irreligious and sinful. Prophetic religion, it is true, places our highest religious and moral desires in the centre of prayer, but it has room also for childlike primitive requests for life and food, rain and sunshine. There is no question here of the religious and ethical rightness of naïve prayer, or of the metaphysical possibility of the influence of man upon God. When prayer is nothing but a simple outpouring of the heart, a " casting of all care from our hearts upon the Heart which formed us " (so Tholuck defines prayer), all objections of philosophy and mysticism are silenced. Only a harsh piety, grounded in a sombre, penitential disposition, like that of Bunyan or Pascal, excludes the sincere petition for temporal things — and according to William James, such personalities belong to the " sick-soul " type. Bunyan says: " Right prayer, as it runs only to God through Christ, so it centres in Him and in Him alone." Bunyan gave this rule upon his death-bed: " Before thou enterest into prayer, ask thy soul, ' Is thy business slight, does it concern the welfare of thy soul? ' " And under the influence of Jansenism, Pascal prays: " I know that I know but one thing: that it is good to follow Thee, and that it is evil to grieve Thee."

(c) *Means of Persuasion*

Petition, as in the prayer of primitive man, is reinforced by persuasion. The ingenuous petitioner not only presents his desire to God, but he " bolsters it well with particulars," as Luther puts it; he gives motives and reasons; he seeks by every indication and argument to move God to fulfil his wish. With Luther, who is perhaps the most naïve, original, and childlike of the great men of religion, this realistic desire to influence God, this seeking to change His will, assumes such primitive forms that to the superficial observer his piety appears to sink below the purity and moral greatness of the devotional spirit of the New Testament. Many turns of speech in his prayers are almost literally identical with the expressions of early peoples.

Homage, praise, and thanksgiving arise chiefly from spontaneous emotions; they may be — as is the rule with primitive man — at the same time a means for prevailing upon God. Very frequently the appeal is to God's own interest, for the matter is not one of selfish caprice but of ideal ends and tasks divinely willed and appointed. Luther prays: " Do good to me, O Lord, for Thy name's sake. Thou knowest that the matter toucheth Thee; Thy name, Thy word, Thy honour I praise, but they blaspheme; if Thou desertest me, Thou forsakest also Thy name, but that is not possible, therefore, deliver me." In a prayer against the Turks he prays: " They are Thy enemies more than ours, and if they persecute and beat us, they persecute and beat Thyself. For the word which we preach, believe, and confess is Thine, not ours, all the work of Thy Holy Spirit in us." Similarly Calvin prays: " Do not permit the memory of Thy name to be abolished from the earth; do not let those perish over whom Thy name is called, nor let the Turks and heathen boast themselves." As primitive peoples remind their God that if He allows His worshippers to perish there will be no longer any one to make offerings to Him, so the psalmist reminds Jahve that if God's people are destroyed there will be none to extol His wonders: " Shall they that are deceased arise and praise Thee: shall Thy lovingkindness be declared in the grave? Or Thy faithfulness in destruction? Shall Thy wonders be known in the dark? " The author of the Apocalypse of Baruch cries to Jahve: " If Thou lettest Thy city perish and givest Thy land to our enemies, how then can Israel's name be remembered? Or how can one tell of Thy glorious deeds? " Mohammed pleads with God that if it were not His will to give him the promised victory, He would have no worshippers.

The perfect naïveté which expresses inner vexation as freely as need, trust and joy, which discloses every impulse of the soul, does not shrink even from threatening God. Yet, frequently, as with primitive man, threat and rebuke give place to soothing entreaty. Luther, challenging God: " If we should finally become angry towards Thee, no longer bring honour and tribute to Thee, how wouldst Thou then continue? " changes suddenly: " Ah, dear God, we are Thine; do what Thou wilt, but grant us endurance."

God is also to be induced to give aid at the present time by being reminded of His previous kindnesses, His graciousness and answers to prayer. " Our fathers trusted in Thee, they trusted and Thou didst deliver them," writes the author of the twenty-second Psalm. The poet of the *Dies irae* sings:

> " Thou the sinful woman savedst;
> Thou the dying thief forgavest;
> And to me a hope vouchsafest."

Luther prays in his sickness at Smalkald: " O Thou faithful God, as Thy name has helped so many people, do Thou help me also! " A still more effective method for persuading God to hear, consists in the claiming of His promises; the petitioner lays hold of God through His own words. Moses speaks to Jahve: " Remember Abraham, Isaac, and Israel, Thy servants, to whom Thou swearest, by Thine own self, and saidst unto them, I will multiply your seed as the stars of heaven, and all this land that I have spoken of will I give unto your seed, and they shall inherit it forever." Reference is made also to the fact that God has expressly commanded men to pray. The objective, historical character of prophetic as distinguished from mystical devotion, appears in this citing of the former deeds, commands, and promises of God. This historical feature of this type of prayer becomes clearer when God is reminded of divine occurrences connected with sacred places. Old Testament petitioners rested upon the covenant of Sinai, through which Jahve and His people were indissolubly united. Jeremiah prays: " Break not Thy covenant with us." Christian suppliants make mention of the sacrificial atonement of God's Son on Golgotha. Calvin prays: " We have a much better covenant to which we can appeal. It is that which Thou hast concluded and ratified through Jesus Christ our Redeemer. . . . Therefore, O Lord, we trust not in ourselves nor in any human hope whatever, but we take refuge in this blessed covenant by our Lord Jesus Christ who has reconciled us to Thee. Look, therefore, O Lord, on the face of Christ and not on us."

The simple use of the name of Jesus in prayer is an appeal to the great redemptive deed of His atoning death. The early Church always prayed to the Father " in " and

" through " Jesus, " in the name of Jesus." Luther prays:
" Look not on our sins but on Thy Son, Jesus Christ, in whose
name we come now before Thee." Prophetic prayer, too,
plainly reveals how the evangelical doctrine of salvation centres in Christ: " Christ is the way through whom the soul
hath admittance to God and without whom it is impossible
that so much as one desire should come into the ears of the
Lord " — so writes Bunyan.

Reference to social relationship with God, found in countless
primitive prayers and especially to man's relation as a child
of God, appears literally in prophetic petition. A post-exilic
worshipper cries to Jahve: " For Thou art our Father, though
Abraham knoweth us not, and Israel doth not acknowledge
us: Thou, O Jahve, art our Father." A striking example is
to be found in a prayer of Calvin's: " O Lord, Thou art our
Father, and we are only mire and earth; Thou art our Creator
and we are the work of Thy hands; Thou art our Shepherd
and we are Thy flock; Thou art our Redeemer and we are
Thy people whom Thou hast purchased; Thou art our God
and we are Thine inheritance. Wherefore be not angry with
us nor punish us in Thy displeasure."

Mention of one's piety and goodness is also among the means
used to move God to hearken. This is frequently met with
in primitive prayer, together with the worshipper's pride in
his sacrificial offerings. The pious Jew presumes upon his
zeal for the law and his trust in God, his righteousness and
good works; the prophet reminds God of his obedience and
ardour in his calling. The evangelical Christian, while rejecting justification through works, yet lays stress upon his own
good will. Even Luther, who assailed all righteousness based
upon good works, in his illness calls upon God to remember his
diligence in preaching: " Thou knowest that I have taught
Thy word diligently." The psalmist prays: " Judge me, O
Jahve, according to my righteousness, and to mine integrity
that is in me."

Appeal to God's pity, too, which belongs to primitive worship, recurs in the prayer of prophetic leaders. " Have mercy
upon me," is a frequent prayer of the psalmist and of others.
Constant unwearied importuning of God that He may be

brought to yield meets us both in primitive religion and the devotional life of the prophetic type. The mystic is wholly immersed, absorbed, lost in God, all desire and craving are stilled in the beatific vision of the Divine. But prophetic natures entreat God with passionate vehemence; they wrestle with Him with a perseverance that will not let go and seek to compel Him through unceasing cries and supplications to fulfil their ardent longings and desires. A pious Jew says: "Presumption obtains results even with Heaven." The same idea underlies Jesus' parable of the persistent friend and the importunate widow. These parables wonderfully illustrate how effectual and certain of being heard are such unwearied fervent pleadings. The urgent demand of Jesus for such prayer [1] has been modified and restricted by theologians of ancient and modern times, who have thus weakened it in re-interpreting it. It awakens in the philosophic mind the same confusion as in the contemplative mystic, for it represents the sharpest contrast to the mystical and philosophic ideal of prayer. And yet, its direct form of expression is psychologically natural.

Jesus' exhortation to vehement prayer contains as its essence that naïve belief in the power of prayer, that loyal, childlike trust in God the Father, that anthropomorphic realism in intercourse with God which, in contrast with all philosophy and mysticism, prophetic petition has in common with the prayer of primitive man. Those parables which encourage the importunate spirit of prayer argue from the less to the greater. If unfriendly and unjust egotists are to be led through persistent prayer and supplication to grant what has been asked, how much more shall the kind Father in Heaven bestow willingly upon those who call upon Him in faith? Jesus has in mind not foolish, childish requests but the greatest and most important to which His hope is directed, the Kingdom of God, which forms the central object of the Lord's Prayer. When the reviled and persecuted cry day and night to Heaven, the great day of Judgment, which shall bring them justice, cannot delay much longer. Luther's soul is fired by the earnest exhortation of Jesus; he finds still more drastic and forceful words for "importunate prayer." His indefatigable

---

[1] πάντοτε προσεύχεσθαι καὶ μὴ ἐγκακεῖν.

zeal borders on defiance, the primitive character of such petition seeming to imperil the purity and exalted character of the
filial relationship evident in the New Testament. " One should
not only pray for an hour, but one must cry out and knock;
you must forthwith compel God to come." " As God continues to hide Himself, so begin to knock and cease not until
thou hast burst open the door which incloses Him." " Such
audacious prayer, which perseveres unflinchingly and ceases
not through fear, is well-pleasing unto God." Tradition brings
us similar utterances from Mohammed: " God loves those
who are truly importunate in prayer." In a Taurât verse
Allah himself says: " He who hopes for my blessing should
present his prayer in a forward manner."

All these different methods of persuasion are meant to support and fortify the prayer and lend it efficacious power.
Closely considered, however, they are more than mere attempts to influence and alter the attitude of God. The appeal
to God's own interest, like the mention of His former mercy
and His promises, His deeds of redemption, and His relation to His children, have as their purpose an actual effect
upon God's will. Yet, they are, at the same time, a strong
expression of confidence and hope, already acting as a cause,
motivating the prayer. Here is manifest the transition, typical
of prophetic prayer, from complaint and petition, to the expression of trust.

(d) *Expression of Weakness and Dependence: Confession of
Sinfulness*

In primitive prayer the acknowledgement of one's own
weakness and of the succouring power of God, as well as the
confession of one's own unworthiness, nothingness, and sinfulness, is one of the methods of winning God to the fulfilment of a desire. Both these are found again in prophetic
prayer in direct connection with petition. Nevertheless, here
the naïve tendency to make the most of a situation, to give
reasons for the request, are not so much in the foreground as
in the means of persuasion mentioned above; here is rather
the natural expression of an elementary psychic experience.
The petitioner is much less concerned with rousing God to aid

and securing favour by casting himself humbly in the dust before His might and acknowledging His absolute power, than he is with giving utterance to the consciousness of complete dependence on Him, the sense of creatureliness, which wholly possesses him. Neither the confession of one's sinfulness nor the admission of guilt has as its object the appeasing of God's wrath and awakening of His pity through self-abasement. This is the object generally of the penitential prayers of primitive and ancient peoples, but here they are the spontaneous expression of sincere self-condemnation, the unreserved confession of one's own unworthiness.

In the sixty-fourth chapter of Isaiah we read: " We are the clay, and Thou our potter, and we are all the work of Thy hand." And Mohammed prays: " O God, Thou hast created my soul and wilt take it to Thyself; to Thee belong its death and its life." " I pray Thee by Thy might, I implore Thee for Thy grace; for behold, Thou art mighty, I have no might; Thou hast knowledge, I have none." " What art Thou but mercy itself; but what am I but misery? Behold, O God, Thou who art mercy, misery is before Thee," are the words of Savonarola. The psalmist cries:

> " Against Thee, Thee only, have I sinned
> And done that which is evil in Thy sight;
> That Thou mayest be justified when Thou speakest,
> And be clear when Thou judgest."

And Pascal confesses: " Thou gavest me health that I might serve Thee but I have misused it for worldly ends. I have abused my health and Thou hast with justice punished me therefor."

(e) *Expression of Trust*

The chief content of prophetic prayer is the utterance of need. This is not all of it, however; it is more than mere supplication and complaint. It begins with the expression of need, but it rises to a height where want and desire are forgotten and trust, joy, and surrender prevail. A wonderful metamorphosis takes place in the prayer itself, unconsciously, involuntarily, often quite suddenly. The harassing, painful emotion, the ardent desire, pass; with a sudden bound the spirit finds itself in a mild, pleasurable mood of confidence and peace, of hope and trust; the feeling of uncertainty and instability is replaced by the blissful consciousness of being cared for, hidden in the hand of a protecting higher Power. Thus assurance issues forth from doubts and questionings, confidence from dread, courage which rejoices in the future from hesitancy and fear; wish and will give place to the calm of inward possession. This change of mood frequently does not occur all at once — especially if lamentation and supplication had their origin in overwhelming fear and passionate longing — but for some time anxiety and hope alternate. The petitioner carries on an internal conflict between doubt and certainty, hesitation and assurance, until finally faith and trust break through with victorious power. This psychic struggle in which hope, timid at first, asserts itself against all the feelings of fear and rises to unshakable confidence, is frequently enacted in naïve individuals, but only very rarely does the trusting mood which there arises from the prayer plainly come to expression. This it is which is new, creative in the prayer-life of prophetic persons, that all the changing emotions, moods, and feelings, not only fear and desire, but faith and trust also, express themselves in the spontaneous words of prayer. Everything which struggles and conquers in the soul of the petitioner is revealed and poured out before God.

Jacob's wrestling with Jahve in the Genesis narrative is the prototype of the prophetic prayer of conflict: " I will not let thee go, except thou bless me." So far as prayer is a striving with God for the soul's salvation and its confidence, it has its origin with Jeremiah, the " father of Christian prayer." " The certainty of his personal communion with God," says Wellhausen, " arose amid pain and sorrow. In his desperate struggles he in no way attained to rest and peace, but rather to the consciousness of victory in defeat." His prayers are a contest for the true ground of faith, a toilsome pressing forward toward religious assurance. They express both his soul's " infrahuman misery " and its " superhuman confidence."

The torturing question addressed to Jahve: " Why shouldest

Thou be as a man affrighted, as a mighty man that cannot save? " yields to the joyful certainty: " Yet Thou, O Jahve, art in the midst of us and we are called by Thy name; leave us not." The prophet seeks to know why Jahve has cast away His own people; he occupies himself profoundly with this fearful paradox, which threatens the prophet's inmost faith in God, bound up with the history of his people. So in despair he interrogates Jahve: " Hast Thou utterly rejected Judah? Hath Thy soul loathed Zion? Why hast Thou smitten us, and there is no healing for us? " " We looked for peace, but no good came; and for a time of healing, and behold, dismay! " Then there comes to him insight that Israel's sins and faithlessness toward Jahve are the causes of her outer catastrophe. " We acknowledge, O Jahve, our wickedness and the iniquity of our fathers; for we have sinned against Thee." A ray of hope shines into the darkness of his despondency. Jahve cannot forsake His people, for then He should have to betray Himself — and a prayer arises to the prophet's lips: " Do not abhor us, for Thy name's sake; do not disgrace the throne of Thy glory; remember, break not Thy covenant with us." His confidence increases: " Jahve is the only God, only He has power among all the gods." " Are there any among the vanities of the nations that can cause rain? or can the heavens give showers? " Thus at last hope has attained to the comforting assurance that Jahve is the Lord of Israel. " Art Thou not He, O Jahve, our God? Therefore, we will wait for Thee, for Thou hast made all these things."

A great number of the Psalms in which this same spirit of prayer finds poetic expression, and which reflect in artistic form the devotional experiences of the community of Jewish exiles, show the same conflict between fearful uncertainty and hopeful courage, the violent alternation of feeling from trembling anxiety to bold confidence. In the Psalms, too, the vehement prayer shifts suddenly to heartfelt outpouring of trust, of praise and rejoicing. Or the Psalm begins with troubled question and moving lament, passes over into fervent prayer for help and salvation, and closes with vigorous words of joyous, unshakable faith in God.

In the thirty-first Psalm we read:

" In Thee, O Jahve, do I take refuge:
Let me never be put to shame.

. . . .

For Thou art my rock and my fortress;
Therefore, for Thy name's sake lead me and guide me.

. . . .

Into Thy hand I commend my spirit:
Thou hast redeemed me, O Jahve, thou God of truth.

. . . .

Have mercy upon me, O Jahve, for I am in distress,
Mine eye wasteth away with grief, yea, my soul and my body."

And the author of the twenty-second Psalm cries:

" My God, my God, why hast Thou forsaken me?

. . . .

But be Thou not far off, O Jahve:
O Thou, my succour, haste Thee to help me.

. . . .

I will declare Thy name unto my brethren; in
the midst of the assembly will I praise Thee."

Luther's prayer at Worms is a typical example of the ebb
and flow of moods and feelings in passionate, spontaneous
prayer. It begins with a woeful consideration of himself in
his grievous situation. His fate is uncertain; no reliance is to
be placed upon man: " The bell has been already cast, judgment has been pronounced." The anxious thoughts mount up
a cry of complaint: " Ah God, ah God, O Thou my God."
Passionate entreaty for help is wrung from the soul of the
tortured man: " Stand Thou by me; do this, Thou must do it,
Thou alone! " His trust increases with the thought of the
worth and justice of his cause: " The matter is not mine, it is
Thine." Growing confidence is again stifled by rising doubts,
which burst forth in vehement questioning of God: " O God,
dost Thou not hear? My God, art Thou dead? " The petitioner threatens God with losing faith in Him, but his in-
domitable trust banishes doubt: " No, Thou canst not die;
Thou only hidest Thyself." He prays afresh, " Stand by me."

Once again uncertainty and fear gain the upper hand: " Lord, where tarriest Thou? Where art Thou, O my God? " Finally, all doubts are scattered; the strain is relaxed; faith triumphs over uncertainty; hope is victorious over fear. Heroic determination fills him who but lately hesitated and trembled, who complained and questioned: " Come, come! I am ready, even to forsake my life for this, submissive as a lamb, for righteous is this cause which is Thine." He faces death boldly, for whether living or dead, he feels himself under the protection of the Most High; nothing evil can come to him. " And should my body perish for this cause, should it fall to the ground, yea, be broken to fragments, yet Thy word and Thy spirit are enough. And all this can happen only to the body; the soul is Thine and belongs to Thee and will remain forever with Thee."

Mystic prayer is silent yearning, blissful absorption, ecstatic vision, passing over into an equable state of feeling which has breadth and depth. Prophetic prayer is the conflict of the soul just as the entire life of prophetic individuals is a constant struggle for the certainty of God and the consolation and salvation of the soul. There is dramatic tension, a rise and fall of moods and feelings, dualistic power and vitality, even as the whole life of such natures reveals a harsh and stern dualism of contrasts and tensions. For this reason prayer is not easy, but, as Luther says, " the hardest work of all " — " a labour above all labours, since he who prays must wage a mighty warfare against the doubt and murmuring excited by the faintheartedness and unworthiness we feel within us." " This is the conflict which the saints have to maintain, those who imagine that the rope may even now break, and yet they continue their heartfelt groaning." " This is that unutterable and powerful groaning with which the godly rouse themselves against despair, the struggle in which they call mightily upon their faith." Bunyan, in a similar strain, remarks: " Right prayer is accompanied with a continual labour after that which is prayed for." And Calvin derives from this psychological fact this rule for prayer: " In the midst of doubt, fear, and trembling, we should compel ourselves to pray until we are aware of a relief that tranquillizes us. We ought not to relax when our hearts waver and are disturbed, until faith comes forth victorious from the conflict."

Hebrew and Christian prayers give positive expression to the confidence obtained or revived in the struggle through prayers by means of the word *Amen,* that is, *so it is.* Originally a response with which the people of Israel took up the words of their leader, it became the regular ending for a petition as " an expression of firm, sincere belief," as Luther remarks, " for at the end, as you say Amen, with a genuine faith and trust, so certainly the prayer is assured and heard."

The *Amen* stands not in vain at the conclusion, for the spirit of faith is the victory which is won through the conflict within prayer; the faint hope which at the beginning of the petition annexed itself to the painful emotion and released the prayer, has suppressed the anxiety and has become complete certainty. Yet, inasmuch as the worshipper is forever renewing through prayer his faith and trust, his fundamental vital feeling may become so joyous, his assurance of life so strong and immovable, that if he opens his mouth in prayer, desiring to bring a request to God, words of confidence force themselves to his lips. Thus the expression of certitude, which customarily and originally stands at the close of prayer, appears at the beginning:

" Yea, though I walk through the valley of the shadow of death,
  I will fear no evil, for Thou art with me;
  Thy rod and Thy staff, they comfort me."

" Withhold not Thou Thy tender mercies from me, O Jahve;
  Let Thy loving kindness and Thy trust continually preserve me."

" But I am poor and needy;
  Yet the Lord thinketh upon me:
  Thou art my help and my deliverer
  Make no tarrying, O my God."

Mohammed prays: " O God, to Thee have I yielded myself, in Thee do I believe, in Thee do I trust . . . forgive what I have done."

As the following prayer of Luther shows, the expression of confidence may precede the petition, to which in turn it grants discharge: " Thou art my God, but I myself am nothing; I hope in Thee and trust not myself; in Thee I shall not be put to shame, but in myself I am already put to shame." Or the prayer is scarcely formulated before it disappears and gives place to words of firm trust: " Lord, reckon up my flight, hold my tears in Thy vessel! Doubtless Thou numberest them. Although no man will think upon my distress, Thou lookest so carefully upon it that Thou countest every step in my flight, how far I am hunted, and forgettest none of the tears which I shed; but I know that Thou inscribest them all in Thy book."

Even the introductory invocation to the Father may be an expression of true confidence. Luther calls attention to Jesus' use of " My Father," as if, in the midst of death and under the wrath of God, He would affirm the fact of God's fatherhood and love to Him.

Many of the Psalms of the Bible, and non-Christian prayers too, are nothing else than direct utterances of entire trust, containing no petition or want. Such prayers fully resemble those of mystic contemplation and yet are fundamentally different. The disposition toward confidence, certainty, sureness, is something quite other than the experiencing of inner unity, tranquillity, and bliss, the ecstatic contemplation of the supreme good. A prayer which originates with Nanak, the founder of the mixed Islamic-Hindu sect of the Sikhs, found in the canonical book, *Adigranth,* reads: " Thou art my Father, Thou art my mother, Thou art my cousin, Thou art my brother, Thou art everywhere my protector. What fear or care can come near me, O Lord? Through Thy mercy I have felt Thee. Thou art my support; Thou art my trust. All that is created is Thine; nothing, O Lord, is ours! " Luther prays: " Dear Lord, I know that Thou hast still more, Thou hast much more than Thou canst ever bestow; in Thee I shall never want, for if there were need, the heavens would rain guilders. Be Thou my treasury, my cellar, my storehouse; in Thee have I all riches; if I have Thee, I have enough."

(f) *Expression of Resignation*

Where the suppliant's distress yields to trust, the wish expressed in the prayer is inwardly sustained and affirmed. Yet a passionate desire does not always maintain its right in prayer. The association of the wish with the thought of God sometimes presents it in an entirely new light; it loses its absolute inner validity and is no longer upheld. The petitioner completely renounces his desire and retracts the petition to which he has given utterance, or he leaves the wish suspended, no longer insisting upon its fulfilment; his request becomes what Luther calls " abandoned prayer." Calvin speaks of " waiting patiently on the Lord with suspended desires." [2] This, however, in no way alters the sense of solace in which the prayer dies away; in this case, too, the same psychic drama is enacted in its entirety, the struggle between hope and fear, certainty and uncertainty. The tense, painful emotion resolves itself into a mood of joy. This change of mood consists solely in the petitioner's renunciation of the absolute fulfilment of his individual wish; he regards its non-fulfilment with resolution and courage; he subordinates his will with humility and fortitude to the will of God, sustained by the confident belief that every external event serves a good and worthy purpose, determined by God, " that," as Calvin remarks, " even if it does not so appear, God always stands by us and in His own good time will permit us to know how little He has turned a deaf ear to the prayers which in the sight of man have seemed to remain unanswered." Yet it is only after hard struggle that the suppliant leaves his wishes and longings with God; the natural will resists every apparent hindrance and menace, and finds no rest until the holy will of God, the challenging and constraining power of religious and moral duties and values, has disclosed itself to him.

Old Testament piety knows only the wish transformed into a hope sustaining the desire; its prayer rarely passes into the complete surrender in which the wish is suppressed. The prayer which culminates in resignation is the creation of Jesus. His prayer of conflict in Gethsemane is the classic example of the transformation of urgent desire into the confident yielding of oneself to the will of God. Overpowered by the terrors of death Jesus breaks forth into a passionate cry of prayer, He pleads that the decree of death shall be turned away,

---

[2] *Suspensis desideriis patienter exspectare Dominum.*

but the thought of the Father diminishes and mitigates the vehemence of the natural desire. He prays that the cup may pass from Him, but with a qualification, " if it be possible." Yet He has scarcely given voice to the plea when He amends it through the words of entire submission: " Nevertheless, not as I will, but as Thou wilt." The thought of the Father's will, of the necessity that one should die for " the many," silences His own wish. Not at once, it is true, does the natural impulse give place to the spirit of sacrifice; three times must He utter the same cry of distress before He attains within Himself complete firmness and resolution to be ready for death.

The fourth Gospel gives a striking variant of the prayer in Gethsemane, which contains likewise an analysis of the idea of suffering. Jesus recognizes plainly and unequivocally the inevitability of His death and atonement: " Except a grain of wheat fall into the earth and die, it abideth by itself alone; but if it die, it beareth much fruit. He that loveth his life loseth it, and he that hateth his life in this world shall keep it unto life eternal." The thought of death rouses in Jesus a thoroughly healthy, human fear: " Now is my soul troubled, and what shall I say? " " Father, save me from this hour," arises to His lips. But at once He is aware of the contradiction in this prayer to the divine mission. " But for this cause came I unto this hour." Then He forgets every trivial fear and selfish wish; He sees only the supreme end which His sacrifice will serve, the establishment of God's kingdom, and He speaks: " Father, glorify Thy name."

Luther's daring prayer for the sick elector Johannsen displays the abrupt change from vehement insistent clamour into willing surrender of his own wishes. He first threatens God that he will throw down his keys and bring no more honour or tribute; then he speaks softly and humbly: " O Lord, we are Thine, do with us as Thou wilt, only give us patience! " Pascal's prayer for the right use of his illness shows progressive elevation. First, he complains of his sinfulness and his previous worldliness, then asks that he shall rightly know himself and repent of his sins; he pleads for consolation and strength,

for power and steadfastness to endure. Finally, he rises to a
complete surrender to God, which testifies to his great heroism.
This submission might be called mystic resignation, if it were
not for Pascal's virile nature and the uncompromising moral
dignity of his endurance: " Thou art Lord of all; do what
Thou wilt. Grant me, take from me, but make my will con-
form to Thine; that being sick as I am, I may glorify Thee
in my sufferings."

Originally, the expression of resignation is the outgrowth of
true prayer. But frequent experience of this transition of the
wish into subordination to God's will finally, if the emotion is
not too intense, produces a type of prayer in which the wish
is only conditionally formulated beforehand, or the expression
of surrender already precedes it, just as we have seen in the
case of hope and assurance. Luther devises out of his mode
of conditional prayer a rule, although it is not in complete
accord with his actual manner of prayer, to the effect " that we
should place our will under that of God in everything which
concerns the body. Inasmuch as only God knows what is good
for us and can be of use to us, we should put His will before
ours and show obedience with patience." Such prayer, to be
sure, has to do with earthly blessings; it does not affect religious and ethical values, which are experienced as the will
of God. " But where the matter is not one of earthly goods
but of eternal welfare, that God will forgive us our sins,
save us, and grant us the Holy Spirit, and life everlasting, there
God's will is plain and certain. Therefore, it is not necessary
when one is praying for these things that one should ask for
them only as though it were a question whether God willed
them or not."

Submission to God's will attained through prayer may become a permanent attitude, so much so, in fact, that an attempt to bring a desire to God in prayer fails utterly, and
only words of surrender come to the lips. Luther prays during pestilence: " Lord, I am in Thy hand; Thou hast bound
me here. Thy will be done, for I am Thy poor creature; Thou
canst slay me here or preserve me." Kierkegaard confesses:
" Gradually I have become more and more mindful of this,
that to be loved by God and to love God means to suffer.

But if that be the case, then I have no right to ask for happiness and success." This paradoxical faith in the value of suffering reduced to silence the wishes which pressed for expression in prayer: " If a wish awoke within me and I wanted to pray, all my burning fervour was as it were blown away, for it was to me as if God looked on me and said, Little friend, do you consider well what you are doing and is it, then, your will that I do not love you? "

The prayer of Jesus: " Not as I will, but as Thou wilt," has been considered by all Christian mystics to be the prototype of mystic resignation. And yet His surrender to the will of the Father differs psychologically and fundamentally from stoic or mystic resignation — even though, naturally, as a result of the mixture of the two types, the fervour of Christian submission to God has lent to mystic resignation a touch of its own enthusiasm. Pure mystic surrender, as required by Stoicism and Buddhism, and as it echoes from the prayers of Christian mystics, is the absolute renunciation of every desire of one's own, complete absence of emotion, a mood of cool indifference, passive, negative, quietist. Christian submission, on the contrary, is not the absolute giving up of every wish, absence of will, but it is renunciation, the yielding of a definite desire and craving in the interests of a higher good; frequently, indeed, it is not complete renunciation but the leaving of the fulfilment of one's own wish to the free judgment and discretion of God, an actual subordination of oneself to God's will. It is, in a way, illogical of mystics to speak in Scriptural terminology of the will of God, for will is attributed only to the God of prophetic religion.

In contrast to the indifference of the mystics, free from joy or sorrow, prophetic surrender is active and positive; there is no suppression of the desires, but confidence, assurance that God, even if He denies us our unimportant wishes, still knows what is best for us. Höffding says strikingly of submissive Christian prayer: " The will is given up, but even this surrender is a positive wish, or it is only the negative side of a positive wish." The resignation of prophetic and evangelical piety, moreover, unlike the mood of indifference of the mystics, is not a result of systematic, purposeful suppression of the emotional life of choice, the " blotting out " of the living will; it is the outcome of a psychic struggle and is won through the discharge of emotion, its unreserved outpouring before God. Christian resignation, differing from that of mysticism, presupposes the simple expression of a concrete wish; it is the spontaneous result of true prayer and therefore does not arise from a state of unconcern which rejects at the threshold every desire, every request. The " holy indifference " of mysticism is artificial, or at least it is artificially prepared by conscious premeditation; the submission of prophetic religion, on the other hand, is quite unintended, for the petition begins with the naïve and spontaneous request; the undesigned result is a creative act. This, to be sure, pertains only to the great petitioners of the prophetic type, for the simplicity and absence of intention of the ordinary worshipper who takes these men as his models may be obscured by emulation and imitation.

The fact that resignation emerges spontaneously out of the expression of need makes it impossible to comprehend it under a rule of prayer. The injunctions both of prophetic leaders and of the theologians who scientifically interpret the prophetic religion of the Bible, are contradictory and this, psychologically considered, is unavoidable. Rules of prayer seeking to reduce religious experience to an authoritative standard are never able to lay primary stress upon more than one of its two elements, the naïve utterance of distress or the expression of trust, that is, submission. This contradiction is quite evident in what Jesus says about prayer. On the one hand He exhorts to trusting, even vehement persisting prayer; on the other, He warns against the using of many words, " for your Father," He reminds His hearers, " knoweth what things ye have need of before ye ask Him." Luther in similar manner encourages on the one side to importunate prayer, on the other desires that prayer for earthly things shall be restricted. These are two phases of one and the same exercise of prayer, and any attempted rule of prayer will exalt one at the expense of the other. Wilhelm Herrmann sees in the inner connection of these two antagonistic elements, naïve wish and joyous

worldliness, then asks that he shall rightly know himself
and repent of his sins; he pleads for consolation and strength,
resignation, the characteristic quality of biblical and Christian prayer. " Two spiritual movements," he says, " are
bound together in vital unity which no human effort could
unite; the heartfelt desire to experience help from God, and
the humble joyous submission to God's will. We cannot accomplish this union by a mere command: ' thou shalt indeed
ask God for a concrete boon, but also thou shalt always be
ready to renounce it.' This union comes about of itself in
him who believes. Our faith sets us in the presence of a God
whose help is certain. . . . The natural desire of the distressed
creature to influence God's will in its own favour vanishes in
Christian prayer because we feel that our petition is laid upon
a God who loves us with a love greater than that of father or
mother."

(g) *Thanksgiving*

The expression of confidence and resignation presupposes
that the need has found voice in complaint or petition; these
are genetically connected. The expression of assurance that
one has been heard rises to a prayer of thanksgiving. When
Paul exhorts the Philippians " in everything by prayer and
supplication with thanksgiving let your requests be made unto
God," he probably means that words of praise should be
mingled with every prayer; that every petition should pass
into an expression of gratitude. Not infrequently the very
expression of the petition awoke in the worshipper such a
confidence that he thanked God in anticipation of the granting of the request. There is a certain justification for the
conventional division into petition and praise. " The two
parts of prayer are petition and thanksgiving " — so runs a
theological axiom of Calvin. Zwingli's definition runs thus:
" Prayer is first praise and glorifying, and then a trustful
appeal for aid in our necessity." The giving of thanks is the
joyful acknowledgment that God has granted His grace or
benefit. The worshipper confesses that his outer or inner happiness is God's free gift, his gratitude is thus a sign of his
entire dependence upon God. As at the primitive level, the

prayer of thanksgiving frequently stands in intimate relation with the prayer of petition; that is, when a request has already been heard. The objects of thanksgiving are likewise pre-eminently religious and ethical blessings.

The psalmist expresses gratitude for the nation's deliverance by Jahve: "I will give thanks unto Thee, for Thou hast answered me, and art become my salvation." And Paul thanks God for the steadfastness and growth of his young Churches: "I thank my God upon all my remembrance of you . . . for your fellowship in furtherance of the gospel from the first day until now." Augustine gives thanks for the sin-forgiving grace of God: "I will love Thee, O Lord, and thank Thee and confess unto Thy name; because Thou hast forgiven me so great and heinous sins of mine. I attribute it to Thy grace and mercy that Thou hast melted away my sins as it were ice." Pascal with his love of paradox prays: "I give Thee thanks, my God, for the good impulses which Thou givest me, and for this very one which Thou hast given me to give Thee thanks."

God is thanked also for what is trivial and everyday: "Giving thanks always for all things in the name of our Lord Jesus Christ, and God, even the Father." As request is made for daily bread, so acknowledgment is made for the same. Jesus Himself always carried out the Jewish custom of giving thanks at the breaking of bread or the drinking of wine. Paul probably used the Jewish formula for grace at meals. . . . It is very significant that the offering of thanks at table gave the name "Eucharist"[3] to the early Christian Communion.

(h) *Praise*

The purely contemplative prayer of adoration directed exclusively to God with no reference to oneself appears only here and there in prophetic devotion. If God is praised, it is for His benefits to mankind. Most of the Old Testament psalms of praise and most Christian hymns are genuine prayers of thanksgiving. In only a few of the Psalms is God glorified for Himself, for His greatness and might or for

---

[3] εὐχαριστία.

the beauty and wisdom of His creation. In these, the worshipping poet, astounded and enraptured, stands in the presence of God and loses himself in wondering contemplation of
the marvel of His nature:

> "Bless Jahve, O my soul,
>   O Jahve, my God, Thou art very great;
>   Thou art clothed with honour and majesty;
>   O Jahve, how manifold are Thy works!
>   In wisdom hast Thou made them all! "

The content of many of the Psalms, such as the ninety-ninth,
is the concrete, poetic contemplation of nature, directed
towards the entire animate and inanimate creation. We perceive here the same enthusiasm for nature which marks individual hymns of antiquity, only it is rendered more genuine
and vivid by the prophetic spirit of prayer. The absolutely
selfless meditation, the solemn exalted adoration of the Infinite, the passing of the sense of dependence audible in
prayers of thanksgiving, and of invocation into pure contemplation — all these characteristics are common to the Old
Testament psalms of praise as well as to various ancient
hymns, and show signs of similarity to the true mystic form
of prayer. Nevertheless, there is an unmistakable difference.
Self-oblivious contemplation never becomes mystic or pantheistic absorption in the contemplated object; the distance
between man and God emphasized in early Semitic and
prophetic religion is dissolved through no mystic union. Contemplative adoration as contrasted with actual mysticism is
thus not directed to the absolutely ideal *summum bonum*, unrelated to any concrete values, or merely imperfectly reflected in them; but God and nature, the highest good and
concrete beautiful things stand in intimate connection; nature
is the " work of His hands." Nature never becomes the
Divine All, neither is she in the neo-Platonic sense a mere
imperfect image of the perfect original, ideal form. " O Jahve,
our Lord, how excellent is Thy name in all the earth."

(i) *Yearning and Vision*

The mystic's prayer is in part ardent longing for the One,
the Highest, and in part a beatific vision and joy in the infinite

God. Yearning and vision are also the content of many prayers in prophetic worship. "Show me, I pray Thee, Thy glory," is the prayer of Moses, in the Jahvist source of the Pentateuch. The longing for the blessed vision of God meets us often in the Psalms, as, for example, the sixteenth, forty-second and sixty-third, revealing an astonishing similarity to the words of mystic prayer, yet containing another meaning. It is true that the desire expressed includes just as in mystic contemplation the assurance of the supreme reality, the only guaranty of happiness to the devout man. But the religious men of the Old Testament do not seek to become one with God, to be submerged in the Infinite, a condition which the mystic attains through complete separation from all creation and through the annihilation of his natural will. The distance between God and man does not permit a dissolution of the human personality into God. The worshipper craves not ecstatic union with God, but only to feel His presence in blessed, living communion with Him. Consciousness of the immediate nearness of God produces a firm confidence in life and a certainty of salvation. "But it is good for me to draw near to God," says the psalmist. Originally the longing for the vision of Jahve's countenance was nothing but the desire to visit the temple, in which, according to Israelitish belief, Jahve tarried, and where one became aware of His protecting aid. With the spiritualization of God, the connection of His presence with an external spot disappeared; God's nearness was a purely inner experience in sincere believing prayer. Thus the fundamental characteristic of prophetic devotion is revealed in such seemingly mystic prayers; the strong vital assurance is based upon the certainty of God's effectual presence.

IV. The Conception of God which Underlies Prophetic Prayer

"Might" and natural human characteristics are the two attributes of the God of primitive man; the prophets know God as will and personality. The personal human picture of God is never absent during the prayer of the devout worshipper. The gross anthropomorphic features of this conception such as form the basis of primitive prayer are discarded: God is neither bound to place nor limited in sphere of action. He is supersensuous. It is not with human eyes and ears that He sees and hears. He has no human needs and desires which man may gratify through sacrifices and offerings. He is not a capricious and revengeful being, although as a righteously zealous God He is angry, He judges and punishes. And yet the essential traits of personality, thinking, willing, feeling, are as vital to the prophetic conception of God as to that of the primitive man. The worshipper is able to pour out the needs of his heart to none but a God with human feelings; none other could comfort and help him; surely not a superpersonal, spiritual ideal. God is not the Sole Existent, the Limitless One, the Supreme Good, as in mystic prayer, but the " Helper in time of need," the " Hearer of prayer," in the simple terms of Luther's piety. The psalmist says: " O Thou that hearest prayer, unto Thee shall all flesh come." Savonarola prays: " To take away misery, to raise up the miserable, that is Thy work." Luther says: " This is the peculiar work of our Lord God, that He hears prayer and helps those who cry to Him." Nor is the God of prophetic worship a static, final Good, but a dynamic Will whom one can expect to take part in the world and in the life of men. He rules the universe and brings the things which should be into being. The contrast to the idea of God presupposed in mystical prayer and the agreement with primitive man's idea of God cannot be denied.

V. Belief in the Presence of God

All primitive prayer is rooted in the belief that a God is near who hearkens. This belief persists in a spiritual form, yet with undiminished realism, in prophetic prayer. For prayer is an actual speaking with a personal " Thou." Moses is distinguished as one " whom Jahve knew face to face," and this idea finds echo in the language of later devotional life. The psalmist confesses: " Jahve is near unto all them that call upon Him, to all that call upon Him in truth." To pray is for Calvin " a conversation with God," for Luther " to come into God's

presence and to speak with Him," for Zwingli " to go to God,"
" to be acquainted with Him and speak with Him." Bunyan
speaks still more clearly: " By prayer is our most direct and
immediate personal approach to the presence of God." Pascal
knows himself in prayer to be " alone in God's presence "; and
Kierkegaard writes: " In still loneliness God lets me weep,
since I weep my pain out again and again before Him."

The drawing near of an insignificant personality to the
great God contains the same paradox for the prophetic and
mystic worshipper alike. " I have taken upon me to speak
unto the Lord, who am but dust and ashes," are the words of
Abraham according to the Jahvist writer. Luther loses
himself in this amazing contrast: " That I who am only
dust and ashes and full of sins should speak to the true,
living, eternal God." The dying Bunyan exhorts: " Before thou enterest into prayer, consider that thou art only ' dust
and ashes ' and He the great God and Father of our Lord
Jesus Christ, who clothes Himself with light as with a garment,
that thou art a vile sinner and He a holy God."

In primitive prayer God's presence is always associated
with a sensuous object, a concrete natural phenomenon — it
may be only the bright sky, or the work of man's hands, an
image or a fetish. Even the pious Israelite longs for the
temple upon Mount Zion, where Jahve is throned in power
and glory. The later prophets break through this conception:
" Thus saith Jahve, ' Heaven is my throne, and the earth
is my footstool; what manner of house will ye build unto
me? ' " And Jesus says, " . . . when neither in this mountain, nor in Jerusalem shall ye worship the Father . . . the
true worshippers shall worship the Father in spirit and in
truth," yet this is not the philosophers' weakening of simple
faith in the nearness of God: God is much closer than if He
were in external objects when He dwells in the hearts of His
believers. " Know ye not that ye are a temple of God and
that the Spirit of God dwelleth in you? " Calvin draws the
logical consequence: " Since we are the true temples of God,
we must pray within ourselves if we would invoke God in
His holy temple." This greater individualizing of the thought
of the actual presence of God makes prayer universal, severs

the primitive association with locality. As Luther says: " A Christian is bound to no place and may pray anywhere, in the street, the fields, or the church." The prophetic and Christian thought of prayer knows as little as the mystical of the local limitations of primitive and ancient devotional religion.

Nevertheless, the individualism which underlies belief in God's presence in the human heart makes the lonely spot the most suitable for prayer. Plotinus's " alone with the Alone " is the ideal of prayer, and in this, mystical and prophetic piety are completely one. Hezekiah in prayer " turns his face to the wall," an involuntary expression of his wish to be alone with God. In post-exilic Judaism pious persons when praying withdrew to an upper chamber. Jesus prays alone on the quiet mountain top, in desert places, in the darkness of night. He considered the solitude of prayer so important that He raised it to a normal requirement. " But thou, when thou prayest, enter into thine inner chamber, and having shut thy door, pray to thy Father, who is in secret."

The mystic craves solitariness because " withdrawal " from the world and man is the condition of blessed union with the Infinite; prophetic natures seek not to isolate themselves permanently, but only to speak unhindered with their God. They receive thus the impulse which sends them to work among their brethren for the kingdom of God. His infinite power, holiness, goodness are manifested to them to be proclaimed to the world, His will to be made known to their fellows. The prophetic individual knows God near at all times, in the turmoil of everyday life and among his associates, as well as in intimate communion with God.

VI. The Relation of God and Man as Revealed in Prayer

Prayer in prophetic piety, as in mysticism, is a real communion, a vital relation between man and God; its social character contrasts with the mystic's tendency to be swallowed up in meditation and contemplation. The forms of prayer, invocation, petition, giving of thanks, in prophetic and primitive worship, are genuine expressions of a relationship of man to God which reflects the relationships of earthly society. Prayer is not, as with the mystic, elevation to the supreme good, but a request for help and grace, the fulfilment of desire. The term "hearing of prayer" is quite foreign to mysticism. God is for the mystic the supreme, changeless Reality whom man cannot influence by prayer even if he should pray for the highest moral blessings. The primitive conception of a real influence of man upon God lies at the root of the prophetic belief in the hearing of prayer. In the Pentateuch we read: "And Moses besought Jahve his God," and then a prayer follows. "And Jahve repented of the evil which He said He would do unto His people." Amos confesses: "Then I said, O Lord Jahve, forgive I beseech Thee. Then Jahve repented concerning this: ' It shall not be,' saith Jahve." The psalmists of Israel repeatedly assert that Jahve has heard their prayer, that because of it He has granted them help and salvation. Jesus speaks most plainly: " Ask, and it shall be given you; seek, and ye shall find; knock, and it shall be opened unto you."

The transferring of the relationships of human society to the relation of man to God through prayer is present in the parables which are found in the eleventh and eighteenth chapters of Luke, concerning the importunate friend and the persistent widow. They reveal the active, effectual nature of prayer; this is also strikingly brought out in Paul's exhortation to the brethren to " strive together with me in your prayers to God for me." To the Church at Philippi he writes: " I know that this shall turn to my salvation through your supplication."

Luther's writings are full of psychologically valuable testimony to belief in the actual power of prayer. He ascribes to prayer even magic virtues. " No one believes how strong and mighty prayer is and how much it can do except he whom experience has taught and who has tried it. It has raised up in our time three persons who lay in danger of death, myself, my wife Katha, and Philip Melanchthon in 1540 at Weimar." " A Christian knows that what he has prayed for is not denied him, and indeed he experiences help in all necessities." " The prayer of a Christian is an almighty thing." For Luther prayer without an answer would be valueless. " If

I did not know that our prayer would be heard, the Devil may pray in my stead." " If a Christian heart earnestly prays, sighs and beseeches and continues to do so, it is impossible that such a prayer should not be heard by God." " Prayer brings it about that God hastens since otherwise He would not so hasten." He says plainly that God's will may be influenced and altered, an idea that, less directly expressed, underlies Old and New Testament utterances in regard to prayer. His bold and unshakable belief is that which is held both by the Old Testament prophets and by Jesus and His apostles, while it continues also among evangelical Christians of more recent times. Kierkegaard writes in his diary: " The archimedean point outside the world is the little chamber where a true suppliant prays in all sincerity — where he lifts the world off its hinges." As C. H. Spurgeon has put it, " Prayer is able to prevail with Heaven and bend omnipotence to its desires."

Even Christian mysticism has not entirely escaped the powerful influence of Biblical Christian belief in answered prayer. This latter plays a striking part in the monasticism of the Eastern Church, which is full of mystic tendencies. The peculiar power of " the spiritual fathers " in prayer, denoted by the word *parrhesia*, that is, frank confidence expressed in prayer, becomes in the great charismatically endowed men nothing less than the right to ask from God any extraordinary gift. So great a mystic as St. Teresa made intercession firmly believing that her prayers were heard. She relates in her autobiography frequent marvellous answers to prayer: " How often the Lord has heard my prayer, I could never tell. If I should count, I should only weary myself, as well as every one who might read it."

The turning of the mystic in prayer to the Supreme Good is an act placed far above all earthly social relationships; only in emotional mysticism do the yearning and beatitude take the form of the bridal relationship. Prophetic prayer, as well as that of primitive religion, unquestionably reflects a human social relationship. Man talks with God as with a friend, master, father. Moses speaks with Jehovah as with a friend; with later prophets this motive is found mixed with the relationship of bondsman, arising out of early Semitic religion. The Psalms most frequently express the idea of servant:

"Behold, as the eyes of servants look unto the hand of their master,
  As the eyes of a maid unto the hand of her mistress;
  So our eyes look upon Jahve our God."

The word "Lord" became the chief form of address with the Jews of the Septuagint, whence it entered Christian devotional language. The filial relation to God the Father, so often found in primitive prayer, became more and more prominent in Israelitish worship. The closeness of the two forms of relationship is revealed in Jahve's words to Malachi: "A son honoureth his father, a servant his master; if then I am a father, where is mine honour? and if I am a master, where is my fear?" The almost invariable use which Jesus makes in His prayer of the term "Father" so impressed itself upon His disciples that the Greek authors of the Gospels repeat it in the Aramaic form of the word, *Abba*. The conception of the filial relationship, which had faded away under the influence of the philosophical and mystical ideas of the late Greek world, blossoms again in the biblical Christianity of the Reformation.

The devotional attitude is a social relationship towards God. The seer or prophet, in friendship with God, manifests, in spite of his reliance upon God, a proud self-consciousness and self-confidence, a manly freedom and openness, an earnestness and sense of worth. Fear is as remote as a puerile assurance. A stronger feeling of dependence is present where God is addressed as Lord and King. The attributes given Jahve by Israelitish worshippers — "Lord of Hosts," "Judge of all the earth," "the great and dreadful God," are all correlated with the awe and fear which are always present in their prayers. In the Old Testament, the "fear of God" is synonymous with religion and piety.

This religious filial relationship includes the humility and reverence of the servant and the frank affection of the friend. The worshipper, conscious of his own littleness, poverty, and helplessness, feels himself totally dependent upon the Father's

goodness, yet united to this humble attitude there is a boldness with which the petitioner, like a child, carries to the
Father fearlessly and trustingly whatever moves him.   It
is a confidence based not upon one's own moral force and
goodness, but upon the truth of God's promises.

The kind of social relationship in which the worshipper
believes he stands to God gives the prayer its tone; manifest
in the choice of words, sound of voice, plays of expression,
the disposition, made known in audible prayer, passes over
to those who listen.   The naïve prayer of primitive man makes
a deep impression upon eye and ear witnesses.   European
ethnographers relate how greatly they have been moved by
the prayer of savages.   Still more profound and lasting must
have been the impression received by those who were present
when the great religious leaders prayed.   Unfortunately, we
possess no testimony as to the effect of the prayers of the
greatest prophetic personalities upon their followers and intimate associates; only about the peculiar quality of Luther's
praying have we some information: Veit Dietrich says: " What
a spirit, what faith, was in his words!   He prayed so devoutly, as one who talked with God with the hope and belief
of one speaking to his Father. . . . When I heard him at a
distance praying in clear tones, my heart burned within me
for joy, because I heard him speaking in so friendly and reverent a manner with God; chiefly, however, since he leaned so
hard upon the promises in the Psalms, as if everything must
certainly come to pass which he desired."

VII. Prophetic Standards of Prayer

Prophetic spirits see, as do the mystics, in their own devotional life the ideal of prayer, prayer according to the will of
God.   But judged by the prophet's standard, the mode of
prayer which stands below the level of the ideal is not considered as merely an incomplete, earlier stage of the pure,
sincere petition, but is stamped as a false and irregular one.
Prophetic teaching about prayer has always a keenly polemic quality.   Furthermore, in contrast with mystic prayer,
prophetic prayer is directed not only to the benefit of those

bound in spiritual kinship, but of all men without distinction. The ideal of prayer appears as a divine obligation everywhere valid. It knows no gradations as does mystical prayer; it is an unqualified *thou shalt;* it is the holy will of God. Prophetic discipline is therefore a struggle for ideal prayer.

This struggle is first against prayer from irreligious motives, such as seeking to be seen in prayer, to obtain the praise of men. The inner devoutness of the prophetic nature protests sharply against mechanical, unthinking, unfeeling babbling of long formulas. Isaiah is zealous against mere praying with the lips: " When ye make many prayers I will not hear." The son of Sirach exhorts: " Repeat not thy words in thy prayer." Jesus warns against the vain repetitions of the heathen. The Reformers carried on an unwearied polemic against undevout and unthinking prayer. " He who prays," says Luther, " prays from the heart and does not turn over a great number of pages or rattle many rosary beads." " If thou prayest from the heart only ' Hallowed be Thy name,' it is more than if thou prayest a hundred psalms without the heart." Zwingli says: " Prayer is nothing other than a lifting up of the mind to God." " There," says Bunyan, " is the life of prayer where in or with the spirit a man who feels his sinfulness comes in the power of the Spirit and calls ' Father ' ! That one word spoken in faith is better than a thousand so-called prayer words, written and read in a formal, cold, and luke-warm fashion." On his death bed he exhorts: " When thou prayest let rather the heart be without the words than the words without heart." Prophetic suppliants find the ideal in spontaneous prayer welling up from the heart, in perfectly free prayers. Bunyan and Fox have opposed still more ve-hemently than others the use of formulas for prayer, chiefly the *Book of Common Prayer.* " Only the Spirit can teach us how we must pray," writes Bunyan. " Without the Spirit, though we had a thousand Common Prayer books yet we know not what we should pray for as we ought." The spirit of the Reformation is opposed to legal and meritorious prayers as a form of atonement or good works, of value in itself as an achievement of man towards God, putting an obligation upon Him to do something in return. This is sinful profanation of the most sacred mystery of devotion, the " outpouring of the heart "; it is the degradation of worship to a mechanically imposed performance.

Positive instruction in mystic prayer consists in a careful psychological analysis of the devotional experiences at the different stages, with an oft-refined technique for the creation of a sure basis for this experience. Prophetic discipline offers no method, no analysis, but a direct, " After this manner, therefore, pray ye." A fuller, more concrete guide may be given in the enumeration of the good things for which one shall pray. Jesus, like the Jewish Rabbis, taught His disciples thus: not through a binding formulary, but in a prayer which has been a model throughout the Christian Church. Augustine says in his instruction in prayer for the widow Proba: " When we pray rightly and properly we shall ask for nothing else than what is contained in the Lord's Prayer. It is, to be sure, left to our choice to pray with other and different words for the same things as are contained in the Lord's Prayer, but we are not free to pray for other things." Luther says: " The Lord's Prayer is the highest, noblest and best prayer; all other prayers should be suspected which do not have or comprise the content and meaning of this prayer." " A Christian has prayed abundantly who has rightly prayed the Lord's Prayer." Calvin writes: " Written in this formula which has been handed down from the best Master is everything which we must ask from God and in general can ask. And this prayer is in every way so perfect that whatever foreign and alien element is added to it but cannot be traced back to it, is impious and is unworthy to be heard by God." " No one," says Rothe, " will ever outgrow the school of the Lord's Prayer, this truly pattern prayer and primary type of all Christian prayer in matter and form."

VIII. Comparison of Mystical and Prophetic Prayer

The difference between mystical and prophetic prayer is manifest in every way: in motive, form, and content, in the conception of God and in the relation to God implied and in the standard of prayer. Mystical prayer has its roots in the yearning of the devout person for union with the Infinite; prophetic prayer arises from the profound need of the heart and the longing for salvation and grace. Mystical prayer is artificially prepared through a refined psychological technique of meditation; the prophetic petition breaks forth spontaneously and violently from the subconscious depths of the religious soul that has been deeply stirred. Mystical prayer is silent, contemplative delight; prophetic prayer a passionate crying and groaning, vehement complaint and pleading. Mystical prayer is solemn exaltation of the spirit to the highest good; prophetic prayer, a simple outpouring of the heart. Mystical prayer is a passing out of oneself, an entering and sinking into the Infinite God; prophetic prayer is the utterance of the profound need that moves the inmost being.

Mystical prayer is a weary climbing by degrees to the heights of vision and union with God; prophetic prayer a stormy assault upon the Father's heart. Mystical prayer represents advances in a straight course, continuous progress, purification, enlightenment, union; prophetic prayer comprises inner transformation, radical revolution; anxious fear and eager longing pass over into serene trust and the joy of calm surrender. The God of the mystic is the Infinite One, the *summum bonum*, in whom the mystic is completely absorbed; the God of prophetic prayer is the living Lord, to whom the worshipper is bound with every fibre of his being, the kind Father to whom he clings in absolute trust and confidence.

Mystical prayer is the consuming of self in the flame of God's love, dissolving into the glow of the Infinite, melting into the stream of the Immeasurable; prophetic prayer is a mighty wrestling with a challenging and commanding God. Mystical prayer is the passing away in desire for the divine Loved One and then again a blessed tranquillity and ecstatic delight in the tender embrace of the Heavenly Bridegroom; prophetic prayer is humble reverence before the majesty of the eternal King and Lord, a timorous pleading of the guilt-laden soul before the stern Judge, a heartfelt, trusting approach of the child to the loving Father. Mystical prayer is something totally new as compared with that of primitive man: the complete detachment from one's ego, absorption in the *summum bonum;*

in prophetic worship primitive prayer reappears, greatly refined, it is true, and ennobled, but yet with all its original force
of passion and *naïveté* and its dramatic vitality. Like primitive prayer, prophetic petition is essentially the expression of
need, desire for salvation and blessing; it is belief in a God who
will hearken and aid.

Yet both types, despite all these differences, reveal a final
common quality. All mystic prayer is a rising to the highest
good; all prophetic prayer finds its culmination in the desire
for the coming of the Kingdom of God, that is, the realization
of all spiritual values. Here it differs strikingly from primitive prayer, for like mystical devotion it is directed not to a
fleeting, temporary good, but to an ultimate supreme good.
Nevertheless, there exists here an essential distinction. The
end of the latter is a static final good; that of the former, a
vital, dynamic magnitude, the Kingdom of God. The final
good which the mystic seeks is beyond all concrete reality, beyond all manifoldness, the " One," " the Only "; that towards
which prophetic piety looks, which controls and permeates
all reality, manifests itself in multiplicity, " God who is all
in all." [4]

[4] ὁ θεὸς πάντα ἐν πᾶσιν.

CHAPTER X

THE PERSONAL PRAYER OF GREAT MEN
(POETS AND ARTISTS)

THE prayer of men of religious genius is the most living, the most powerful, the most profound, and the most fervent species of prayer; it towers as the loftiest peak among the various types. If we exclude the prayer of the early Christian Church, there stands next to it, in psychic depth and native energy, the prayer of those great and creative men whose thought and life, like that of men of religious genius, belongs to a higher sphere, yet to a sphere other than the strictly religious, that of the poet and the artist, the statesman and the military leader. Whilst in the case of religious genius the spiritual life, that is, the life of values, culminates in the religious realm or is exclusively limited to it, the element of religion does not occupy the central, dominating place, but stands beside artistic creation or the shaping of political policy. Prayer, therefore, has not that controlling place in their lives and thought which it has in the lives of prophets and saints; it is not, as it is with them, " a praying without ceasing," an abiding *life of prayer*. Nevertheless it can be matched with the prayer of great religious leaders in vital vigour, freshness, spontaneity, and originality; it reveals the same forcible individualism which is the outstanding characteristic of the prayer of religious geniuses. As prayer for the great spirits in the realm of religion is the soil of all religious perceptions and revelations, so it is also for the men of poetic and plastic arts a chief source of their productive activity, a spring of artistic ideas and inspiration. As in the prayer of religious genius, so here two types are to be distinguished: an aesthetic, contemplative and an ethical, emotional mode of prayer. The former is close to the mystical, the latter is similar in struc-

ture to the prophetic type, and like this type it resembles the
primitive form of prayer in emotional quality, simplicity, and
realism. Both forms, however, are not mutually exclusive
but may be bound up together in one and the same personality. Thus, for instance, both types are exhibited in Beethoven's illustrations of prayer.

I. THE AESTHETIC, CONTEMPLATIVE TYPE

Doubtless aesthetic and romantic mysticism is not religious
mysticism in the strict sense of the term. The deepest difference between them is that the former is without that limitation
to the religious domain which is essential to all genuine mysticism. Yet the mode and method of its religious experience
from a psychological point of view, is so closely related to
mysticism proper, that we are justified in speaking of it as a
variant or parallel to mysticism. Pre-intimations of this
mystical type are already found in the personal hymnology
of ancient peoples and in not a few Old Testament Psalms.
The piety of the Persian Sûfis and Jewish Chassids, of St.
Francis of Assisi and Suso reveals strains of this mysticism.
Its proper representatives, however, are among modern poets
and poet-philosophers such as Rousseau, Goethe, the roman-
ticists, Emerson, Ruskin, Amiel, Paul de Lagarde, and Mal-
wida of Meysenbug. This aesthetic religion is the religion of
many cultured people to-day who reject the identification
of religion with morality. The esteem which the mediaeval
mystics enjoy at the present time, as in the age of romanticism, rests on the correct understanding of the relationship
of modern religion to mysticism.

Aesthetic, artistic mysticism, in contrast to the purely religious type rejects a negative, pessimistic estimate of the
world; it reveals a thoroughly optimistic feeling for life. As
the watchword of the Jewish Chassids has it: — " Let only joy
rule." Amiel defines religion as enthusiasm. Healthy joy in
the world and life admits of no isolation from the world, no
mortification of the senses, no suppression of the emotional
life, no painful self-concentration and self-hypnosis. Joy in
life is not burdened with any feeling of insignificance, any

consciousness of being miserable sinners. There is just as little of an ascetic element as there is of any training of the soul; quietism and passiveness is secondary. Modern mystics are creative personalities penetrated by faith in values and in ideal tasks. Aesthetic mysticism is clarified, harmonious, free from all that is ecstatic and visionary, from all emotional confusion. It believes in the value and rights of human personality, which are denied and annulled by radical mysticism.

This latter type, which "closes" the entire world of the senses, is insensitive and indifferent to all aesthetic values, especially to the beauty of Nature. Madame Guyon says of the woman mystic: "If she walks through the most glorious scene of Nature, she can distinguish nothing; the trees do not blossom for her, the flowers do not exhale their fragrance for her." On the contrary, the contemplative enjoyment of concrete, artistic values is essential to aesthetic mysticism, and just because Nature conceals in itself a plenitude of such values, aesthetic experiences especially are determined by Nature. The unreserved surrender to the value of beauty can take place only in a high-wrought mood of unity, a feeling of being at one with the object contemplated, still more deeply, a feeling of infinitude, an absorption in the All. These aesthetic moods and experiences clearly reveal a relationship with genuine mystical experiences; they have a religious tone, the feeling for Nature glides into a mystical, ecstatic consciousness of God, the One and Only. But the great distinction between this and genuine mysticism is this, that the mystical experience of union with God is kindled in the contemplation of the world, that the "numinous" experience of values is linked up with an aesthetic experience of values, that the "holy" is identified with the "beautiful." The God of this mysticism does not stand behind the delusive reality, without vital relation to it; on the contrary, He is immanent in the world. His nature shines through everything that is aesthetically valuable. The God of this religion is of necessity pantheistic, a God who "reveals" Himself in all that is noble and beautiful. "In everything which man beholds, he beholds the countenance of the Friend," says Ferîd-ed-dîn-Attâr. "Do you not see God?" says Goethe. "By every quiet spring, under every blossoming tree He meets me in the warmth of His love." In all *Nature* — in wood and meadow, fountain and lake, mountain and sea, sunshine and storm and starry night — but also in *man* — in the simplicity of a child's eyes and the charm of a maiden's face, in the tender embrace of a lover, and in the anxious look of a mother — not merely in *art*, in the world of colours and tones, of rhythms and rhymes — but everywhere does the enthusiastic mystic find his God. In all that is beautiful and noble he beholds the unity and the harmony of the All. "Creation," says Amiel, "is an immense symphony, glorifying the God of goodness by the exhaustless riches of its harmonious tones and praises."

What the aesthetic mystics call "prayer," "adoration," "devotion," shows an unmistakable similarity to the contemplative absorption of the genuine mystic. Devotional contemplation, however, is nearly always concentrated on something without, is directed on a concrete natural object as representing a value, in contrast to the inner contemplation of the prayer genuinely mystical. Strong aesthetic impressions of Nature call forth spontaneously a prayerful mood. Rousseau writes in his *Confessions:* "I rose every morning before the sun and passed through a neighbouring orchard into a pleasant path which led by a vineyard and along the hills towards Chambéry. While walking I prayed, not by a vain motion of the lips, but with a sincere lifting up of my heart to the Creator of this beautiful Nature whose charms lay spread out before my eyes. I never like to pray in my chamber; it is to me as if the walls and all the little works of man came between God and myself. I like to contemplate Him in His works, whilst my heart lifts itself up to Him."

With fixed gaze he who prays beholds the beauty of Nature and sinks down in contemplation into deep delightful peace and sweet day dreams, or he is seized by astonishment and admiration, borne away by ecstasy and bliss. He glides into feelings of sublimity and blessedness; he is "inundated by sensations," "submerged in sensations." All discords are absent; "work, tears, sin, pain, death are no more"; "the joy of being able to admire is the governing feeling; gratitude is mingled with enthusiasm "; " one adores in the amazement of ecstasy and in the ardent humility of love." " To be is to be blessed: life is happiness," as Amiel says. Intoxicated with rapture he who gives himself to the object by which he is entranced even to self-oblivion believes that he passes out beyond himself, enters into the object of contemplation and dissolves away in it. In the disappearance of clear self-consciousness and the unreserved losing of oneself in an object of æsthetic value, he experiences an enlargement of his own constricted ego; a feeling of the infinite comes over him, a " cosmic consciousness "; it is to him as if, in the phrase of Amiel, " he bore the world in his bosom." As Friedrich Braig sings:

> " In the deep night I rest
> On world's foundation,
> Giant I am, primeval mountain
>   Midst roaring sea,
> Forests I bear and on my breast
> Rivers are rolling.
> My brow is rock
> My eyes are stars."

This solemn mood, this fervent feeling for Nature, may express itself spontaneously in the free words of prayer, but more frequently the aesthetic contemplation remains dumb, a speechless, enraptured vision and joy. " I am silent, I bow myself, I adore," as Amiel says. The emotional mood is not set free, its energy remains pent up within itself. " Silence," says the same writer, " is the divine state because every word and every gesture are limited and transient."

Contemplative adoration, praise, surrender, longing, union, form the content of this type of prayer. The parallelism to mystical prayer in the strict sense is everywhere apparent. " O let me ever feel love eternally ! " " Thou all-loving who didst create sun and moon and stars, heaven and earth and me ! " " Upwards to Thy breast, all-loving Father ! " " Praise is my only prayer." These cries come from the lips of Goethe.

The romanticist mystic, in his powerful moods, experiences contact with the Unity that rules the All; a *tête-à-tête avec l'infini*, a *converser avec Dieu* — so Amiel calls the ardent contemplation of Nature. Paul de Lagarde calls prayer " an inhalation in the divine air, a realization that the atmosphere of the human soul is the eternal Holy Spirit." The feeling of the immediate presence of the divine which is essential to all religious experience forms also the underlying religious note in the devotional moods of aesthetic mysticism. Nevertheless contemplative devotion never becomes realistic, simple communion of prayer which presupposes the idea of a personal God. Even the address of " Thou " to the infinite universal divinity cannot delude one as to its non-personal or superpersonal character. The Infinite does not wear human features like the God of the simple-minded worshipper; the relation to Him, therefore, cannot be along the lines of the human and the social.

II. THE EMOTIONAL, ETHICAL TYPE

Among modern poets prayer is a contemplative self-absorption in the infinite beauty of the God who reveals Himself in Nature. Its similarity to the sacred vision of the *summum bonum* to which the praying mystic is uplifted is very obvious. As compared with this exalted mystically tinged method of prayer there is in the devotional religion of great poets and artists a simpler, more purely human method which has affinity with prophetic piety and with the natural prayer of primitive man. Here prayer is not the enraptured vision and enjoyment of the glories of Nature, not a floating and feasting in the infinite All, but a simple expression of whatever touches the heart, of need and longing, of moral struggle and artistic effort. Simple petition and complaint forms the focus of the prayer as we have encountered it in primitive religion and in the piety of men of prophetic genius. In impulsive, unrestricted words the great geniuses pour out their hearts before God. Take, for example, the prayer of Oliver Cromwell on his death-bed: " Lord, though I am a miserable and wretched creature, I am in covenant with Thee through grace. And I may, and I will, come to Thee for Thy people. Thou hast made me, though very unworthy, a mean instrument to do them some good and Thee service. . . . Lord, however Thou do dispose of me, continue and go on to do good for them. Give them consistency of judgment, one heart and mutual love; and go on to deliver them, and with the work of reformation; and make the name of Christ glorious in the world. Teach those who look too much upon Thy instruments, to depend more upon Thyself. . . . And pardon the folly of this short prayer: Even for Jesus Christ's sake. And give us a good night if it be Thy pleasure. Amen."

Great men have poured forth their yearning and desire not only in extempore words of devotion, but sometimes they have had recourse to venerable forms of prayer. A little poem of the Russian poet Lermontow teaches us what vital power issues from the devout repetition of a formula of prayer:

" When in a gloomy hour
   My heart with grief was fraught,
A half-forgotten prayer
   Some wondrous message brought.

A bliss beyond expression
   Lies in those sacred words,
Mysterious life is flowing
   To me from magic chords.

And from my soul the burden
   Of anxious doubt doth flee —
A sigh sent up to Heaven
   Sets all my being free."

It is not small selfish wishes and commonplace fancies that form the subject of prayer among great men; it is the high aims and ideal values to which they aspire in the strain of seeking and struggling. They cannot realize by their own will and effort alone the lofty ideal of personality which hovers before them, or moral greatness, inner freedom, self-conquering power; hence the ethical ideal of life becomes for them an object of petitional prayer. No one can bestow upon himself the productive energy to create and put into form the matter created; it is an endowment of genius, a divine gift of grace. The extraordinary suggestions, impulses, ideas in which artists and poets conceive their works of genius cannot be generated by intending and willing them; genius passively receives them as from a higher Power; they are, just as much as the deep experiences of religious persons, breathed, infused into them, divine donations. Let them be wanting — what happens? The springs of artistic creation fail. Hence great poets and artists supplicate with such fervour and passion for high thoughts and deep feelings, for faith in themselves, for the joy and power of invention and creation. Petition for the realization of the personal ideal is always closely bound up with petition for grace and blessing in the ideal work of the vocation. To illustrate this, take the prayer of Michelangelo: " O let me behold Thee in every place! When I feel myself inflamed by mortal beauty, my ardour for Thy beauty is extinguished and I am enkindled by it as formerly I was by Thine. O my true Lord, to Thee alone I call for help against my blind, useless torment, for Thou alone canst inwardly and outwardly renew my senses, will and power which are weak and languid."

All simple hearted prayer is an unrestrained " outpouring of the soul "; the pious man expresses unreservedly to God all his distress and anxiety, whether the need be spiritual or physical. The limitation of petitionary prayer to the sphere of moral and religious values is not compatible with the frankness and confidence of a childlike religion. In hours of painful disillusionment and deep depression Beethoven poured forth the misery of his heart in passionate cries to God and called upon Him for help and compassion. " O God, God, look down upon Thy unhappy Beethoven; let it not remain so any longer!" " O God, help! Thou seest me forsaken by all mankind, for I will commit no unrighteous thing. Hear my entreaty!" " O God, God, my Refuge, my Rock, O my All! Thou seest my inmost soul.". . . " O Thou ever ineffable One, hear me! Hear me! Thy unhappy, most unhappy of all mortals."

Every morally healthy person who turns in his affliction and necessity to the mighty God, begins his prayer with lament and supplication. But the expression of whatever weighs very heavily upon the heart achieves a remarkable inner relief and uplift. The vehement emotions of anxiety, worry, depression, mourning dissolve away in the gentle mood of trust, good hope, resignation. In Beethoven's diary we come upon the following prayer: " Serenely I will submit to all changes and I will put my whole confidence, O God, only in Thy unchangeable goodness." Benvenuto Cellini, ill-treated in prison, cried to Christ in the bitterness of his heart: " Righteous God, who on the Cross hast paid all our debts, why should my innocence make amends for debts which I know not? Yet let Thy will be done." Edward Mörike prays in childlike trust and simple resignation:

> " Lord, what Thou wilt, command,
>   Heart's gladness or heart's grieving,
> I will rejoice, believing
>   That both are from Thy hand."

All these prayers which poets and artists wrote down in simple prose or in stately poetry are not drawn-out meditations or self-contemplation in the guise of prayers, but impressive and powerful utterances of the heart. Because these great men with all the gifts of genius were yet simple, sincere childlike natures and because their fresh, spontaneous life was not troubled by rational reflection nor corroded by philosophical criticism, they could pray with fervour and passion of heart, they could cry to God their Lord and beseech Him as did the great men of religion. Their praying is a converse, an interchange of thought with the personal God sustained by faith in answers to prayer and in the possibility of man's influence on God. Prayer is not a means for bringing about a subjective, psychological influence on oneself; it is an objective force which penetrates the heavens and conquers the heart of God. Nay, it is more, it is itself a revelation of God in man. The thought of the God-inspired gift of prayer which the great religious leaders never are tired of uttering reappears in the confessions of modern poets. Hebbel says: " When man prays God breathes in him." Centuries ago the devout Persian Jalâl-ed-dîn-Rûmî had expressed this wondrous religious paradox thus:

> " I looked for God — He was not there.
> Begging for light I cried in prayer,

Then, turning back with many a tear
I felt my shoulder touched: 'Behold, I'm here.'
' I looked for thee, I am with thee.'
And the great God went home with me."

Thus in the religion of great men we are always coming upon parallels to the devotional life of men of religious genius: spontaneity and emotional power, the free expression of all impelling experiences, the central place of petition in prayer, petition for great ideal values, the transition from the wish expressed in the prayer to trust and resignation, faith in the personality of God and in the granting of prayer, the thought of prayer as a gift — all these characteristic peculiarities of the prophetic type repeat themselves here. Nevertheless there is a great difference between the praying of eminent artists and poets and that of prophetic personalities. In the former there is at the centre of prayer the artistic ideal of personality and life, artistic creation and embodiment, in the latter, fulness of religious and moral values, God and His Kingdom, the eternal redemption of the individual soul and of all humanity; in the former, we see a struggle for the realization of what is humanly great, noble and beautiful, in the latter, a consuming passion for the God-given, moral and religious task of life. Thus the prayer of great men, in spite of all its depth, fervour, and passion, is different from the prayer of religious geniuses, as art is different from religion, civilization from the Kingdom of God, the secular from the holy.

CHAPTER XI

PRAYER IN PUBLIC WORSHIP

I. Public Prayer as Related to the Devotional Life of Prophetic Personalities

Mysticism is from its very nature non-social. " God and the soul," " God in the soul " — in these words all mystical religion is comprised. In mystical prayer the individual soul, set free from the world and society, lifts itself up to God in order to be perfectly at one with Him. A strong and lively feeling of fellowship such as rules a religious association, a tribe or a people, a sect or a church, is incompatible with the quiet contemplation, the inner absorption, the rapturous bliss of the mystic. There is no room, therefore, in mysticism for congregational prayer, which is the elementary expression of the religious social consciousness. Neither neo-Platonism nor Sûfism, neither the religion of the Vedas nor Buddhism was in a position to create congregational prayer. The prayer of public worship is rather the creation of the spirit of prophetic piety. To be sure, that splendid individualism which characterizes the mystic's prayer, animates also the prayer of the prophetic genius. Are there more personal prayers than those of Jeremiah or Jesus? Is there a more inward and personal relation of man to God than that of the unhappy prophet to his Jahve, or of God's Son to His Father, or of St. Paul to his exalted Lord? And yet it was these who gave the impulse to the rise of prayer in congregational public worship.

Prophetic, in contrast to mystical religion, is strongly social. Here the concern is not about the salvation of the individual; it is about the salvation of the people, the Church, humanity. The great goal of religious yearning is not the blessed union of the individual soul with the infinite Deity, but the realization of His universal sovereignty. The social character of prophetic religion is unmistakably expressed in the life of prayer. With the petition for one's own salvation is coupled the intercession for a brother's; the petition in our own need and the intercession for our neighbour are united in the supplication for the coming of the Kingdom of God, which is the central subject of prayer in prophetic ideal religion. Intercession is the form of prayer for which prophetic spirits contend, they must carry other men also to the heights of their own devotional life. Even the insignificant and the weak should renounce external, worldly, and selfish praying, and learn to call on God in spirit and in truth. Thus the living intercession for the brethren is an unwearied work of education in true prayer and reveals the social feature which is peculiar to the spirit of prophetic as distinguished from mystical prayer.

This social spirit of prayer which asks for another's salvation as for one's own, which would have all men share in one's own experiences in prayer, cannot stop at mere intercession and training in prayer; rather, it presses on of itself to *united* prayer. The common yearning for redemption seeks expression in common petitions; the common experience of redemption, in common praise and thanksgiving. Where there is a living consciousness that " the many are one body," individual prayer must expand into common prayer, without, however, becoming absorbed in it or losing its own vital energy in this enlargement of itself. Thus the prayer of congregational worship is rooted in the spirit of prophetic poetry; it issues directly out of the personal, prophetic, devotional life.

II. Historical Survey

Before we investigate more closely the content, form, and idea of common prayer in public worship, it is necessary to make a survey of its historical relations. The congregational prayer of Judaism is one of the abundant religious fruits which the hard period of the Exile in Babylon brought to maturity. The pre-exilic worship of the Israelites was a national sacrificial worship such as we meet with in all primitive and ancient peoples, consisting of the offering of gifts, slain beasts, burnt offerings, acts of consecration, ceremonies of purifications, and rites of *tabu*. Against this complicated ritual the prophets Amos, Hosea, Micah, Isaiah, and Jeremiah, raised a protest and demanded a pure, moral worship of Jahve. The deuteronomic reform uprooted all tendencies to polytheism in Israel by confining the offering of sacrifice, which from ancient times had taken place all over the land, to the central sanctuary at Jerusalem. But this very centralization meant a powerful strengthening of the old sacrificial cult against which the prophets had fought. A common pure devotional service such as corresponded to the prophetic ideal of religion became possible only in the Exile. In a foreign land the Israelites could bring no bloody sacrifices and offerings to Jahve, for He dwelt far away and the foreign soil on which they lived was unclean, *tabu*, the property of demons. But the consciousness that they were the people of Jahve, and the impulse to adore the God of their fathers, remained alive in their hearts, even among strangers; nay, the yearning for home and the God of their home forced the children of exile, with heightened energy, to common devotion and common prayer. They came together in special houses for the reading of their books of history and law and the writings of their prophets.

It was the confessions of Jeremiah especially that awoke in their hearts fresh courage; in his sad fate as a prophet they recognized their own destiny. Touching hymns inspired by the devotional religion of Jeremiah in which individual pious singers expressed the deep suffering and unbroken trust of God's exiled people, rang out again in their assemblies. The psalter became the prayer book of the exiled community. The power and passion of Jeremiah's devotional spirit poured through the psalms into the piety of the Jewish Church.

Thus had arisen on the shores of the Euphrates a nonsacrificial, purely spiritual congregational worship, consisting of the reading of Scripture and prayer. The community of the Exile had learned that Jahve neither desired sacrifices nor had pleasure in burnt offerings, but that the genuine offering consists rather in a humble and contrite spirit. It is true that after the return from the Exile the Temple rose in new splendour, the old sacrificial system was revived in the deuteronomic sense, the Temple ritual became, as is seen from the Levitical law book, immensely complicated; but the spiritualized public worship, the service of the Word and prayer which was born of exilic religion, could never again be dispossessed by a sacrificial cult. Everywhere in the land of the Jews and in the Dispersion, " meeting-houses," " houses of prayer " [1] were erected, and in them every day, but especially on the Sabbath and on festival days, pious people gathered together to hear the Scriptures read, and to pray. Even in the Temple at Jerusalem the holy Scriptures were interpreted, and the lofty prayers of the psalmists resounded. The post-exilic religion reveals side by side the old sacrificial cult and the new spiritual worship of the Word and prayer. Only after the destruction of the sanctuary of Jahve in the year 70 A.D., when the sacrificial cultus ceased, did the synagogal service of prayer become simply public worship, and succeeded to the old sacrificial system.

Jesus, a true son of the religion of His fathers, thoroughly conservative in His attitude towards the religious inheritance of the past, zealously shared in this common worship. We meet Him on the Sabbath in the Synagogue teaching and explaining the holy Scriptures. The disciples followed His example after the Resurrection and the descent of the Spirit, by attending the customary Jewish worship in the Temple. But from the birthday of the Church, at the feast of Pentecost, they assembled together daily for a special Christian service, a common meal, and giving of thanks. In the simple parabolic act of the breaking of bread, and the passing round of the cup of blessing, as Jesus had prescribed at His last supper, they represented His surrender to death for the salvation of the " many." They entered into intimate communion with their exalted Lord who dwelt in their midst by eating of the same bread and drinking of the same cup, and not with Him only but with the brothers and sisters round the table. This common meal became a foretaste of that glorious table fellowship which awaited them in the Kingdom of God soon to appear. The singing of psalms and solemn prayers of thanksgiving, similar to the blessing which the Jewish head of

[1] συναγωγαί, προσευκτήρια, οἶκοι προσευχῆς.

the house spoke over the bread and wine, accompanied the Christian " Lord's Supper." The eucharistic prayers contained in the *Didache* give a fairly accurate picture of the eucharistic liturgy in the early Church at the time when the disciples still belonged to the Jewish communion and took part in the divine service of the Temple or the Synagogue.

Thus the primitive Church knows a double congregational worship; the general Jewish services on Sabbath or festival days in Temple or Synagogue, and the special Christian eucharistic service for which the disciples gathered in their houses. Whilst the primitive Church at Jerusalem maintained communion in worship with the Jewish Synagogue, the Gentile churches founded by Paul had no relation from the beginning with the public worship of Judaism. After the final breach of the Palestinian Church with synagogal Judaism, here also participation in Jewish worship ceased. This independence of the Christian Church first accomplished in Paul's Gentile churches and later in the Mother Church of Jerusalem, led to the rise of a peculiarly Christian liturgy. The Christians took over from the Synagogue the service of Scripture reading and prayer and bound it up with the eucharistic meal. From the fusion of these two heterogeneous elements arose the Christian Mass. The division into the catechumens' Mass and the believers' Mass strictly so-called, as it still appears to-day in the mass-liturgies of the Eastern churches, shows clearly enough the traces of its origin. As the eucharistic prayers of thanksgiving in the *Didache* are connected with the Jewish blessing at table, so the prayers of praise and petition which in the Christian service follow the reading of Scripture are in closest contact with the Jewish synagogal prayers. The general prayer of intercession which Clement the Roman bishop inserts in his letter to the Corinthians and which may stand as a type of early congregational prayer, shows an unmistakable similarity to the main prayer of the synagogue, the *Schmone 'Esre*. In a similar way, the basic form of the *Anaphora* in the Eastern liturgies of the Mass shows clear points of contact with the framework of the *Shema* and the various literary documents of the early congregational prayer. All the early Christian liturgies demonstrate how clearly the prayer language of the nascent religion is dependent on that of the Synagogue. Nevertheless the devotional language in the worship of early Christianity reveals creative originality as compared with the traditional Jewish terminology. It was Paul who radically changed the stereotyped doxologies of the synagogal liturgy, who gave them a Christian stamp, and breathed into them the power of his Christian experience.

The prayer of the early Church was more free from all conventional bonds than even the prayer of the Synagogue; it was as much a living thing as the personal devotional life of the early Christians. Early Christianity, in contrast to ancient temple rituals and mystery cults, knew no binding formularies. It was only in the second half of the third century that the gradual stabilizing of prayer in public worship began along with the formation of fixed ecclesiastical institutions. Different formularies originate in East and West without, however, as yet being prescribed.

In the fourth century was begun a comprehensive liturgical reform. The simple celebration of the mysteries in the early Church was surrounded with a gorgeous ceremonial borrowed in part from the disappearing ancient rituals. The liturgical forms of prayer were worked over from a dogmatic point of view. The old doxologies and forms of prayer in the language of a Christology that subordinated the Son to the Father, and of belief in a Trinity of three manifestations for the work of redemption, were the fixed points behind which Arians and other heretics entrenched themselves in their battle against ecclesiastical dogmas. In order to deprive them of these supports, all dogmatically offensive passages in the text of the prayers were expunged and they were replaced by theologically correct formulas. Thus the liturgy entered the service of dogmatic instruction and of the conflict with heretics.

From the fourth century onward, indeed, every larger church had a standard liturgical formulary of its own. But gradually the liturgies of the great metropolitan churches crushed out those of the smaller neighbouring churches: and thus arose whole liturgical provinces. The Roman liturgy of the Mass attained the widest extension. With the strengthening of the Roman primacy went hand in hand the suppression of the other Western liturgies until, finally, Gregory VII made the Roman liturgy the liturgy of the Christian West.

The Reformation brought very great changes in the sphere of public worship. Already the pre-Reformation Wycliffites and Hussites celebrated the Mass, in part at least, in the vulgar tongue. In all countries in which the Reformation gained a footing, the living language of the people took the place of the dead Latin of the Church. In Germany it was Thomas Münzer who in Altstedt introduced the first German Mass. But the Reformation did more: it substituted for the old liturgy of the Mass new forms of worship which proscribed the Eucharist *as a sacrifice*. With the rejection of the Catholic idea of sacrifice the idea of the Communion, the mysterious fellowship with the exalted Lord at His table, was pushed into the background. The non-sacrificial, purely spiritual worship, with the Word as its centre, which the Synagogue maintained, was revived by the Reformers. In it the connection with the prayers of the Mass was in part piously preserved and in part logically dissolved. The founders of sects and the Swiss Reformers were the most radical. They made the Bible the exclusive formal and material principle of divine worship and quenched every recollection of the Roman liturgy. In the evangelical sects and free churches, the free prayer of the minister or of the members of the congregation prevailed; the individualistic spirit of the sects tolerated no binding of common prayer by stiff rules and formulas. It is true the Swiss reformers created fixed forms of service, but these were quite independent of the Catholic liturgy. Zwingli's order of public worship betrays a certain poverty. The central point of the service is the preaching of the Word; the prayer of the congregation forms only the introduction to and the conclusion of the sermon. Calvin's liturgical formula is richer. It leans upon the order of service of Martin Bucer, but is distinctly original, revealing deep religious fervour and genuine moral power. Much more conservative is Luther's " German Mass and Order of Service " published in 1526. It takes over numerous prayers from the Roman Missal, but all those texts in which the thought of sacrifice is expressed are excluded. In spite of various Calvinistic insertions, the Anglican Book of Common Prayer stands in close connection with the Roman liturgy of the Mass. All the evangelical rituals and liturgies, like the developed liturgies of the old Church, show fixed orders of service and prayers obligatory for minister and congregation.

Pietism brought no particular reform in the traditional service, but with the period of rationalism a far-reaching change took place. The prayers of the old Church and of the Reformers stand in sharp contradiction to the rational and moralistic ideal of the Enlightenment. New liturgical products in a rationalistic spirit were substituted for them. A shallow modern poetic speech took the place of the stately early Christian, Pauline language of prayer. " The tone of the salon entered the Church." One even dared to paraphrase the Lord's Prayer and the Creed in the spirit of rationalism. At the beginning of the nineteenth century an evangelical movement rose up with primitive religious power in protest against the tendency to allow the evangelical faith to evaporate in a vague highly cultured religion of reason.

The struggle for liturgical reform which flamed up at the beginning of the last century has not died down even to-day. The liturgical problem is one of the most important and most difficult domestic problems of modern Protestantism. The individual congregation demands the right to determine independently the order of service and the form of liturgical prayer. The individualistic piety of the present day is not satisfied with the liturgical formulas of the old Church or of the Reformation age; it longs for an independent expression of its own. We want to get rid of the contradiction which exists between modern religious views and the intellectual content of the traditional liturgical formularies of prayer. With all pious feeling for the precious liturgical inheritance of the past, we ask for the liturgist freedom in the selection and wording of the prayers. In accordance with the laws of " the psychology of the congregation " we would shape an ideal form of liturgy which, suited to the thought and aspiration of modern man, should lead him to the very heart of Christian prayer.

Common prayer in public worship, in the full sense of the word, is peculiar to the Jewish and Christian religions. Outside the Jewish Synagogue and the Christian Churches and sects only traces of such a thing can be found. Among less civilized peoples we frequently meet common prayer of a social group which in external form resembles that of Jewish and Christian congregations. The content, however, of the prayer betrays the same native eudaemonism which marks the personal prayers of primitive man. Common prayer is here not the expression of a *religious* assembly but of the *secular* political association of families, of the village or the tribe. It does not subserve the religious yearning for salvation but the worldly interests of everyday life. We may not therefore here speak of common prayer in public worship. Ancient cults know only priestly prayers and hymns which accompany a sacred act. The syncretist mystery cults of the Roman Empire, so far as we can judge from our scanty sources, were familiar with common prayer. This, however, does not take the central place in the public solemnity which it occupies in the Jewish Synagogue and Christian Church; the mysterious sacred act occupies this place, which the priests and the initiated accompany with mysterious, archaic formulas. Only in the Egyptian religion of the new kingdom do we come upon a trace of a public service of prayer. Islam which, in its rules of prayer, is wholly dependent on Judaism, observes public congregational prayer; according to the prescript of the Koran it is said in the mosque every Friday at noon. Fundamentally, however, this prayer is only the offering in common of the individual obligatory prayer (*salât*). In India only the modern Brâhma Samâj has, after the pattern of western evangelical churches, a divine service with Scripture reading, prayers and hymns. Keshub Chunder Sen is the author of the order of public worship observed to-day by the adherents of this sect.

Thus outside Judaism and Christianity only meagre traces and germs of common prayer in public worship may be found. Christianity is " the religion of prayer " — this phrase is verified as much in the divine service of Christian Churches and sects as in the devotional life of great Christian personalities.

Just as prayer is in Christianity the central point of personal piety, it is also the focus of congregational worship.

III. Motive and Purpose of Common Prayer in Public Worship

All prayer is originally the immediate expression of up-springing emotions, of deeply moving religious experiences. The common prayer of public worship is also originally not the intentional creation of a more or less pious individual, but the fervent necessary utterance of the common religious experiences of a group closely bound together. In times of great religious excitement when existing religious communions bind themselves more closely together or new ones are formed, the spirit of religious devotion does not remain limited to individuals of creative genius, but is poured out upon all the members of the congregation. "We, the many, are one body" — no word demonstrates the fervid feeling of communion, which penetrates all these religious movements, more vitally than this Pauline assertion. One great experience dominates the old Jewish Church, the assurance of Israel being the elect people of Jahve and hope in Israel's lordship over the heathen. One great experience dominates the primitive Church: the assurance of salvation bestowed in Christ and the yearning for the speedy fulfilment of the Kingdom of God. This common experience spontaneously urges to expression in prayer just as every emotional religious experience of an individual longs for relief through prayer. The congregation, assured of its salvation, will glorify God "with one mind and one mouth." As Ignatius says: it "will sing praise to Him as a great choir."

Congregational prayer is not only the expression of the collective religious experience, it contributes to the mutual edification of the members of the congregation. "Edification"[2] is the awakening, intensification, and vitalization of the religious feelings, moods, and volitional tendencies. "Let everything be done for edification" is the maxim which Paul holds up in his discussion of the common worship. He would

[2] οἰκοδομή.

keep the speaking with tongues as much as possible out of
religious services because no edifying influences issue from
it to those who are assembled. The brethren are not moved
to common prayer by an emotional prayer expressed in confused verbal fragments or in unintelligible, strange forms of
speech. " For thou verily givest thanks well, but the other
is not edified."

The *pedagogic* purpose of common prayer is allied to that of
edification. The prayer of the congregation is meant to lift
the individual to a higher stage of devotion. Narrow self-
seeking wishes should be silenced in the presence of the congregation. The little and the weak who come to the meeting
with low and earthly thoughts, should be carried to heights
of religious yearning, should pray as the strong and the creative pray; those who do not know what true prayer is, should
here learn to pray and practise the art. This pedagogic aim
of common prayer was put by the reformers in the foreground,
and was emphasized ever more clearly by the old Protestant
orthodoxy as by modern theology. " Prescribed prayers read
by the minister," says von der Goltz, " are not properly
prayers but an introduction to common prayer." This educational aim is, however, subordinate. All common prayer is
meant to be rather the direct utterance of a common religious
experience and to serve for the mutual edification, that is,
strengthening and enhancement of this experience.

Congregational prayer is the centre and climax of congregational worship. It is always preceded by the reading and
exposition of Scripture, the preaching of the Word, which is
meant to prepare the hearts of believers for common prayer.
As the prayer of the mystic is kindled in meditation and by
it is nourished, so the prayer of the congregation is kindled
by being steeped in the Word as set down in Scripture.

Not infrequently, however, already in Alexandrian Judaism
and later in many Protestant Churches, preaching takes the
dominant place in divine service and gives prayer a secondary
place. As Theodore Harnack says, " the independent character and the equal dignity of prayer with the sermon is lost,
the liturgical prayer of the congregation sinks down to a mere
appendix of the sermon." Nevertheless, originally the read-

ing of Scripture and the homily had only a subordinate and preparatory value. Not speech *about* God but speech *to* God, not the preaching of the revelation of God, but direct intercourse with God is, strictly speaking, the worship of God.

Common prayer in worship was originally the immediate expression of common religious experiences and served for common edification. But the regular return of meetings for prayer and the continual identity of the motives of prayer led to a gradual weakening of the experiences and a progressive condition of apathy. As, among primitive peoples, the free expression of an emotion hardened into a piece of complicated ritual, so also the congregational prayer of Jew and Christian, ceasing to be the living product of a collective religious experience, became a stiff, cultual institution, a traditional order of service valued as an end in itself, inviolable in form, and the observance of which is obligatory. Nevertheless, the spirit of vital communion lives on in liturgical forms of prayer and kindles again and again in many a devout heart that feeling of fellowship of which it was the original expression.

IV. THE FORM OF COMMON PRAYER IN PUBLIC WORSHIP

The liturgical prayer of the Jewish Synagogue and of the Christian Church, when compared with the common prayer of primitive tribes, shows nothing essentially new in its *form*. All the characteristic forms in which the primitive village, family, and tribe expressed their common concerns reappear.

The consciousness of the presence of God and the effort after mutual edification by common prayer demands some order in the conduct of worship. Paul exhorts the Christians — " Let all things be done decently and in order." Common prayer does not consist in a confusion of voices each addressing God in its own words — that would be the individual prayers of many, but not at all *common prayer*. This latter is the prayer of *one* member of the congregation which the others follow with attention and devotion. In the primitive Church every male Christian, when moved by the Spirit, had the right to preach and to pray. The custom of general free prayer is the clear background of the fourteenth chapter of First Corinthians in which the Apostle reviews the problems of public worship: "When ye come together each one hath a psalm." Paul does not question the right of the free prayer of the laity; he only demands that each should use this right as a means of edifying the congregation, and should pray in language generally understood and not in unintelligible *glossolalia*.

The early Christian enthusiasm soon began to die away. Originally all the members of the Church were "possessors of the Spirit," endowed with charismatic gifts; but very soon their number grew small. The ministry, the episcopate, and the presbyterate took the place of personal possession of the Spirit. The bishops and presbyters are now the official leaders in worship who, in the name of the assembled congregation, say the public prayers. Ignatius speaks in the same breath of "the prayer of the bishop and the congregation" — a sign that already at the end of the first century the bishop took a pre-eminent part in the public prayers of the Church. At first the eucharistic thanksgiving seems to have been reserved for the "president." According to the *Didache*, the prophets, that is, the possessors of the Spirit, utter the eucharistic prayer in perfectly free fashion. In the description of public worship given by Justin Martyr it is exclusively the "president"[3] who speaks the prayer of petition and thanksgiving at the presentation of bread, wine, and water. The pre-Communion prayers, on the contrary, which came in between the Scripture reading and sermon and the celebration of the Eucharist, seem to have been, according to Justin's description, the free prayers of individual members of the congregation. Here, therefore, exist side by side the free prayers of the laity, and the official prayer of the priest. Later, all the prayers in public worship passed into the hands of officials, bishops, or deacons. But along with and after the regular leader in prayer the president and his helpers, the men of the Spirit, had for a long time the extraordinary right in the public assemblies to rise and offer prayers of their own. The sects in which the early Christian enthusiasm flared up anew have again and again attempted to reproduce the public

[3] προεστώς

worship of the primitive Church; they have even revived the free, unlimited lay prayer in the assemblies for worship. But since the enthusiasm lasts only a relatively short time, and the possession of the Spirit is the gift of only a few devout persons, even in the sects those tendencies always prevail which in the worship of the early Church led from lay prayer to priestly prayer. Even the Quakers, who reject root and branch all clerical offices and rules of worship, give to such members of the congregation as are more frequently moved by the Spirit in the Assemblies, the commission to preach and pray. These " recorded ministers " have, however, no privileges as leaders of the assemblies, much less any ecclesiastical office in the proper sense of the term.

The words of the congregational prayer were originally as free, as much the inspiration of the moment, as the spontaneous prayer of the individual. The enthusiasm which in times of religious beginnings and revolutions flames up, tolerates no binding of common prayer to hard and fast forms. " The Spirit bloweth where it listeth." According to the *Didache* the possessors of the Spirit in the Early Church pray " what they will," as the Spirit inspires them. Tertullian, the energetic champion of the Montanist movement, testifies that the Christians in their meetings pray freely from the heart. But even when the congregational prayer had become the business of bishops and priests, the setting and scope of the prayer for a long time remained free. Justin says that the president prays at the celebration of the Eucharist " as he is able," [4] that is, in such manner and at such length as is within his ability. Whilst, however, the prayer of the Spirit-possessed layman reveals always a strongly personal note, the prayer of the priestly leader, in spite of all formal freedom in particulars, shows a fixed scheme which is related to the scheme of prayer of the Synagogue. The general outlines, the order of thought and so the framework, as well as certain recurring forms of expression, remain fixed; only the detailed setting forth in language is the personal work of the moment. Here we have to do with a transitional type of prayer, an intermediate form which we have already discovered in the praying of primitive man.

---

[4] ὅση δύναμις αὐτῷ.

The need arose early for formulated models of prayer which, however, exhibit no binding formularies but are merely examples for imitation. The *Didache* contains such models for the celebration of the Eucharist. From these pattern prayers handed down orally or in writing arose gradually fixed liturgical formulas which were recited in public worship. Previous to the fall of the Temple the Jewish Synagogue already had such formal prayers. The famous " Eighteen Prayers " received its present arrangement after the destruction of the Temple, but had certainly attained formal fixity a long time before. Yet the law forbidding the writing down of liturgical texts which was in force till the closing of the Talmud ensured a place for free or half-free prayer in synagogal Judaism for a long time.

In the Christian Church the final transformation of free into fixed prayer took place in the third century. In the fifth century we find everywhere fixed rules for divine service and obligatory forms of prayer. The liturgist no longer " prays from the heart " but recites a sacred text from memory or reads it from the book of ritual. Where in the first century stood the prayer of the charismatically gifted layman, in the fifth century stands, consecrated by tradition, the formulary of the church official.

Once liturgical prayer has become an inviolable formula binding on the conscience, it possesses immense stability. The ceremonial prayers which to-day are murmured or sung at the Mass of the Catholic Church and of the orthodox Churches of the Orient go back, in their composition, to the sixth century and much further. Many prayers of the Roman Mass have been received unchanged or only slightly modified, into evangelical prayer books. Thus we meet here the same fact that we meet in ancient religions. The liturgical formula lasts through hundreds, nay, thousands of years; it is almost immortal. It can even survive the greatest religious upheavals and revolutions.

The evangelical sects have protested with all their might against the binding of common prayer by prescribed rules and forms. The English Independents considered fixed prayer or a statutory liturgy as a denial of the Holy Spirit, as blasphemy against God. Even the Lord's Prayer was not excluded from this rejection of all formulated prayer. Milton, in his *Defensio pro populo Anglicano*, has expressed in eloquent terms the anti-liturgical spirit of these Independents. In Calvinism touched by the spirit of the sects free prayer predominates. The most radical form of free congregational prayer is seen in Quaker meetings. The Quakers demand not only prayer that is unrestricted by any formulation, they insist on prayer that is perfectly spontaneous, breaking forth in power out of inspired conditions. This Spirit-inspired prayer of the Quaker meetings is a border-line form between purely individual prayer and collective public prayer.

The language of common prayer in public worship is quite different from that of individual prayer. The minister who addresses God in the name and in place of the congregation feels himself in a totally different mental attitude from that of the pious man who pours out his heart to God in the stillness of his chamber. The consciousness of the presence of many people brings about an involuntary limitation of the individual experience, a certain emotional repression. The devotional stillness with which the assembly listens to his words produces an elevated tone of mind.

This special state of the feelings finds expression as much in the variety of tone and accent of the voice, as in the choice and connection of the words. While the personal, emotional prayer (to this belongs, in many instances, the enthusiastic prayer of the lay charismatics, and lay possessors of the Spirit of primitive Christianity, also to many sects) is uttered in incoherent cries and sighs, the liturgical prayer is recited in slow, solemn tones, and in an impressive regular rhythm, or even sung in a uniform, reciting note or majestic melody. Personal prayer, corresponding to the change of emotions and feelings, shows an impulsiveness or irregularity of the thoughts; liturgical prayer reveals, corresponding to the uniform mental mood, a clear progress in thought, and perspicuous construction. If the language of the emotional prayer discloses an elementary passion, an irresistible impulse, the language of the liturgical prayer reveals solemn gravity and measured dignity.

The numerous biblical terms and ornate phrases lend to the prayer diction of public worship a venerable and antique character. Thus we can speak of a sacerdotal style in liturgic prayer, which is manifestly removed from the unstudied style of spontaneous individual prayer. However, this solemn sacerdotal style has no connection necessarily with the impulse of the artistic, the specially composed, and the unnatural. On the contrary, the language of the early Christian prayers, such as the Clementine, or *Didache* prayers, show a natural simplicity, unpretentiousness, and power; it is suited to grip the hearer directly and to awaken that living disposition to prayer from which it flowed of old. The Roman missal, and numerous evangelical orders of service, have preserved this peculiarity of the classic Christian common prayer. Brevity and weight distinguish the *Gloria* and *Prefaces*, in which the early Christian patterns of prayer live on.

In contrast with this, the Synagogue prayers, the prayer formulas of the *Apostolic Constitutions* and most liturgies of the Eastern Church, reveal a copious diction, an oppressive accumulation of resounding epithets, a rhetorical pomp — all peculiarities reminiscent of ancient ritual prayers and cultual hymns. In their reflective tone, they reveal themselves at times rather as catechisms and homilies than as prayers of the congregation. The modern evangelical movement for ritual reform seeks to introduce a religious revival and psychological deepening of the liturgic style of prayer, and thus to renew the common prayer of divine service in the early Christian sense.

The minister in public worship prays not as an individual for himself; he is much rather the representative and accredited agent of the congregation, who turns to God in their name and at their bidding. The praying subject, as indeed is shown by the use of " we " in liturgical prayers, is the assembled congregation. It listens devoutly to the words of its representative, inwardly appropriates them, and in silence accompanies them in prayer. The early Christian community evidenced this inward participation in the prayer of their leader by posture and gestures; standing up, the faithful raised their hands. It is only this joint praying of the assembled congregation

with their accredited prayer leader, that makes its praying a
real common prayer. Hence the leader prefaces his words
with an express summons to prayer to those present.[5] " Praise
Jahve," cried the leader of the congregation in the Jewish
Synagogue. In the Egyptian order of service it is the deacon
who, before prayer, exhorts the assembly: " Pray," or " Ye
who stand there, bow your heads." In the *Apostolic Constitutions* we meet with the following formulas, as the deacon's
invitation to prayer: " Pray," " Let us pray," " Let us give
heed," " Let us rise." In the Roman missal, numerous prayers
are preceded by the simple invitation: " *Oremus*," which also
is found in the evangelical liturgies. This short summons is
expanded at times to a formal exhortation, by which the
faithful are to be prepared for the prayer to follow. Time-
honoured in the Eastern and Western Churches, is the usual
antiphonal prayer and response between Bishop and people,
which introduced the chief eucharistic prayer: " The Lord
be with you " — " And with thy spirit "; " Lift up your
hearts " — " We lift them up unto the Lord "; " Let us give
thanks unto our Lord God " — " It is meet and right so to do."
The unity in prayer between minister and people nowhere
creates such an overpowering impression as in this wonderful
antiphony, in which the congregation joyfully re-echoes the
invitation to prayer of its leader.

The most usual form in which the congregation manifests
its inward participation in the prayers of its representative,
is the " response," a short prayerful exclamation, with which
it chimes in at the conclusion of a prayer, or of a portion of it.
The Psalm singing in the temple of Jerusalem was concluded
by the people present with a doxological formula: " Blessed
be Jahve for evermore! Blessed be Jahve, the God of Israel,
from everlasting to everlasting! "

In the old Jewish " Eighteen Prayers," there follows after
every benediction, or prayer, the cry of the congregation:
" Praised be Thou, O Lord! " concluded by an adjunct which
takes up the closing words of the song of praise, and shortly
summarizes its contents.

In the eucharistic prayer of the *Didache*, a doxological

[5] προσφώνησις, *indictio precum.*

response of the assembly follows each sentence of the prayer leader. The whole prayer consists of an almost litany-like exchange of sentences between leader and people, which brings before our eyes the dramatic liveliness of the early Christian common prayer.

As regards the Eucharist, give thanks thus: first as regards the cup:

Leader: " We thank Thee, our Father, for the holy vine of Thy servant, David, which Thou hast made known to us through Thy Son Jesus."

Congregation: " To Thee be the glory for ever and ever! "

Then as regards the broken bread:

Leader: " We thank Thee, our Father, for the life and knowledge which Thou hast revealed to us through Thy Son Jesus! "

Congregation: " To Thee be the glory for ever and ever! "

Leader: " As this broken bread was strewed on the mountains and being collected became one, so let Thy Church be brought together from the ends of the earth into Thy kingdom! "

Congregation: " For Thine is the glory, and the power, through Jesus Christ, for ever and ever."

In harmony with the character of the eucharistic prayers as prayers of thanksgiving, each sentence rings out in a solemn note of praise; both in the petitions and intercessions, the responses of the people contain in any case a petition. In the Clementine liturgy of the *Apostolic Constitutions* and other oriental liturgies, the choir of the faithful strengthens each request with a litany-like cry: " Lord, have mercy upon us! " a form of response which dates back to the earliest period of Christianity.

Herein lies an important difference between the primitive Christian liturgy and the later, viz., that in the former the responding congregation broke much more often into the leader's prayer than later, when the living contact between both was dissolved, and the chief part at public service fell to the praying priests. Other antiphonal formulas are the *Alleluia* and *Hosanna*, cries of praise which the Christian community took over in their early Hebrew form from the Jewish Synagogue, as well as the *Maranatha* (" Come, Lord "), the early Christian cry of longing which re-echoed in the Hellenistic congregations in the old Aramaic dialect.

Following these antiphonal utterances came the concluding cry " Amen," with which the congregation ends every prayer. With this Hebrew particle, which means " truly," " so is it," the congregation acknowledges what its representative has spoken in prayer; identifies itself with his words, solemnly strengthens the inner unity between them and the officiant. In all probability the " Amen " was usual as a choral conclusion of prayer, even in old Israel. Even other peoples in primitive stages of culture know similar assenting cries, with which a group closes the prayer of its representative. This primitive method of response was retained by the exilic and post-exilic community, and taken over in a primitive Hebrew form from early Christendom. The Corinthian Church in its assembly answers every prayer of a brother with this short cry. The Apocalypse shows that the Church associates itself with the prayer of praise of the Highest by an " Amen." Justin's description of the observance of the Eucharist in the Roman Church teaches us the same thing.

In the Catholic Church of East and West, as in the Evangelical Churches and sects, this primeval liturgical cry of prayer has become a permanent concluding sentence of every congregational prayer; nay, even individual piety has adopted it as an expression of living trust in the prayer-hearing grace of God.

All these short responsive prayers are stereotyped, formal and unchangeable; for owing to their fixed connection, they are suited for recitation by a choir. They are those elements in Jewish and Christian public worship which long ago possessed formal fixedness, before the prayer of the leader had lost its free character.

Besides these short responses, permanent prayer-texts of slight extent are spoken rhythmically in chorus by the assembled congregation. According to the *Apostolic Constitu-*

tions the *trisagion,* following the *preface,* is prayed by the whole people. The natural rhythm which runs through this prayer of praise facilitates its choral recitation. According to the same order of divine service, the congregation utters a solemn prayer of praise before the Communion. According to the liturgy of St. James, the whole congregation prays the Lord's Prayer. The Psalms, which were employed in Jewish and early Christian congregational worship and later in conventual hours of prayer, were, in consequence of their poetic structure, suitable for dramatic and antiphonal recitation by a prayer leader and the whole assembly, or by two half-choirs. According to Zwingli's order of service, the *Gloria* and *Apostles' Creed* were recited antiphonally by two half-choirs, one of men, and one of women.

Along with the spoken, i.e., solemnly rendered, choir prayer, there was from the beginning the melodic chorus singing. We have already learnt about the choral prayer of praise as a form of primitive prayer. Its introduction into the liturgical service must have proceeded principally from practical needs; with its fixed forms of presentation, rhythm and melody, singing is the simplest form of choral prayer, simpler and easier than the common recitation in the speaking voice. The hymn has taken, at all times, and in all Churches, a special place in the service. In contrast to liturgical prayer, it shows a much greater variety. While the latter, in the course of its development through centuries, reveals only relatively small changes, the hymn shows constant change: in it is reflected the individual pious mood of the moment. While the liturgical prayers are super-personal in character — it is only occasionally that we know the authors of Church prayers — hymns are the poetical creation of sharply defined religious personalities, who in them have uttered their profoundest feelings.

If we compare a Jewish piut, a hymn of Ambrose, a sequence of Bernard, a Lutheran choral, and a spiritual poem of Zinzendorf, then we recognize indubitably that the hymn is not a specifically social, that is, churchly matter; it is essentially individual. In the hymn, personal devotional piety makes its way into the collective worship of the congregation, and becomes the common possession of many. The content of common prayer is by no means exhausted by the enumeration of the various prayers pronounced aloud by the leader, the responses and the singing of the congregation. *Silent prayer* is a not unimportant element in genuine public worship. Vocal prayer imposes limits on the thoughts and feelings of the worshipper; they are confined within the framework of the given liturgy even when the leader utters a free prayer. At certain moments of worship the personal life must transcend these limitations.

The worship of the Synagogue allowed moments of silent prayer, and traces of the same usage are to be found in the *Apostolic Constitutions*. It is prescribed that at the Offering " all the people shall stand and pray silently." The Roman Catholic Church gives opportunity, especially at the Mass, for silent prayer. In the worship of Protestant Churches it has not been wholly suppressed but it has certainly been reduced to a minimum. Only the Quakers give it a large place in their services. Rudolph Otto has recently voiced the growing demand for a larger measure of silent worship in Protestant assemblies.[6]

V. The Content of Common Prayer in Public Worship

The essence of mystical prayer is the exclusive turning of the soul to the highest good; the essence of prophetic prayer is the expression of the deep need of the soul and the cry for salvation. At the heart of liturgical prayer is praise of God's greatness and power, and thanksgiving for the salvation bestowed by Him.[7] The response with which the congregation in the Synagogue takes up the words of the leader in the " Eighteen Prayers " is a cry of praise: " Praised be Thou, Jahve! " The response with which, according to the *Didache*, the assembled congregation replied to the leader, is a doxology: " Glory be to Thee forever! " The author of the Acts describes the eucharistic service of the primitive Church of Jerusalem as " the praise of God." Ignatius calls the Christian assembly for worship a " meeting for thanksgiving and praise."

---

[6] [In the Protestant Episcopal Church of the United States "silent prayer" is growing in favour. The above paragraph is taken from the appendix.]

[7] αἶνος, δόξα, εὐχαριστία.

The numerous stately doxologies and formulas of thanksgiving in the Pauline letters is the clear reflection of the prominent place which prayers of praise and thanksgiving assumed in public worship. Origen is under the influence of the liturgical custom of the Early Church when, in his theological plan of prayer, he names praise and thanksgiving as the two first topics of Christian prayer. Nay, it corresponds thoroughly to the central place of praise and thanksgiving in the public prayer of the Church when the celebration of the Christian Mysteries is simply called " Eucharist," that is, thanksgiving. In the worship of the early Christians praise and thanksgiving take a larger place than in the later liturgies. When enthusiasm had passed away and the assurance of salvation had become weaker, the prayer for salvation took the prominent place.

The prayer of praise and thanksgiving bears always a contemplative character: he who prays is realizing the greatness, power, holiness, and goodness of God. Here the common prayer of the Church touches the prayer of the mystic who sinks in meditation and vision into the divine infinitude. Yet there exists an unmistakable difference. The mystic looks with steadfast eye on God the highest Ideal as the *summum bonum* at rest, complete in Himself beyond all that is; the congregation of Jews or of Christians contemplates God as living at work in nature and history, as the Creator, Ruler, Guide, and Benefactor.

The " Eighteen Prayers " begin with the words: " Praised be Thou, Lord, our God and God of our fathers, the God of Abraham, the God of Isaac, the God of Jacob, great, mighty and terrible God, most High God, thou who bestowest rich grace, and hast created all things and callest to mind the favours and promises of the fathers. . . ." Response: " Praised be Thou, Lord, Shield of Abraham." " Thou art mighty to help; Thou who sustainest the falling, healest the sick and settest free those in prison, and art true to Thy word to those who sleep in the dust. Who is like to Thee, O King, Thou who killest and makest alive. . . ." Response: " Praised be Thou, Lord, who makest the dead to live."

The simple congregational prayer in the fifty-ninth and

sixtieth chapters of the First Epistle of Clement of Rome moves in the same circle of ideas: " Thou hast opened the eyes of our hearts, that we may know Thee, the One who abidest Highest among the high, Holy among the holy . . . who makest rich and makest poor, who killest and makest alive, who alone art the Benefactor of spirits, the God of all flesh. . . . Thou Lord, hast created the earth, Thou art faithful in all generations, righteous in Thy judgments, wonderful in Thy might and splendour."

Prayer in public worship is the living expression of the consciousness of redemption which a religious communion possesses. But redemption is, for the Jewish and Christian faith, indissolubly bound up with history; hence definite, God-ordained historical facts are the motives and supports of faith and hope. The saving acts of God form, therefore, an important subject of liturgical praise and thanksgiving. The central deed of redemption in the Jewish faith is the exodus of Israel from Egypt. In Christian common prayer the redemption bestowed in Christ forms the chief subject of praise and thanksgiving. The praise of the greatness and power of God, as also thanksgiving for the salvation bestowed, widens out in Jewish and early Christian liturgical prayer into an epic contemplation of God's creative and redeeming deeds. The detailed prayer which Ezra, after the return from the Exile, offers at the giving of the law begins with the remembrance of the creation of the world and then runs through the entire history of Israel. The early Church took over this mode of prayer. The epic of creation and of the wonderful deliverance and guidance of God's people was sung at the public celebration of the Christian Eucharist. The echo of this kind of prayer is perceivable in the entire early Christian literature from the second to the fourth century in East and West.

The chief eucharistic prayer of the ancient Church as given in the *Apostolic Constitutions* comprehends the whole world-drama in a systematic philosophy of history; it proceeds from the fulness of being of the eternal God, and from the generation of the Logos before all time, and then reviews the whole history of creation and redemption: the creation of the angels, of the world, of living beings, of mankind, of the happy primitive condition of Adam, his fall, and expulsion from Paradise, God's pity on fallen man, His punitive and rewarding righteousness in history, His giving of the law by Moses, His wonderful leading of the chosen people, the incarnation of the Son of God, His birth of a virgin, His teaching and healing, His suffering and death, His Resurrection and Ascension, His coming again. In its all-embracing unity of view, the ancient Church's prefatory prayer is the grandest creation of Christian liturgies. As Baumstark remarks, " Preaching and prayer, narration and hymn together, it unfolds the picture of world happenings from the first day of creation till the last Day of Judgment."

Since the fourth century, the ancient Church epic of the eucharistic thanksgiving has become merged into the liturgies of the Eastern and Western Churches; in the Roman Mass, it is completely effaced. The Western Church, in its liturgical prayers, makes constant reference to the feasts of the Church's year, which correspond to the single acts of the great historical drama of redemption. The Preface of the Western liturgies of the Mass does not embrace, like the ancient Church Thanksgiving Prayer, the whole history of creation and redemption, but only a single redeeming act, that special secret of redemption which the Church calls to mind at a special festival — the incarnation of the Son of God, His redeeming death, His Resurrection, Ascension, and the sending of the Spirit. (Many evangelical service-books have retained the prefaces of the Roman missal in the liturgy for the Lord's supper and feast days.)

CHRISTMAS (according to the Gothic missal): " Truly worthy and right, just and salutary is it that we thank Thee, Holy God, Almighty Father, Eternal God; for to-day hath our Lord Jesus Christ deigned to visit the earth. He proceeded from the sanctuary of the Virgin's body, and came down meekly from Heaven. The angels sang: ' Glory be to God on high! ' when the humanity of the Redeemer shone forth; the whole angel host shouted, because the earth received the eternal King. Holy Mary became a precious temple which bore the Lord of lords! She conceived for our sins the glorious life, so that bitter death was driven away. That womb which knew no human taint was worthy to bear God. Into the world was born Jesus Christ, who ever has lived, and lives, Thy Son our Lord. Through Him the angels praise Thy majesty," etc.

PASSION TIDE (Roman missal): "Truly worthy and right, just and salutary is it that we Thank Thee always and everywhere, Holy Father, Almighty Lord, Eternal God; Thou who hast fastened the salvation of mankind to the wood of the Cross, so that from the place whence death sprang, life may arise, and so that death which conquered on the Cross might also be conquered on the Cross; through Christ our Lord; through Him the angels praise Thy majesty," etc.

EASTER (ibidem): "Truly worthy and right, just and salutary is it, to praise Thee, O Lord, at all times; but on this day we are bound to worship Thee still more gloriously, since Christ our Pascal Lamb is sacrificed. He is verily the true Lamb, that has taken away the sins of the world, who by His dying destroyed our death, and by His rising again has restored to us everlasting life. Therefore with angels and archangels, with Thrones and Powers, and with the whole army of Heaven, we sing the hymn of Thy glory, and cry without end," etc.

WHITSUN (ibidem): "Truly worthy and right, just and salutary is it, that we thank Thee ever and at all times, Holy Lord, Almighty Father, Eternal God, through Christ our Lord; who ascended above all Heavens and sitting at Thy right hand poured forth the Holy Spirit of promise upon men adopted as children. Therefore, the whole of mankind on the earth exults with a common joy; but also the Powers above and angelic Principalities sing a Hymn of Praise to Thy glory, and cry without end," etc.

The Thanksgiving Prayer in public worship, the direct expression of the living consciousness of salvation, is always a calling to mind of the history of redemption. Whether it refers to the entire chain of the divine deeds of redemption, as in the ancient Jewish and ancient Church liturgy, or to a single redemptive deed as in the Western Mass, or to a unique redeeming, historical personality, as in the evangelical servicebooks — there is always something historically real which forms the subject of praise and thanksgiving. The historical character of Jewish and Christian piety never comes out so forcibly as in the prayer of public worship; redemption is rooted in history.

Praise and thanksgiving form the first part of public prayer. There follows, according to Origen's scheme, the acknowledgment of sinfulness connected with the prayer for the forgiveness of sins, and the destruction of sinful propensities.

Ezra's great, historical prayer of praise ends with an acknowledgment of sin: " Thou hast dealt truly and we have done wickedly; neither have our Kings, our princes, our priests, nor our fathers kept Thy law, nor hearkened unto Thy commandments."

In Daniel's prayer at the rebuilding of the Temple is reflected the liturgical confessional prayer of the post-exilic community: " O Lord, the great and dreadful God . . . we have sinned and have dealt perversely and have done wickedly; neither have we hearkened unto Thy servants, the prophets. . . . O Lord, righteousness belongeth unto Thee, but unto us confusion of face as at this day."

The feeling of sin which finds expression in the confessional prayer of the Christian congregation is purer and more personal in comparison with the Jewish. The Jewish consciousness of sin is super-personal; the individual feels himself answerable for the sins of his people and of his forefathers. The Christian consciousness of sin is personal, the individual feels himself sinful, although his inclination to evil is rooted in original sin. The Jewish consciousness of guilt shows a strong eudaemonistic strain; the Jewish people feels itself deserving of frightful national misfortune, of God's great punitive visitation. The Christian consciousness of sin is purely ethical; the Christian experiences his infinite distance from the God-ordained moral ideal. The Christian community knows itself, indeed, assured of salvation bestowed in Christ, but it feels its continual weakness and sinfulness; it must, therefore, recognize ever and again its moral unworthiness and pray for the remission of sins and new moral power.

The confessional prayer of Clement contains the words:

" Forgive us our iniquities and unrighteousnesses, our transgressions and shortcomings, our error and stumbling. Lay not
every sin to the account of Thy servants and handmaids, but
cleanse us through the purification of Thy truth, and guide
our steps into the path of holiness." The liturgical collection
of prayers of Bishop Serapion contains the following acknowledgment of sin: " We acknowledge before Thee humbly, O
gracious God, our weaknesses, and call Thy power to help.
Pardon us our earlier sins, overlook all past errors, and make
us new men. Make us holy and pure servants. We surrender
ourselves to Thee, accept us O God of Truth, accept Thy
people, and let them become entirely holy; grant that they
may walk blameless and pure. May they, when fitted for
Heaven, be numbered among the angels; may they all become
Thy chosen and holy ones! "

Sin and Grace are the corner stone of the Reformed piety
defined by the Pauline experience of redemption. This piety
rings out yet more intimate tones occasionally in acknowledgment of sin and prayer for forgiveness than does the old
Church.

The Sunday Divine Service begins in most Reformed
Service-books with the Confessional Prayer of Oecolampadius:
" O Heavenly Father, eternal and compassionate God, we
acknowledge and confess before Thy Divine Majesty, that we
are poor, miserable sinners, conceived and born in corruption,
inclined to all evil, incapable without Thee of good, and that
we have daily and on many occasions transgressed Thy holy
commandments, by which we draw down upon us Thy wrath,
and according to Thy righteous judgment draw upon us death
and destruction. But, O Lord, we suffer sorrow and pain that
we have angered Thee, and bewail ourselves and our sins and
pray that Thy grace come to the help of our misery and
suffering. Wilt Thou on this account have mercy on us, O
most gracious God and Father, and pardon us all our sins
through the holy suffering of Thy dear Son, our Lord Jesus
Christ? Forgive us our sins, and grant and increase in us
daily the gifts of Thy Holy Spirit, that we may unreservedly
acknowledge our unrighteousness, and experience in ourselves
sincere sorrow, which may destroy sin in us, and bring forth

the fruits of innocence and righteousness that may be pleasing to Thee for Jesus' sake!"

The Introductory Prayer of the Swedish High Mass is formed by the following confessional prayer:

"I, a poor sinful man, who am born in sin, and also later through all the days of my life and in various manners have offended against Thee, confess with a full heart before Thee, O holy and just God, loving Father, that I have not loved Thee above all, nor my neighbour as myself. Against Thee and Thy holy commandments have I sinned in thought, word, and deed, and know that therefore I am worthy of eternal damnation, if Thou wouldst judge me as Thy righteousness requireth, and my sins have deserved. But now, dear Heavenly Father, hast Thou promised to receive all repentant sinners with compassion and grace, if they turn to Thee with living faith in Thy fatherly pity, and take refuge in the merits of Jesus Christ, the Redeemer. With Him Thou wilt overlook offences which they have committed against Thee, and never more reckon their sins to them. On this, I, a poor sinner, rely, and pray Thee with confidence that Thou wouldst deign, according to this Thy promise, to have pity on me, to be gracious unto me, and forgive me all my sins, to the praise and glory of Thy holy Name."

Unreserved self-condemnation and self-depreciation rings out here in unshakable, joyous trust in God's forgiving grace.

The acknowledgment of sin with the prayer for forgiveness following on it, leads up to petition proper. Origen's division joins on to the Confession " the prayer for great and heavenly concerns, individual as well as universal." The consummation for which Jewish and early Christian piety yearned is the full accomplishment of the divine sovereignty; the coming of God's Kingdom is, therefore, the most important subject of prayer in the Synagogue and the early Christian Church. The Jewish hope of the Kingdom of God has a politico-national colouring. What the Jewish Church longs for, is redemption from the oppression of foreign lordship, renewal of the splendid Davidic Kingdom, the overthrow of Israel's enemies, and of its present oppressors.

In the *Schmone 'Esre* the Jewish Synagogue prays: " Look

on our misery and guide our affairs and redeem us for Thy name's sake, for Thou art a strong Redeemer. Proclaim with loud trumpets our freedom, and raise a banner to collect our scattered ones, and gather them from the four corners of the earth. . . . Set up again our Judges as formerly, and our Counsellors as in the beginning: and take from us sorrow and sighing; and rule over us, Thou Lord, alone in grace and pity; and justify us in the Judgment . . . and may there be no hope for the slanderers; and may all who do evil come quickly to destruction, and all be rooted out very early; and cripple, dash to pieces, and overthrow them, and quickly bow down the proud in our days. . . . And come back in pity to Jerusalem Thy city, and dwell in its midst as Thou hast said; and build it up soon in our days an everlasting building; and set up soon the Throne of David in the midst thereof. Let the seed of David Thy servant soon shoot forth, and exalt his horn through Thy help; for on Thy help we wait all the days. . . . Have good pleasure, O Lord our God, in Thy people Israel, and in their prayer; and bring back again the sacrificial service to the Holy of Holies of Thy house, and accept the sacrifice of Israel and their prayer in love and good pleasure; and may the daily sacrifice of Israel Thy people be acceptable. O that our eyes might see Thy return to Zion in pity!"

In primitive Christianity a spiritualization of the idea of a divine Kingdom was accomplished. To be sure, the primitive Christian community also expected the Kingdom of God here on earth, not in Heaven beyond, but this Kingdom is no national lordship of the Jews, no earthly Kingdom of happiness, but a universal, divine moral sovereignty, the victory of God over the powers of Satan, of good over evil. The hope of the primitive Church was not the enthronement of a worldly ruler from the stem of David — but the advent of the exalted Lord and Son of God, Jesus Christ, on the clouds of Heaven. In words similar to those of the Jewish Synagogue, the primitive Christian community prayed for the early fulfilment of their ardent longing, for the coming of the Lord and for the consummation of all things.

Thus we read in the eucharistic prayers of the *Didache:* "Remember, O Lord, Thy Church to redeem it from all evil and to perfect it in Thy love; so gather the Church (which has been sanctified) together from the four winds into Thy Kingdom which Thou hast prepared for it; for Thine is the power and the glory, for ever. May grace come, may the world pass away! Hosanna to the Son of David! . . . Maranatha (Come, Lord!) Amen!"

The hope of the immediate nearness of God's Kingdom lost its heaven-storming power about the end of the first century; in a weakened form it still lived on in the two following centuries, then to disappear almost entirely; only in the sects of all ages has it flared up again and again in a mighty flame. For later Christianity, the Church, an institute of salvation, all-embracing, amazingly stable and affluent, became the visible Kingdom of God. Hence, in the Church's public prayers, the eschatological petition for the Kingdom of God, which still is the central prayer of the *Didache,* disappears. Its place is taken by the prayer for the Church, for its preservation and outward extension, its inward strengthening and unity.

With special clearness is this inward change of the Christian believing consciousness to be recognized in the prayer of the *Euchologium* of Serapion. It contains the wording of the *Didache* prayer almost entirely, and imperceptibly changes the prayer for the Kingdom of God into the prayer for the unity of the Church. " As this bread was strewn over the mountains and gathered up into one, so gather also Thy holy Church from all peoples, all lands, all cities, villages and houses, and make them one living Catholic Church."

In the early Eastern liturgies, the prayer for the Church stands at the head of all general intercessions. Thus it reads in the ideal liturgy of the eighth book of the *Apostolic Constitutions:* " Let us pray for the Holy Catholic and Apostolic Church, which is spread abroad from one end of the earth to the other, that the Lord may protect it, founded on the rock, from storms and waves, and keep it till the fulfilment of eternity." A similar tone runs through the prayer in the liturgy of St. Basil: " Remember, O Lord, Thy holy Catholic and Apostolic Church, which stretches from one end of the earth to the other. As Thou hast won it with the precious blood of Thy Christ, so grant it peace and preserve this holy house till the end of the world." The Roman Good Friday liturgy contains the powerful prayer: "Let us pray for the Holy Church of God, that its God, our Lord, may grant peace, and be willing to unite and protect it over the whole earth, subject unto it the authorities and powers and grant us to glorify God, the Almighty Father, in a still calm life. Almighty, Eternal God, Thou hast revealed Thy glory to all peoples in Christ, protect the works of Thy compassion, so that Thy Church, which is scattered over the whole earth, may abide with steadfast faith in Thy knowledge."

The primitive Christian prayer for God's Kingdom sounds with a duller echo in these prayers, for the strength and unity of the Church.

Prayers offered in common for individual, religious, and moral benefits form the greater part of petitions in public worship, as we have already found them in the individual prayer life of prophetic personalities.

Justin says in his description of the Baptismal Communion: "We offer prayers in common that we may be found worthy to understand the truth, and may be found in good conduct of life and in the fulfilment of Thy commandments, so that we may attain everlasting salvation." The *Euchologium* of Serapion contains the prayer: "Give us knowledge and faith and piety and holiness. Destroy all passion, all lust, all sin in this people, grant that they all may become clean. . . . Give us a holy disposition and perfect enjoyment. Grant that we may seek and love Thee. Grant that we may search and explore Thy holy words; stretch forth Thy hand, O Lord, and raise us up. Raise us up, O God of mercies, grant that we may look upwards, open our eyes, grant us courage, grant that we be not ashamed or fear or condemn. Do away with our debt of guilt. Inscribe our names in the book of life. Reckon us among Thy holy prophets and apostles through Thine only-begotten Son, Jesus Christ."

The Collect of the Roman liturgy of the Mass, which also was frequently taken over into the evangelical liturgies, is distinguished by its general setting and powerful brevity. Like the chief *Thanksgiving* of the Mass, the *Preface*, this chief petitionary prayer in the Western liturgy has a reference to the current festival or festival period of the Church Year. The contents of the prayer strikes the special note of the Feast or festal period; the longing of Advent, and the joy of Christmas, the serious penitence of Lent, the rejoicing of Easter Day, and the spiritual power of Whitsuntide.

In the petitions of the Evangelical liturgies, we find expressed the thoughts and temper of reformed piety, in so far as they are not taken over from the old Church but are creations of the Reformation. The firm hold on God's Word, which underlies their writings, the consciousness of forgiveness, the pure trust in God, on account of Christ's merit, form the most important subject of the petition.

A prayer of the old Strassburg Order of Service, from the Reformation period, runs thus: " Almighty, gracious Father, since all our salvation lies in this that we have a true understanding of Thy Word, grant to us all that our hearts being set free from worldly affairs, we may with all zeal and faith hear and apprehend Thy holy word, so that we may rightly know and love Thy gracious will, and live in all sobriety to Thy praise and glory." Like personal prophetic piety, the piety of Synagogue and of the early Church makes no distinction between earthly and heavenly, material and spiritual petitions. All matters which the congregation has at heart are expressed in public prayer. Just as the Lord's Prayer contains the simple petition for daily bread between the petitions for the Kingdom of God and the forgiveness of sins, so the Jewish *Schmone 'Esre* contains among weighty and spiritual petitions prayer for the increase of the fruits of the field and for an abundant harvest: " Bless us, O Lord, this year, let all turn out well, and give Thy blessing to the land; and satisfy us with Thy goodness and bless our year like the good years." In the liturgy of the eighth book of the *Apostolic Constitutions* we repeatedly meet with the petition for good weather and for the fruitfulness of the earth. Similar prayers are to be found in the *Euchologium* of Serapion.

The congregation supplicates not alone the great benefits of salvation to which all its members aspire, and for the daily bread which all need; it thinks in similar fashion of the special circumstances and needs of its individual members. One of the most important portions of the early Christian service is the general intercessory prayer, whose echo we meet in numerous parts of early Christian literature. These intercessory prayers are not, however, as may often be the case to-day, impressive, pious turns of speech, but the genuine and direct expression of the religious feeling of the community. The consciousness that all are members of one body, that each has to bear the burden of the others, makes the needs and concerns of one individual brother become the need and concern of the assembled congregation.

Clement of Rome prays:

" We pray Thee, O Lord, become a helper and deliverer to us: help those among us who are in tribulation, have pity on the poor, raise up the fallen, show Thyself to those who are in need, heal the sick, lead back the strayed ones of Thy people, feed the hungry, free our prisoners, raise up the weak, comfort the faint-hearted."

In similar fashion the petition for brethren suffering and in danger, recurs in all liturgies of the Eastern Church. It meets us also in the Orders of Service of the Evangelical Church; here, however, it is no longer limited, as in the ancient Church, to the members of the congregation, but is conceived in universal terms.

The prayer for brethren who are in need and danger forms the kernel of the early Christian intercessory prayer. The prayer for the leaders and servants of the congregation, accompanies or precedes this. With the progressive differentiation of Church officials, this intercession is developed into the prayer for all ecclesiastical grades from interpreters up to the Bishop.

The intercessory prayer of the Jewish and early Christian Church reaches out over the whole circle of devotees of the faith. An important place is occupied in it by the petition for the heathen rulers, and heathen officialdom. The Jewish community prayed for the great Persian King, and later for the Ptolemies. Early Christianity took over this Jewish custom which, moreover, the syncretistic cult of Isis had also adopted. The composer of the Pastoral Epistles calls on

Timothy to pray for all kings and magistrates. Clement of Rome prays:

" Thou, O Lord, gavest to them the authority of sovereignty through Thine excellent and inexpressible might, so that we may acknowledge the glory and honour which is given them by Thee, and subject ourselves to them, and not oppose Thy will. Grant them, O Lord, health, peace, concord, prosperity, so that they may exercise without offence the lordship entrusted to them by Thee. For Thou, O Heavenly Ruler, King of the ages, givest to the children of men glory, honour, and power over those dwelling on the earth. Do Thou, O Lord, guide their counsels to what is good, and well pleasing by Thee, so that they may exercise the power entrusted to them by Thee, in peace and gentleness with piety, and find grace before Thee."

When the government of the world had come into Christian hands, after the victory of Christianity, the intercessory prayer of the Christian Church for the " most Christian " Ruler, who was their protector, took on a still greater importance. The Reformation brought an intimate connection of the Church with the individual State; the universal Christian fellowship narrowed itself down into the State Church. The early Christian petition for Ruler and State, thus received a strongly politico-national colouring. A clear example of this State-Church form of prayer is offered by the Prussian liturgy.

The simple Christian petition for the secular authority is expanded here into a long-winded, political and patriotic exhortation, intended to implant firmly in the hearts of the assembled believers the sense of subjection to monarchs. A much deeper, really religious spirit is expressed in the prayer of intercession of the Calvinistic liturgy. The type of sect which Calvinism has preserved, has prevented the absorption of religious community life into the politico-national State Church establishment.

" We pray Thee, Heavenly Father, for all princes and lords to whom Thou hast entrusted the rule of Thy righteousness, especially for the governors of this town, that it may please Thee to impart to them Thy Spirit, which alone is good and truly princely, and daily to increase it, so that they may acknowledge Thy Son our Lord, Jesus Christ, in real faith, as the King of kings, and Lord of all lords, to whom Thou hast given all power in Heaven, and on earth, and may seek to serve Him, and to exalt His lordship through their own lordship, while they lead their subjects, who are the creatures of Thy hand and sheep of Thy flock, according to Thy goodwill, in order that we, living here, and on the whole earth, in goodly peace, and rest, may serve Thee in all holiness and honour, freed and assured from the fear of our enemies, may be able to praise Thee throughout our whole life."

The Christian intercessory prayer knows no limitation of creed or nation. The commandment of the Lord, " Love your enemies, pray for those who persecute you and despitefully use you," was also fulfilled by the early Christian Church in its assemblies at public worship. In the middle of the prayer for brethren who are in need and distress, is inserted the petition for the salvation of the Jews and heathen.

In the prayer of Clement of Rome we find:

" Lead back those of Thy people who have strayed. May all peoples know that Thou art the only God and Jesus Christ Thy Son, and we are His people and the sheep of His flock." In the great intercessory prayer of the Roman Good Friday Service, the love and care of the Church for those far removed from her, as well as the proud consciousness of those who have apprehended the right faith, makes a strong impression. " Let us also pray for heretics and schismatics, that our God and Lord may draw them out of their errors and lead them back to the Holy Mother, the Catholic and Apostolic Church. Almighty, Everlasting God, who bestowest salvation on all, and willest that no one should be lost, look down on the devilish delusion of blinded souls, in order that the hearts of those who have erred may lay aside all heretical wickedness, and return to the unity of Thy truth. Let us also pray for the unbelieving Jews, that God our Lord may remove the veil from their hearts, that they also may recognize Jesus Christ, our Lord. Almighty, Eternal God, Thou who dost not reject Jewish faithfulness from Thy compassion, hear our prayers, which we bring before Thee, on account of the blindness of that people, so that they may acknowledge the truth of Thy light, which is Christ, and may be drawn out of their darkness — Let us also pray for the heathen, that God the Almighty may take away wickedness from their hearts, so that they may forsake their graven images, and betake themselves to the living and true God, and to His Only Son, Jesus Christ, Our God and Lord. Almighty, Eternal God, Thou who art intent, not on the death of sinners, but ever on their life, graciously accept our prayer, and free them from the worship of their graven images, and make them members of Thy Holy Church, to the praise and glory of Thy name."

The intercession for those who are strangers to Christian truth passed over also into the evangelical liturgies. In the Calvinistic Sunday Service is found: " We pray Thee, all gracious and merciful Father, for *all* men that Thou who desirest to be acknowledged as the Redeemer of the whole world wouldst lead back those who still linger in darkness and ignorance, through the illumination of Thy Holy Spirit and the preaching of Thy Gospel, to the right way of Thy gospel, that is, that they may acknowledge Thee, the only true God, and Him whom Thou hast sent, Jesus Christ."

The intercession of the Christian congregation covers not only the living but also the departed; for the living and dead belong to the all-embracing communion of saints, who together form, indeed, the Church of Christ. Serapion's *Euchologium* contains the following Prayer for the Dead: " We pray, also, for them that have fallen asleep, of whom we now think (Here follows the list of names). Sanctify these souls for Thou knowest them all; sanctify all who have fallen asleep in the Lord, and number them henceforward among Thy holy angelic hosts, and give them a place and position in Thy Kingdom."

The intercessory prayer in the worship of Christian congregations, is thus the expression of universal, neighbourly love, which the Lord commanded His disciples, which the apostle of the Gentiles preaches and the primitive Church practised. Hence it is as wide and all-embracing as this love itself; living and dead, those present and those at a distance, friends and foes, Christian and heathen, orthodox and heretic, saints and sinners, strong and weak; healthy and sick, masters and slaves, spiritual leaders and worldly potentates — the congregation of brethren assembled in the Lord, remembers them all in common prayer to the Father.

Praise and thanksgiving form the culminating point of common prayer in public worship. Solemn praise forms also the effective conclusion of all liturgical prayers of the Synagogue, and of early Christianity; every petition and intercession rises at the conclusion to a resounding expression of praise, the Doxology.

The contemplative praying of the mystic is impassioned with a rapturous vision of the Highest Good, the simple petition of prophetic genius rings out in strong words of confidence or resignation; the liturgical prayer of the Jewish and Christian assemblies ends in a solemn acknowledgment of the sovereign majesty and boundless might of God. The response which concludes every verse of the *Schmone 'Esre* is a mighty cry of praise: " Praised be Thou, O Lord! " The closing section of this prayer is a richly worded hymn of praise. The primitive Christian Church adopted this use of the Doxology as a conclusion to prayer; but it simplified an expanded form of homage into a plain, powerful, and pithily brief expression of praise. St. Paul, in the commencement and close of his letters, regularly falls into solemn liturgical language; the doxologies with which the congregation in Jerusalem, Corinth, Rome, and Ephesus ended their prayers may be found in Philip 4:20, I Tim. 1:17, Rom. 16:27, Eph. 3:21, I Clement 60.

VI. THE INVOCATION IN CHRISTIAN COMMON PRAYER

Prayer in Jewish and Christian congregations, like the personal prayer of great religious leaders, is addressed not to " gods many and lords many," but to the one true God. It is true that the early Christian faith in the revealing and redeeming Son of God and in His Spirit continuing to work in the Church, broke through the rigid monotheism which threatened to fade into a form of deism. Nevertheless, in primitive Christianity, prayer in public worship is addressed only to God the Father, never to Jesus. But the naming of the name of Jesus

belongs to every liturgical prayer, because in the primitive
Christian experience of redemption God is indissolubly bound
up with Christ as the Revealer, Redeemer, and Finisher of
our faith. This naming of Jesus' name is, however, not a
direct address to Him, a strict invocation, but purely a " joint-
reference to Him." This peculiarity in the public prayer of
the Early Church may be traced especially to Paul. He exhorts the Church at Colossae in these words: " Let the word
of Christ dwell in you richly . . . and whatsoever you do, in
word or in deed, do all *in the name of the Lord Jesus Christ*,
giving thanks to God the Father through Him." The fourth
evangelist calls this mode of prayer — in which is implied the
assurance of being heard — prayer " in the name of Jesus."
The first form in which the name of Jesus occurs in public
prayer is the inclusion of His name in the invocation to
the Father; and this we find already in the Pauline letters, as,
for example, " Blessed be the God and Father of our Lord
Jesus Christ." The *Apostolic Constitutions* has the phrase:
" God and Father of Thy holy Son Jesus, our Saviour."

The second and much more frequent form is the organic
incorporation of the name in petition or thanksgiving. Moreover, it belongs already to the New Testament period. Thus
Paul: " I thank my God through Jesus Christ." Ignatius
exhorts the Roman Church: " Sing praise to the Father in
Christ Jesus." The formula " through Jesus," less frequently
" in Jesus," is so closely bound up with the closing sentence
of the prayer or section of the prayer that it forms a material
part of this sentence and at the same time leads to the final
doxology.

Nowhere is the primitive belief in the mediatorship of Jesus
so clearly revealed as in public prayer. He is not the object
of praise and thanksgiving, He is not the " Hearer " of the
prayers to whom the worshipping congregation turns for help.
Praise and thanksgiving, petition and intercession are addressed exclusively to the Father, yet not to the infinite and
mighty God enthroned in the highest heavens, but to the God
who through Jesus has created the world and by Him bestows
upon His chosen, grace and redemption, justification and
blessedness. Jesus is the intercessor who on behalf of His

believing people presents their petitions to the Father. " There is one God and one Mediator between God and man, the man Christ Jesus," writes Paul. " The Son of God," says Origen, " is the High Priest of our sacrifices and the Advocate with the Father; He prays with him who prays, and supplicates with him who supplicates." Wherever this faith in Christ, to which Paul gave classical expression, is living there can be no prayer which leaves unnamed the name of Jesus. The stated common prayer of early Christianity was always addressed to God through Christ. But from the first days of the religion, the oppressed hearts of Christians sent up brief ejaculations to the exalted Lord Jesus, the earliest specimen of which we have in the prayers of the dying Stephen. There can be no doubt that, in view of the importance of personal enthusiastic prayer in the primitive assemblies, direct prayers to Christ were not confined to personal devotion. " He who prays in the name of Jesus will pray, sooner or later, *to* Jesus." The response in the original Aramaic *Maranatha* and the hymns in use from the earliest times bear witness to this fact. The Apocalypse contains hymns of this kind. Ignatius says that " Jesus Christ is unanimously celebrated in song," and even Pliny bears witness that " the Christians sing hymns antiphonally to Christ as to a god." Clement of Alexandria in his *Protrepticus* has transmitted such a hymn which is addressed directly to Christ. The earliest example in liturgical prayer of direct address to Christ is to be found in the *Gloria in excelsis:* " O Lord God, Lamb of God, Son of the Father, that takest away the sins of the world, have mercy upon us." But it is a question whether in all probability there may not be here a working over of an old prayer of adoration addressed only to God the Father. A manuscript of the *Apostolic Constitutions* has this noteworthy reading: " Lord God, Father of Jesus Christ, the spotless Lamb, that takest away the sin of the world, receive our prayer." Protestant Churches hold fast to the rule of the Early Church of addressing prayers to the Father through Christ. Nevertheless, various prayer-books took over from the Roman Mass those prayers which are addressed directly to Christ, the *Gloria*, the *Agnus Dei*, and the Communion prayers.

VII. The Idea of Prayer in Public Worship

Common prayer is not a common meditation but, precisely like individual prayer, a real intercourse with God who is invoked and experienced as present. To be sure, it is not an individual self that comes into relation with God, but an ideal fellowship with which every member of the congregation feels himself identified. Wherever common prayer wells up with native energy out of the experience of religious unity, as in the ancient Jewish Church, in primitive Christianity, and in the sects, there is the consciousness that the living God is present and that the congregation is in direct communion with Him. This is felt as strongly and profoundly as in the prayer-life of the great men of religion who in the silence of the inner chamber call upon their God. In the Babylonian Talmud it is written: " Wherever ten persons pray, the Shekinah dwells among them." " God Himself is in the synagogue." Common prayer, therefore, in so far as it is a living thing of the mind, is really what in outward form it appears to be, a calling upon God, a speaking with God.

Common prayer is first of all, as has been shown, pure adoration, praise, and thanksgiving, a solemn acknowledgment of the might and majesty of God and also of the gifts and blessings of salvation which the congregation has received from God. An element of contemplation inheres in liturgical prayer. The congregation is absorbed in the fulness of blessings which are implied in the being and working of God, and which are vouchsafed it as gifts of grace. This glorifying of God, in contrast to the eulogies of primitive prayer and cultual hymn, is not dictated by hidden selfish desires with a view to flatter Him and to persuade Him to change His mind; it is the welling forth of those strong and genuine feelings of worth which rise up in the hearts of the assembled believers. Schleiermacher is, therefore, in a certain sense, right when he describes common prayer as " nothing but a representation of the aroused religious consciousness of the congregation." Of course, this definition is not at all exhaustive; it forgets to bring out the relation in which the congregation, which praises and gives thanks, stands to God. The glorifying of God for

His own sake, as also for the sake of His manifestations of grace to men, is not a mere representation of feelings that have been experienced, but in the strict sense " a service of God " to which the congregation feels itself bound. The congregation held in the grasp of God's goodness and glory would offer Him something, would present to Him a symbol of their devout reverence and fervent gratitude. The common prayer of praise and thanksgiving thus becomes an " offering." It is, of course, no sacrifice of animal or food such as primitive man and ancient priests offered, but a purely spiritual offering. Jewish and early Christian writings overflow with statements in which prayer in public worship is described as an " offering."

The thought of " offering " appears here in its sublimest and most spiritual form. The mystic regards his unreserved renunciation of all earthly things, the perfect surrender of his own will to God's as an offering; the Jewish and Christian assemblies of worshippers see in their solemn praise and thanksgiving an offering made to the Most High. Thus offering and sacrifice in personal religion at its highest as of collective worship, are fused into the unity in which they were already bound up in primitive religion.

In the contemplative character of liturgical praise and thanksgiving, the common prayer of public worship reveals a certain relationship to personal, mystical prayer. In petition and intercession the prophetic type of devotion shows itself. As has been shown, the primitive idea of the influence of prayer on the will of God lies at the basis of prophetic prayer. This same idea underlies common prayer in so far as it is petition and intercession. In it, as in all simple prayer, is an indestructible faith in its being heard and answered. The congregation unified in the worship of God has the confident hope that its petitions and intercessions will be realized, nay, it believes that the prayer of many will move God sooner to an answer than that of an individual. " In the solidarity of prayer," writes von der Goltz, " there is a mutual supplementing of the individual's weakness which also can be conceived as a joint-struggle against the power of the Adversary."

The faith of the primitive Church in the power of common prayer already finds expression in a saying of the Lord.

" Again I say unto you that if two of you shall agree on the earth as touching anything that they shall ask, it shall be done for them of my Father who is in heaven; For where two or three are gathered together in my name, there am I in the midst of them." Ignatius remarks in connection with this passage: " If the prayer of one individual and of a second has such power, how much more the prayer of the bishop and the entire church." This thought returns again almost literally in Luther when he remarks: " Jesus says that when two on earth are at one about something for which they pray, it shall be done unto them; how much more should they obtain that for which they pray when a whole city comes together unitedly to praise or to pray. . . . We can and we ought, indeed, to pray in all places and at all times; but prayer is nowhere so vigorous and so strong as when a great number pray in unison."

Thus in common prayer a mystical and prophetic element can be shown. Contemplative praise resembles the mystical manner of prayer. The petition and intercession sustained by faith in answers to prayer arises out of prophetic religion. Miss A. L. Strong, an American psychologist, is therefore plausibly in the right when she explains common prayer as a mixture of the " contemplative-aesthetic," that is, the mystical, and the " practico-ethical," that is, the prophetic type. But this characterization is, nevertheless, not entirely correct, for the relation of common to mystical prayer is not an inward one; the religious spirit which speaks out of it is rather purely prophetic. The God to whom the Jewish Synagogue and the Christian Church pray is not the supreme spiritual Value which shines upon the mystic estranged from the world and himself, but the living, creating, ever-active Will to whom men of prophetic genius turned for help. This same ethical activity which is the mark of the prophetic type of devotional religion, animates also the common prayer of Jew and Christian. The prayer of public worship is not, like mystical prayer, a fading away of the finite spirit in the infinite God, but the active expression of the assurance of and yearning for salvation. It is not the tender union of a solitary soul with the heavenly Saviour and Bridegroom, but the solemn homage of believing people before their God, who is also their

King, the heartfelt supplication of the great family to their gracious Father-God. Jewish and Christian common prayer is then nothing else than the overflow of the prophetic devotional religion into the worship of those religious communions which have originated in the prophetic spirit.

VIII. Special Types of Common Prayer in Public Worship

(a) *Prayer in the Public Worship of the Early Church.* Public worship in primitive Christianity as it was celebrated in Jerusalem from the Day of Pentecost and was transplanted by Paul into the Christian Churches of the Roman Empire, is a mystery in a double sense. It is, like the celebration of mysteries in the syncretist religions of redemption, a something done, a sacred drama which is played before the eyes of the devout fellowship, nay, which is consummated by those who take part in the mysteries. This sacred drama is the redeeming death of Jesus which is " preached," as Paul says, everywhere and as often as the Christian Church celebrates the Eucharist — preached not in mere words of grateful remembrance, but in a sacred act. The bloody suffering and death of the Son of God is " renewed unbloodily." This latter theological formula touches the core of the primitive Christian conception. If we want to express it in terms of the modern science of religion we must say that the eucharistic mystery act is a mimetic, that is, an imitative ritual act. The thankful congregation unceasingly represented the saving death of Jesus with the same parabolic action which on the night before His death He performed — the breaking of the bread and the passing round and emptying of the cup — and with which in touching symbolism He set before the eyes of His disciples His sacrificial death for " the many." But this " remembrance " by way of imitation is no mere symbolic exhibition, no mere picturing to oneself of an historical fact by an analogy; it is a mysterious, real renewal, no mere shadow of a reality but the full reality itself. It is an idea common to the religion and magic of all peoples and times that through the mimetic act, the thing imitated, intended, and represented is itself effected, that the copy and the model are bound together by mystic bonds of identity. All ancient mystery liturgies would establish supersensuous realities by an act of imitation. The early Christian celebration of the Eucharist has also the same intention; it exhibits a real renewal of the saving deed of Christ. The act which renews the saving deed of the Cross is accompanied by the repetition of the Scriptural account of the Lord's Supper; the narrative of what Jesus said and did exalts living faith in the transcendent reality of the sacred act that is performed.

And yet again in another sense the primitive Christian worship is a mystery. The Eucharist is a sacred meal by which the communicants come into immediate bodily and spiritual communion with their Lord and Redeemer.[8] The breaking and eating of the bread is a communion of the body of Christ, the drinking from the cup of blessing is a communion of the blood of Christ. The primitive Christian celebration is therefore called " the Lord's Supper." Thus communion with the exalted Son of God, the Head of the Church, follows upon renewal of the Lord's sacrificial death. The primitive Christian service is accordingly a mystery celebration, a sacramental worship, a " liturgy," though in contrast to ancient mystery liturgies, it does without all hard and fast forms.

The double mystery of the Eucharist, the remembrance of the saving deed of Jesus and the communion with the Lord, is the focus of primitive Christian congregational worship. Common prayer is intimately related to this mystery, it is a part of its celebration. The prayers are grouped round the sacred act, which is the centre and climax of the service. Yet the common prayer is no sacred formula which lends mysterious and magical power to the ritual act, something like the *brahma,* the spell with which the Vedic priest accompanies the sacrificial act, or like those archaic sentences which the initiated recite in the syncretist and secret mysteries. It is a real, collective prayer, a common praise, thanksgiving, petition, and intercession, more alive, powerful, and passionate than anything the history of religion has known before or since. It is no priestly prayer to which the congregation listens, without

---

[8] τραπέζης κυρίου μετέχειν.

understanding it, but common prayer, the prayer of gifted possessors of the Spirit who carry their brethren with them in their enthusiasm. It is the entire congregation that prays, not an isolated official priest; it is the entire congregation, not an isolated official who celebrates the mystery. By prayer and by the sacred act the entire congregation in which "the many are one body" come into most intimate communion with the Father and the exalted Lord. Speech and act, prayer and sacrament are bound together in perfect harmony.

(b) *Prayer in Catholic Public Worship.* In the public worship of the Catholic Church (the Roman, as also the various Churches of the East), the living worship of the congregation has become a rigid, cultual institution. The Mass of the Western and Eastern Churches is in original character identical with the primitive Christian congregational worship; it is sacramental, a celebration of a mystery. The same mystery which was celebrated in Christian houses in Jerusalem, Corinth, and Rome is celebrated daily in the cathedrals and chapels of the East and the West, namely, the setting forth of the atoning death of Jesus and the coming into communion of believers with their Lord. But out of the simple act of breaking bread and drinking from a cup has grown a complicated liturgy under a rigid rule, even to the smallest details, which in pomp and splendour is in no way behind the ancient temple-rituals and syncretist mystery liturgies. The thing done, the cultual act has become the principal thing; the spoken word accompanying the act, the liturgical prayer, hardened into a stereotyped formula, has but a secondary value. Not a few of the prayers in the Mass which sound on the lips of the priest are indeed the same as those with which the primitive Church gave thanks and offered supplications. But the liturgical prayer of the Mass is no longer common prayer. By the use of an ancient language, half understood or not understood at all, the bond between the officiant and the congregation is torn asunder. The priest prays in the name of the people; the congregation do not pray with him, but by themselves. It is not the people but the acolyte or the choir that takes up his prayer in the responses. Nay, the greatest part of the Mass is spoken by the celebrant silently or in a murmur, so that even he who understands the ecclesiastical language is unable to follow his words. The congregation has become a dumb spectator of the holy mystery which is enacted before their eyes. The congregation does, it is true, feel itself inwardly at one with the officiant and so shares in his prayer, but this inner sympathy is not revealed outwardly in the common utterance of prayer. The prayer of the people present at the Mass is not *common* but *individual* prayer. The devout feelings of reverence and love, humility and trust, which arise in the hearts of those present at the contemplation of the sacred drama and at the hearing of the solemn hymn or of the mysterious, monotonous murmur, are expressed in silent, personal prayer. Thus an individual mysticism springs up in the midst of public worship. Thus the individual soul rises in a bold flight to God; it is absorbed in the great mystery of redemption, revealed before it in liturgical symbol; and without the bonds imposed by common prayer, it cherishes spontaneously devout converse with God.

In the Roman liturgy of the Mass there is a further element. The dissolution of direct contact between the congregation and the officiant representing it transforms liturgical worship into a sacramental act, valuable in and for itself, which can be performed by the priest alone and does not need the presence of the congregation. The ancient idea of sacrifice which already at an early time had invaded the world of Christian ideas was strengthened still more by this separation of the liturgy from the living consciousness of the Church. The dramatic exhibition and the real renewal of the saving death of Jesus Christ is now considered a sacrificial offering brought to God which by itself, *ex opere operato,* has wonderful effects of grace for believers. The application of the ancient thought of sacrifice to the Mass, as also the self-sufficiency of liturgical worship making it a priestly, ritual act quite apart from the congregation, gave occasion to the rise of private Masses in the Western Church. As the pagan priests offered sacrifices for the private interests of individual believers, so also the Catholic priest offers the sacrifice of the Mass for definite individuals and purposes, as for example, recovery of a sick person or for the repose of the soul of one who has died. The private Mass is alien to the orthodox Churches of the East, which in their conservative temper hold fast to the old ecclesiastical traditions. Thereby the late rise and secondary character of this western institution is made evident.

The liturgical worship of the Roman Church and its eastern sister-churches is no common worship, but a mystery liturgy at which the devout congregation is present in dumb devotion and profound reverence, but not in active participation. The congregation, originally the active agent in every act of worship, is lost in passivity: to it and before it the cultus is performed which, apart from the cultual officiants, the priests, is not conceivable. The living prayer of the congregation has made way for the ritual prayer of the priest. Nevertheless, at least in the western Church, common prayer in worship has not wholly perished; it was merely moved from the central liturgical service to forms of service of a secondary character. The rise of forms of devotion in the Middle Ages and their richer development in recent centuries, shows clearly how deeply the need was felt in western Christendom. This is especially true in the countries of German speech, where these forms saved common prayer for public worship after liturgical prayer in the proper sense of the term had been hardened into a formula of priestly ritual. The thought and the mood of these common forms of " devotions " in church is, of course, quite different from that of the liturgical prayers of the Early Church. All the forms of " devotions " familiar to Catholic People are rooted in the contemplative devotional piety of mediaeval mysticism, especially in the Jesus-mysticism of Bernard of Clairvaux. The substance of Catholic " devotion " is at bottom only mysticism carried over into the cult. Even in these subordinate forms of divine service the eucharistic mystery is not wanting. All " devotions " are performed before the " exposed holy of holies," the pyx which conceals the eucharistic body of Christ, or on ceremonial occasions, the ornate monstrance in which the consecrated host is plainly visible, is taken from the tabernacle and placed in view of the faithful. Thus the eucharistic mystery is the central point, not only of the liturgical service, but also of the other secondary services. The consciousness of the sensuous yet transcendent presence of the Lord heightens the vitality of the prayerful mood in the congregation.

The Catholic Church has not lacked attempts to revive the early Christian ideal of liturgical common prayer by the Introduction of the vernacular into the service of the Mass. Finally the Old Catholic Church, which sought to reconstruct the public worship of Early Christianity, celebrates the Roman Mass in the German language with delicate changes and simplifications. All prayers, even the so-called " prayer of silence," the canon, together with the words of consecration, are spoken aloud; not the choir or the acolyte, but the assembled congregation responds.

(c) *Prayer in the public worship of the synagogue and of the Evangelical churches and sects.* Whilst the mystery stands as the central feature of primitive Christian and Catholic worship, it is completely absent from the worship of Mohammedans and Jews, and it is preserved among Evangelicals only in a rudimentary fashion. The relatively infrequent occurrence of the celebration of the Lord's Supper is the only relic of the mystery-service of primitive Christianity. The worship of the synagogue and of the Reformation was a perfectly *spiritual and ethical service of the Word*, consisting of Scripture reading, sermon, prayer and hymn. No sensuous sign supports and animates the experience of God's immediate nearness; no sacred act fills the congregation with dread and reverence; no tremendous mystery shakes the devout faithful to their inmost souls. The Lord's Supper in the reformed Churches is not a dramatic renewal of the redeeming deed of Christ and mystical union with the exalted Lord, but a mere sign and pledge of the comfort of forgiveness and assurance of salvation, as in the Lutheran Church or as in the reformed Churches, " an act of thanksgiving and confession raised to a high degree of intensity." The evangelical congregational worship has, just like that of the Synagogue, not a cultual and sensuous, but a personal and spiritual quality. Söderblom says: " The individual's personal reverence for God is unified into common thanksgiving and adoration. The evangelical service is, therefore, individual communion with God occurring with a number of people at the same time." We can only therefore speak inexactly of a synagogal and evangelical *liturgy;* for " liturgy " [9] according to the sense of the word is a holy, sacramental act which brings the believer into a sensuous yet spiritual communion with the divine.

In the Judaism of the Exile and the Dispersion non-sacrificial worship was a hard necessity because one could bring a sacrifice only to the central sanctuary on Zion. What hovered before the minds of the reformers in the revival of the synagogal worship was the overflow of the purely spiritual devotional life of the great prophetic geniuses into the worshipping assembly: even the praying of the congregation should be as the praying of Jeremiah, Jesus, and Paul, " a worship in spirit and in truth," a personal, though collectively exercised, communion with God. But this overflow of the individual spirit of prayer into the life of worship of a great congregation takes from prayer something of its immediate power and vitality. All genuine simple prayer is rooted in the experience of the mysterious, immediate presence of God. In the religious genius as in the restricted communion of the newly converted and awakened, this experience is kindled spontaneously, as something purely spiritual, without any sensuous supports or external symbols. But a great congregation which is composed for the most part of persons of average piety needs, in order to perceive more palpably God's nearness, a sensuous stimulus, a visible sign, an acted parable. It receives from the contemplation of the holy performance of a mystery and from the sight of a cultual object, in which God's presence is visible, the most powerful impulse to fervent and passionate prayer. With the exclusion of mystery from divine service the Reformers have also weakened the primal religious emotions of reverence before the *numinous* and of wonder before the *fascinosum.* The " holy " in evangelical worship belongs only to the Word, to the living voice of the preacher and leader in worship. But with the suppression of the *numinous* and with the resultant rationalizing of worship, it follows that the educational purpose, a subordinate aim of common prayer, is made its main purpose; and thus, instead of being the living expression of a common conscious-

---

[9] λιτή = *litare*, to offer, and ἔργον, an act.

ness of salvation, it becomes mere instruction in individual devotional life. If we look at the mass of average religious people we must judge that the delicate and chaste spirituality of the Evangelical service, the logical renunciation of everything primitive, sensuous and magically mystical signifies only an apparent purification and deepening of congregational worship. The charm and power of public worship lies precisely in the mysterious, the sensuous, the primitive. Wherever the primitive element is destroyed in prophetic bluntness and sober severity, the appointed sources of the life of worship in the Church are dried up. It is true that in the Catholic as in the orthodox Churches of the East, the early Christian liturgy is hardened into a complicated ritual, the free common prayer into sacred formulas, the living speech of prayer into a dead, sacrosanct language. But even in the Churches of the Reformation, there is, as some evangelical theologians confess, " too little of the spirit of prayer and of adoration," nay, according to the unjust, over-generalized judgment of Vilmar " in them the living prayer of the congregation is almost everywhere extinct." Only in narrow sectarian conventicles and in the family worship of pious evangelical families is the early Christian common prayer perpetuated in its original warmth and power. Whilst the liturgy of the Catholic Church approximates to the ancient temple ritual and the syncretist mystery-liturgies, the evangelical congregational worship means a return to the synagogal worship of Judaism. Both the Catholic and Evangelical forms of worship have, though in different ways, abandoned the primitive Christian form of worship and have modelled themselves on pre-Christian forms. But whilst the intellectual sobriety of evangelical worship can only with difficulty set free the vital forces of personal piety, the Catholic liturgy of the Mass with its numinous, mysterious quality and its wealth of sensuous and aesthetic stimuli, has been for centuries the starting-point of mystical prayer and contemplation. Nevertheless the ideal of public worship is that of Protestantism. The spiritual adoration of God by an assembly of spiritually mature personalities is the highest and purest form of worship, the true divine service.

CHAPTER XII

PERSONAL PRAYER AS A LAW OF DUTY AND GOOD WORKS

THE religion of the book and the law takes its place as an independent form beside primitive religion, ritual religion, the reconstructed religion of philosophy, creative personal religion, and the living religion of social fellowship. Its roots are to be found in personal prophetic religion and in the immediate, vital piety of the communion in which prophetic religion lives and works. The fresh, upspringing religious experience of prophetic geniuses, and that of the young community inspired by prophetic enthusiasm, stiffens into unconditionally obligatory ideal and law. Religion and piety cease to be free creative experience, a " being driven by the spirit," and become obedience to a holy law laid down in an inspired book which contains the closed and final revelation of God, for there is no continuously operative revelation through prophets and saints. It is true that the religious and ethical ideals as a whole may remain at the high point to which they were elevated by the original vital power, but the freshness and vigour of this power are gone. The motives of religion and morality cease to be either the deep anguish of the heart and the trembling consciousness of guilt, or the inner longing for the salvation and joyous confidence and trust, but have become fear of divine punishment and hope of a divine reward. Emphasis is laid not on a radical change of mind, but on a doing of external works. The religious man is ever seeking to enhance the sum of the obligatory religious duties he has performed by heaping up a mass of voluntary " good works." The idea of authority becomes sharply stressed. This idea is indeed already an essential element of prophetic religion, but in the religion of law the personal authority of religious genius is displaced by the super-personal authority of the law, the book, the official teacher.

The history of religion knows four great legalistic religions: Persian Mazdaism, post-exilic Judaism, Islam, and fully developed Catholicism as it appears about the close of the third century. Nevertheless, it would be wrong to believe that this characterization exhausts the peculiarity and historical significance of these religions. In Judaism and Islam a stiff legalism covers a tender, ardent mysticism. An incomparably deep mystical piety blooms in the Catholicism of all centuries, indeed in it the spirit of the early church has never died out, although it continues to live only in the religious orders in a form amenable to ecclesiastical authority. If we describe these systems of religions as legalistic religions we are merely perceiving their official form, their general external aspect, and we leave unconsidered a great variety of undercurrents.

A new concept of prayer is common to all legalistic religions. Prayer is looked upon as a service rendered by the individual to God, first as a duty and then as a meritorious good work. Still, in saying this, we do not mean that this is the only kind of prayer in these religions. On the contrary, side by side with the legally prescribed and meritorious prayer, there exist the primitive and artless prayer of the masses, the personal prayers of great saints, and the prayers of public worship.

It is in Islam that obligatory prayer appears in its most stringent form. The individual prayer (du'a) as well as the prayer of public worship is secondary to the prayer of obligation (salât). In Talmudic Judaism likewise, the prayer of obligation plays a more important rôle than the congregational prayer of the synagogue. Owing to the deepening of the devotional life by Christianity, prescribed and meritorious prayer is given only a subordinate place in Catholicism, and is, in the main, limited to the masses of the people who are influenced only a very little by the devotional life of the saints and by the prayers of the Church's liturgy.

Legal and meritorious prayer is a service of man to God which has value in itself. God claims this service, and he who omits it, is ensnared in sin and incurs the divine judgment. The prescribed prayer is the confession of faith which distinguishes the godly from the godless, the believing from the unbelieving. " He who neglects the performance of the *salât*," says a Mohammedan theologian, " is an unbeliever." But he who, going beyond the minimum of prayers divinely commanded, performs prayers voluntarily, is assured of a divine reward in this world and in the world to come. The idea of service which underlies meritorious prayer signifies a revival of the primitive idea of sacrifice. It is significant that prescribed and meritorious prayer appeared in Judaism precisely when, through the centralization of worship, general sacrifice had disappeared, and assumed still greater proportions when altar and temple were laid in the dust. The Talmud expressly teaches that the daily prescribed prayers took the place of the daily sacrifice of earlier times. The formulated prayer in the mind of the pious person is simply an offering which he presents to God. The prayer ordained by law is the regular tribute which man owes to God as to a king, a service which he is obliged to discharge as a servant to his master. As an ancient Jewish text has it: " Just as the service at the altar is called '*abodâ* (that is, hard service), so prayer is called a '*abodâ*." Whilst the regular obligatory prayer is equivalent to the primitive tribute-offering, all further prayer has a function similar to the free will offering of gifts; this free will offering is called in later Judaism quite simply, " prayer of donation." Man does that which is well pleasing to God; and in return he hopes that God will grant him the fulfilment of definite wishes or quite generally, earthly happiness and heavenly blessedness. Ahura Mazda promises: " He who recites to me in this material world, O holy Zarathustra, this portion of the *Ahuna vairya*, his soul I bring three times over the bridge to Paradise, I who am Ahura Mazda, to the best place, the most perfect purity, the best lights." The fundamental thought of all sacrificial offerings *do ut des* is here present in a spiritualized form.

Since prayer is a sacrificial offering, a " good work," it can be strengthened with other " good works," especially by fasting and almsgiving. There is thus a triad bound together in the closest way, a triad which Christianity took over from the mother-religion, Judaism, and which also recurs in Islam under the name of the "Five Foundation Pillars."

But not only does the thought of sacrifice underlie meritorious prayer; there is in the background the idea of magic. The Jewish *shema*, the Christian Lord's Prayer, the opening and closing suras of the Koran — they all share the same fate, they were all obliged to serve as magic formulas the self-seeking aims of men. The religious valuation of these formulas, belief in their holy quality, led to the idea of their magical efficacy. Because they were deemed "holy" they were also deemed to be imbued with immanent, supernatural "might" (*Mana*). Their words were the most powerful incantations, the strongest conjurations. Thus does meritorious prayer sink down to the level of primitive magic; from a reverent offering to the great God it becomes a mere mechanical device in the service of human selfishness.

The *content* of prescribed prayer is precisely at the spiritual level of the religions whose adherents recite these formulas. It contains no petition for the little needs of daily life, but a solemn confession of the greatness and holiness of God; no materialistic wishes and cravings, but a bringing home to oneself of great religious duties; no imposing of one's wishes on God, but a humble praise of His power. Thus whilst the content of prescribed prayer reveals religious depth and purity, its *formalism* of necessity deprives it of spirituality, and inwardness. To be sure, religious law does require a devotional prayer, a recitation of the words with full inner sympathy. Jewish law demands of the praying individual *kawwannas*, Christian law asks for "attention" and "devotion," but when the stress is laid on the wording of the formula, when the formula itself is considered holy the spirit can not but escape from it. Its every day use, the endless repetition of one and the same formula, tends to make prayer mechanical; in the end it becomes a mere thoughtless babbling of the words. The religious authorities themselves make concessions to mechanical prayer. A teacher in the Talmud explains that if one can not pray the entire *shema* with devotion, one can do so for the first part, and for the second part pronunciation of the words

will suffice. A second factor which leads to the externalizing
of prescribed prayer is the fear of punishment and hope of reward. The primitive eudaemonism which is excluded from
the content of the prayer reappears in the motives of fear
and hope with which it is used. The praying man does not
obey a native inner impulse, but the external compulsion of
the law; fear of punishment affrights him, hope of reward
allures him. And so it comes to pass that legalized and meritorious prayer, the substance of which lifts up the soul to
God and the blessings of salvation, becomes by the motives
that inspire it an expedient for winning or retaining the divine
favour. Such prayer is for man not a liberating joy but an
oppressive burden, in so far as constant repetition has not
made the psychic experience so mechanical, so that the worshipper no longer suffers from the disagreeable feelings which
it produces.

In spite of all tendency to de-spiritualization, prescribed or
meritorious prayer has a religious value. There are always
devout persons who, animated by a personal religious impulse,
give themselves up to the meaning of the prescribed prayers,
and pray with thought and concentration; they penetrate
through the words to the spirit in which the prayer was composed. And so even legal formularies of prayer can kindle,
strengthen, and purify the religious life. And even prayers
recited without complete understanding are not entirely without some religious quality. Even the mechanical pray-er is
conscious, though indistinctly and vaguely, that he has to do
with something holy; that the words which he uses bear a religious value, that they bring him into relation with God, and
confirm and advance his soul's salvation. All these thoughts
are mingled in a weak and dim devotional experience and
yet it is a genuinely religious experience. The same mood
of reverent and joyous confidence which animated primitive
man when he whispered mysterious incantations, possesses also
the Mohammedan zealot for law who performs his *salât* with
meticulous care, or the Torah-loving Jew, who with hand
swathed with phylacteries, recites his *shema,* or the pious
Catholic who says his rosary, allowing bead after bead to
slip through his fingers, and stringing together *ave* to *ave.*

Unthinking prayer, that is, that prayer which does not concentrate on the meaning of the words, is not at all an impious prayer so long as it is sustained, however vaguely and indistinctly, by spiritual moods and feelings. Even the theology of the Church distinguishes between prayer with *attentio* or the strain of attention, and prayer with *devotio*, that is, devotional feeling. Only that prayer which is without any undercurrent of feeling is absolutely undevout. Of course it is always a lower type of religion to which the mental and emotional implications of a prayer or confession are perfectly alien and unintelligible and which remains at least poor in devotional tone, although not entirely devoid of it.

The great prophetic leaders who have passionately fought for the ideal of prayer in spirit and in truth, brand this unthinking type of prayer as impious and sinful. The mystics on the other hand with their fine psychological insight and large-heartedness discover even in the unintelligible muttering of sacred formulas a crude and dark presentiment of the sublime experience of mystical prayer.

It was at the Reformation that the most incisive protest against prescribed and meritorious prayer was raised. The attempt to imprison the God-given spirit of prayer within narrow legalistic limits and the use of prayer in the service of those seeking self-righteousness by works seemed to them a shameful misuse and profanation of the holiest things. This protest puts the dangers of this form of prayer in the most disagreeable light, but hardly does justice to the educational values inherent in it. Only a few divinely favoured souls are able to reach fully to the lofty ideal of pure and spontaneous prayer as it can be experienced in the individual soul. The great mass of average people need fixed religious forms to which in their spiritual dependence they can cling; they need some stern compulsion to drive them away from the concerns of daily life and lift them up to a higher world. They need the motives of hope and fear which spur them on to a religious life and to the discharge of their moral duties. In spite of all externalism, want of thought, and selfishness, prescribed and meritorious prayer in the universal legalistic religions has acted at all times as a mighty lever in the spiritual life.

CHAPTER XIII

THE ESSENCE OF PRAYER

PRAYER appears in history in an astonishing multiplicity of forms; as the calm collectedness of a devout individual soul, and as the ceremonial liturgy of a great congregation; as an original creation of a religious genius, and as an imitation on the part of a simple, average religious person; as the spontaneous expression of upspringing religious experiences, and as the mechanical recitation of an incomprehensible formula; as bliss and ecstasy of heart, and as painful fulfilment of the law; as the involuntary discharge of an overwhelming emotion, and as the voluntary concentration on a religious object; as loud shouting and crying, and as still, silent absorption; as artistic poetry, and as stammering speech; as the flight of the spirit to the supreme Light, and as a cry out of the deep distress of the heart; as joyous thanksgiving and ecstatic praise, and as humble supplication for forgiveness and compassion; as a childlike entreaty for life, health, and happiness, and as an earnest desire for power in the moral struggle of existence; as a simple petition for daily bread, and as an all-consuming yearning for God Himself; as a selfish wish, and as an unselfish solicitude for a brother; as wild cursing and vengeful thirst, and as heroic intercession for personal enemies and persecutors; as a stormy clamour and demand, and as joyful renunciation and holy serenity; as a desire to change God's will and make it chime with our petty wishes, and as a self-forgetting vision of and surrender to the Highest Good; as the timid entreaty of the sinner before a stern judge, and as the trustful talk of a child with a kind father; as swelling phrases of politeness and flattery before an unapproachable King, and as a free outpouring in the presence of a friend who cares; as the humble petition of a servant to a powerful master, and as the ecstatic converse of the bride with the heavenly Bridegroom.

In considering these varied contrasts and in the survey of the different leading types of prayer, the problem emerges: what is common to all these diverse kinds of prayer, what underlies all these phenomenal forms, in a word, what is the essence of prayer? The answer to this question is not easy. There is the danger of fundamentally misinterpreting prayer by making its essence an empty abstraction. If we would understand the essence of prayer we must look attentively at those types in which we see it as the naïve, spontaneous utterance of the soul; we must, therefore, separate the primary types from the secondary. This separation is easily effected. The primary types which cannot be confounded with the others are these: — the naïve prayer of primitive man, the devotional life of men of religious genius, the prayers of great men, the common prayer of public worship in so far as it has not hardened into a stiff, sacrosanct institution. In all these instances prayer appears as a purely psychical fact, the immediate expression of an original and profound experience of the soul. It bursts forth with innate energy. Very different are the secondary types. They are no longer an original, personal experience, but an imitation or a congealment of such a living experience. The personal prayer of the average religious man is a more or less true reflection of the original experience of another; it remains inferior to the ideal model in power, depth, and vitality. The philosophical idea of prayer is a cold abstraction built up in harmony with metaphysical and ethical standards; by it living prayer is subjected to an alien law, to the principles of philosophy, and is transformed and revised in accordance with this law. The product of this amendment is no longer real prayer, but its shadow, an artificial, dead simulacrum of it. The ritual forms of prayer, the cultual hymn, liturgical common prayer as an institution of the cultus, all these types are phenomena of congelation in which the upspringing personal life has been transmuted into objective, impersonal forms and rules. The penetration into their inner meaning may indeed give rise in devout, susceptible souls to new experiences of prayer, their recitation in public or private worship may take place in a devotional mood, but they themselves are not the direct expression of a personal experience. The essential features of prayer are never visible in these disintegrated, dead, secondary forms, but only in unadulterated, simple prayer as it lives in unsophisticated, primitive human beings and in outstanding men of creative genius. In determining the essence of prayer, therefore, we must fix our attention exclusively on prayer in its primitive simplicity. Only then can we take into consideration the secondary types and inquire how far the essence of prayer is expressed by them.

To answer our question, we must first of all discover the essential motive of prayer, its common psychological root. What moves men to pray? What do men seek when they pray? Da Costa Guimaraens, a French psychologist, defined it thus: " To pray means to satisfy a psychical need." The definition is superficial and is, moreover, insipidly formulated, but it is on the track of a correct psychological motivation. Prayer is the expression of a primitive impulsion to a higher, richer, intenser life. Whatever may be the burden of the prayer, to whatever realm of values it may belong, whether to the eudaemonistic, the ethical, or the purely religious realm — it is always a great longing for life, for a more potent, a purer, a more blessed life. " When I seek Thee, my God," prays Augustine, " I seek a blessed life." His words uncover the psychical root of all prayer. The hungry pygmy who begs for food, the entranced mystic, absorbed in the greatness and beauty of the infinite God, the guilt-oppressed Christian who prays for forgiveness of sins and assurance of salvation — all are seeking life; they seek a confirmation and an enrichment of their realization of life. Even the Buddhist beggar-monk, who by meditation works himself up into a state of perfect indifference, seeks in the denial of life to attain a higher and purer life.

The effort to fortify, to reinforce, to enhance one's life is the motive of all prayer. But the discovery of the deepest root of prayer does not disclose its peculiar essence. In order to get to the bottom of this, we should not ask for the psychological motive of prayer; we must rather make clear the religious ideas of him who prays in simplicity, we must grasp his inner attitude and spiritual aim, the intellectual presuppositions which underlie prayer as a psychical experience. What does the simple, devout person, undisturbed by reflection, think when he prays? He believes that he speaks with a God, immediately present and personal, has intercourse with Him, that there is between them a vital and spiritual commerce. There are three elements which form the inner structure of the prayer-experience: faith in a living personal God, faith in His real, immediate presence, and a realistic fellowship into which man enters with a God conceived as present.

Every prayer is a turning of man to another Being to whom he inwardly opens his heart; it is the speech of an " I " to a " Thou." This " Thou," this other with whom the devout person comes into relation, in whose presence he stands as he prays, is no human being but a supersensuous, superhuman Being on whom he feels himself dependent, yet a being who plainly wears the features of a human personality, with thought, will, feeling, self-consciousness. " Prayer," says Tylor, " is the address of a personal spirit to a personal spirit." Belief in the personality of God is the necessary presupposition, the fundamental condition of all prayer. The anthropomorphism which is always found in primitive prayer and which often appears in the prayer of outstanding religious personalities, the prophets among them, is a coarsening and materializing of this belief in God's personality; it does not, however, belong to the essence of prayer as faith does. But wherever the vital conception of the divine personality grows dim, where, as in the philosophical ideal or in pantheistic mysticism, it passes over into the " One and All," [1] genuine prayer dissolves and becomes purely contemplative absorption and adoration.

The man who prays feels himself very close to this personal God. Primitive man believes that God dwells in a visible place; to this place he hastens when he would pray, or he turns his eyes and hands towards it. The religious genius experiences the divine presence in the stillness of his own heart, in the deepest recesses of his soul. But it is always the reverential and trustful consciousness of the living presence of God, which is the keynote of the genuine prayer-experience. It is true that the God to whom the worshipper cries transcends all

---

[1] ἐν καὶ πᾶν.

material things — and yet the pious man feels His nearness with an assurance as undoubted as though a living man stood before him.

Belief in God's personality and the assurance of His presence are the two presuppositions of prayer. But prayer itself is no mere belief in the reality of a personal God — such a belief underlies even a theistic metaphysic; — nor is it a mere experience of His presence — for this is the accompaniment of the entire life and thought of the great men of religion. Prayer is rather a living relation of man to God, a direct and inner contact, a refuge, a mutual intercourse, a conversation, spiritual commerce, an association, a fellowship, a communion, a converse, a one-ness, a union of an " I " and a " Thou." Only an accumulation of these synonyms which human speech employs to make clear the innermost relations of man to man, can give an appropriate picture of the realistic power and vitality of that relation into which the praying man enters with God. Since prayer displays a communion, a conversation between an " I " and a " Thou," it is a social phenomenon. The relation to God of him who prays always reflects an earthly social relation: that of servant or child or friend or bride. In the praying of primitive man, as in the devoutness of creative religious personalities, the religious bond is conceived after the analogy of human society. It is just this earthly social element that lends to natural prayer its dramatic vivacity. Wherever, as with many mystics, the religious relation no longer exhibits an analogy to social relations, prayer passes over from a real relation of communion to mere contemplation and adoration.

As anthropomorphism is only a crude form of belief in the personality of God, so belief in the real influence of prayer on the divine will, in the winning over of God to our side as it appears most clearly in primitive and prophetic prayer, is only a crude form of immediate, vital, and dynamic intercourse with God. It does not belong to the essence of prayer. The miracle of prayer does not lie in the accomplishment of the prayer, in the influence of man on God, but in the mysterious contact which comes to pass between the finite and the infinite Spirit. It is by this very fact that prayer is a genuine fellow-

ship of man with God, that it is something not merely psychological, but transcendental and metaphysical, or as Tholuck
has expressed it, " no mere earthly power but a power which
reaches to the heavens." In the words of Söderblom: " in the
depths of our inner life we have not a mere echo of our own
voice, of our own being, resounding from the dark depths of
personality, but a reality higher and greater than our own,
which we can adore and in which we can trust."

*Prayer is, therefore, a living communion of the religious
man with God, conceived as personal and present in experience, a communion which reflects the forms of the social relations of humanity.* This is prayer in essence. It is only imperfectly realized in the subordinate types of prayer. In
ritual prayer, cultual hymn, in liturgical prayer, as in prayer
regulated by law and deemed a thing in itself meritorious, the
experience of the Divine presence is, for the most part, weak
and shadowy. Here we have prayer as a more or less external
action, not as an inner contact of the heart with God. But
also in the philosophical ideal of prayer and in certain forms
of mystical communion, we can discern but faintly the essence of prayer. If we are to distinguish clearly between the
religious experiences and states of mind related to prayer,
which play an important part in the religion of philosophers
and mystics, and prayer itself considered simply from the
point of view which makes it to be prayer, some elucida-
tion of what we mean by " adoration " and " devotion " is
necessary.

Adoration (or reverent contemplation) and devotion are absolutely necessary elements in religious experience. Both
terms stand for conceptions much wider than that of prayer;
both denote religious experiences and states, the nature of
which is obviously different from that of prayer; nay, we
may go further and say that they comprehend psychical events
and experiences which belong to the " secular," not to the
strictly religious realm, or are on the borderland of both.

Adoration is the solemn contemplation of the " Holy One "
as the highest Good, unreserved surrender to Him, a mingling
of one's being with His. We see this even in the religious life
of primitive peoples. The awe which primitive man evinces by

speech and gesture as he stands in the presence of a " holy object," that is, an object filled with supernatural and magical power, is " adoration," although in a crude and imperfect fashion. The " holy " object has for him ideal worth: yes, even supreme value in the moment when, overcome by awe and wonder, he sinks in the dust before it. But it is in the personal experience of the poet and the mystic that we find adoration in its absolute purity and perfection. It is the soul-satisfying contemplation of the highest good, the very climax of mystical prayer: it is the unreserved losing of one's self in the glory of Nature as seen in the sacred poetry of ancient peoples and in the aesthetic mysticism of modern poets. Compared with it primitive ceremonial adoration is but a preliminary form. Now, a personal God can be the object of this adoration, just as He is the object of prayer. The God whom primitive man worships is an anthropomorphic being; the *summum bonum* of a mysticism centering in a personal God shows the traits of a spiritual personality. But the note of personality is by no means essential to the object of adoration. Primitive cults knew not only spiritual beings made after man's image, but also lifeless objects which being " holy," that is, as *mana* and *tabu*, lay claim to worship. Moreover, the object in which the poetic spirit sinks in an ecstasy of adoration, is not personal: it is the life-giving sun, creative and nurturing Mother Nature, the Alone and the Infinite as revealed in the beautiful. There is, nevertheless, something that is beyond experience, something which shines through Nature as through a translucent medium. Just as the God whom the worshipper invokes, is felt to be palpably near and immediately present, so also the object of adoration which the pious spirit regards with awe is felt to be equally near and present. The relation to God into which he who prays enters, resembles in its intimacy the relation which subsists between the adoring person and the object of his adoration.

Subsidiary to religious adoration is the " secular." Ordinarily we indicate by the word " adoration " the state of being laid hold of by a supreme good, the complete surrender to it, whether this good be religious (*numinous*) or " secular," natural or supernatural, earthly or heavenly. Everything

which man experiences as a supreme good, whatever is the
object of "love" — a person, an association of persons, an
abstract idea — can also in the wider sense of the word be an
object of adoration. The young lover adores his beloved, the
patriotic citizen his fatherland, the loyal working man his
class, the creative artist his muse, the high-minded philosopher
the idea of the true and the good If love means the belief of
a man in his supreme good, adoration is this belief at its highest point of intensity, the culmination of love. The adoring
person steadily contemplates his ideal object; he is filled with
inspiration, admiration, rapture, yearning; all other thoughts
and wishes have vanished; he belongs only to the one object,
loses himself in it, and in it dissolves away. *Adoration is the
contemplative surrender to a supreme good.*

Devotion (*Andacht*) is a necessary presupposition and foundation alike of prayer and adoration. The praying man who
converses with God, the adoring man who is absorbed in his
highest ideal — both are devout, self-collected, concentrated.
But the state of a soul in contemplation can just as well dispense with every reference to God or a supreme good. Devotion is, to begin with, concentration of the mind on a definite
point, a wide-awake state of consciousness whose field is
greatly circumscribed. But the mathematician who solves
a geometrical problem also experiences this state of concentration, or the designer who constructs a model. Devotion, as
distinct from mere mental concentration, from intensity of
attention, is a solemn, still, exalted, consecrated mood of the
soul. The philosopher experiences devotion when the mystery
of the human spirit rises up before him in its autonomy and
freedom: the scholar when he deciphers ancient documents
and recalls to life long-forgotten men and peoples; the lover
of nature when he stands before some lofty mountain peak or
when he delights in the contemplation of some modest wild
flower; the artist when suddenly a new idea forces itself upon
him; the lover of art when he admires Raphael's Madonna or
listens to a Symphony of Beethoven; the man engaged in a
moral struggle when he searches his conscience, judges himself, and sets before himself lofty aims and tasks; the pious
man when he participates in a holy act of worship or ponders

on a religious mystery; even the irreligious man when he enters into the still dimness of a majestic cathedral or witnesses the solemn high mass in a Roman Catholic church. Devotion may rise into complete absorption; the field of consciousness is narrowed, the intensity of the experience grows; the concrete perceptions and ideas which aroused the experience of devotion wave themselves in a mood that is at once deep and agreeable. The states of absorption appear in the religious as in the "secular" experience. They meet us just as much in the mystical devotional life as in scientific investigation and artistic creation. In absorption the mystic experiences perfect stillness and serenity, holy joy and equanimity — all of them experiences which may be clearly distinguished from contemplative adoration. Yet in them there lives in some manner the thought of an ultimate and highest state, though not so vividly as in adoration. Even in Buddhist absorption the idea of an ultimate and a highest — Nirvana — is operative.

Devotion is, therefore, the quiet, solemn mood of the soul which is caused by the contemplation of ethical and intellectual, but especially of aesthetic and religious values, whether of external objects or of imaginative conceptions dominated by feeling. Whilst adoration is concerned inwardly with an ideal object and holds it fast with convulsive energy, the objective presupposition of the experience of devotion acts purely as a stimulus. Devotion itself tends to depart from its objective presupposition, and to become wholly subjective, concentrated, and absorbed. In short, adoration has an objective, devotion a subjective character.

The analysis of adoration and devotion enables us to set the essence of prayer in the clearest light. Prayer is no mere feeling of exaltation, no mere hallowed mood, no mere prostration before a supreme good. It is rather a real intercourse of God with man, a living fellowship of the finite spirit with the Infinite. And just because the modern has no correct conception of the immediacy and tenderness of the relation effected by prayer in which the simple and devout soul stands to God, he is constantly confusing with genuine prayer these more general religious phenomena — adoration and devotion — which have their analogies even outside the religious sphere.

Because the man of to-day, entangled in the prejudices of a rationalistic philosophy, struggles against the primitive realism of frank and free prayer, he is inclined to see the ideal and essence of prayer in a vague, devotional mood and in aesthetic contemplation. But the essence of prayer is revealed with unquestionable clearness to penetrating psychological study, and it may be put thus: *to pray means to speak to and have intercourse with God*, as suppliant with judge, servant with master, child with father, bride with bridegroom. The severely non-rational character of religion nowhere makes so overwhelming an impression as in prayer. For modern thought, dominated by Copernicus and Kant, prayer is as great a stone of stumbling as it was for the enlightened philosophy of the Greeks. But a compromise between unsophisticated piety and a rational world-view obliterates the essential features of prayer, and the most living manifestation of religion withers into a lifeless abstraction. There are only two possibilities: either decisively to affirm prayer " in its entirely non-rational character and with all its difficulties," as Ménégoz says, or to surrender genuine prayer and substitute for it adoration and devotion which resemble prayer. Every attempt to mingle the two conceptions violates psychological veracity.

Religious persons and students of religion agree in testifying that prayer is the centre of religion, the soul of all piety. The definition of the essence of prayer explains this testimony; prayer is a living communion of man with God. Prayer brings man into direct touch with God, into a personal relation with Him. Without prayer faith remains a theoretical conviction; worship is only an external and formal act; moral action is without spiritual depth; man remains at a distance from God; an abyss yawns between the finite and the Infinite. " God is in heaven and thou art on the earth." " We cannot come to God," says Luther, " except through prayer alone, for He is too high above us." In prayer man rises to heaven, heaven sinks to earth, the veil between the visible and the invisible is torn asunder, man comes before God to speak with Him about his soul's welfare and salvation. " Prayer," says Mechthild of Magdeburg, " draws the great God down into a small heart; it drives the hungry soul up to God in His fulness." Similarly Johann Arndt says: " In prayer the highest and the lowest come together, the lowliest heart and the most exalted God."

As the mysterious linking of man with the Eternal, prayer is an incomprehensible wonder, a miracle of miracles which is daily brought to pass in the devout soul. The historian and psychologist of religion can only be a spectator and interpreter of that deep and powerful life which is unveiled in prayer: only the religious man can penetrate the mystery. But in the final analysis scientific inquiry stands under the same overwhelming impression as living religion. It is compelled to agree with the confession of Chrysostom: " There is nothing more powerful than prayer and there is nothing to be compared with it." [2]

[2] Οὐκ ἔστιν οὐδὲν εὐχῆς δυνατώτερον οὐδὲ ἴσον;

SELECT BIBLIOGRAPHY

(Where English translations are known to exist, the English title only is given.)

ADDIS, W. E. Hebrew Religion. London, 1906.

ALTHAUS, P. Zur Charakteristik der Evangel. Gebetsliteratur im Reformationsjahrhundert. Leipzig, 1914.

AMES, E. S. The Psychology of Religious Experience. Boston, 1910.

AMIEL, H. F. Amiel's Journal. Trans. by Mrs. Humphry Ward. London, 1885.

ANGELUS SILESIUS. Cherubimischer Wandersmann. Halle, 1895.

ANON. The Cloud of Unknowing. London, 1912.

ARNDT, J. Vier Bücher vom wahren Christentum. (See Koepp, W.) Berlin, 1840.

ATHANASIUS, ST. Life of St. Antony. (Library of Nicene and Post-Nicene Fathers.) Oxford, 1892.

ATTAR, FERID-ED-DIN. Selections from the Seven Valleys. London, 1910.

AUGUSTINE, ST. Works ed. by Marcus Dods. Edinburgh, 1876.

BAKER, A. Holy Wisdom or Directions for the Prayer of Contemplation. London, 1908.

BATCHELOR, J. The Ainu and their Folklore. London, 1901.

BAUMSTARK, A. Die Messe in Morgenland. Kempten, 1906.

BERNARD, ST. On loving God. Caldey Abbey, 1909.

BOEHME, J. The Way to Christ. London, 1911. The Threefold Life of Man. London, 1909. Life of Boehme by F. Hartmann. London, 1891.

BÖHMER, H. Die Bekenntnisse des Ignatius von Loyola. Leipzig, 1902.

BONAVENTURA, ST. Opera Omnia. Paris, 1864.

BOUSSET, W. Die Religion des Judentums im neuesten Zeitalter. Berlin, 1903.

BREASTED, J. H. Development of Religion and Thought in Ancient Egypt. London, 1912.

BRIGHTMAN, F. E. Liturgies, Eastern and Western. Vol. I. Eastern Liturgies. Oxford, 1896.

BROWN, W. A. The Life of Prayer in a World of Science. New York, 1927.

BRUCE, W. S. The Psychology of Christian Life and Behaviour. Edinburgh, 1922.

BUNYAN, J. Works. London, 1736.

BUTLER, DOM. C. Monasticism. (Ency. Brit. 11th ed. vol. XVIII.) Cambridge, 1911.

BÜTTNER, H. Meister Eckhart's Schriften und Predigten. Jena, 1903–1910.

CAIRNS, D. S. The Faith that Rebels. London, 1929.

CALLAWAY, C. The Religious System of the Amazulu. Natal, 1868–1870.

CALVIN, J. Works 48 vols. (Calvin Translation Society.) Edinburgh, 1843–1855.

CARPENTER, J. E. Comparative Religion. (Home University Library). London, 1916.

CATHERINE OF GENOA, ST. The Treatise on Purgatory. London, 1858.

CATHERINE OF SIENA, ST. The Divine Dialogue. London, 1896.

CHRIST, P. Die Lehre des Gebets nach dem neuen Testament. Leyden, 1886.

CLEMENT OF ALEXANDRIA. Works, trans. by W. Wilson. Edinburgh, 1869.

CLODD, E. Tom-tit-tot: Savage Philosophy in Folk-Tale. London, 1898.

COATS, R. H. Realm of Prayer. London, 1908.

CODRINGTON, R. H. The Melanesians. Oxford, 1891.

COE, G. A. The Psychology of Religion. Chicago, 1909.

COHU, J. R. Oremus, or the Place of Prayer in the Modern Religious Life. London, 1908.

CUMONT, F. The Oriental Religions in Roman Paganism. Chicago, 1911.

CUTTEN, G. B. Psychological Phenomena of Christianity. London, 1909.

DA COSTA GUIMARAENS. Le besoin de prier et ses conditions psychologiques. (*Revue philosophique*, 1902.)

DALMAN, G. H. The Words of Jesus. Edinburgh, 1902.

DE GROOT, J. J. M. The Religion of the Chinese. New York, 1910.

DEISSMANN, A. Evangelium und Urchristentum. Munich, 1905.

DAVIDS, RHYS, MRS. Buddhism. (Home University Library.) London, 1916.

DAVIDSON, A. B. Theology of the Old Testament. Edinburgh, 1890.

DIBELLIUS, O. Das Vaterunser. Giesen, 1903.

DIETERICH, A. Eine Mithrasliturgie. Leipzig, 1910.

DIONYSIUS THE AREOPAGITE. Works, trans. by J. Parker. Oxford, 1897.

DORNER, A. Grundiss der Religionsphilosophie. Leipzig, 1903.

DUCHESNE, L. Christian Worship. London, 1903.

ECKHART, MEISTER. Meister Eckhart. Ed. by Pfeiffer. Göttingen, 1906.

ELBOGEN, J. Studien zur Gesch. des jüdischen Gottesdienstes. Berlin, 1907.

ELLIS, A. B. Ewe-speaking Peoples. London, 1890.

FARNELL, L. R. The Evolution of Religion. London, 1905. Higher Aspects of Greek Religion. London, 1912.

FEUERBACH, L. The Essence of Christianity. Trans. by George Eliot. London, 1854.

FOWLER, W. W. The Religious Experience of the Roman People. London, 1911.

FOX, GEORGE. Journal. Ed. by N. Penney. Cambridge, 1911.

FRANK, SEBASTIAN. Paradoxa. Jena, 1909.

FRAZER, J. G. The Golden Bough. London, 1900.

GALLOWAY, G. Principles of Religious Development. London, 1909.

GAMBLE, J. Christian Faith and Worship. London, 1912.

GARDNER, E. St. Catherine of Siena. London, 1907.

GARDNER, PERCY. Modernity and the Churches. London, 1909.

GIRGENSOHN, K. Reden über die christliche Religion. Munich, 1913.

GOLDZIHER, J. Zauberelemente im islamischen Gebet. Giessen, 1906.

GOLTZ, VON DER. Das Gebet in der ältesten Christenheit. Leipzig, 1901.

GREIFF, A. Das Gebet im Alten Testament. Münster, 1905.

GRUNERT, M. Das Gebet in Islam. Prague, 1911.

GRUPPE, O. Die griechischen Kulte und Mythen in ihren Beziehungen zu den orientalischen Religionen. Leipzig, 1887.

GUTHRIE, W. N. Offices of Mystical Religion. New York, 1927.

GUYAU, J. M. L'irreligion de l'avenir. Paris, 1904.

GUYON, MADAME. The Autobiography of Madame Guyon. Trans. by T. Allen. London, 1897. Moyen court et très facile de faire oraison. Cologne, 1704.

HANNAY, J. O. Spirit and Origin of Christian Monasticism. London, 1903.

HARNACK, THEODOR. Der christliche Gemeindegottesdienst. Erlangen, 1854.

HARRISON, MISS J. E. Prolegomena to the Study of Greek Religion.

HARTMANN, E. VON. Das religiöse Bewusstsein der Menschheit. Berlin, 1882.

HEILER, F. Die Buddhistische Versenkung. Munich, 1918.

HEPHER, C. The Fellowship of Silence. London, 1915.

HERRMANN, W. The Communion of the Christian with God. London, 1910.

HOCKING, W. E. The Meaning of God in Human Experience. Yale University Press, 1912.

HÖFFDING, H. Philosophy of Religion. London, 1906.

HOUET, A. L. Die Psychologie des Bauerntums. Tübringen, 1905.

HOWITT, H. W. The Native Tribes of South-Eastern Australia. London, 1904.

HÜGEL, F. VON. The Mystical Element of Religion as studied in St. Catherine of Genoa and her friends. (2 vols.) London, 1908. Essays and Addresses on the Philosophy of Religion. London, 1921.

IGNATIUS LOYOLA, ST. The Spiritual Exercises. London, 1880.

INGE, W. R. Christian Mysticism. London, 1898. Faith and Its Psychology. London, 1902. Studies of English Mystics. London, 1905. Personal Idealism and Mysticism. London, 1907.

JACAPONE DA TODI. Laude di frate Jacapone da Todi. Roma, 1910.

JACKSON, A. V. W., Zoroaster, the Prophet of Ancient Iran. New York, 1899.

JALÂL-ED-DÎN-RÛMÎ. Selected Poems. Trans. Nicholson. Cambridge, 1898.

JAMES, W. The Varieties of Religious Experience. London, 1902.

JOHN OF THE CROSS, ST. The Dark Night of the Soul. Trans. Lewis. London, 1908.

JOLI, H. Psychologie des Saints. Paris, 1898.

JONES, RUFUS, M. Studies in Mystical Religion. London, 1909.

JULIAN OF NORWICH. Revelations of Divine Love. Ed. G. Wanack. London, 1914.

JUNOD, H. A. The Life of a South African Tribe. (2 vols.) Leipzig, 1912–1913.

JUSTIN MARTYR. Works. The Ante-Nicene Fathers Series. Edinburgh, 1880.

KANT, IMMANUEL. Religion within the Bounds of Reason only. Trans. by Semple. London, 1838.

KENNEDY, H. A. A. Philo's Contributions to Religion. London, 1919. St. Paul and the Mystery Religions. London, 1916.

KIERKEGAARD, S. Noten zu Kierkegaard's Lebensgeschichte. Halle, 1876.

KING, L. W. Babylonian Magic and Sorcery. London, 1896.

KINGSLEY, M. H. Travels in West Africa. London, 1897.

Köberle, J. Die Motive des Glaubens an die Gebetserhörung im Alten Testament. Erlangen, 1901.

Koepp, W. Johann Arndt. Berlin, 1912.

Köstlin, H. A. Geschichte des christlichen Gottesdienst. Freiburg, 1887.

Lang, A. The Making of Religion. London, 1900.

Langlow-Parker, K., Mrs. The Euahlayi Tribes. London, 1905.

Laurence, Brother. The Practice of the Presence of God. London, 1906.

Law, William. The Liberal and Mystical Writings of William Law. Ed. W. S. Palmer. London, 1908.

Le Roy, A. La religion des peuples primitifs. Paris, 1909.

Luther, Martin. Luther's Primary Works. Ed. Wace and Buchheim. London, 1890.

Mânikha Vâçagar. The Tiruvâçagam. Ed. G. V. Pope. London, 1900.

Marcus Aurelius. Marcus Aurelius Antoninus to Himself. Trans. by G. H. Rendall. London, 1898.

Marett, R. R. The Threshold of Religion. London, 1909.

Masson, F. Fénelon et Madame Guyon. Paris, 1907.

McComb, S. A Book of Modern Prayers: With Introductory Essay on " Prayer: Its Meaning and Value." New York, 1926.

Mechthild of Magdeburg. Offenbarungen der Schwester Mechthild. Regensburg, 1869.

Ménégoz, F. Le problème de la prière. Strassburg, 1925.

Missale Romanum. The Roman Missal in Latin and English. Tournay, 1911.

Monier-Williams, M. A. Indian Wisdom. London, 1876.

Monod, A. Sermons. (3 vols.) Paris, 1881.

Monrad, D. G. (Bishop). Aus der Welt des Gebets. Trans. from the Danish. Gotha, 1878.

Moore, G. F. History of Religions. New York, 1913.

Müller, Max. On Ancient Prayer. Berlin, 1897.

Nagelsbuch, C. F. Die homerische Theologie. Nürnberg, 1840.

Nassau, R. H. Fetichism in West Africa. London, 1904.

Nicholson, R. A. The Mystics of Islam. London, 1914.

Novalis. Schriften. Ed. by J. Minor. Jena, 1907.

Oldenburg, H. Buddha. Berlin, 1914. Die Religion des Veda. Stuttgart, 1917.

Oman, J. C. The Mystics, Ascetics and Saints of India. London, 1903.

Orchard, W. E. Divine Service. London, 1921.

ORIGEN. Library of Works. Ante-Nicene Fathers. Edinburgh, 1869–1872.

OTTO, R. The Idea of the Holy. London, 1924.

PASCAL. Works. Trans. O. W. Wight. New York, 1859.

PATERSON, W. P., and others. The Power of Prayer. London, 1921.

PAULSEN, F. Introduction to Philosophy. New York, 1895.

PERLES, F. Das Gebet im Judentum. Frankfort, 1904.

PETER OF ALCANTARA, ST. Das goldene Büchlein. Trans. from the Spanish. Würzburg, 1900.

PFENDER, R. De la prière juive à la prière chrétienne. Geneva, 1905.

PHILO. Works. Trans. by Yonge. London, 1854.

PLOTINUS. The Ethical, Physical and Psychical Treatises. Trans. by Stephen MacKenna. London, 1917–1921.

POULAIN, A. The Graces of Interior Prayer. London, 1910.

PRATT, J. B. The Religious Consciousness. New York, 1921.

RÉJÉGAC, E. Essay on the Bases of Mystic Knowledge. London, 1899.

REITZENSTEIN, K. Poimandres. Leipzig, 1904.

REVILLE, A. Les religions des peuples non civilisés. Paris, 1883.

RIETSCHEL, G. Lehrbuch des Liturgik. Berlin, 1900.

ROBINSON, T. H. The History of Religions. London, 1926.

ROHDE, E. Psyche. Tübingen, 1903.

ROTHE, R. Theologische Ethik. Wittenberg, 1867.

ROUTLEDGE, W. and K. With a Pre-historic People; The Akikuyu of British East Africa. London, 1910.

RUYSBROECK, J. The Adornment of the Spiritual Marriage. Ed. by E. Underhill. London, 1906.

SABATIER, AUGUSTE. Outline of the Philosophy of Religion. New York, 1913.

SABATIER, PAUL. Life of Francis of Assisi. London, 1901.

SAVONAROLA, G. (See under Villari.)

SAYCE, A. N. The Religion of Ancient Egypt. Edinburgh, 1913.

SCHEEL, O. Die Anschauung Augustins über Christi Person und Werk. Tübingen, 1901.

SCHMIDT, L. Die Ethik der alten Griechen. Berlin, 1882.

SCHULTZ, H. Old Testament Theology. Edinburgh, 1885.

SCHUTZ, H. Urgeschichte der Kultur. Leipzig, 1900.

SEARS, A. L. The Drama of the Spiritual Life. New York, 1915.

SEGOND, I. La Prière: Étude de psychologie religieuse. Paris, 1911.

SKEAT-BLAGDEN, W. W. Pagan Races of the Malay Peninsula. London, 1905.

SMITH, MARGARET. Studies in Early Mysticism in the Near and Middle East. London, 1931.

SNEATH, E. H., and others. At One with the Invisible; Studies in Mysticism. New York, 1921.

SODERBLOM, N. Studiet av Religionen. Stockholm, 1908.

STRAUCH, PH. Margaretha Ebner und Heinrich von Nördlingen. Tübingen, 1882.

STREETER, B. H., and APPASAMY, J. J. The Sadhu: A Study in Mysticism and Practical Religion. London, 1921.

STREETER, B. H., and others. Concerning Prayer. London, 1916. Reality. London, 1916.

SUSO, HENRY. Die Schriften des Seligen H. Suso. Ed. by H. S. Denifle. Munich, 1876. Life by Himself. Trans. by T. F. Knox. London, 1913.

TAULER, JOHN. The History and Life of Doctor John Tauler. Trans. by Susannah Winkworth. London, 1906.

TERESA, ST. Life of St. Teresa, written by Herself. Trans. by D. Lewis. London, 1904.

TERSTEEGEN, G. Geistliche Lieder. Ed. W. Nelle.

THEOLOGIA GERMANICA. Trans. by Susannah Winkworth. London, 1907.

THOMAS À KEMPIS. Of the Imitation of Christ. Trans. by C. Bigg. London, 1901.

THOMAS AQUINAS, ST. Of God and His Creatures. Trans. by J. Rickaby. London, 1905.

TIETLE, C. P. Elements of the Science of Religion. London, 1897.

TILESTON, M. W. Great Souls at Prayer. London, 1913. Prayers, Ancient and Modern. Boston, 1928.

TYLOR, E. B. Primitive Culture. (2 vols.) London, 1903.

TYRELL, G. Lex Orandi. London, 1907. Lex Credendi. London, 1906.

UNAMUNO, MIGUEL DE. The Tragic Sense of Life in Men and in Peoples. London, 1917.

UNDERHILL, EVELYN. Mysticism: A study in the Nature and Development of Man's Spiritual Consciousness. London, 1912. The Mystic Way. London, 1913. The Life of the Spirit and the Life of To-day. London, 1922.

UPANISHADS, THE. Sacred Books of the East. Trans. by Max Müller. Oxford, 1879–1884.

VALENTINE, C. H. Modern Psychology and the Validity of Christian Experience. London, 1926.

372 BIBLIOGRAPHY

VILLARI, P. Life and Times of Girolamo Savonarola. Trans. by
L. Villari. London, 1889.

WARNECK, J. Die Religionen der Batak. Berlin, 1897.

WARREN, F. C. Liturgy of the Ante-Nicene Church. London, 1897.

WEINEL, H. St. Paul: The Man and His Work. Trans. by G. A.
Bienemann. London, 1906.

WELLHAUSEN, J. Israelitische und Jüdische Geschichte. Berlin,
1897.

WERNLE, P. Jesus. Tübingen, 1916.

WHITEHEAD, A. N. Religion in the Making. Cambridge, 1927.

WIEMAN, H. N. Methods of Private Religious Living. New York,
1929.

INDEX OF NAMES